SIGN LANGUAGE
Interpreting and Interpreter Education

PERSPECTIVES ON DEAFNESS

Series Editors
Marc Marschark
Patricia Elizabeth Spencer

SIGN LANGUAGE
Interpreting and Interpreter Education
DIRECTIONS FOR RESEARCH AND PRACTICE

EDITED BY
Marc Marschark,
Rico Peterson,
and
Elizabeth A. Winston

CONTRIBUTING EDITORS
Patricia Sapere,
Carol M. Convertino,
Rosemarie Seewagen,
and Christine Monikowski

OXFORD
UNIVERSITY PRESS

2005

OXFORD

UNIVERSITY PRESS

Oxford University Press, Inc., publishes works that further
Oxford University's objective of excellence
in research, scholarship, and education.

Oxford   New York
Auckland   Cape Town   Dar es Salaam   Hong Kong   Karachi
Kuala Lumpur   Madrid   Melbourne   Mexico City   Nairobi
New Delhi   Shanghai   Taipei   Toronto

With offices in
Argentina   Austria   Brazil   Chile   Czech Republic   France   Greece
Guatemala   Hungary   Italy   Japan   Poland   Portugal   Singapore
South Korea   Switzerland   Thailand   Turkey   Ukraine   Vietnam

Published by Oxford University Press, Inc.
198 Madison Avenue, New York, New York 10016
www.oup.com

Oxford is a registered trademark of Oxford University Press

Library of Congress Cataloging-in-Publication Data
Sign language interpreting and interpreter education: directions for research
and practice/edited by Marc Marschark ... [et al.].
    p. cm.—(Perspectives on deafness)
  Includes bibliographical references.
  ISBN-13 978-0-19-517694-0

    1. Interpreters for the deaf—Training of—United States.   2. Sign language—Study
and teaching—United States.   3. Deaf—Means of communication—United States.
I. Marschark, Marc. II. Series.
  HV2402.S54   2005
  419'.7'080221—dc22   2004012885

9 8 7 6 5 4 3 2 1

Printed in the United States of America
on acid-free paper

Preface

Sign language interpreting, by history if not by definition, puts individuals in a somewhat awkward position. Interpreters need to be impartial in what they interpret, but they need to be involved and invested enough to ensure that communication is accurate and successful. They work for both deaf and hearing participants in any given situation, and both deaf and hearing participants lose if an interpreter is not involved or is not successful. However, often the general public's view is that interpreters work "for" deaf people and are solely "responsible for them."

Interpreting situations sometimes involve intensely private information of the sort that might be hard to share with one person (e.g., a lawyer or a doctor), and yet both parties have to depend on a third person who is expected to maintain objectivity and confidentiality regardless of the stress or personal conflicts created by the interaction. As such, although sign language interpreters are essential intermediaries, facilitating communication between individuals who use different languages and may be from different cultures, they have to resist directing or controlling the interactions or injecting their own views of the participants or the content they are interpreting.

Finally, in educational interpreting, where interpreters are supposed to facilitate the effective flow of classroom communication, they are often perceived as being solely responsible for it, bestowing on them a role in the education of deaf children that is neither wanted nor appropriate. This is not for want of caring or trying. Educational interpreters may or may not be familiar with the content of a particular class, they may have lesser educations than the students they are interpreting for (e.g., at the college level), or they may have sign language and interpreting skills that are inappropriate for the audience or setting.

Questions concerning all of these issues have been raised in a variety of settings and publications, but their answers are surprisingly elusive. In part, this is because the field is young, the issues themselves are not well defined, and the extent to which they raise problems or elicit questions at all depends on the experience and perspective of those involved. More interesting, perhaps, is the sensitivity of the issues—for interpreters, interpreter educators, and the deaf (and hearing) individuals they serve. It is not surprising that some of these issues are difficult; there is no doubt that they have the potential to cause discomfort or harm to all involved. What is surprising is the lack of serious inquiry about these issues and the paucity of research about even the most basic of questions (e.g., how effective is interpreted communication?). And that brings us to the beginning of the story.

The National Sign Language Interpreting Project was established in 2002 with funding from the National Science Foundation to conduct research on interactions of interpreter characteristics, student characteristics, and settings as they relate to providing students with access to education. We already knew that there was little information available about how much deaf students understand in various academic contexts, but we were unprepared for the apparent lack of interest about what seemed essential questions about the effectiveness of sign language interpreting, its effects on the various participants, and ways to improve it. Certainly, there was no shortage of opinions. After all, interpreter-training programs routinely teach students about strategies to support and enhance communication and factors that are assumed to underlie successful interpreting. But the lack of any empirical foundation for such teaching, as well as our early findings that educational interpreting is not as successful as interpreters, students, and teachers assume, was both surprising and frustrating. It also led us to seek out broad expertise in establishing an agenda for research in interpreting, and especially educational interpreting, in order to improve our understanding and practice of interpreting, interpreter education, and academic opportunities for deaf and hard-of-hearing students.

And, thus, the Workshop on Educational Interpreting and Interpreter Education was conceived. Invitations to participate were sent to a variety of individuals who were known for their intimate knowledge of interpreting and interpreter education and their research orientation. Almost all of those invited agreed to attend the February 2004 workshop and to circulate first drafts of the chapters found in this volume prior to that meeting. As planned, the meeting included discussion of the chapters and the need for a research agenda, but beyond that, there was little that went as expected.

One surprising aspect of the workshop discussion, at least for some participants, was the implicit—and sometimes explicit—admission that interpreting is both not as well understood as might be expected and often of poorer quality than most people assume. Such confessions led participants to some emotional discussions, and several participants argued that "no interpreting is better than bad interpreting." Coming from recognized experts in the field, such views are remarkable—both refreshing in their honesty and somewhat frightening for those who depend on interpreters or seek to educate deaf students in mainstream settings. But they also reflect feelings of frustration in trying to improve the situation, a shared understanding that led to frequent workshop references to "the interpreter as Venus de Milo."

With regard to the training of interpreters, Winston (this volume) clearly articulated the responsibility of interpreter educators in this situation:

> In spite of years of teaching interpreting, in spite of curriculum changes, in spite of a recognized failure to adequately educate interpreters, we continue to do what we do. We accept students into interpreting programs because we are told to, ignoring evidence that it does not result in competent interpreters. We graduate students into the community, acknowledging that they are not qualified, that there is a gap, and that they need at least a year or two to achieve even "entry level" competence. We recognize that we are barely able to teach them the facts, when what we need are interpreters who can go far beyond the facts; who can go beyond the most simple cognitive skills of remembering and understanding.

In his historical introduction to this volume, Cokely provides a broader context, describing the situation that we, as investigators, found when we looked to the literature for the foundations of interpreting and interpreter education. Describing repeated attempts to encourage sharing of information and the establishment of a research basis for interpreting and interpreter education, Cokely notes that "to this day, there continues to be a lack of coordinated, basic research that can inform the practice of interpreting and transliterating and the preparation of interpreters and transliterators."

With regard to the basis for certifying individuals (including those lamented by Winston) as interpreters, Cokely pointed out:

> It is now 40 years after the founding of RID and the rejection of calls for conducting research before implementing a certification process. It is almost 25 years after leading practitioners of the day were ignored in their request for significant federal funding for research into interpreting and transliterating. Nevertheless, legislative and programmatic initiatives continue without the necessary research base

upon which to develop those initiatives in order for them to be successful.

If there was broad agreement at the workshop that interpreting and interpreter education are based more on instinct and experience than factual information obtained from research and study, there was much less agreement on what, if anything, should be done about it. As the chapters of this volume reveal, there were at least three perspectives, which divide these chapters rather equally. One set of chapters clearly reflects the authors' views of the importance of research for better understanding of interpreting, improving teaching of both interpreting students and deaf students, and improving interpreting overall. The second set describes linguistic approaches to interpreting, an orientation expressed at the workshop in terms of the belief that if interpreting students were only taught more about sign language linguistics, their interpreting would be more accurate and of higher quality. The remaining chapters focus on specific areas in which the contributors have expertise or interest and believe they might provide a broader impact on interpreting and interpreter education.

Despite the diversity of perspectives evident in this volume, the workshop produced a clear agenda for research that will be apparent throughout the chapters. Specific research questions are offered on a variety of topics; indeed, all contributors were asked to include the questions they felt were in greatest need of exploration. In other cases, however, clear gaps in our knowledge are indicated, either explicitly or implicitly, and those gaps circumscribe their own questions about what it is we need to know and why we have not already asked the *whys*, *hows*, and *whats*.

The shape of the research agenda emerging from the workshop was defined in part by the flow and character of the discussion itself. The final chapter of this volume provides a partial summary of that discussion, but not all of the workshop's most important aspects can be captured explicitly in writing. Some are expressed in the way the chapters fit together; others in the musings of contributors who found the discussion threatening as well as enlightening. And there were certainly some awkward moments. Confessions about the poor quality of interpreting and interpreter education, for example, were sometimes accompanied by defensive postures and laments that we bear little responsibility for the current state of interpreting (politics, educational administrators, "laws," and other interpreters were among the villains). Suggestions that the roles of interpreters might need to change were seen as obvious by some and an affront by others. Even the titles given to interpreters in different settings (e.g., mediators, communication specialists, language specialists) became a hot topic of debate, as though a rose by some other name might not smell as sweet.

One of the more fascinating threads running through the workshop lay in the interpreting of the proceedings itself. Because attendees included deaf participants and several hearing participants who were not fluent users of American Sign Language (ASL), the organizers sought out highly respected local interpreters, gave them drafts of the chapters in advance, and offered opportunities to meet with presenters. Yet, when it became clear that there were numerous communication breakdowns despite the skills and experience of all involved, there was an atmosphere of helplessness. The issue was discussed among the deaf and hearing "consumers," and there were private discussions with the interpreters, but no one was able to provide a solution. Most notable, however, was the lack of comfort (i.e., prohibition) in discussing the matter publicly, even though it provided a prime example of what the workshop was all about! Several participants indicated that it was the norm, to be expected; others claimed it was solely the responsibility of the consumers to solve it. While this may all be correct, it is still wholly unsatisfying.

In one late-night post mortem of the workshop, one group of participants agreed that they would never allow such a situation to occur again (why now?) and devised some innovative methods for ensuring effective communication in such settings. Still, the fact that the participants in a conference focusing on the effectiveness of interpreting would feel helpless in such a situation is a powerful statement about the field and those of us involved in it. From a scientific perspective, it was fascinating to watch the exact situation we were discussing unfold in real life, although to an all-wise observer it might have seemed bizarre. As one participant put it much later: "If *we* couldn't resolve this, how can we expect others to do it!"

Beyond recognizing the lack of empirical research on interpreting and the need for it, one of the few points of universal agreement among workshop participants was that many deaf students, and young deaf children in particular, are not receiving high-quality interpreting in the classroom. There was broad acknowledgment that interpreters working in K–12 classrooms are often the least skilled and/or least experienced, with the university classroom positions going to the better established and more skilled interpreters. Clearly, this is backward.

Educational interpreting was perceived to be, in general, less esteemed (by other interpreters) than community interpreting, not that there has been any empirical consideration of the extent to which the knowledge and skills involved in one domain necessarily transfer to the other. At the same time, the concern of most workshop participants about the ethics of the current state of affairs, in which the students most in need of fluent language models and clear communication are the least likely to receive them, is something that comes through in only a few of the chapters that follow. Once again, there may be feelings of helplessness among those who are neither consumers nor the parents of student consumers, but the contrast between the magnitude of complaint at the workshop and the lack of consideration in this written product deserves red-faced mention.

Finally, we come back to the issue of the research agenda. The goals of both the workshop and this volume, explicitly stated in the invitation to participate, indicated the need to do the following:

1. Present cutting-edge research and research needs relevant to educational interpreting;
2. Describe opportunities for and potential barriers to expanded research and implementation, both immediate and long term; and
3. Discuss ways in which basic and applied research can have more direct influence on both educational interpreting and interpreter education.

The extent to which each of the chapters and the volume as a whole accomplish these goals will vary with the perspective of each reader. What is provided, in any case, is an accurate assessment of where we are, where we are going, and where we need to go with regard to interpreting and interpreter education. Despite differing vantage points, the contributors to this volume all recognize (explicitly or implicitly) that it is only through knowledge and investigation that we can improve interpreting and better serve our consumers. Although some contributors might be more interested in practice, research, or pedagogy, all agree that we could be doing "more better good" in all three areas and that the present situation sorely needs improving.

To the extent that this volume opens eyes, focuses attention, or motivates research, we will consider our efforts in organizing the workshop and this book successful. Most important, it is a first step in taking control of our own field, identifying the variety of stakeholders with whom we need to be collaborating, and establishing a research agenda to guide us in the near future. A journey of a thousand miles begins with a single step, and both of these lie before us.

Marc Marschark
Patricia Sapere
Rosemarie Seewagen

Acknowledgments

The organizers of the Workshop on Educational Interpreting and Interpreter Education and the editors of this volume gratefully acknowledge support for these activities from the National Science Foundation, Research on Learning and Education Program, through Grant REC-0207394 (National Sign Language Interpreting Project, Marc Marschark, PI); the U.S. Department of Education, through Grant #H160C030001 (Project TIEM.Online, Elizabeth A. Winston, PI); the Department of Research, National Technical Institute for the Deaf (NTID); and Oxford University Press. We also wish to express appreciation for the support provided by the Department of American Sign Language and Interpreter Education at NTID and the Office of the Vice President/Dean for NTID at Rochester Institute of Technology. Any opinions, findings and conclusions, or recommendations expressed in this material are those of the contributors and do not necessarily reflect the views of these agencies and organizations.

Contents

Contributors

Dennis Cokely
ASL Program
400 Meserve Hall
Northeastern University
Boston, MA 02115–5000

Carol Convertino
National Sign Language
  Interpreting Project
National Technical Institute for
  the Deaf
96 Lomb Memorial Drive
Rochester, NY 14623

Jeffrey E. Davis
Department of Theory and
  Practice in Teacher
  Education
University of Tennessee
Knoxville, TN 37996–3442

Robyn K. Dean
URMC Deaf Wellness Center
300 Crittenden Boulevard
Rochester, NY 14642

Eileen Forestal
Union County College
1033 Springfield Ave.
Cranford, NJ 07060

Laurene Gallimore
Department of Education
Gallaudet University
800 Florida Avenue NE
Washington, DC 20002

Doni LaRock
National Sign Language
  Interpreting Project
National Technical Institute for
  the Deaf
96 Lomb Memorial Drive
Rochester, NY 14623

Robert G. Lee
Boston University
Modern Foreign Languages &
  Literatures
American Sign Language
  Linguistic Research Project

718 Commonwealth Avenue
Boston, MA 02215

Patricia Lessard
Ohlone College
ASL/Interpreter Preparation
   Program
43600 Mission Boulevard
Fremont, CA 94539

Marc Marschark
Department of Research
National Technical Institute for
   the Deaf
96 Lomb Memorial Drive
Rochester, NY 14623
and
Department of Psychology
University of Aberdeen
Aberdeen AB24 2UB
Scotland

Christine Monikowski
Department of ASL and
   Interpreting Education
National Technical Institute for
   the Deaf
52 Lomb Memorial Drive
Rochester, NY 14623

Jemina Napier
Department of Linguistics
Macquarie University
NSW 2109, Australia

Rico Peterson
Department of ASL and
   Interpreting Education
National Technical Institute for
   the Deaf
52 Lomb Memorial Drive
Rochester, NY 14623

Robert Q Pollard, Jr.
URMC Deaf Wellness
   Center
300 Crittenden Boulevard
Rochester, NY 14642

David Quinto-Pozos
Department of Speech and
   Hearing Science
University of Illinois at
   Urbana–Champaign
MC–482
901 South Sixth Street
Champaign, Illinois 61820

Patricia Sapere
National Sign Language
   Interpreting Project
National Technical Institute for
   the Deaf
96 Lomb Memorial Drive
Rochester, NY 14623

Rosemarie Seewagen
National Sign Language
   Interpreting Project
National Technical Institute for
   the Deaf
96 Lomb Memorial Drive
Rochester, NY 14623

Graham H. Turner
Department of Education &
   Social Science
University of Central
   Lancashire
Preston, PR1 2HE
United Kingdom

Elizabeth A. Winston
1613 Leila Drive
Loveland, CO 80538

SIGN LANGUAGE
Interpreting and Interpreter Education

1

Shifting Positionality: A Critical Examination of the Turning Point in the Relationship of Interpreters and the Deaf Community

Dennis Cokely

Interpreters have always occupied a unique social and cultural position relative to the communities within which they work. It is they who are positioned "between worlds" and who make possible communication with "outsiders." While there is emerging literature on the positionality of those who provide access to another spoken language world (e.g., Karttunen, 1994; Valdes, 2003), there is surprisingly little literature in this regard on sign language interpreters/transliterators.[1] Given that sign language interpreters/transliterators are positioned between sign language and spoken language worlds, there are critical aspects of their social and cultural positionality that have no counterpart among interpreters who are positioned between two spoken language worlds. Although this chapter focuses on the shifting positionality of sign language interpreters/transliterators in the United States, the observations developed here will, I believe, hold relevance for Deaf Communities and sign language interpreters/transliterators in other countries.[2]

OUR HISTORIC FOOTING

In order to fully appreciate the dramatic shifts in positionality that have occurred, it is important to understand that the roots of the practice of sign language interpreting/transliterating lie squarely within the aegis of Deaf Communities. Before the early 1970s, interpretation/transliteration was seen as a voluntary and charitable activity that fell to those non-deaf persons with some level of competence in sign language. This usually meant that the pool of prospective interpreters/transliterators consisted of the daughters, sons, siblings, or extended relatives of deaf adults or those who lacked any blood ties to the Deaf Community but who were engaged in an occupation that placed them in regular interaction with members of the Community (e.g., teachers, social workers, ministers).[3]

Ultimately, however, members of the Community would determine for themselves whether and when someone possessed sufficient communicative competence and had also demonstrated sufficient trustworthiness that they would be asked to interpret/transliterate. Absent any external, objective criteria that might serve to validate someone's competence as an interpreter/transliterator, the Community relied on the judgment and experience of its members to determine who could function effectively as an interpreter/transliterator. This judgment, it would appear, was based more on one's overall fluency in sign than one's technical skill at interpreting/transliterating (Fant, 1990) and, perhaps more important, a sense that the individual would act in the best communicative interests of the deaf individual. This resulted in a rather limited pool of prospective interpreters/transliterators.

Thus, it is no wonder that as the communicative needs of the Community increased, the number of those judged capable was insufficient to meet the Community's needs. The notion of Community selectivity raises an interesting series of questions about those who presumably would be judged most trustworthy by the Community: children of deaf adults (CODAs). One wonders, for example, what were the factors that led some CODAs to shun the Community and avoid interpreting altogether, and what were the factors led the Community to choose some CODAs but not others. For their part, those individuals, both CODAs and non-CODAs who were asked (or, given the times, perhaps "chosen" better captures the reality) to function as interpreters/transliterators perceived their work as "just another way of helping deaf family members, friends, co-workers, or complete strangers. It was a way of contributing to the general welfare of deaf people...." (Fant, 1990, p. 10).

This view of "interpretation/transliteration as my contribution" is certainly in keeping with the Community's expectations of reciprocity (Smith, 1983) and the characterization of the American Deaf Community as a collectivist culture (Mindess, 1999). Interpreters and transliterators not only became part of the fabric of the Community, but advice on who was considered a competent practitioner or a promising interpreter/transliterator-in-the-making was part of the received wisdom of the Community passed along by older Deaf adults to younger members in much the same way advice was given about "Deaf friendly" doctors, dentists, or other needed service providers.

Fant (1990) also asserts that this view of "interpretation/transliteration as my contribution" was in keeping with societal norms of the time in which good deeds were a matter of private, and not corporate, concerns. It is probable that such a view of "interpretation/transliteration as my contribution" has existed since there have been Deaf people with non-deaf relatives and friends. However, in the United States at least, during the decade of the sixties, this view of interpreter/transliterator volunteerism occurred within a wider societal context of Kennedy's Camelot and Johnson's Great Society. It is not too farfetched to believe that the "ask what you can do for your country" infectious spirit of the times contributed to the founding of the organization that is now known as the Registry of Interpreters for the Deaf (RID).

In this view of "interpretation/transliteration as my contribution," few people actually called themselves interpreters or transliterators. They were asked to do the work, but the work of interpreting did not define them or their relation to the Community. Individuals who worked as interpreters or transliterators were employed as schoolteachers, educational administrators, rehabilitation counselors, or religious workers; many worked as housewives. The assumption was that no one earned a living by doing the work of interpreting/transliterating, largely because there was no expectation of compensation. "We did not expect to be paid, we did not ask to be paid, because we did not do it for the money. We felt it was our obligation, our duty to do it, and if we did not do it, the deaf person would suffer and we would feel responsible" (Fant, 1990, p. 10).

Interpreting/transliterating was not even viewed as an occupation, much less a profession. This was underscored, even in the mid-seventies, when individuals were expected to volunteer their services as interpreters/transliterators at local, regional, national, and international conferences and conventions. A case in point that demonstrates the expectation of "interpretation/transliteration as my contribution" is the Seventh Congress of the World Federation of the Deaf, held in 1975 in Washington, DC. At that Congress, sign language interpreters/transliterators were expected not only to volunteer their services but also to register for the Congress and pay for all of their own expenses. Spoken language interpreters (Spanish, French, and German), however, were well compensated and given working conditions in accord with prevailing international conference standards.

That interpreting/transliterating was viewed neither as occupation nor profession was evident at a 1964 meeting that would result in the founding of the organization that is now known as the Registry of Interpreters for the Deaf (RID).[4] Of the 73 participants (15 of whom were deaf) and 6 observers at that meeting, 90% were actively engaged in the field of education. Most of the non-deaf educators present could and did interpret/transliterate, but "they did not think of themselves as interpreters" (Fant, 1990, p. 7). It is noteworthy (and serves to underscore the discussion thus far) that only two of the participants even called themselves "interpreters." Typically, professionals come together to create an organization that will serve their goals and needs. In the case of interpreters/transliterators, this sequence was reversed and the organization appeared before there was a commonly recognized understanding of the work of interpreters/transliterators and certainly before practitioners thought of themselves as "professionals."

"At a workshop on interpreting for the deaf conducted at Ball State Teachers College, June 14–17, 1964, in Muncie, Indiana, the National Registry of Professional Interpreters and Translators for the Deaf was organized"[5] (Quigley & Youngs, 1965). However, within 6 months of the organizational meeting, the name had been changed to the Registry of Interpreters for the Deaf. Fant states that dropping the word "professional" better expressed the organization's intent to recruit, train, and maintain a registry. There were eight stated purposes of the organization, the third of which was to recruit "qualified interpreters and translators." According to Fant, "We were eager to recruit, train, and verify the competence of interpreters, but I do not believe that we thought they would become full-time interpreters. It is my opinion that we perceived the new interpreters functioning in much the same way as we had, that is, holding full-time jobs and interpreting on the side" (1990, p. 7).

It is quite likely, however, that another, perhaps more significant, force contributed to the name change. I believe a compelling case can be made that at the time the notion of a "professional interpreter" was, for the Community, the antithesis of "interpretation/transliteration as my contribution." If the prevailing view of "interpretation/transliteration as my contribution" rested on an assumption of Communal proximity, perhaps the notion of "interpreter/transliterator as professional" was seen as the embodiment of distance and detachment. Although it seems clear that the original intent of including the word "professional" was to reflect individuals who were skilled and competent, perhaps it was felt that the popular understanding of a "professional" (well compensated and aloof) would be perceived negatively by the Deaf Community which, after all, had a centuries-old history of being maltreated by "professionals."

This name change, a generally unheralded event, can be seen as the organization's first collective response to a shift in positionality of interpreters/transliterators vis-à-vis the Community. The name change was certainly influenced by the fact that the work was seen as only a part-time endeavor. However, in light of the well-documented historic oppression experienced by the Community at the hands of "professionals," and given the importance of social proximity to the

Community, the original organizational name may have been perceived as too dramatic and negative a shift away from the Community. Creating an organization was one thing; creating an organization of "professionals" was something quite different.

SHIFTING PLATES OF POSITIONALITY

Just as the earth's tectonic plates move uncontrollably and alter the relationship of landmasses to each other, so too events within society at large, the Deaf Community, and the newly formed organization altered the societal and Community positionality of interpreters/transliterators. While the Ball State organizational meeting is often viewed as a critical turning point in the positionality of interpreters/transliterators and the Deaf Community (e.g., Stewart, Shine, & Cartwright, 2004), there is compelling evidence that subsequent events, and not the founding of the organization, would irrevocably alter the social and cultural positionality of interpreters/transliterators as a group.

The organizational event that occurred in 1964 marked the beginning of a shift away from the relationship that interpreters and transliterators had enjoyed with the Community. However, events that occurred between 1972 and 1975 marked a pivotal period resulting in an irreversible widening of the fissure between interpreters/transliterators and the Community that had begun to appear in 1964. In 1972, the grant that had provided organizational support for RID ended. That grant was prepared by the National Association of the Deaf (NAD) and submitted to the Vocational Rehabilitation Administration of the Department of Health, Education, and Welfare. The grant provided funding to hire RID's first executive director (a Deaf man, Al Pimentel) and support staff. The grant also made it possible to house the organization's home offices within NAD's home offices. Thus, on an organizational level, the grant made possible the symbolic realization of the prevailing relationship between interpreters/transliterators and the Deaf Community.

When the grant expired in 1972, RID had a membership of fewer than 400 members. Many did not contribute to the Community as interpreters/transliterators but were supporters of the idea of an organization of practitioners. Thus, membership dues were insufficient to sustain salaries and rent. RID was forced to reduce its staff to only part-time (non-deaf) secretarial support, move out of the NAD home offices, and relocate to available, rent-free space at Gallaudet College. In hindsight, the physical relocation away from NAD, the inability to renew the Deaf executive director's contract, and the retention of non-deaf support staff were signs of growing separation from the Community. The organizational separation and attendant decisions represented a type of "separation by proxy" of interpreter/transliterators and the

Community and would be widened and reinforced by other events that also occurred that same year.

1972 also marked the beginning of RID's program to test and certify the qualifications of interpreters/transliterators. In October, a workshop was held in Memphis, Tennessee, to launch the certification system. Its primary motivation was the fact that an alarmingly high number of members did not possess what was felt to be minimally acceptable skills, and yet they were card-carrying members of RID. At that time, membership was gained simply by having two RID members sign an application that they would vouch for the applicant's abilities. In its early stages, this procedure may have had some validity since, according to Fant, "most of the members were skilled interpreters and quite adept at spotting other skilled interpreters, or they were consumers who were sophisticated at identification of skilled interpreters" (1990, p. 41).

In one sense, this process might be viewed as an organizational attempt to mirror the Community's "received wisdom" practice that had served it well for many years. However, as the number of new RID members grew over a relatively short period of time, it became clear that more and more of these newer members were unable to sustain a level of quality that was acceptable to the Community. As a result, the number of RID members with marginal skills (and no vested support from the Community) increased, and RID became quite suspect in the eyes of the Community. While the crucible of Community work attested to an individual's competence, in the eyes of society at large, mere membership in the organization of practitioners became a sufficient testament to one's competence.

This practice of RID members vetting new members represented another subtle shift in positionality vis-à-vis the Community. It is understandable that this vetting model would have elements of the prevailing model used by other certifying bodies (i.e., only members of the organization are able to vet those who would be certified) and of the model used by the Community (membership based on judgment of and acceptance by the members). However, the lack of overt, research-based criteria meant that intuitive judgments, which formed the original basis for membership and certification decisions, could neither be uniformly applied nor sustained. Consequently, a growing number of individuals were deemed worthy of RID membership and of holding its certification but who did not or could not conform to the Community's notion of competence. RID certification was, after all, only the organization's certification; it was not an independent, research-based, Community-validated assessment of an individual's competence. By joining the RID one could, without having the Community's imprimatur, have membership within the organization of interpreters and thus claim the title of "interpreter."

For society at large, the issue of qualifications of RID members was not a matter of question. "State officials, knowing little about deafness and less about interpreting, were easily convinced that everything was in order, simply because there was a registry of interpreters" (Schein, 1984, p. 112). It seems quite clear now that, from the perspective of government agencies, the *fact* that RID conducted testing and certification was of far greater significance than questions about its validity and reliability. This is clear from reports of pressure exerted on RID by the Vocational Rehabilitation Administration to begin a national certification program immediately after the RID grant ended in 1972. As will be addressed later, the research basis upon which to build a valid and reliable testing and certification system was simply not available at the time, and yet this seemed not to be a matter of concern.[6]

With the 1972 implementation of a national testing program aimed at certifying interpreters/transliterators, the processes involved in weaning and vetting practitioners were removed from the Community. What had essentially been a process of demonstrating competence and trustworthiness *over* time (control over which was vested in the Community), became a process of demonstrating competence at a single point in time (control over which was vested in examination boards). Given the absence of an adequate research base in the field, the now-predictable result was a great variability in the judgments of evaluation teams. The initial evaluation design called for Deaf people to be represented on evaluation teams. This, no doubt, was an acknowledgment of the importance of the Community's judgment in qualifying interpreters/transliterators. However, those Deaf people who agreed to serve on evaluation teams (and who were also RID members) were placed in the untenable position of upholding the standards of the Community in a testing situation that did not well reflect the expectations of the Community.

The position of and pressures on these representatives of the Community should not be discounted lightly. Lacking an empirically supported base for their work, they could not be the successful distillate of the Community's wisdom on evaluation teams. Some local evaluation teams gained a reputation for being stricter than others; as a result, it was not unusual for candidates to take the test in areas where teams were reputed to be more lenient. The critical issue then became one of credentialed incompetence. Individuals who otherwise would not be deemed qualified by the Community could, in effect, be credentialed in the eyes of society. This perception became more critical given other events begun in 1972.

The widespread proliferation of Manual Codes for English began in the United States in 1972. These artificially created systems of signing (e.g., Anthony, 1971; Gustason & Zawolkow, 1972) not only purported to represent English manually, but also claimed to be easier to learn than American Sign Language (ASL).[7] Given the historic oppression of ASL and the long-standing failure of educational systems to create appropriate environments in which Deaf students could become fluent in reading and writing English, it is not surprising that these systems would gain popularity. Unfortunately, such coded systems appealed to administrators faced with research demonstrating that the use of manual communication (i.e., signing) in the classroom is not detrimental to a Deaf child's educational experience.[8] They also appealed to parents who, in their naiveté, believed the advertising campaigns that using a system that purports to manually mirror spoken English will result in academic success, and to those individuals who were seeking an easy way to "learn to sign."[9]

At the time, RID's testing and certification system was not sufficiently sensitive to the differences between the signing of the Community and signs that were English-like. It is my belief that the early failure to capture this difference led to heightened dissatisfaction within the Community with services rendered by RID members. For example, an increasing number of RID members were certified who were unable to sign using the language of the Community, but who could sign using English-like signs. The early RID testing system tried to capture this dichotomy by establishing two certificates—one a certificate of interpretation and one a certificate of translation (later renamed transliteration)—but in many overt and subtle ways seemed to place greater value on the latter. The directions given to candidates taking the certification test are revealing. Before being given the testing materials for the certificate of interpretation, individuals were often instructed to "sign like you would for Deaf children or Deaf people with limited language skills." But before being given the testing materials for the certificate of translation, individuals were instructed to "sign like you would for the Deaf people on this panel." The difference is non-trivial. ASL, the "other language" used in interpretation, was thus characterized by the organization of interpreters as infantile, fit only for children and those without language; use of more English-like signing would be the behavior appropriate for those who were adults, those "without language problems," and those sitting in judgment of a candidate's skills.

However, while individuals could be certified for using English-like signing only, prevailing hiring and referral practices of the day were largely insensitive to the differences that mattered to the Community. Thus, for example, referral agencies often failed to solicit the interpreting or transliterating needs and preferences from members of the Community who were requesting services. This situation was exacerbated by the failure of RID and its members to be explicit in their use of terminology in order to differentiate between the tasks of interpreting and transliteration. In addition, the widespread use of the terms "interpreter" and "interpreting" as generic terms to refer to any facilitation of communication involving a Deaf person did not serve the Community well (Cokely, 1982).

The unwillingness or reluctance to be precise in this area is rather ironic given that the work of interpreters is fundamentally concerned with precision of meaning and intent. Partially as a result of this lack of clarity around the type of services that an "interpreter" could provide, the number of Community complaints regarding interpreter/transliterator incompetence began to increase. It is true that as the sheer volume of interpreting services being provided increased, one would expect an increase in the number of complaints. However, one has only to read the Community publications of the day and the issues raised by Deaf RID members at its conventions to realize that the type and volume of complaints cannot be accounted for solely by an increase in volume. Not only was there a lack of a solid research foundation upon which to base practice, including such critical questions as Community need and satisfaction, but the general reluctance to at least communicate with precision about distinctions in the work would prove problematic. The lack of a solid research foundation on interpretation and transliteration that would serve to enlighten and frame the issues loomed large and, in fact, this lack remains largely unaddressed to this day (see Marschark et al., this volume; Napier, this volume).

Ironically, 1972 also marked the first instructional text designed to teach ASL—Lou Fant's *Ameslan*. This text, which was a significant departure from previous picture books of signs, represented the first attempt to popularize learning the syntactic structure of the language of the Community. Even though Bill Stokoe's pioneering work in ASL was published in 1965, Deaf people, particularly at Gallaudet, who were the classic victims of prevailing hegemonic views on language and signing, initially resisted his work (see, e.g., Baker & Battison, 1980; Maher, 1996). Until the late 1970s and early 1980s, it would be safe to say that Stokoe's work was viewed largely as the province of researchers. In another ironic twist, 1972 would also mark the first year of publication of *Sign Language Studies*, a publication intended to disseminate research on the Community and its language. It also marked the first year that colleges and universities accepted ASL in fulfillment of their language requirements.[10]

Thus, during this period, there was movement on several fronts toward recognition of the language of the Community and acknowledgment of the status of the Community as a linguistic and cultural minority.[11] However, the popular appeal of Manual Codes for English served to reinforce for those unacquainted with the Community the historic pathological views of the Community and its language as deficient, deviant, and defective. This popular appeal was, in large measure, based on the perception that these codes were easier to learn than the language of the Community. In a very real sense, philosophical camps were drawn at this time and the general inability or unwillingness to be clear and definitive in this area would create further divisions between interpreters/transliterators and the Community—divisions that continue to this day.[12] This issue, perhaps more than any other, symbolizes the divide that had begun and would widen over the next decade or so. Would interpreters/transliterators accept the Community by embracing its language or would they inadvertently further oppress the Community by rejecting its language?

INTERPRETATION BY LEGISLATIVE FIAT

Legislative institutionalization of interpretation and transliteration began between 1972 and 1975. Section 504 of the Rehabilitation Act Amendments of 1973 would prove to have far-reaching implications for the Community and interpreters/transliterators. Although it was not immediately implemented,[13] this piece of legislation provided "handicapped individual[s]" with access to any "program or activity receiving federal financial assistance." For members of the Community, this meant increased access to aspects of society in general that had previously been denied or unavailable to them. For example, attending public colleges and universities was possible to a far greater extent than ever before. Importantly, such access could only be made possible if these colleges and universities employed interpreters/transliterators. While the Community generally viewed this piece of access legislation as a positive step forward, another piece of legislation passed during this period would not be so positively received.

The Education of All Handicapped Children's Act (P.L. 94-142) was passed in 1975 and was seen by many in the Community (and continues to be, even in its present iteration as the Individuals with Disabilities Education Act) as a piece of oppressive, normalization legislation. The effects on the Community—oppression by separation, communicative insensitivity, and the slow decline of residential schools for deaf students—have been discussed elsewhere (e.g., Lane 1992; Wrigley, 2002). While promoted by society in general as educational access legislation, many in the Community have concluded that in reality only the illusion of access and equality has been created. Given the value of cohesion to the Community,[14] this view of illusionary access should not be surprising. For interpreters/transliterators, this legislation would further alter their relationship with the Community. Interpreters/transliterators had now, albeit unwittingly, become the very instruments used to oppress the Community by creating and fostering this illusion of educational access and equality.

The passage of P.L. 94-142 and, to a lesser extent, Section 504 of the 1973 Rehabilitation Act also meant that for the first time on a wide scale, national-level control over who would be employed and retained in the position of interpreter/transliterator no longer rested in the hands of the Community. Prior to the passage of these pieces of legislation, members of the Community would typically arrange for interpreters/transliterators for activities or events. During the era of "interpretation/transliteration *as my contribution,*" the Community had some control over who would be asked to interpret or transliterate, given the restrictions of individuals' availability. The Community also had control over whether and when it would accept a would-be interpreter/transliterator. However, that vetting process would change with the era of "interpretation/transliteration *as legislative fiat.*"

In this new era, people who were not Community members (and who were unaware of reasonable expectations for practitioners' skill sets) were responsible for the hiring and supervision of interpreters/transliterators. One striking consequence of "interpretation/transliteration by legislative fiat" was that the demand for interpreters/transliterators quickly outpaced the supply. Nowhere was this more apparent than in K–12 educational settings where "interpreters" were, and often continue to be, hired and "supervised" by individuals who know nothing about the Community and its language and where deaf children are often isolated from the Community.

The explosion in the number of individuals claiming the title of interpreter or transliterator was nothing short of staggering. In 1974, RID had approximately 500 members; 6 years later well over four times that number held one or more forms of certification (Rudner, Getson, & Dirst, 1981). It must be borne in mind that the RID membership numbers do not include the many so-called interpreters who were hired by K–12 schools but who had no form of certification. This almost fivefold increase in the number of interpreters and transliterators could only come as a result of significant changes in the Community's relation to interpreters/transliterators. The era of "interpretation/transliteration as legislative fiat" brought with it full-time employment opportunities that had not previously existed. Slightly more than 10 years after the founding of RID and the prevailing view of "interpretation/transliteration as my contribution" to the Community for which no monetary compensation was expected, it was now possible for individuals to earn a living by interpreting or transliterating. Not only was monetary compensation possible, but it was becoming the norm. Ironically, legislation would begin to evoke the very result that founding RID members sought to avoid when they changed the organization's name: interpreters and transliterators were moving toward becoming "professional." While practitioners viewed this shift positively, members of the Community were considerably less enthusiastic. One has only to read the national and local Community publications (e.g., *The Deaf American*) and the RID newsletters of the time to gain an appreciation of the differences in how various issues were viewed—for example, rates of payment, ethical conduct, diminished sense of loyalty to the Community, and deteriorating quality control in certifying interpreters/transliterators.

ACADEMIC INSTITUTIONALIZATION

Another change that began during this era was a dramatic increase in the academic institutionalization of the language of the Community. The instruction of "sign language"[15] began to shift from churches and community centers, where it had been largely situated, to colleges and universities. This was partially a result of changes in the prevailing educational methodologies of the time. An increasing number of schools and programs for deaf children began to encourage and expect that "sign language" would be used in classrooms. Schools and programs began to expect that teachers would use "simultaneous communication," and a number of schools and programs adopted "total communication" (Holcomb, 1973). As a result, teacher preparation programs began to revise their curricula to include "sign language" classes. That led to an increase in the number of colleges and universities offering "sign language."

In many colleges and universities, instructors who were not Deaf were hired to teach because Deaf people often lacked the necessary academic credentials. Academic institutionalization was a significant change in how people who were not members of the community could gain access to the language of the Community. Up until this era, access to language of the Community had generally been by legacy or reward (Cokely, 2000). Individuals came to the language through blood ties (Deaf parents or siblings) or because they had learned the language directly from members of the Community (in nonacademic settings). The academic institutionalization of the language of the Community, while positive in many respects, brought with it another level of loss of Community control. The Community attempted to exert some measure of control in this regard through the 1974 founding of the Sign Instructors Guidance Network (SIGN) organization that is now called the American Sign Language Teachers Association (ASLTA). In an interesting case of history repeating itself, SIGN/ASLTA (like the RID before it), was closely linked with the NAD and established itself as the certifying body for sign language teachers. (SIGN/ASLTA has disaffiliated with the NAD and is seeking recognition on its own as an independent professional organization of sign language teachers.)

Given the precedent of academic institutionalization of language access, it is not difficult to understand how academic institutionalization would be seen by society at large as a viable response to the widespread increase in demand for interpreters/transliterators. Sensing the growing demand for interpreters/transliterators, the Rehabilitation Services Administration (RSA) created and funded the National Interpreter Training Consortium (NITC) in 1974. This consortium, which consisted of six colleges and universities,[16] was created to address the shortage of interpreters/transliterators. Among the consortium's goals was the development and implementation of 3-month training courses for individuals without prior interpreting experience. It is again noteworthy that, as was the case with development of the RID certification test, there was no meaningful research base upon which to properly understand the linguistic, cognitive, and sociolinguistic demands of interpretation and transliteration. Thus, not only the initial instructional premise, but also the curricula that were developed by the NITC, lacked the level of rigor that would be needed to replace or even to approximate the results produced by the experiential education that a prospective practitioner received from within the Community.

By 1980, the number of colleges or universities with interpreter training programs throughout the country had grown to over fifty, including the six original NITC members (Schein, 1984). Most of these were housed in community colleges and had grown in response to non-deaf students who wanted more advanced sign language courses. Since there was a growing demand for interpreters/transliterators, and since existing extensive language curricula were non-existent, sign language programs responded by adding "interpreting" courses. These interpreter training programs often were based on the only material available—the 1965 report of a Workshop on Interpreting published by the U.S. Department of Health, Education, and Welfare (Fant, 1990).

Partially in response to the need to gain information about prevailing practices, the National Academy of Gallaudet College convened a 1979 meeting of individuals with "experience and expertise in interpreter training" (Yoken, 1979). At the conference, participants identified topics related to interpreting and transliterating as well as pertinent publications. Sixty-three publications or initiatives were listed. An indication of the lack of basic research that existed at the time is that fewer than six of the listings directly related to the tasks of interpreting or transliterating. Following the 1979 "state-of-the-art conference," a second conference was held about a year later. At that conference, participants (again, individuals with "experience and expertise in interpreter training") identified over 100 specific topics for research that they felt were critical in order to inform training and education programs as well as certification and testing procedures. The primary recommendation was that the federal government fund co-ordinated, focused research in interpreting and transliterating. In 1980, the federal government announced that it would replace the NITC with ten federally funded programs and would greatly increase the funding level.

Conference participants recommended that one of these newly authorized programs be devoted to research. Nothing came of the recommendation, and to date there continues to be a lack of coordinated, basic research that can inform the practice of interpreting and transliterating and the preparation of interpreters and transliterators. It is unfortunate that current funding agencies fail to realize the critical need for basic research in order to effectively execute the very activities that their funding supports. Indeed, some of the available funding for interpreting and transliterating (e.g., the current RSA grants) expressly forbids research in grant activities. The lack of a research base to shape training and education programs and to inform assessment meant that the Community was becoming functionally marginalized as a locus of quality control in terms of the competencies of those who would interpret and transliterate. This marginalization was further increased by the fact that few Community members held faculty positions within training and education programs.

With implementation of this era's legislation, it was now increasingly possible in the eyes of society at large for individuals to earn a living by interpreting or transliterating without having been involved with or vetted by the Community. This meant that students with no prior contact with Deaf people could undertake a course of study to become an interpreter or transliterator. Prior to this time, as a result of one's "interactive" footing in the Community, "interpretation/transliteration as my contribution" was the orientation to the task. During this new era, however, the collective relationship continued to change from one based on communal obligation to one based on economic opportunity; from one based on personal relations to one based on business relations.

A gap had formed between the Community and interpreters/transliterators that could perhaps best be characterized as an emergent crisis of identity. As interpreters/transliterators began to forge an identity that was distinct from the Community, and one viewed by many as independent of the Community, it became increasingly easy for society and the Community to view them as service providers *for* the Community instead of service agents *of* the Community. In the now burgeoning era of academic footing, "interpretation/transliteration as compensated service" was becoming the primary orientation to the task. Prospective students were recruited into training and education programs because of growing demands in the "job market." As a result, members of the Community were no longer friends for whom one interpreted or transliterated; they were now "consumers" or "clients." Certainly this change in orientation contributed to the shift in prevailing "models" of the task—that is, from helper to machine. Since many interpreters/transliterators were no longer from the Community, the Community sought protection in urging ersatz interpreters/transliterators to function in more of a mechanistic manner because they had not yet proven that they were trustworthy.

As "interpretation/transliteration as compensated service" became the norm, issues of compensation became yet another facet of the "love/hate" relationship between the Community and interpreters and transliterators. Members of the Community resented the fact that interpreters and transliterators now routinely expected to be compensated for their services even though members of the Community were unemployed or underemployed. The Community also feared that rising hourly fees demanded by interpreters and transliterators would result in a denial of access and services because agencies and service providers would resist paying these fees.

The academic institutionalization of the Community's language as well as a shift in the process by which interpreters and transliterators would be trained and employed marked a significant loss of control for the Community. Certainly there were, and continue to be, significant advantages to the academic acceptance of the language of the Community, but those advantages carry with them a significant cost to the Community. Legislation had appropriately mandated societal access for Deaf people, but the gate-keeping function that the Community had long held in shaping the pool of individuals who would interpret or transliterate no longer resided within the Community. Employment opportunities for interpreters/transliterators were increasing dramatically. In yet another significant shift and loss of control, it was no longer the Community that was requesting interpretation and transliteration services. In fact, by 1980, most interpreters/transliterators were being requested by and employed by non-deaf people (LaVor, 1985), further underscoring the view of interpreters/transliterators as being *for* the Community. A survey of 160 certified interpreters and transliterators at the 1980 RID convention (Cokely, 1981) revealed the extent of this shift. Ninety-eight percent of the respondents reported that they interpreted regularly on a paid basis, those with Deaf parents for an average of 9.5 years (i.e., since 1970) and those whose parents were not Deaf for an average of 4.5 years (i.e., since 1975) with educational/classroom work being the most frequent setting by a margin of five to one.

Given the increase in academic footing as an entrée to interpretation and transliteration and the fact that would-be practitioners often have no requisite connections to the Community, the responsibility for ensuring that the Community is not merely an object of study and theoretical curiosity rests with those responsible for an education or training program. Programs bear the burden of seeking out a variety of ways in which their students can become actively involved with the Community. Activities that provide avenues of Community connect-edness are quite varied, but as Monikowski and Peterson (this volume) point out, there is a critical issue that must be considered with any such activity: The Community must perceive that it is being served by the activity rather than being taken advantage of by the activity. The ac-tivity must be such that it directly benefits the Community; benefits to the students should be viewed as by-products of the activity. This is particularly crucial given the shift in positionality of interpreters/transliterators. If these would-be practitioners are no longer perceived as "of the Community," then it is essential that programs begin to be perceived as "of the Community." If would-be practitioners no longer view "interpretation/transliteration as my contribution," then it is es-sential that programs begin to seek ways that they and their students can contribute to the Community. Programs unable or unwilling to be "of the Community" and unable or unwilling to contribute to the Community should examine their raison d'être.

ACTIVITY QUA ACCOMPLISHMENT?

As one reviews the events during the pivotal 1972–1975 period, and the consequences of those events, it seems clear that activity was mistaken for accomplishment. When one examines the initiatives of the era, one is struck by the virtual absence of research upon which to base those initiatives. Clearly there is value in the anecdotal experiences of prac-titioners of the day and the received wisdom of the Community in shaping interpreter/transliterator assessment and training programs. Clearly there is value in federal legislative and programmatic initiatives that increase societal access for the Community. However, without the prerequisite research base, necessarily rooted in the Community, it is unclear whether such initiatives can truly be effective.

Unfortunately, it seems clear that this pattern of mistaking move-ment as a measure of success continues. It is now 40 years after the founding of RID and the rejection of calls for conducting research be-fore implementing a certification process. It is almost 25 years after leading practitioners of the day were ignored in their request for sig-nificant federal funding for research into interpreting and transliterat-ing. Nevertheless, legislative and programmatic initiatives continue without the necessary research base upon which to develop those ini-tiatives in order for them to be successful.

One need only consider the early RID evaluations to realize the shortcomings of well-intentioned activities that were uninformed by research. Consider, for example, that "Speed/Time lag" was among the rating criteria used in RID evaluation process from 1972 until 1983 (Rudner et al., 1981). This rating category meant that candidates were penalized if, in rendering their interpretations or transliterations, they lagged behind the stimulus test material. This directly influenced interpreter training programs (ITPs) and resulted in notions of accuracy that were quantitative, not qualitative. In fact, early interpreter training programs, such as the Gallaudet College ITP, developed and purchased materials that were "speed graded," and individuals were judged competent if they could "interpret" audiotaped material at speeds approaching 120 words per minute. As one practitioner put it, "I was brainwashed to believe that accuracy was in volume of information and if it took seven hundred and fifty words to say this, then it should take seven hundred and fifty words to sign it and if it didn't then somehow I was jeopardizing accuracy" (*Interpreters on Interpreting*, 1989). As a result, synchrony of interpretation and source message became highly valued, and candidates were marked down if their performance did not maintain temporal synchrony with the original message. This meant that evaluation candidates were penalized if they did the very thing (i.e., seeking to increase comprehension which often is in an inverse relationship with temporal synchrony) that subsequent research would show was necessary for more accurate work (Cokely, 1986).

Another more recent movement that poses interesting questions for the relationship between interpreters/transliterators and the Community is the emergence of certified deaf interpreters (CDIs). As Forestal notes in this volume, Deaf people were originally certified by RID in order to function as evaluators in the RID testing system. Within the past two decades, however, there has been a growing demand for and presence of Deaf individuals working in a team with non-deaf interpreters/transliterators in a range of dialogic interactions (e.g., mental health and medical settings) and at a limited number of conferences. In a clear case of history repeating itself, RID has recently implemented a national certification test for these Deaf individuals and yet there is virtually no research that investigates what it is Deaf people actually do when they work with a non-deaf colleague in facilitating communication.

On the surface, it appears that the cognitive, linguistic, and communicative processes that are at work in such interactions are fundamentally different for Deaf people and for their non-deaf teammates. Anecdotal evidence to support this comes from a series of meetings held during the 2001–2002 academic year. During that year, I was fortunate enough to meet 1 day a month with a dozen Deaf people from all over New England, all of whom worked as CDIs. During the course of these meetings, it became clear that excepting those rare platform opportunities, their regular work as CDIs occurred whenever there was a perceived "language problem" such as an immigrant Deaf person or a Deaf person with minimal communication skills. None of the Deaf persons ever recalled working in a situation in which there was no perceived language or communication "problem." This reality also conditions how the Community perceives CDIs. A perfect example is an incident related by one of the Deaf people in the group who was sent to work at a Deaf child's Individualized Educational Program (IEP) meeting. When the CDI entered the meeting room, the Deaf child's mother, who was herself Deaf, turned to the CDI and signed, "We don't need you here. My child doesn't have any communication problems."

During the yearlong series of meetings with this group of Deaf people, it also became clear that the linguistic and communicative strategies that CDIs commonly employ are markedly different from what has become expected, conventional practice among non-deaf interpreters/transliterators. These observations suggest that there is much about the work of our Deaf colleagues that we do not yet understand and that they may not be able to fully articulate. One wonders then how it is possible to assess and certify competence in the absence of such fundamental research. Our history of presuming we know what to do despite the lack of research has not been positive.

Another interesting question that emerged from this series of meetings with CDIs is the wisdom of using the job title "Certified Deaf Interpreter." The job title "CDI" attempts to frame the communicative work of Deaf people by linking it to the communicative work of non-deaf interpreters/transliterators. However, Deaf people reported repeatedly that it was often difficult to convince employers or clients of the need for two "interpreters," particularly when one of them is Deaf. This is made doubly difficult since the view of the general non-deaf public is that interpreters are "for" Deaf people. The group of Deaf colleagues also reported significant resistance from non-Deaf interpreters and transliterators who felt that the presence of a Deaf teammate called into question their own skills and ability to do the task at hand. If, however, as I believe to be the case, the tasks are different, then framing the task differently can bring a greater level of respect for the task and an increase in the job market for Deaf colleagues. A differently framed and more precise job title, such as "Visual Language Specialist," automatically creates new expectations within which differentiated tasks can be more readily understood and accepted by society in general. This "frame differentiation by title" might also assist non-Deaf interpreters/transliterators who feel that the presence of or need for a Deaf colleague is somehow an affront or challenge to their own competence.

Job market cultivation is essential, but it can only occur with a clear notion of what it is Deaf team members actually do. Ultimately, however, the value in more accurately reflecting the communicative work of our Deaf colleagues can only happen in a meaningful way if it is rooted in descriptive and empirical research. In the absence of descriptive and empirical research on the communicative tasks performed by CDIs, we are unable to address successfully the economic objections of employers who see the presence of a second interpreter as unnecessary and the presence of a CDI as impractical or inconceivable. Unfortunately, as Forestal notes in this volume, there is presently little support for developing careers for Deaf people in this area.

Perhaps nowhere have the consequences of mistaking activity for accomplishment and proceeding without a sufficient research base been more glaring and more devastating than the decades' old movement to mainstream Deaf students begun with passage of P.L. 94-142. Not only did this movement alter the relationship between the Community and interpreters/transliterators, but it also radically altered the social and cultural nature of the Community. From the Community's perspective, P.L. 94-142 (and its later incarnations) is a prime example of the legislated consequences of hegemony and the implementation of views proffered almost a century earlier. Mainstreaming legislation, which passed by appealing to the values of democratic inclusivity and maximizing one's potential, failed to consider properly and fully the linguistic and communicative demands of interpreted/transliterated education as well as the social and psychological costs of mainstreaming deaf students. Ironically, while the integrationist rhetoric of the day obscured the social and psychological costs, the very presence of an organization of interpreters/transliterators and growing national certification of its members served to minimize concerns about linguistic and communicative demands of mainstreaming Deaf students.

In a relatively short period of time, K–12 settings became, and remain, the most frequent employment opportunities for interpreters/transliterators. The fact that interpreters and transliterators, as a group, did not take a strong stand against this disabling legislation may have been seen by some in the Community as self-serving, because of the very increase in employment opportunities. The employment impact on practitioners can be better understood when one considers the fact that at the present time, it has been estimated that 60% of interpreters and transliterators work in K–12 settings (Burch, 2002). Mainstreaming legislation that was, and is, viewed as a symbol of destruction for many in the Community (e.g., Jankowski, 1997) had co-opted interpreters/transliterators into enabling this destruction and thus further distancing them as a group from the Community.

Once again, activity, absent fundamental research, was taken as the measure of success. The illusion of access had been created, and the symbol of that illusion for many was, and remains, interpreters/transliterators. RID, acting on the premise that the organization should adhere to the same expectations of neutrality and impartiality it expected of practitioners, took no significant stand. School districts and individual schools, compelled by force of law (and with little desire to or knowledge with which to fight for meaningful changes in the law), coupled with a rapidly shrinking supply of "qualified" interpreters/ transliterators, had no choice but to hire anyone that they felt could function as an interpreter/transliterator, including those that the Community felt were "signers" but clearly not interpreters/transliterators. To the uninformed and uneducated educational establishment, these were "prima facie interpreters," but they often had no affiliation with the RID and thus were neither vetted by the organization nor compelled to abide by its Code of Ethics.

Beginning in the mid-seventies, the number of Deaf students who were thrust into mainstream educational programs began to increase exponentially. This "legislatively forced Deaf diaspora" yielded nothing short of catastrophic consequences for residential schools for Deaf students and, as a result, the Community, its language, and its culture (see, e.g., Lane, 1992; Lane, Bahan, & Hoffmeister, 1996; Wrigley, 2002). In a relatively short period of time, a sizeable number of individuals were employed as interpreters/transliterators in K–12 settings who were even further removed from being vetted to any degree by the Community. That the majority of these individuals lacked RID certification or any other competency credentials led to a perception that those working in K–12 settings represented the least competent among us. This perception is only strengthened by surveys that reveal that a large number of individuals view working in K–12 settings as a "stepping stone" until they become state screened or nationally certified and thus are able to work in other venues.

For example, a 2002 survey of K–12 interpreters/transliterators working in Massachusetts revealed that fully two-thirds envision themselves working in the K–12 setting for 5 years or less, with almost a third envisioning their K–12 careers lasting 3 years or less.[17] Another significant finding is that fully one-third of those surveyed had been working as interpreters/transliterators for 2 years or less. If these data can be generalized nationwide, then not only is a significant portion of the K–12 interpreter/transliterator population rather inexperienced, but the K–12 establishment confronts a significant work force turnover and an extremely high level of instability on an annual basis. So too, then, they reveal that the least experienced among us and, to the extent that there is a correlation, the least competent among us are working in settings that have significant consequences for the future of deaf students and the Community.

Given that the educational lives of so many Deaf students were, and are, determined by what in some cases can best be described as "ersatz practitioners," it is astounding that we continue to have such little research on the work of those who function as K–12 interpreters/ transliterators. Consider, for example, that in a review of almost sixty refereed research articles dealing with interpretation and transliteration from 1986 to 1996, only five studies are focused on the actual working of interpreters/transliterators in K–12 settings.[18] Beginning with the passage of P.L. 94-142, we have been witness to a legislative initiative based on a series of presumptions, none of which has been empirically supported. Three decades later not only do we still lack empirical research that can address essential questions regarding mainstreaming of Deaf students and the work of interpreters/transliterators in K–12 settings, but we lack any concerted and coordinated effort that can address these questions (Marschark et al., this volume).

The explicit and implicit research questions in this volume stand not only as a chronicle of what we do not know about interpreting and transliterating in general, and about interpreting and transliterating in K–12 settings in particular, but they also serve as suggestions that might guide a research agenda. Clearly a systematic, coordinated program of research, properly involving members of the Community and other stakeholders, would reveal additional areas of critical inquiry. Unfortunately, the reality is that we have not had a nationally coordinated, properly supported and sustained research initiative that can inform practice in these critical areas. Undeterred by our lack of knowledge, society continues to place Deaf students in mainstream settings, often in isolation from other Deaf peers. A cynic would hold that this educational "integration by separation" of Deaf people has been a deliberate maneuver to further marginalize Deaf people and foster the dissipation of the Community. The same cynic would also hold that the hegemonic "powers that be" see little value in seeking answers to necessary and fundamental research questions because the answers would only challenge the status quo and upset the illusion that access has been created. Finally, the same cynic would hold that schools and school districts faced with legal mandates, and yet realizing the true cost of integrating Deaf students into their programs, have responded by spending the minimum amount necessary to create the illusion of access and compliance.

As a society we invest far greater resources in researching initiatives that are hardly as valuable to our future as the educational lives of children of the Community. It is certainly perplexing and troubling that, given the educational and life-trajectory stakes for Deaf children, there has not been more of an outcry for such bedrock research from the Community, including parents, practitioners, administrators, legislators, interpreters/transliterators, interpreter educators, and those who have been the victims of the illusion of educational access. Individual practitioners surely bear some responsibility for challenging the historic pattern of practice that has used the mere physical presence of an interpreter/transliterator as an indication of the likely success of an interaction. Ultimately, however, the decisions surrounding educational placement for Deaf students rest with parents. It is they who, in their desire to seek the best for their children, need to make the best-informed decisions possible. Their quest to make these decisions must necessarily seek to address the questions of whether an interpreted education is an equivalent and appropriate education; whether the choice of an interpreted education is more a parent-centered or a child-centered option; and, of utmost importance, whether the interpreters/transliterators provided by the school have been independently qualified and credentialed. The lack of fundamental research in this area should be of paramount concern to parents, and the demand for such research should be spearheaded by parents.

Programs designed to train and educate interpreters/transliterators also bear significant responsibility in this regard. Clearly both programs and practitioners have an obligation to question activities within the field that are not supported by solid empirical and theoretical research. But programs bear a heavier responsibility since it is they whose perspectives and actions will shape the future interpreters/transliterators. Just as programs should seek to be "of the Community" and should seek opportunities to create Community connectedness for their students, they also have an obligation to demand a greater theoretical and empirical research foundation within the profession and education and training programs. In short, programs bear the responsibility for challenging the historic pattern of practice that has valued action over evidence and has viewed activity as accomplishment.

SUMMARY AND CONCLUSIONS

This chapter has examined the relationship between interpreters/transliterators and the Community and the forces that altered that relationship. Although the 1964 creation of an organization of interpreters/transliterators might be seen as a pivotal event, this chapter suggests that a series of events between 1972 and 1975 would irrevocably alter the position of interpreters/transliterators vis-à-vis the Community. What began as a relationship largely evolved from personal connections with members of the Community became a relationship based on commerce and often rooted in detachment. The shifted positionality was heightened by the exponential growth of employment opportunities brought about by federal legislation. The most significant consequence of this shift was a loss of Community control over who would be viewed as interpreters/transliterators. Ironically, the presence of the organization of interpreters and transliterators and its certification system served as evidence to society at large that competent interpreters and transliterators existed in sufficient number to implement legislation passed during this period.

From 1972 to 1975, interpretation and transliteration as an occupation clearly moved from an activity in which the time-tested imprimatur of the Community was of paramount importance for practitioners to an activity in which legislatively mandated employment for practitioners required little or no involvement from the Community. Of particular significance was the large-scale employment opportunity for interpreters and transliterators created by P.L. 94-142, the very legislation that would bring about a forced deaf diaspora. From the Community's perspective, the relationship was altered even more by the academic institutionalization of its language and the subsequent institutionalization of programs designed to train and educate interpreters and transliterators. The academic institutionalization has further exacerbated the shifted relation in large measure because most members of the Community lack the academic qualifications required to work at academic institutions.

Underscoring and enabling each of these position-altering events has been a persistent lack of empirical research; fundamental research necessary to inform practitioners and the programs that seek to train or educate them. While individual practitioners bear some responsibility for questioning practices that are not rooted in research, programs bear a much heavier burden of responsibility. The greater burden arises from the position that programs now occupy as the primary source of Community connectedness for would-be interpreters/transliterators. As the gate keeping for interpretation and transliteration becomes more rooted in academia and further removed from the crucible of Community interaction, programs have the responsibility to be "of the Community" rather than "for the Community." In large measure, discharging this responsibility requires that programs not only demand a greater level of research to guide their educational activities, but also that they question practices not substantiated by research. Ultimately, it means that action absent empirical evidence can no longer be taken as accomplishment.

NOTES

1. I have chosen to use the terms "interpreter/transliterator" and "interpreting/transliterating" throughout this chapter. While this may be slightly more cumbersome than the generic "interpreter" and "interpreting," I believe that the generic terms not only fail to accurately capture differing skill-sets required of practitioners, but also fail to capture the competencies required by different members of the Deaf Community.

2. I am keenly aware that dealing with issues of positionality and identity relations is incredibly complex and prone to overgeneralizations. These issues are made even more complex when one of the groups involved, the Deaf Community, is a historically oppressed minority. Clearly I make no claim to speak for the Deaf Community in offering these observations, and I also fully

recognize that it is often difficult to distinguish "speaking about" from "speaking for." My "knowledge claims" in this arena stem from my own experience of almost four decades of interactions with Deaf people and interpreters at local, regional, national, and international levels.

3. I use the term "the Community" in the full knowledge that the Deaf Community is not, by its very nature, monolithic and that there is wonderful linguistic, social, ethic, socio-economic, and other diversity within the Community.

4. The notion of an organization of interpreters did not occur in a vacuum; in 1963, the Texas Society of Interpreters for the Deaf (TSID) was established. TSID would become the first local affiliate chapter of RID.

5. The actual organizational meeting took place the evening of June 16, 1964.

6. Interestingly, Fant (1990) notes that in January of 1965, at a Follow-Up Workshop on Interpreting, the vice president of The Psychological Corporation, a company specializing in the development of certification programs, made a presentation to the participants. According to Fant, "He made it abundantly clear that much research must precede any attempt to construct an instrument for certifying competence" (p. 44).

7. A growing body of literature has not only revealed linguistic and performance problems with these Manual Codes for English (e.g., Cokely and Gawlik, 1973; Marmor and Petitto, 1979), but has also failed to substantiate causal claims of improved academic performance of students using these codes (see, e.g., Lederberg, 2003; Schick, 2003).

8. Most notable among this research were Meadow (1968) and Schlesinger and Meadow (1972). The latter work was quite prominent in the proceedings of the 1972 Special Study Institute on "Psycholinguistics and Total Communication" held at Lewis and Clark College, Oregon.

9. In fact, in their advertising, several of the authors made clear their belief that learning their system was far easier than learning ASL, and this was used as a primary selling point.

10. Among the first were American University, New York University, and the University of Minnesota.

11. It is worth remembering that this positive movement toward acceptance of the language and recognition of the community occurred within a wider social context in which traditionally oppressed groups were beginning to claim recognition and empowerment.

12. I firmly believe that the pervasive notion that RID and its members have to be "all things to all people" has negatively impacted testing, certification, and licensure issues; access legislation issues; the efficacy of referral agencies; and the curricula of interpreter training and education programs.

13. It would take 2 years and several protests, culminating in a sit-in at the offices of the Secretary of Health, Education, and Welfare in 1975, before the federal government finally released implementation rules and regulations.

14. Mindess (1999) discusses the idea of the Community as a collectivist culture in which the group and the received wisdom of the group is held in high regard.

15. The term "sign language" was, and still is, often used in academic settings to refer to any means of manual communication, including American Sign Language or one of the Manual Codes for English.

16. New York University, Gallaudet College, the University of Tennessee, the California State University at Northridge, the University of Arizona, and St. Paul Technical Vocational Institute.

17. This survey was conducted under the auspices of the Interpreter Education Project at Northeastern on behalf of the Massachusetts Commission for the Deaf and Hard of Hearing and the Massachusetts Department of Education.

18. See Seal (2004) for full details; of the 60 articles, 21 focus on the need for and characteristics of K–12 interpreters/transliterators, 15 focus on the work of interpreters/transliterators (but only 5 are in the K–12 setting), 18 focus on interpreters/transliterators working in postsecondary settings, and 7 focus on miscellaneous aspects of interpreters/transliterators.

REFERENCES

Anthony, D. (1971). *Seeing essential English manual.* Anaheim, CA: Educational Services Division, Union High School District.

Baker, C., & Battison, R. (1980). *Sign language and the Deaf Community.* Silver Spring, MD: National Association of the Deaf.

Burch, D. (2002). Essential education for sign language interpreters in pre-college educational settings. *Journal of Interpretation*, 125–149.

Cokely, D. (1981). Sign language interpreters: a demographic survey. *Sign Language Studies 10 (32)*, 261–286.

Cokely, D. (1982). Editor's comments. *The Reflector, 2 (Winter)*, 3–5.

Cokely, D. (1986). Effects of lag time on interpreter errors. *Sign Language Studies 53*, 341–375.

Cokely, D. (2000). Exploring ethics: a case for revising the code of ethics. *Journal of Interpretation*, 25–60.

Cokely, D., & Gawlick, R. (1976). Options: A position paper on the relation between Manual English and Sign. *The Deaf American, 25 (9)*, 7–11.

Fant, L. (1972). *Ameslan: An introduction to American Sign Language.* Los Angeles: Joyce Media, Inc.

Fant, L. (1990). *Silver threads.* Silver Spring, MD: RID Publications.

Gustason, G., & Zawolkow, E. (1972). *Signing exact English.* Los Alamitos, CA: Modern Signs Press.

Holcomb, R. (1973). Total communication is a must. In *Proceedings of the 46th CAID Meeting.*

Jankowski, K. (1997). *Deaf empowerment.* Washington, DC: Gallaudet University Press.

Karttunen, F. (1994). *Between worlds: Interpreters, guides and survivors.* New Brunswick, NJ: Rutgers University Press.

Lane, H. (1992). *The mask of benevolence: Disabling the deaf community.* New York: Knopf.

Lane, H., Bahan, B., & Hoffmeister, B. (1996). *Journey into the deaf-world.* San Diego: Dawn Sign Press.

LaVor, M. (1985). Interpreters: The economic impact. *Journal of Interpretation*, 27–37.

Lederberg, A. (2003). Expressing meaning: from communicative intent to building a lexicon. In M. Marschark & P. Spencer (Eds.), *Deaf studies, language, and education.* New York: Oxford University Press.

Maher, J. (1996). *Seeing language in sign: The work of William C. Stokoe,* Washington, DC: Gallaudet University Press.

Marmor, G., & Petitto, L. (1979). Simultaneous communication in the classroom: how well is English grammar represented? *Sign Language Studies, 23,* 99–136.

Meadow, K. (1968). Early manual communication in relation to the deaf child's intellectual, social, and communicative functioning. *American Annals of the Deaf, 113 (1),* 29–41.

Mindess, A. (1999). *Reading between the signs.* Yarmouth, ME: Intercultural Press.

Quigley, S., & Youngs, J. (1965). *Interpreting for deaf people.* Washington, DC: U.S. Department of Health, Education and Welfare.

Quigley, S., Basel, B., & Wilbur, R. (1973). A survey of interpreters for deaf people in the state of Illinois. *Journal of Rehabilitation of the Deaf 6 (1),* 7–11.

Rudner, L., Getson, P., & Dirst, R. (1981). Interpreter competence. *RID Interpreting Journal 1 (1),* 10–18.

Schein, J. (1984). *Speaking the language of sign.* New York: Doubleday.

Schick, B. (2003). The development of American sign language and manually coded English systems. In M. Marschark & P. Spencer (Eds.), *Deaf studies, language, and education.* New York: Oxford University Press.

Schlesinger, H., & Meadow, K. (1972). *Sound and sign: Childhood deafness and mental health.* Berkeley: University of California Press.

Seal, B. (2004). *Best practices in educational interpreting.* Boston: Allyn and Bacon.

Sign Media, Inc. (1989). *Interpreters on interpreting: Identity.* Burtonsville, MD: Sign Media, Inc.

Smith, T. (1983). What goes around comes around: Reciprocity and interpreters. *The Reflector 5 (Winter),* 5–7.

Stewart, D., Schein, J., & Cartwright, B. (2004). *Sign language interpreting: Exploring its art and science.* Boston: Allyn and Bacon.

Stokoe, W. Casterline, D., & Croneberg, C. (1965). *A dictionary of American sign language on linguistic principles.* Washington, DC: Gallaudet University Press.

Valdes, G. (2003). *Expanding definitions of giftedness.* Hillsdale, NJ: Lawrence Erlbaum Associates.

Wrigley, O. (2002). *The politics of deafness.* Washington, DC: Gallaudet University Press.

Yoken, C. (1979). *Interpreter training: The state of the art.* Washington, DC: National Academy, Gallaudet College.

2

Toward Real Interpreting

Graham H. Turner

As British Sign Language (BSL)–English interpreting has developed on a professional footing over the past two decades, much has been made of the non-routine nature of professional interpreting work. One of the characteristics that distinguishes professions from other occupations appears to be that, for the professional, it is a realistic truism that "no two jobs are the same." It is the non-routine nature of the work that ensures that every day, every encounter, every turn at talk is indeed fundamentally unknown terrain.

This chapter summarizes how an informed interpreting practitioner can negotiate such terrain effectively. In doing so, it takes a step toward promoting what I have called "real interpreting" (Turner & Harrington, 2001)—interpreting that takes into account the range of contextual factors that, from moment to moment, guide the choices that interpreters make in designing their contributions to communicative exchanges. To engage in real interpreting means, as a practitioner, to know your options well and endeavor to select appropriately from among them, according to the prevailing circumstances. With this comes the responsibility to make informed choices and to be accountable for them.

TYPOLOGIES AND PARAMETERS

Interpreting is nothing if not a multifaceted activity. Students of the discipline benefit greatly from the opportunity to build a rounded awareness of how their experiences or expectations form part of a much larger "jigsaw" or map. Standing back from immediate knowledge and concerns, it is possible to take a broader view of the field, to enlarge one's perspective, and to identify a wide range of elements closely intertwined to create an entire interpreting landscape. To the intellectual good fortune of the field, several interpreting scholars have attempted to develop the necessary panoptic field of vision in an effort to capture in print an overview of this territory.

Heidemarie Salevsky proposed a relatively early typology of interpreting (and translation) events, based on a set of seven parameters:

- Repeatability of the activity,
- Proportion of the relevant text available to the interpreter,
- Timeframe in which the activities or tasks of the interpreter unfold (e.g., does reception of the message unfold in parallel to its reperformance?),
- Time constraints (e.g., are there restrictions on the speed at which the process must occur?),
- Spatial constraints relating to the physical location of participants,
- Channel or mode via which the original text is received (e.g., visual or auditory), and
- Channel or mode in which the relayed text is delivered. (1982, pp. 80–86)

Subsequently, Salevsky (1993) set out a structural account of interpreting studies, with subdomains defined according to situational variables: varieties of interpreting (consecutive or simultaneous), the medium (human, machine, computer-aided interpreting), area or institution (legal interpreting, health interpreting, etc.), text relations (text type, degree of specialization, etc.), partner relations (source-text producer vs. target-text addressee), combinations of languages involved, and combinations of cultures invoked.

In 1997 Bistra Alexieva, a scholar specializing in Bulgarian-English interpreting, produced further work building on these foundations (2002). Alexieva directly challenged a history throughout which interpreter-mediated events have typically been categorized according to single parameters, such as by the communicative situation or context in which the interpreting occurs ("conference interpreting," "court interpreting," or "TV interpreting," etc.). Alexieva commended Salevsky's model, which she described as a "multiparameter" approach, and sought to include two kinds of additional parameters: (a) elements of the communicative situation (i.e., *who* speaks to *whom* about *what*, *where*, *when*, *why*, and for *what purpose*), and (b) the nature of the texts involved in the event, including questions of orality versus literacy, proportion of the text available, topic(s) addressed, and questions of intertextuality and relationships with relevant macro-texts.

Alexieva developed the proposed typology by grouping the parameters under two broad headings:

- Mode of delivery: this allows us to distinguish between (i) a non-stop delivery of the source text and simultaneous production of the target text, and (ii) a consecutive delivery of the source text (in chunks of varying lengths) followed by the production of the target text. This distinction also involves differences in the use, or non-use, of ancillary equipment, the specificity of the setting, and the nature of the contact or distance between participants.
- Elements of the communicative situation, namely: the primary participants (Speaker and Addressee), the secondary participants (Interpreter, Organizer, Moderator), the topic discussed and the way it relates to the communicative context, the type of texts used in the communication, the spatial and temporal specificities of the communication, and the purpose of the communication goals pursued by the participants. (2002, pp. 221–222)

Alexieva detailed each of these elements in turn, aligning them under six key parameters and stressing, in addition, that since interpreting is always inherently a matter of inter*cultural* communication, it will also constantly be necessary to consider how issues of "universality" versus "cultural specificity" interact with other parameters in determining the nature of an interpreted event.

In a synthesis of mapping, integrating the diverse elements of the *gestalt* of interpretation, Franz Pöchhacker has established a careful and well-founded definition of interpreting as "a form of Translation in which a first and final rendition in another language is produced on the basis of a one-time presentation of an utterance in a source language" (2004, p. 11). Pöchhacker suggested that the concept of interpreting can be broadly differentiated according to *social* contexts and institutional *settings* (inter-social vs. intra-social settings) as well as situational *constellations* and formats *of interaction* (multilateral conference vs. face-to-face dialogue). Reviewing previous attempts to generate a typological overview of interpreting practices, he described a more detailed typology by applying the parameters of language modality (signed vs. spoken-language interpreting), working mode (consecutive vs. simultaneous interpreting), directionality (bilateral, relay interpreting, etc.), use of technology (remote interpreting, machine interpreting), and professional status ("natural" vs. professional interpreting).

In concluding his overview, Pöchhacker adopted the following set of eight dimensions to map out the theoretical territory of interpreting studies: Medium, Setting, Mode, Languages (cultures), Discourse, Participants, Interpreter, and Problem.

Pöchhacker suggested that one can distinguish and "plot" types of interpreting (conference interpreting, community-based interpreting, etc.) on a multidimensional grid by taking these eight parameters as axes of a conceptual graph, but stressed that, given the many facets of the diverse phenomena to be covered, this schematic approach cannot be equated with a combinatorial map of features.

INTERPRETERS' CHOICES

As valuable as these high-level overviews and maps of the territory undoubtedly are, they primarily address the theorist's requirements for a broad understanding of the field rather than provide a framework for practitioners to use in their everyday work. In order to move toward such a framework, the interpreter's focus in this context can be reduced to one key question: In what ways might I interpret this?

At first glance, this appears to be an absurdly simple question. How does this advance the interpreter's cause any further at all? The important point here is the presupposition required in order to ask this question at all, which is that *the interpreter has a choice* about what to do. To be asking this question at all, one must be assuming a theoretical position that affords the interpreter a role, not as a "conduit" through whom messages pass (without being in any significant way transformed), but as an *active* third participant in interaction. If it is accepted that interpreters do not act as conduits, then of necessity they *must* engage as communicative participants. They are *obliged* to make choices (Turner & Harrington, 2001). This is an understanding that has developed within the field as a whole over a considerable period of time, but one rooted in the work of Anderson (2002), Wadensjö (1992, 1993, 1995, 1997, 1998, 2001a, 2001b), and Roy (1989, 1993a, 1993b, 2000).

It is also crucial to note that the choice-making activity in which the interpreter engages is a *dynamic* process. This is not a matter of "tuning in" to one of a range of preset stations (as one might on a radio) and then sitting back while the tunes wash over and through the listener. The choices that an interpreter makes are a moment-by-moment matter, decisions made and remade to reflect the prevailing circumstances of the interaction. It is the intensity of attention required in order to undertake this process effectively that lies behind the oft-cited claim that performance levels decrease after 20 minutes of simultaneous interpreting.

Interpreting is here taken to be an activity the nature of which can shift significantly at any time within an interactional event. The typological distinctions discussed above are, in this context, seen not as static or monolithic reifications, but as elements in an impressionistic, kaleidoscopic engagement in communicative interaction. Such a position extends the analysis of Alexieva, who noted that "the boundaries between these phenomena are likely to remain fluid...we cannot expect to delineate clear-cut categories....Rather than attempt to describe these events as rigid categories, we should approach them as 'families,' with central members (prototypes) and peripheral members (blend-forms)" (2002, p. 221). This is an approach I have sought to develop with reference to the notion of "hybrid" forms of interpreting (Turner & Pollitt, 2002). That article examined sign language–interpreted performances in the theatre, exploring questions about their categorization within one frame of reference as "literary translations" and within another as "community interpreting." We suggested that, *pace* Alexieva, rather than see interpreter-mediated activity that simultaneously combines features associated with several different normative categories as "peripheral," it should perhaps be considered quite common-place, or indeed consistently predictable. Here, though, I am arguing that this notion should be pressed further in order to conceptualize the dynamic nature of interpreter decision-making as a reflection of the *kaleidoscopically* hybrid essence of the process.

"In what ways might I interpret this?" is the primary question in the practitioner's scheme of action, but it can be answered, in essence, with reference to the following four sub-questions. These sub-questions provide, when answered, the principles upon which any particular interpretation might be constructed.

1. Who Are We?

This question is designed to frame the interpreter's awareness of issues of identity in the construction of all communication. Notice that if this is conceived as a moment-by-moment issue, then what is really being asked is "who are the participants in this interaction being now?" or, in other words, how are they seeking to construct and present their identity at this point in the exchange. It is clear from scholarship to date that these questions of identity should be seen not as absolutes (people do not have fixed identities; the contingent nature of identity presentation is always relevant to interpreting), but that we must think of participants' identities *relative* to each other. (Monikowski and Peterson, in this volume, seek to reinvigorate interpreting students' awareness of the need to develop an appropriate and finely judged relationship with deaf service users in particular.) In doing so, we highlight particular issues of power that research on sign language interpreting has made a recurring, strong theme (e.g., Baker-Shenk, 1991). In addition, there is a re-emerging strand of analysis (e.g., Sperlinger & Bergson, 2003) that foregrounds the emotive state and responses of participants as a crucial variable partly defining the interpreting context. At issue here, too, is the matter of who is considered to be an "interested party" in any particular interaction: a broad, socially constructed understanding of interpreting as action suggests that this should not necessarily be confined solely to those present and contributing directly to the talk exchange.

2. What Are We Trying to Do?

This sub-question highlights the function of the interaction in which the participants are engaged. This should be understood to subsume functions at several levels of analysis: the overall function of the discourse framework (e.g., to conduct a trial in law), the intent of a particular passage of interaction (e.g., to cross-question a witness), the pragmatic target of a particular turn at talk (e.g., to generate a certain implication in the minds of the attendant jury), and so forth. Part of the interpreter's work, when possible, is also to anticipate where a given stretch of talk may be heading: in other words, not only "what are we trying to do?," but also "what might we be doing next?"

3. What Can We Do With Our Languages?

In this sub-question, the focus is on the language resources that are in use or otherwise available to the participants (an issue explored with particular reference to interpreters' sign language skills by Lee and by Quinto-Pozos in this volume). This question includes both productive and receptive resources; that is, what is or may be understood as well as articulated. The key reason for this question is to retain awareness that what can be uttered and comprehended, as banal as the observation may seem, will in significant part define the progress of the interaction. This is both a matter of how the structures of different languages (with reference to the cultural environments in which they operate) reflect the world in unique ways, and of the particular combinations of knowledge of language that individuals command. It is also important to note here that these language resources, too, are not static reservoirs. Clearly, individuals' abilities and preferences change over time, and particular resources are foregrounded as a result of processes of inter- and intra-textuality.

4. What Kind of Exchange Do We Think This Is?

This final sub-question emerges from the previous three. In less everyday terms, it might be recast as "How do we conceive of the structure and texture of this interactional event?" Part of the response to this question concerns the constraints or characteristics of the setting; that is, the physical location of the exchange and its institutional context. Equally important for the interpreter, though, will be the expectations held by participants about what an interpreter does, and experienced interpreters often expect the worst on this issue—as Anderson notes: "The interpreter's position is also characterized by role overload... [since she is] frequently expected to do more than is objectively possible" (2002, p. 211). Again, it should be noted that the answer to this question will be subject to the same dynamic forces at play across the board: not least, this will be so because each participant's expectations about the interpreting process will be constructed in relation to the way other participants respond, moment by moment, to the interpreting activity.

These questions have been constructed in everyday terms in order to demystify the interpreting process. The questions reflect the range of contextual factors involved in guiding the choices that interpreters make in designing their contributions to communicative exchanges.

It is crucial to note that framing the questions to focus on what "we" do is a reflection of the position already established of the interpreter as an active participant, on her own terms, in the talk exchange. It is vital that the interpreter has the self-awareness to consider with integrity the identity that she is presenting, the objectives that she has for the interaction, the language resources at her command, and her own conception of the interactional patterning at play. Of course, this is only the beginning. Since her job is to act as the pivot enabling communication to take place between the other participants, the quality of her interpretation will also depend on her ability to reflect actively on her understanding of all other participants' positions in relation to these issues.

PROJECTION AND FOCUSING

Le Page and Tabouret-Keller (1985) produced the seminal volume, *Acts of Identity: Creole-based Approaches to Language and Ethnicity*, which espoused the idea that language is absolutely and always a social process in which meaning derives from interaction between *people* rather than from either the words or the utterer.

But how do people ever arrive at shared understandings of meanings in their talk—or, at least, meanings sufficiently shared to permit communication that they consider meaningful enough to act upon? (It will be important for us to bear in mind this issue of "sufficient understanding" when we seek to measure service users' comprehension of interpreted output—see Marschark, Sapere, Convertino, & Seewagen, this volume.) The answer depends on the banal observation that no two interlocutors can ever share total experience of words-in-action; banal but not insignificant. Our personal experiences contribute to our notions of the appropriate contexts for use of any particular word: when a word comes to mind, the resonance of its connections and interrelationships with other words provides the intertextual background: as Johnson-Laird put it taking a simple semiotic case, "If the reference of a sign is an object perceivable by the senses, my idea of it is an internal image, arising from memories of sensory impressions which I have had and acts, both internal and external, which I have performed. Such an idea is [also] often saturated with feeling" (1983, p. 183).

How do we get from here to communicating using these highly personal concepts? Le Page taught, taking the cinema as his metaphor, that using language to communicate was a matter of *projection* and *focusing*: "We engage in activities I call projection and focusing: we project onto the social screen the concepts we have formed, by talking about them, so as to furnish our universe and try to get others to acknowledge the shape of the furniture; we in turn try to bring our concepts into focus with those of others, so that there is feedback from the social screen through language" (1980, pp. 15–16).

Each participant in talk thus "projects" an understanding or a vision of the universe onto the screen and, through talk-in-interaction, interlocutors aiming to achieve effective communication seek to generate a "focused" shared image or notion of the world as expressed in their co-talk. The more focused the outcome, the greater the mutual understanding achieved. Le Page and Tabouret-Keller elaborated:

> The speaker is projecting his inner universe, implicitly with the invitation to others to share it, at least insofar as they recognize his language as an accurate symbolization of the world, and to share his attitude toward it. By verbalizing as he does, he is seeking to reinforce his models of the world, and hopes for acts of solidarity from those with whom he wishes to identify. The feedback he receives from those with whom he talks may reinforce him, or may cause him to modify his projections, both in their form and in their content. To the extent that he is reinforced, his behaviour in that particular context may become more regular, more focused. (1985, p. 181)

The same ideas about projection and focusing apply in the context of interpreted communication. In such a case, the attempt to construct shared understandings needs to take place across a language boundary. As "message producers," the primary participants "project," in their own languages, an understanding of the universe, particular messages about or relating to this universe that they seek to convey, identity characteristics that they wish from time to time to highlight, and particular intentions they may hold for the outcome of the talk exchange. As "message receivers," primary participants use their understanding of what the other may be seeking to project, aiming to attune themselves as far as possible to the frequency he or she may be using. However, there is a difference, of course, created by the presence of the interpreter. For the interpreter is, in effect, actively articulating her understanding for every turn at talk. This means that the interpreter enacts the task of reprojecting, based on her own understanding, what each participant independently generates, aiming to engineer a focus that permits both participants to share a perception of the co-constructed image.

The most ready metaphor to adopt here is not cinematic but, rather, is based on the alternative optical context of a visit to the optician. When one is being fitted for glasses, each eye is considered independently for information about the lenses that will best enable the eye to achieve an assisted focus on images projected onto a screen. When both lenses have been successfully positioned, the result is a sharply focused image and two eyes that have no trouble in agreeing what they are seeing. Likewise, in the interpreted talk exchange, each primary participant projects word images into the shared communicative space (cf. the [social] screen). Although they are set on a trajectory toward the screen based on the individual utterer's conceptual framework, once "out there" they are independent of any one person's control. It is the interpreter whose principal task it is to "read" the indicators of how utterances will "look" to the primary participants once on the screen and to select, moment by moment through their recasting of talk into another language, those "lenses" that will permit the achievement, to the greatest extent possible in the circumstances, of a shared focus to the talk proceedings for the primary participants.

SOME RESEARCH UNDERPINNINGS

Ethics and Role

A paradigm shift that has fundamentally advanced research in sign language interpreting was informed initially by the kind of ideas presented by Anderson (2002, but first published in 1976) and cited earlier. The key to Anderson's contribution was the renewed focus on interpreting as a profoundly social rather than an essentially psychological process. Anderson noted that the interpreter's role as a sociolinguistic actor involved ambiguity, uncertainty, and confusion to all concerned. Confirming this situation still to be the case in the United Kingdom within BSL-English interpreting in the 1990s provided me with evidence of the considerable challenge still facing the field.

In 1992, a group of researchers at the University of Durham, England, created a survey of BSL-English interpreters. There were a total of 103 replies to the survey questionnaire: 51 registered trainee interpreters, 48 registered qualified interpreters, and 4 others, representing approximately a third of practicing interpreters in the United Kingdom at that time. One element of this survey sought to explore interpreting ethics and practitioners' understanding of their role. A series of hypothetical dilemmas were put to interpreters for their anonymous responses.

The researchers included experienced interpreting practitioners, and we tried to draw upon situations from our own experiences and from those passed on to us by other interpreters. Respondents were asked to try to answer in terms of what they felt they really *would* do—rather than what they felt they were *supposed* to do—if they found themselves in these situations. The respondents' articulation of *why* they had given particular answers was most significant.

The four dilemmas presented in the published article that drew upon this study (Tate & Turner, 1997) all revolved around some aspect of interpreters' views of the role model to which they orientated their practices: specifically, all four pertained to the mechanistic nature, or otherwise, of interpreter behavior, the use of professional judgment, and interpreter-generated *input* to the interactional event. The dilemmas included the following:

(a) You are interpreting with a deaf mother-to-be when she goes for a scan [ultrasound]. You know that she doesn't want to know the sex of her baby, but the gynecologist suddenly comes out with the information that it's a boy! What do you do, and why?

(b) You are interpreting with a deaf patient visiting her GP. She is prescribed a drug called Visapan (which the doctor says is powerful) to be taken once a day. In your interpretation, you fingerspell the name. The deaf person nods calmly and signs "Is it okay to take several vitamins at once?" You interpret the question to the doctor and she says "Yes, of course, that's no problem." You are aware that there has been a misunderstanding, that is, that the deaf person is referring to the Visapan as vitamins. You have interpreted everything by the book. What do you do, and why?

Tate and Turner found that many interpreters appeared to claim that they did not always abide by their reading of the Code of Ethics, but that they habitually drew a veil over such courses of action, amounting to what we suggested was a "conspiracy of silence." A frequent response to the dilemmas was that there needed to be a fuller reworking of the code that would guide interpreters more explicitly on how to respond in the face of situations such as these. This view shifted over time, evolving into the argument that it was not so much the *code* that needed to change so much as the professional *culture* that it was designed to reflect and engender. Pivotal to such change were (a) the educational processes by which practitioners are enculturated and (b) the articulation of the ethical values that underpin the wording of the published code. At the same time, the study gave evidence that interpreters were typically very ready to relate their actions to the Code of Ethics: They frequently made direct reference to its precepts in accounting for their (hypothetical) choices. Such responses were taken to indicate a real willingness among practitioners to accept a fully regulated professional approach, giving grounds for a very solid institutional foundation for the national field. In concluding, Tate and Turner argued:

> At present, our experience is that we face a situation where many interpreters actually expect the Code to guide them in some simple black-and-white fashion: they want the Code to tell them exactly what to do. If our perception is accurate (and we feel that this survey helps to confirm that it is), then it needs to be better established during the education of interpreters that grey goes with the territory, and that would-be professionals had better learn to live with it, and indeed to embrace it. Being able to act competently within the grey zone is an integral part of their professionalism. (1997, p. 33)

The term "grey zone" may suggest to some a rather negative image, but the ability to operate autonomously in complex, uncertain conditions is actually an indicator of professional maturity or a marker that "an interpreter or other professional has 'cracked the code' of the profession—or that they have managed to get through our (teachers') gate keeping and figured out the secrets we keep" (Elizabeth Winston, personal communication).

Linguistic Resources and Interpreting Choices

Issues relating to differences in the structures of BSL and English, as the two languages that British interpreters need to "reconcile" if they are to find ways of focusing meanings for the primary participants in the interactions which they mediate, have always been prominent for me as a researcher of interpreting.

In 1993, I began working on a project entitled *Access to Justice for Deaf People in the Bilingual, Bimodal Courtroom*. This three-year project is reported in detail by the project directors Brennan and Brown in the 1997 volume, *Equality before the law: Deaf people's access to justice*, plus a number of further papers (Reed, Turner, & Taylor, 2001; Turner, 1995; Turner & Brown, 2001). The services of a BSL-English interpreter are, of course, essential if deaf people are to have fair and proper treatment when they appear in court as defendants or witnesses. The objectives of the project were to explore the access to justice afforded to deaf people within the courts, the role of interpreters in mediating such access, problems inherent in the process of interpreting courtroom discourse, and sociocultural influences on the nature of courtroom interactions. The outcomes from this study have fed into both interpreter training and policy-making with respect to justice and the Deaf community.

The project had three main parts: (1) to gather and collate evidence from records and interviews with deaf people, interpreters, and others about experiences in the criminal justice process and the roles that interpreters play; (2) to record and analyze courtroom interaction in relevant cases; and (3) to work toward developing outcomes in the form of training materials and programs, guidelines to good practice, and academic reports of the research findings.

The project especially reinforced the impact on interpreting of the pervasive nature of visuality within the structure of BSL, in stark contrast to English, where it is not a necessary part of the linguistic patterning as it is in any signed language.

A down-to-earth example follows: *A man walks into a bar and buys a drink.* In English, we could embellish this account in various ways, but a typical BSL account would include certain types of visual information automatically (i.e., it would be more unusual to exclude than include such information). Thus, we may be able to discern from the signed rendition what kind of doors the bar had at its entrance—double or single swing-door, door with a round knob or a vertical handle, doors needing to be pushed or pulled; or to picture the barman in detail—a large, left-handed man with a laconic air who ceased drying glasses in order to serve the drink; or to tell that the counter was located opposite the entrance, the place was crowded, and the man paid with a bill from the wallet in the left breast-pocket of his overcoat. To include such information in BSL would be unmarked and unremarkable, simply because we take it for granted as part and parcel of the visual encoding inherent in the language structure.

The following examples begin to suggest why this may noticeably matter in legal interpreting situations (Turner, Reed, & Taylor, 2001). In the course of a murder trial, an item of importance to the police enquiries was recovered after having been thrown away by or on behalf of a defendant. On a number of occasions, this action of "throwing away" was mentioned in the police station and court exchanges. Not once did the interpreter find out about the direction in which the item was thrown. Yet it would be impossible for the interpreter to create a visualized signing of the action—required by virtue of the visual-spatial structure of BSL—without being determinate about the direction. It is, at one level, a tiny detail, but given the nature of interaction in legal cases, potentially highly significant given that the BSL rendition, without highly alert processing by the interpreter to produce a circumlocutory explanatory equivalent, must include some apparent details of the physical action and spatial relations in which this part of the case history occurred.

In another instance, a lawyer said in court to a pathologist, "You found (the defendant's) blood—as a possible source—on the trouser leg." The interpreter had to indicate one trouser leg or the other, and opted for the right leg. The pathologist went on to describe the stain on the left leg. The interpreter could go on to refer thereafter to the left leg. Of course, this instance looks trivial from the point of view of a hearing person who knows—if they notice at all—that there has been an understandable and explicable inconsistency. But for the deaf person, this is just one more element of confusion. The stain has suddenly and unaccountably migrated from right to left leg. Should the deaf defendant assume that he was mistaken when he thought he saw the right leg being indicated in the first place? Perhaps he was at fault for not paying proper attention. Perhaps the interpreter did change the reference. Perhaps the interpreter accurately repeated what was said in the court, and the court personnel were confused. The deaf person has no more likely explanation for his confusion, given the apparent satisfaction of the court, but to blame himself for lacking concentration. There is no one else to blame, apparently. No one feels that there has been any problem. Is it likely that they are all wrong? If one now multiplies this small example by hundreds for the times that it occurs in one way or another during the days of the trial, the result has to be a disadvantageous and unjust lack of clarity—potentially highly salient to the course of the trial and the verdict reached—in the experience of the judicial process afforded to the deaf defendant.

Besides highlighting the structural contrasts between signed and spoken languages, and the choices which the interpreter is thus obliged to make, research in interpreted courtroom interaction also sheds further light in particular on the interpreter's role as a *coordinator* of talk. With regard to this issue, Turner and Brown (2001) argued that the manner of participation and the institutionalized role of the BSL-English interpreter in court ought to be reviewed. Here we found particular and highly detailed inspiration in the work of Berk-Seligson (1990) and Morris (1989a, 1989b), who provided thorough analyses of bilingual court interaction and were in no doubt about the participation status of the interpreter. Berk-Seligson categorically stated that "the court interpreter is a new variable in the ecology of the...courtroom. She is an intrusive element, far from being the unobtrusive figure whom judges and attorneys would like her to be. Her intrusiveness is manifested in multiple ways.... Together, these intrusions make for judicial proceedings of a different nature" (1990, p. 96).

Berk-Seligson further showed that what the interpreter does, the way she does it, and the choices she is obliged to make have a measurable effect on viewers and listeners. Morris (1989a, pp. 31–32) reaches a related conclusion, saying that interpreters in practice undertake "a role which is not limited exclusively to reproducing participants' utterances, and which may involve their exerting some degree of influence over the proceedings proper, including exercising control over speakers."

And yet the received role norms here disregard all of this as an irrelevance and pretend that the legal proceedings have not changed by virtue of the interpreter's presence. The courtroom is attended by a range of people, each of whom has a part to play in the unfolding talk-event.

To this extent alone, the interpreter's need to manage the exchange is highly significant. The result is what Morris (1989a, p. 31, 1989b, p. 10) calls the "basic dilemma" of court interpretation: both dynamism in interaction and the utmost accuracy in the delivery of messages— structural disparities notwithstanding—are vital to the successful conclusion of the proceedings, yet these often seem to be mutually incompatible aims to the interpreter seeking to maintain them both in parallel. For reasons of both coordination and the recasting of linguistic structure, then, the court interpreter cannot be "invisible" or neutral, but must play an active role in achieving communication. This provides further reinforcement, in a specific, high-stakes context, of the key issue concisely captured by Roy: "All communication is an interactive exchange, and when interpreters are used, they are a part of the interaction naturally. The point is not their neutrality but rather what is or can be their participation in the event" (1989, p. 265).

Communicative Constraints

Choices about the salience of elements of message content and about the most effective way to coordinate talk-in-interaction were highlighted in a different way by a further study completed in 2001 (Atherton, Gregg, Harrington, et al., 2001). That study considered the provision of interpreting services in a context where deaf service users were identified as having "minimal language skills" (MLS), living in sheltered accommodation and engaged in independent-living skills rehabilitation. The study centered on "case review" meetings at which the full range of stakeholders in a particular residents' care—on-site key workers, local authority representatives, medical authorities, family members—met with the resident and discussed progress and plans via an interpreter. Participants were interviewed before and after such meetings, which were videotaped and analyzed. Outcomes were directly embedded into developing training for interpreters and key workers in a cycle of iterations through the period of the study.

For interpreters, seeking to produce language output understandable to a person exhibiting disordered language-processing skills provided a significant challenge, but in many respects the outcomes of the project in terms of identifying recommendations for good practice were generalizable to other contexts. This entails the development by interpreters of their ability to marshal the full richness of the visual resources of BSL and to recognize the absolute necessity of bringing these to bear upon the task of wholly recasting meaning from English into a genuinely accessible signed form. There is a dangerously naïve view that "any" interpreter can cope with MLS work, perhaps precisely because the BSL expected is seen as less "high level" in terms of linguistic complexity. Findings indicated that, far from finding the task straightforward in this respect, interpreters attempted to deal with the specific difficulties of interpreting for this group of residents by making a number of carefully calibrated adjustments. When interviewed about their feelings on the success or otherwise of case reviews they had been working on, interpreters made judgments based on whether they felt the service they had provided had resulted in meaningful communication: "It was successful in terms of my role with the resident"; "I felt the resident was getting a lot of information."

The adjustments fell into four main categories, as defined by Loncke (1995): linguistic (vocabulary and repetition), cognitive (redundancy and repetition), knowledge level (shared reference points), and communication style (modality). Adjustments were not discrete, and overlapping could and did occur across two or more categories. An example of all four adjustments taking place within the same section of interpretation is provided by the following sample.

Speech

FIRST VOICE: Did you say you were going to buy [a television for the resident]?

SECOND VOICE: Yes, but I can't do it unless she has her hearing aids back again...Do you know why then she hasn't got any, because she had them right up until she left Oldville.

FIRST VOICE: To be honest, I didn't even know that she used to wear them. Did she used to wear them?

SECOND VOICE: Yes.

FIRST VOICE: And they didn't [indistinct] when she came here?

SECOND VOICE: No.

THIRD VOICE: She wasn't wearing them when she arrived and she has been here 2 years now.

SECOND VOICE: In her right ear there is partial sound.

THIRD VOICE: Where are they?

Signing (glossed)—interpreter to resident

T-T will pay square object (lip pattern—"television") plug in lead hearing aid television, hear better television, but need you hearing aids. Hearing aids before...

Hearing aids nothing? Hearing aids nothing? Hearing aid [indicates right ear] nothing? Hearing aid (right ear) have?

[repeated] Like [points to hearing aid of deaf staff member sat next to her] have? Now, nothing [repeated several times] [points to hearing aid again] have? Your bedroom have?

The interpreter concentrates on the central concept being discussed, making a cognitive adjustment by making redundant that information she judges would cause communication to be ineffective for the resident. Linguistic adjustment comes through repetition of both vocabulary and placement, and the use of a limited vocabulary. Knowledge level is adjusted by the substitution of "before" for a place name. A second adjustment involves conceptualizing technical details in a form that the resident can understand, by making what is being discussed in abstract terms (having to find hearing aids before a new television can be bought) mean something that the resident understands in terms of her daily life (hearing the television better). Adjustment of communication style occurs when the interpreter uses visual and physical clues (e.g., pointing to hearing aids) to make the communication clearer.

Interpreters can successfully adapt their style of interpreting to match the needs of the residents, but this is still an area that causes the interpreters problems. They report anxiety about doing more of this type of adjustment, as the following quotes from interviews with interpreters indicate:

"I was making decisions on what to interpret. I don't like being put in that position, I would rather be given guidance. People seem to be oblivious to that going on."

"There were lots of times when I wasn't interpreting, because I kept thinking, 'I don't know how to interpret this.'"

The challenge for interpreter educators and those constructing and delivering the service is again to find a way of empowering interpreters to make these decisions, based on their professional assessment of what will work best in providing meaningful communication.

Expectations of Interpreters as "Negotiators" of Meaning

Once again, issues over differing perceptions of the role of the interpreter surfaced significantly in the MLS study. In interviews with case review chairs, the role of interpreters was often seen in relatively stark terms.

"The interpreter's job is to interpret. The Chair should control the meeting and what is being interpreted."

It was clear that the interpreters were doing some monitoring of the resident's ability to comprehend, but when an interpreter considered that non-comprehension was happening, ways of dealing with this were not always apparent. Interpreters stated that they felt unable to resolve the difficulties this caused for a variety of reasons. For example, seeking clarification is a regular and accepted part of normal interpreter working practice. However, in case reviews, interpreters felt unable to seek as much clarification as they required; in some instances, interpreters felt unable to ask for any clarification at all:

"If you were in court...you would ask for clarification. Why don't we do that in case reviews? We do, but not a lot. To have stopped that meeting and have asked, 'What do you mean by shiny tablets?'...maybe I should have, I don't know. Maybe I should have interrupted more?"

"Maybe I should have stopped the group, and asked them to go back. It would have meant a lengthy meeting, but I didn't do it. I abbreviated it so I am not happy with my role there."

Interpreters also felt that on-site staff did not fully understand the particular ways in which interpreters need to work in case reviews.

"I don't think staff necessarily understand the interpreting issues. You ask people to be conscious of language that they use, but they don't understand what that means, because they are not in our shoes."

"I don't feel I can provide meaningful communication...I feel I am colluding with everyone, because they could sit there and say, 'We've done our bit, we've provided an interpreter.'"

"They expected me to translate everything and I felt really deskilled."

The recommendations for changes in working practices made at the conclusion of the MLS project thus focused significantly on interpreting as an activity that cannot be made effective by the interpreter alone. Making interaction meaningful is not a responsibility that belongs only to the interpreter, but is a matter of *co-construction* between/among all participants. The target, in this and all interpreter-mediated settings, is to arrive at a *shared* understanding among key participants of the most effective ways to promote meaningful communication in these exchanges. In addition, interaction is not seen as a matter with a preordained or self-generating form that starts and finishes when conversational participants are face to face; hence, the strong focus in this work on preliminaries and debriefing. The project recommendations therefore entail significant expectations on all participants and are designed to create the *conditions* in which real interpreting can take place. These expectations focus on the following:

- *Preparation* prior to and *debriefing* after case review meetings;
- Communication *management* in case review meetings; and
- Contributions of meeting chairs, interpreters, other professionals, and residents to facilitating effective interaction.

Designing Talk for an Audience

Analysis of interpreting in a quite different context provided further food for thought about the social context within which an interpreter makes her professional choices and, in particular, about how those choices will be conditioned by the way in which the interpreter construes the relevant audience for which she is designing her talk. The study (Turner & Pollitt, 2002) set out to begin an exploration of the nature of the sign language interpreted performance (SLIP) in the theater, and in so doing, to problematize a number of issues embedded within contemporary discourses on community interpreting. An initial description in the article gives a brief scoping account of SLIPs with reference to the wider literature before exemplifying challenges faced by the practitioner (using data drawn from assignments ranging from traditional pantomime to classic twentieth-century drama). We then take this point of departure as a heuristic device to unpack the category distinctions upon which key terms have been identified as resting, and conclude with a discussion of descriptive and theoretical outcomes in relation to the wider field.

The audience for SLIPs might be thought very obviously to consist of those deaf people sitting in the auditorium watching the show, but there is in fact no guarantee that there will even be any deaf person watching the SLIP. This suggests that the interpreting may be supposed to serve some additional function. Who else is the interpreter providing a service for? This goes beyond the question of "audience design" (in the sense of Bell, 1984), to wider issues about the production and consumption of this service and the full range of stakeholder groups or interested parties. The theater setting perhaps highlights this question, but we identified a preliminary list, as follows, by reference to this and other settings:

- The state/taxpayer—this is perhaps particularly evident in legal settings where the costs of the interpreting service are borne by the state (i.e., taxpayers), and where the consequences of outcomes (a guilty or not-guilty verdict, a re-trial in the case of problems, etc.) generate immediate further consequences for the polity; but in the theater also, the taxpayer may ultimately be footing the bill

- The sponsor(s)—for instance, SLIPs may be funded by corporate sponsorship, which presents certain potential obligations to the interpreter
- The local (government) authority—such an authority may subsidize the cost of SLIPs; a more conventional example would be interpreting in a social care setting where the local authority has a statutory obligation to provide social care to Deaf people deemed unable to live independently, and interpreting may be offered to enable the authority to be assured that *its* care requirements are being met
- The host theatre
- The author of the play
- The director
- The actors
- The non-Deaf audience—they are, after all, always present and a majority of the audience, and they frequently do watch the interpreter; some of them may be BSL students who have come specifically for this purpose; most are receiving some informal Deaf Awareness training simply by having their attention drawn to the power of interpretation
- The Deaf audience
- The Deaf community—non-present Deaf persons are nevertheless interested parties here, since the interpreter's actions and approach are taken to be a reflection in some sense of the requirements of their user communities
- And, of course, the interpreter is also a stakeholder—professionally risking a great deal every time she steps into the light so overtly. (Turner & Pollitt, 2002, p. 40).

All of these are potentially parties whose interests the interpreter may need to consider from moment to moment in the choices she makes about the design of her communicative output. It was therefore argued that we needed to reconceptualize the stakeholders in the interpreting project. Especially as interpreting becomes increasingly professionalized on the one hand (since this entails potential relationships with purchasers who may not be direct consumers and may be acting on behalf of wider social groups) and institutionalized on the other, it becomes crucial that the interpreter has an awareness of the demands implicitly or explicitly placed upon her from all quarters. Her understanding of these relationships will have a significant bearing upon her professional choices as a service provider.

The theater setting—in the United Kingdom, at least—also raises particular questions about how the interpreter is positioned as a political agent. In particular, she has a primary relationship with deaf service users: how is this affected by her work in the theater? For, as

Mason articulated, she faces a serious problem of potential role conflict, given the "pressure on interpreters to display some allegiance to their in-group. At the same time, however, they are conscious of acting professionally for an employer whose goals they may or may not feel they should help to achieve. Thus, they are pulled both ways" (2000, p. 222). In the context of the limited resources that the establishment dedicates to deaf people's engagement in theatre, the interpreter's role in facilitating access for deaf people to the cultural heritage of the majority-language community can be seen as directly at odds with the desire to promote Deaf arts. There is rarely sufficient money for theaters to do both. However, one might argue that SLIPs do promote Deaf awareness and some appreciation of the power and capabilities of signed language. So the interpreter has decisions to make about her personal positioning, and, again, it is clear on reflection that such decisions may not be confined to this setting alone.

REFLECTING ON INTERPRETING

Training and practice in a range of professions have been influenced in modern times by the idea of the "reflective practitioner" (Schön, 1983, 1987). Schön argued that the ability to reflect critically when we encounter complexity and unfamiliarity is a vital component of professional practice. Developing this notion, Schön introduced the concepts of "knowing-in action"—actions and judgments carried out spontaneously, without one having to think about them before or during their performance; "reflection-in-action"—the process (often sparked when prescribed action hits its limits) where, while acting, one reflects on what one is doing and what to do next—and "reflection-on-action"—this occurs after action and may be facilitated by such activity as supervision, mentoring, or reviewing recordings of one's work.

Although these terms may not commonly be used in the interpreting field, interpreters will be exploiting knowing-in-action and, to a greater or lesser extent, reflection-in-action, and the development of critical thinking skills in interpreters and interpreter-educators is a recurrent theme of this volume (e.g., Monikowski & Peterson, Dean & Pollard, Winston). Structures of interpreter education and practice have not always encouraged interpreters to engage in reflection-on-action, though, at least in any consistent or systematic fashion (Sperlinger & Bergson, 2003). We have formalized reflection-on-action within our program, seeking to enable interpreters to develop their ability to deal with the unexpected ("no two jobs are the same") and so to enrich their professional competence. The process we have developed for our postgraduate interpreting students to use in presenting such reflection-on-action as part of their assessed work is the production of a "Critical Interpreting Awareness" (CIA) log in which they present an annotated review of their own interpreting performance evidence, accounting for and explaining choices made and undertaking critical analysis in light of scholarly theoretical and conceptual models. In this context, I have defined "critical" as referring to (1) having a critical perspective on *interpreting per se*, (2) having a critical perspective on particular *interpretations*, and (3) being able to make critical readings of wider *social practices, arrangements, and procedures* that are mediated by, made possible by, and partially sustained through transmitting and receiving interpreted "texts."

Students are instructed that they will normally be expected to produce five or six log entries, each between 2,000 and 2,500 words. The entries are to be designed to show (1) that they are exploring issues across a variety of interpreting settings/situations (e.g., health, legal, etc.; solo work, co-working, etc.; monologues, two-party interactions, multiparty interactions, etc.; and so on) and (2) that they can identify, investigate, and appropriately apply ideas relating to a range of levels of analysis (from fine-grained microanalysis of the role of the left eyebrow in rhetorical questions, as it might be, to macrostructural metaprofessional issues).

A CYCLE OF EMPOWERMENT: FROM RESEARCH TO EDUCATION TO PRACTICE TO REFLECTION

The model developed in our interpreting program might be seen, in light of the discussion above, as one that has valued and sought to embed the idea of professional empowerment. Research and scholarship gather and generate knowledge and ideas upon which good practice can be built; the educational curriculum presents and interprets this material; and students are guided in the practical application of the theory. As practitioners, they undertake reflection-on-action, which not only enriches their ongoing practice but is in itself a form of analytical scholarship that can and does give rise to innovation and insight with which to recommence the cycle.

As one whose entry into interpreter education came via working as a researcher, my view is that, in the terms of Cameron and colleagues (1992), research should be conducted "on, for, and with" all stakeholders, including interpreters. Researchers have very real responsibilities to make careful decisions concerning three dimensions of their relationship with other stakeholders in their work. The first dimension (research "on") is about the *ethical* position to be adopted in the course of the research, that is, the manner in which the researchers intend to ensure that due care is taken to protect the interests of those who have traditionally been called the "subjects" of the research. The second dimension (research "for") refers to the researchers' role in *advocating* on behalf of others to achieve social change in light of their studies' findings. Third, the final dimension (research "with") relates to the *empowerment* of others to influence the framing and conduct of the research and to achieve subsequent change independently. Clearly, the third element of this is the key in the context of the relationship between research, education, practice, and reflection. Education can be a key site for empowerment and a catalyst to the renewal of the cycle.

What does it mean to try and put into practice the "on, for, and with" principles? Cameron and colleagues (1992) give three concise and deceptively simple "programmatic precepts" as a springboard: (1) persons are not objects and should not be treated as objects; (2) subjects have their own agendas, and research should try to address them; and (3) if knowledge is worth having, it is worth sharing. Frank Harrington and I considered each of these in turn, relating it to interpreting research through the lens of our own studies. Our summary of key points suggests that researchers should aim to

1. Work with other stakeholders to select and set up projects
2. Consider the advantages of research teams—but take seriously the danger of tokenism
3. Maintain dialogue throughout with all stakeholders—i.e., before, while, and after the study takes place
4. Seek explicit permission from participants, and keep open the option of opting out
5. Minimize disruption to people's real lives
6. Maintain absolute respect for confidentiality
7. Build the outcomes from research into training with all stakeholders
8. Disseminate as widely as possible to all stakeholder groups
9. Where appropriate, be willing to advocate. (Harrington & Turner, 2000, p. 263)

Of the three "programmatic precepts," one—if knowledge is worth having, it is worth sharing— directly leads to implications about research and education. While the present chapter focuses on interpreter education, in the context of the discussion above about differing expectations of the role of the interpreter, it is particularly important to remember the multiplicity of other stakeholder groups who might benefit from learning opportunities that draw upon research outcomes to support and disseminate current thinking about good practice. These include professional consumers, personal consumers, user-group representative organizations, and national bodies (including regulatory bodies and statutory authorities). As researchers, we should be looking to establish learning events for the full range of stakeholders that offer the opportunity for more in-depth assimilation of "the knowledge" accruing from scholarship in order to render it more effectively useable by them for their own professional or community purposes and, one would hope, to maintain the empowerment cycle with their involvement.

It should be stressed here that in respect of interpreter education and its relationship with research, the empowerment cycle is one that behaves as continuously self-regenerating. No research project should be thought of as entirely discrete: Researchers are part of a never-ending trajectory toward knowing-all-there-is-to-know. In just the same way, the cycle of empowerment discussed in this chapter is designed to lead toward the goal of imagining, nurturing, and securing real interpreting.

Some Research and Development Priorities

Finally, I would like to sketch four possible future areas of analysis and examination. These seem to be suggested by other chapters in this volume. In some cases, the issues are not directly highlighted, but they underlie our collective concerns in parts of the analytical territory where the leading edge of curriculum and policy development is exploring options.

First, it is worth underscoring that we do need a great deal more basic research, not only about interpreting, but also about the structures of the languages and communicative practices with which interpreters work (as the chapter by Lee attests). I am certainly acutely aware of the minimal nature of the basic descriptive work on BSL that has been conducted in recent times. Essentially, an initial wave of enthusiasm—captured in key texts by Brennan and colleagues (1984), Deuchar (1984), Kyle and Woll (1985), and Brennan (1990)—was seen to culminate in the production of the first bilingual BSL/English dictionary (Brien, 1992) and an introduction to the linguistics of BSL (Sutton-Spence & Woll, 1999). To all intents and purposes, it seems that everyone except the researchers now considers the description of BSL to be complete. It is, of course, by no means complete, and it is once again indicative of wider attitudes to sign languages that anyone (including many deaf people, it has to be said) should think otherwise.

So we need to know much, much more about BSL. It is fundamental to all of the applications that need to be explored, including interpreting. Educators of interpreters cannot hope to develop an evidence-based curriculum without such basic material (Quinto-Pozos, this volume). We also need to embed habits of dissemination (as noted by Lee, this volume; see also Turner & Harrington, 2000, and Turner & Alker, 2003) to ensure that relevant information about BSL reaches all interested parties. It is also worth noting that the gathering of chapters into this volume, and the process by which the contents were discussed among the authors, points to a need for those interested in interpreting research and interpreter education to work harder at joining up the knowledge that, collectively, we already have. To put it delicately, there is, for instance, in the wider literature, apparently a strong tendency for analysts to confine their sphere of knowledge to the shores of their own continent. This volume, in its way, helps to broaden horizons.

Second, there is a need for research that will support the challenges we wish to pose to certain powerful but misguided drivers of policy and attitudes toward interpreting, especially in the field of educational interpreting. For example, a recurrent theme in this volume is that interpreting provision in the education of deaf children and young people is highly problematic and that institutions provide only "illusionary access" (Cokely, this volume). I also believe that it is necessary to challenge the notion of low-risk interpreting assignments suitable for "beginners" or for what some in the United Kingdom are misleadingly (because they mean to identify people less than fully qualified as interpreters) starting to call "community interpreters": If the interpreting is being done effectively, there is, as Monikowski and Peterson (this volume) strongly articulate, no such thing as a guaranteed "easy" interpreting assignment.

To counter these kinds of problems, we need more action research (cf. Atherton et al., 2001) to demonstrate how much more effective interpreting can be with well-prepared interpreters and informed service users; the development of tools and approaches to evaluate service-user comprehension of interpreting output, in educational settings (see Marschark et al., this volume) and beyond; and enhanced "close-up," thickly descriptive, ethnographic research of interpreting practices to help develop forms of independent quality assurance in the field.

Third, while many chapters in this volume clearly show and participate in the late twentieth-century "turn" toward a model of the interpreter as a "coordinator and negotiator of meanings in a three-way interaction" (Mason, 1999, p. 160), there is progress yet to be made in pushing at our understanding of how triadic, multi-layered, interpreted interactions work. How does the interpreter actively "project" her understanding of every turn at talk and what does that imply for our analyses and therefore for our curriculae? Roy (2000) argued that people act in concert with each other; that is, that meaning is in the shared space between them. So how do triadic interlocutors get it there and how can we, as researchers, find it there? In order to explore these questions, I think we will need more research that continues to apply insights from "mainstream" sociolinguistics and the social sciences in general with as much sophistication as Roy herself did in her initial analyses of the interpreting triad (Roy, 1989). This will be hard, for it requires gigantic leaps of the imagination and real conceptual invigoration to see new connections, but there is evidence in this volume and elsewhere of such innovative theoretical links being both forged and applied to interpreter education.

Finally, I am concerned that we pay urgent attention to the relationship between deaf and hearing people over interpreting and especially to ensuring that those developments in the field that are seen as "hearing led" are demystified so that all stakeholders are in a position to make informed choices about the kind of interpreters required in the twenty-first century and about how best to "co-construct" such interpreters. This will ultimately entail more deaf people needing to be trained and become experienced as interpreters (and translators), partly on the basis that this is the best way to understand the complexities of the role; more opportunities for deaf people to train and practice as interpreting researchers, partly for similar reasons; and more research being done (see Forestal, this volume) on what deaf interpreters currently do. We need to envisage more effective ways of enabling deaf people to "see both sides" of interpreted talk and hence to evaluate interpreting quality. Among other things, this may assist in the spreading of the message that, as Monikowski and Peterson (this volume) suggest, where interpreting is concerned, something is definitely not always better than nothing.

In the long run, the aim needs to be to challenge as fully and inclusively as possible all forms of ignorance about interpreting. This includes the naïve interpreter's blithe assumptions that they are "doing a good job," which are very often founded on nothing more than a lack of awareness about the myriad ways in which things can be (and probably are) going wrong. It also includes stakeholders' willingness to accept "illusionary access," especially in educational and community contexts, and particularly the apparent readiness of some people to tolerate such levels of access even in the long term. Empowering service users and community representatives to deliver informed challenges to received wisdom in these contexts, therefore, is a major and pressing priority, as is the collection of hard evidence about the real demand for interpreting services, since quality compromises are so often predicated upon the mismatch between supply and demand. The research reported here by Marschark and colleagues, exploring the implications of students thinking that they are understanding in classrooms when they in fact may not be doing so, assuredly needs to be explored further and in other settings (e.g., when a deaf person gives a statement to the police).

In all, a fundamental challenge at this time appears to be the task of bringing deaf and hearing people, interpreters, educators, and service users onto the same wavelength, negotiating concertedly and with shared underpinnings their aims for the development and delivery of all aspects of the interpreting profession. To do so will require accessing, at a close-up level, all stakeholders' perspectives on interpreting and their differing experiences of interpreter-mediated talk events. This is a colossal challenge, but one into which many—as this volume attests—are nevertheless willing to throw ourselves with passion, intensity, and commitment.

ACKNOWLEDGMENTS

I have had the good fortune to have worked for and alongside many wise and talented colleagues and teachers from whom I have learned a great deal, with whom I have jointly developed and presented the analyses discussed in this chapter, and to whom I owe a huge debt of gratitude and respect, which I very gladly acknowledge. I am also grateful to the editors of this volume for their comments and to all who participated in the workshop that acted as the launch pad for this volume.

REFERENCES

Alexieva, B. (2002). A typology of interpreter-mediated events. [Originally published in 1997 in *The Translator 3 (2)*, 153–174.] In F. Pöchhacker & M. Shlesinger (Eds.), *The interpreting studies reader*. London: Routledge, pp. 219–233.

Anderson, R.B.W. (2002). Perspectives on the role of interpreter. [Originally published in 1976 in R.W. Brislin (Ed.), *Translation: applications and research*. New York: Gardner Press, pp. 208–228.] In F. Pöchhacker & M. Shlesinger (Eds.), *The interpreting studies reader*. London: Routledge, pp. 209–217.

Atherton, M., Gregg, A., Harrington, F.J., Quinn, G., Traynor, N., & Turner, G.H. (2001). *Addressing communication disadvantage: Deaf people with minimal language skills*. Preston: University of Central Lancashire/Deafway.

Baker-Shenk, C. (1991). The interpreter: machine, advocate, or ally? In *Expanding horizons: proceedings of the 1991 RID convention*. Silver Spring, MD: RID Publications, pp. 120–140.

Bell, A. (1984). Language style as audience design. *Language in Society, 13*, 145–204.

Berk-Seligson, S. (1990). *The bilingual courtroom: Court interpreters in the judicial process*. Chicago and London: Chicago University Press.

Brennan, M. (1990). *Word formation in British sign language*. Stockholm: University of Stockholm.

Brennan, M., & Brown, R. (1997), *Equality before the law: Deaf people's access to justice*. Durham: Deaf Studies Research Unit/University of Durham.

Brennan, M., Colville, M., Lawson. L., & Hughes, G. (1984). *Words in hand: A structural analysis of the signs of British sign language*. Edinburgh: Moray House College of Education.

Brien, D. (1992). *Dictionary of British sign language/English*. London: Faber & Faber.

Cameron, D., Frazer, E., Harvey, P., Rampton, B., & Richardson, K. (1992). *Researching language: Issues of power and method*. London: Routledge.

Deuchar, M. (1984). *British sign language*. London: Routledge.

Johnson-Laird, P.N. (1983). *Mental models: Towards a cognitive science of language, inference, and consciousness*. Cambridge: Cambridge University Press.

Kyle, J.G. & Woll, B. (1985). *Sign language: The study of deaf people and their language*. Cambridge: Cambridge University Press.

Le Page, R.B. (1980). Projection, focusing, diffusion or, steps towards a socio-linguistic theory of language, illustrated from the sociolinguistic survey of multilingual communities, Stages I: Cayo District, Belize (formerly British Honduras) and II: St. Lucia. *York Papers in Linguistics (9)*, 1–32.

Le Page, R.B., & Tabouret-Keller, A. (1985). *Acts of identity: Creole-based approaches to language and ethnicity*. Cambridge: Cambridge University Press.

Loncke, F. (1995). Setting the Scene. *Report of working seminar on minimal language skills*. Ghent: European Federation of Sign Language Interpreters.

Mason, I. (1999). Introduction. *The Translator, 5 (2)*, 147–160.

Mason, I. (2000). Models and methods in dialogue interpreting research. In M. Olohan (Ed.), *Intercultural faultlines: Research models in translation studies 1-textual and cognitive aspects*. Manchester: St. Jerome, 215–231.

Morris, R. (1989a). Court interpretation: The trial of Ivan Demjanjuk: a case study. *The Interpreters' Newsletter, (2)*, 27–37.

Morris, R. (1989b). Eichmann v. Demjanjuk: A study of interpreted proceedings. *Parallèles: Cahiers de L'Ecole de Traduction et d'Interpretation, Université de Genève*, pp. 9–28.

Pöchhacker, F. (2004). *Introducing interpreting studies*. London: Routledge.

Reed, M., Turner, G.H., & Taylor, C. (2001). Working paper on access to justice for deaf people. In F.J. Harrington, & G.H. Turner (Eds.), *Interpreting interpreting: Studies and reflections on sign language interpreting*. Coleford, Glocs.: Douglas McLean, pp. 168–216.

Roy, C.B. (1989). *A sociolinguistic analysis of the interpreter's role in the turn exchanges of an interpreted event*. Unpublished dissertation. Washington DC: Georgetown University, University Microfilms DAO64793.

Roy C.B. (1993a). The problem with definitions, descriptions and the role metaphors of interpreters. *Journal of Interpretation, 6(1)*, 127–154.

Roy, C.B. (1993b). A sociolinguistic analysis of the interpreter's role in simultaneous talk in interpreted interaction. *Multilingua 12 (4)*, 341–363.

Roy, C.B. (2000). *Interpreting as a discourse process*. Oxford: Oxford University Press.

Salevsky, H. (1982). Teoreticheskie problemi klassifikatzii vidov perevoda [Theoretical problems of the classification of types of translation]. *Fremdsprachen, 26 (2)*, 80–86.

Salevsky, H. (1993). The distinctive nature of interpreting studies. *Target: International Journal of Translation Studies, 5 (2)*, 149–167.

Schön, D. (1983). *The reflective practioner*. New York: Basic Books.

Schön, D. (1987). *Educating the reflexive practitioner*. Oxford: Jossey Bass.

Sperlinger, D., & Bergson, M. (2003). Reflections on interpreting in psychotherapeutic encounters. *Deaf Worlds: International Journal of Deaf Studies, 19 (3)*, 6–23.

Sutton-Spence, R., & Woll, B. (1999). *The linguistics of British sign language: An introduction*. Cambridge: Cambridge University Press.

Tate, G., & Turner, G.H. (1997). The code and the culture: Sign language interpreting—in search of the new breed's ethics. *Deaf Worlds, 13 (3)*, 27–34.

Turner, G.H. (1995). The bilingual, bimodal courtroom: A first glance. *Journal of Interpretation, 7 (1)*, 3–33.

Turner, G.H., & Alker, D. (2003). Partnership in British sign language research and policy development. *Deaf Worlds: International Journal of Deaf Studies, 19 (2)*, 47–65.

Turner, G.H., & Brown, R.K. (2001). Interaction and the role of the interpreter in court. In F.J. Harrington & G.H. Turner (Eds.), *Interpreting interpreting: Studies and reflections on sign language interpreting*. Coleford, Glocs.: Douglas McLean, pp. 152–167.

Turner, G.H., & Harrington, F.J. (2000). Issues of power and method in interpreting research. In M. Olohan (Ed.), *Intercultural faultlines: Research models in translation studies 1—textual and cognitive aspects*. Manchester: St. Jerome, pp. 253–265.

Turner, G.H., & Harrington, F.J. (2001). The campaign for real interpreting. In F.J. Harrington & G.H. Turner (Eds.), *Interpreting interpreting: Studies and reflections on sign language interpreting*. Coleford, UK: Douglas McLean, pp. vi–xiv.

Turner, G.H., & Pollitt, K. (2002). Community interpreting meets literary translation: English-BSL interpreting in the theatre. *The Translator, 8 (1)*, 25–48.

Wadensjö, C. (1992). *Interpreting as interaction*. Linsköping: Linsköping University.

Wadensjö, C. (1993) The double role of a dialogue interpreter. *Perspectives: Studies in Translatology, 1*, 105–121.

Wadensjö, C. (1995). Dialogue interpreting and the distribution of responsibility. *Hermes: Journal of Linguistics, 14*, 111–130.

Wadensjö, C. (1997). Recycled information as a questioning strategy: Pitfalls in interpreter-mediated talk. In S.E. Carr, R. Roberts, A. Dufour, & D. Steyn (Eds.), *The critical link: Interpreters in the community*. Amsterdam: John Benjamins, pp. 35–52.

Wadensjö, C. (1998). *Interpreting as interaction*. London: Longman.

Wadensjö, C. (2001a). Dialogue interpreting and ethics: On the impact of communicative genres. Plenary paper presented at The Critical Link 3: The Complexity of the Profession conference, UQAM, Montréal, Canada.

Wadensjö, C. (2001b). Interpreting in crisis—the interpreter's position in therapeutic encounters. In I. Mason (Ed.), *Triadic exchanges: Studies in dialogue interpreting*. Manchester: St. Jerome, pp. 67–85.

3

Educational Interpreting: Access and Outcomes

Marc Marschark, Patricia Sapere,
Carol Convertino, & Rosemarie Seewagen

In his review of the history of deaf education, Lang noted that despite the efforts of scholars and researchers, the field remains plagued by false assumptions and ill-founded attitudes. "This is especially true," he claimed, "with regard to the issue of language and its relationship to academic achievement... [where] misconceptions, as well as insufficient bridging of research and practice, have thwarted efforts to effectively teach language and academic content to deaf children" (2003, p. 9). While the foregoing may be obvious with regard to school placement of deaf students and the modes of communication used in academic settings, in this chapter we suggest that a similar situation has emerged with regard to educational interpreting. Whether through "misconceptions" or simply a lack of relevant research, the assumption that mainstream education—supported by sign language interpreting—can provide deaf students with fair and appropriate public education may be unfounded.

The need for educational interpreting is greater today than ever before, as mainstream academic placement has become the primary means of educating deaf students. In the United States, for example, a requirement in Public Law 94-142 (1975) requiring education in the "least restrictive environment" for all handicapped children has resulted in over 75% of deaf children now being educated in local public schools with hearing classmates. Yet, there is a well-documented shortage of qualified interpreters (Baily & Straub, 1992; Jones, Clark, & Stoltz, 1997), and the headlong rush to mainstreaming has been based more on perceived cost savings than the educational needs of deaf children or our ability to provide them with full access in academic settings (see Easterbrooks, Lytle, Sheets, & Crook, 2004, for the legal consequences of such shortcomings).

The basis for PL 94-142—and the continuing popularity of main-stream placements for deaf children—lies in the belief that we are able to educate deaf children (and others with special needs) in that environment as well as or better than in special settings. Whether or not there are existing data for that position (see Karchmer & Mitchell, 2003; Stinson & Kluwin, 2003), educating deaf children in regular public school classrooms involves two fundamental assumptions that are in need of empirical evaluation. One is that the structure of information communicated by a hearing teacher for a hearing class is commensurate with the knowledge structure and learning styles of deaf students. If deaf students "learn differently" than hearing students, then they may be at a serious academic disadvantage in mainstream classrooms compared to settings designed to account for those special needs. This assumes, of course, that we have identified such differences and developed methods to incorporate them into teaching methods (for discussion of the broader educational issues, see Marschark, Lang, & Albertini, 2002; Ramsey, 1997).

The second assumption underlying mainstream education is that for those students who depend on signed communication, a skilled sign language interpreter will provide them with access to classroom communication roughly equivalent to that of their hearing peers.[1] Yet, despite an increasing research literature concerning sign language interpreting, remarkably little is known about how much of an interpreted message is actually understood by deaf students in the classroom—or deaf individuals in any setting, for that matter (Harrington, 2000; Napier, this volume). As the various chapters in this volume reveal, a number of studies have documented some of the processes thought to underlie effective interpreting and, to a lesser extent, means of teaching and evaluating interpreting skills (see also Monikowski & Winston, 2003). Few investigators, however, have considered explicitly the contributions of student characteristics (e.g., communication preferences, content knowledge, educational level), interpreter characteristics (e.g., education, content knowledge, familiarity with students), instructor characteristics (e.g., experience with deaf students and sign language, use of visual materials), or settings (e.g., social, educational, technical). To what extent do these factors actually influence comprehension of interpreting? Do they only affect the comfort of students, teachers, and interpreters?

Both in mainstream settings and in educational programs designed for deaf children that make use of educational interpreting in various situations, there is a tacit assumption that providing those students with interpreting for lectures and classroom discussion gives them learning opportunities comparable to those of hearing students. Yet, there is almost a complete lack of knowledge concerning how variables like those noted previously might influence learning by students of different ages/grade levels or different class contents. These questions are not new (Harrington, 2000; Jacobs, 1977; Redden, Davis, & Brown, 1978; Stewart & Kluwin, 1996), but surprisingly little progress has been made.

UNDERSTANDING CLASSROOM INTERPRETING

Questions concerning the effectiveness of educational interpreting need to consider the interpreter and the student as well as the instructor and the setting (Ramsey, 1997). On the interpreter side, Schick, Williams, and Bolster (1999) suggested that educational interpreting is unlikely to provide deaf students with full access to instruction. They evaluated interpreters' skills in K–12 educational settings, using videotaped samples of expressive production of classroom content and receptive performance from a standardized interview with a deaf student. Assessments took into account factors such as students' grade levels and modes of communication. Schick and colleagues found that less than half of the 59 interpreters they evaluated performed at a level considered minimally acceptable for educational interpreting. They concluded that many deaf children are denied access to classroom communication because of the skills of their interpreters.

Johnson (1991) investigated challenges faced by deaf students and interpreters in the classroom, reflecting the interactions of all of the contributing factors noted earlier. She videotaped graduate-level, interpreted classes and described several situations in which even when interpreters understood the instructors' message, communication breakdowns occurred. Of particular difficulty were situations in which classes involved material that was unfamiliar to students and interpreters and those in which diagrams and ambiguous descriptions of visual-spatial scenes were involved. Beyond the issue of divided attention between visual materials and the interpreter, Johnson noted that communication via sign language requires visual-spatial detail not required in spoken communication. In interpreting the description of a house built on a platform, for example, an interpreter was seen to establish characteristics of the platform, the house, and other details, some of which conflicted with later information. Not only was the student confused as to the description, but attempts at repair (when the student was unaware that they were repairs) only increased confusion. Furthermore, assumptions on the part of instructors, hearing classmates, and interpreters about what deaf students saw and understood resulted in miscommunications due to the asynchronous nature of "simultaneous interpreting."

Research on students' classroom comprehension of interpreting has most frequently evaluated the use of natural sign languages versus vernacular-based sign systems (e.g., American Sign Language [ASL], British Sign Language [BSL], and Australian Sign Language [Auslan] versus English-based sign or sign-supported English); that is, use of interpreting versus transliteration.[2] Although there is some variability in the literature, and in some cases definitions are left to the imaginations of readers, *interpreting* and *transliteration* are used here rather specifically. Following descriptions used by Frishberg (1986), the Registry of Interpreters for the Deaf (http://www.rid.org/expl.html [accessed January 21, 2004]), and others, *interpreting* here refers to the immediate transmission of productions in ASL or other natural signed languages through the spoken vernacular ("sign to voice") and from the spoken vernacular into the corresponding natural sign language ("voice to sign"). *Transliteration* refers to the transmission of a spoken language into a vernacular-based sign system (e.g., signing with English word order), retaining features of the spoken vernacular but strongly influenced by the natural sign vernacular. Unless otherwise indicated, our use of these terms assumes they are of high-quality in terms of clarity and accuracy, as determined by appropriate methodologies. This is not to say that they always are: only that we will assume for the sake of discussion that they are produced by qualified and skilled interpreters.

One of the first studies to compare interpreting and transliteration was by Fleischer (1975), who found that deaf high school students comprehended more of a lecture communicated via interpreting than by transliteration. Although information on the students' sign language skills was not reported, Fleischer suggested that students' language fluencies might interact with mode of communication. However, Murphy and Fleischer (1977) replicated Fleischer's 1975 study, comparing interpreting and transliteration with groups of deaf students who reported preferring one mode or the other and found no differences in comprehension due either to mode of communication, communication preference, or their interaction.

Livingston, Singer, and Abramson (1994) further explored interpreting and transliteration and the mode-match issue. In that study, college students were designated as "oriented toward ASL or English-like signing" by deaf adults working with the investigators. Looking ahead, it is noteworthy that comprehension scores were quite variable, ranging from 50% to 74%, with an overall mean score of only 62%. More important to Livingston and colleagues, however, was the finding that of the students who had seen an interpreted lecture, those designated as ASL-oriented scored significantly higher overall than students designated as oriented toward English-like signing. There was no advantage of transliteration for students in the latter group, however, and when a narrative presentation rather than a lecture was interpreted, neither comparison was reliable. These results indicate that ASL interpreting is not necessarily (or generally) better for classroom communication than transliteration, nor is the matter one of simply matching the mode of interpreting to student language skills.

Marschark, Sapere, Convertino, Seewagen, and Maltzen (2004) explored the issue of interpreting versus transliteration in greater depth. In three experiments, deaf college students saw lectures accompanied by either interpreting or transliteration. In two experiments, the groups were mixed with regard to whether students were more skilled in and preferred ASL or English-based signing, as determined by a questionnaire following the experiment and by information available from university databases. Regardless of whether students received written comprehension tests (experiment 1) or interpreting-congruent signed tests (experiment 2), there was no effect of mode of interpreting nor any interaction with student skills/preferences.[3] A third experiment that involved a priori (congruent and incongruent) student assignment to interpreting or transliteration conditions also failed to find any overall effect of the mode of interpreting or any interaction with student skills/preferences. These null findings have now been replicated in another larger study (Marschark, Sapere, Convertino, & Seewagen, 2005), and we have considerable confidence in their validity and reliability. Furthermore, our findings that deaf students were comprehending only 60%–75% of interpreted lectures (compared to 85%–90% by hearing peers) is consistent with the averages reported by Livingston and colleagues (1994) and Jacobs (1977), also with deaf college students and multiple-choice comprehension tests.

Two other aspects of Marschark and colleagues' (2004) study are important here. First, regression and other analyses of student demographic characteristics found that comprehension of lectures was not related to reading levels, degree, or age of onset of hearing losses; parental hearing status; use of assistive listening devices; registration in baccalaureate or pre-baccalaureate programs; or the age at which sign language was learned. This result could reflect either the complexity of student-interpreter-setting interactions or the large variability in the language and educational histories of most deaf students. Alternatively, the effects of interpreting versus transliteration may be more subtle than can be discerned on the basis of a comprehension test following a single lecture. It is also likely that some individual deaf students might benefit more from interpreting or transliteration either across settings or in particular contexts, even if such relations do not hold at the group level. This possibility is of particular interest to interpreters and interpreter trainers. After all, why put so much time and effort into providing both ASL and English-based interpreting services if it makes little difference to comprehension? In large measure, this should be considered a rhetorical question, but it is also one that will take on greater importance if further investigation indicates that the same findings are obtained with regard to learning in more extended investigations or in K–12 and community settings.[4]

The second important aspect of the Marschark et al. findings concerns the extent to which deaf students (or other consumers of interpreting services) are aware of how various factors influence their comprehension. Experiment 3 showed that when students were asked to predict their performance on comprehension tests following interpreted lectures, hearing students' predictions were reliably correlated with their actual test scores, while those of deaf students were not. This manipulation followed observations in earlier experiments that deaf students were extremely confident of 100% (or close) correct performance on such tests, only to score closer to 60% on average. One possibility is that the students understood the content of the interpreted lecture, but were less able than hearing peers to accurately judge their performance on the comprehension test. A re-analysis of data available from the study, however, revealed no relation between students' actual test scores and their ratings of either their comprehension or the quality of the interpreter.

Without any evidence to the contrary, it thus appears that the deaf college students generally may be less aware than hearing peers of how much of classroom lectures they understand (see Johnson, 1991; Napier & Barker, 2004). It remains unclear whether such findings indicate that they simply do not understand interpreting as well as we (and they) assume they do, or that they do not apply metacognitive skills to monitor ongoing comprehension (Krinsky, 1990; Strassman, 1997). Although other possibilities are considered in the following sections, these two alternatives are intertwined in such a way that if one is true, both are likely true. They therefore warrant a bit of elaboration.

ON KNOWING WHAT WE KNOW AND WHAT WE UNDERSTAND—OR NOT

A central component of learning for any student involves recognition of when comprehension is successful and when it is not. The role of *metacognition* in the comprehension of sign language interpreting has not yet received significant attention. Seal (2004) noted that interpreting at the secondary-school level might serve as a catalyst for metacognitive and metalinguistic processing by deaf students and discussed the need for such processing by interpreters in order to improve their own performance. Metacognition also has been recognized as important in reading and academic performance for both deaf students (Strassman, 1997) and hearing students (Kruger & Dunning, 1999; Sinkavich, 1995). The general finding in this area clearly indicates that "the rich get richer and the poor get poorer." Students who know more are better able to distinguish what is known and what is new and, if anything, tend to underestimate their performance. Students who know less tend not to realize how much they do not know/comprehend and thus tend to overestimate their performance (Kruger & Dunning, 1999). In metacognition studies with hearing students, however, it can be assumed that the participants are all English fluent. With deaf students, we have to figure out how much of their overestimations are specific to sign language interpreting, the result of less content knowledge, or the product of lower facility in their sign language skills.

Because most deaf students grow up with variable language and education experiences, perhaps it should not be surprising that they are unable to judge accurately whether and how much they comprehend of classroom content (Johnson, 1991). In particular, given the reports of poor interpreting quality in K–12 settings (Jones et al., 1997; LaBue, 1995; Schick et al., 1999) and the likelihood that instructors are unaware of deaf students' level of access to classroom communication (Ramsey, 1997), students who encounter more skilled interpreters in a post-secondary classroom might understandably be delighted at their increased levels of understanding and participation. At that juncture, another aspect of metacognition in the classroom becomes important. While some students recognize gaps in their comprehension and attempt to compensate through reading and meetings with tutors or instructors, others are either unaware of their comprehension failures or simply accept them as normal (see Napier & Barker, 2004). Moreover, reading comprehension is well recognized as being problematic for deaf students, and individual tutoring or advising without effective communication only perpetuates the information-impoverished situation (Harrington, 2000; Lang, Biser, Mousley, Orlando, & Porter, 2004), so the remedial value of these alternatives remains in question.[5]

Another factor affecting comprehension in the classroom is students' prior knowledge, both about course-related content and more general world knowledge.[6] In a series of experiments involving hearing students, Rawson and Kintsch (2002) demonstrated that the role of background information on memory for textual materials lies in its facilitating the organization of new information through existing category superordinates and other semantic links. Rawson and Kintsch noted that "to the extent that organizational superordinates are not developed until further into study trials, fewer opportunities to link content to those superordinates would be available" (pp. 774–775; see also Mayer, 1983). Studies by McEvoy, Marschark, and Nelson (1999) and Marschark, Convertino, McEvoy, and Masteller (2004) demonstrated that such conceptual linkages in the mental lexicon are far more variable across deaf college students than hearing peers, as reflected qualitatively and quantitatively in tasks involving single words. Thus, it is likely that prior knowledge is less effectively applied by deaf students than hearing students in contexts such as reading and interpreting (Jelinek, Lewis, & Jackson, 2001; Oakhill & Cain, 2000).

Taken together, these findings suggest that deaf students may be at a relative disadvantage in a classroom where information is structured by a hearing instructor for hearing students, while at the same time instructors and interpreters would find it more difficult to "tune" instruction to match several deaf students in the same classroom. The findings also suggest that differences observed between deaf and hearing students' understanding of classroom content might be independent of the nature and quality of educational interpreting, but due to inappropriate comprehension/learning strategies or failure to apply content knowledge (see also Lang, 2002; Marschark, Lang, et al., 2002; Richardson, MacLeod-Gallinger, McKee, & Long, 1999). Marschark and colleagues (2004, experiment 3) therefore statistically controlled for the effects of prior knowledge using scores from pretests corresponding to each lecture. Deaf students scored significantly lower than hearing students on the pretest and still scored lower on the comprehension test when the effects of prior knowledge were removed. It is possible that controlling for prior knowledge via content-specific pretests is not sufficiently sensitive to demonstrate its effects, but it appears more likely that the application of content knowledge is only one of several factors affecting comprehension of sign language interpreting. Student sign language skill might be expected to predict understanding of interpreting, for example, but it also will interact with interpreter skill and the setting (e.g., Johnson, 1991), making any simple causal relations unlikely.

In this regard, recall that Marschark and colleagues (2004) found no significant relation between deaf students' comprehension scores and their sign/spoken skills. Many of those students, however, had gained their sign skills in a college environment where there is considerable social pressure to use sign language (Kersting, 1997) and thus may have lesser sign fluencies. Might those students who had appropriate language tools at their disposal throughout development demonstrate the expected language advantage?[7] Evaluation of that suggestion is possible by re-examining data from experiment 3, where 17 students reported learning to sign from birth and 31 reported learning it later. Overall, students who reported starting to learn sign at 1 year of age or before obtained significantly higher scores on the comprehension test than the later signers (81% vs. 73%), although they still scored significantly lower than the hearing students (89%) (see Mayberry & Eichen, 1991, concerning the long-term benefits of early sign language acquisition). A similar analysis was conducted using the data from the Marschark et al. (2005) study in which students saw two different lectures. Using comprehension test scores on two content-knowledge pretests and both comprehension tests, no differences were observed between the comprehension of 23 students who had two deaf parents and 59 others who had either one or no deaf parents. The same result was obtained if a criterion of one rather than two deaf parents was employed.

Summarizing the results described in this section, it appears that both prior content knowledge and sign language skill affect deaf students' understanding of interpreting in the classroom, but neither is sufficient to explain their poorer comprehension relative to hearing peers. Deaf students in the studies reviewed thus far comprehended only about 85% of what was understood or recalled by hearing students. Although growing up with ASL may enhance comprehension, even those students who had deaf parents did not comprehend as much of an interpreted lecture as their hearing peers did. We cannot continue to deal with various aspects of deaf students' educations as though they were independent. Rather, we have to examine possible interactions among characteristics of students, interpreters, instructors, and settings. Let us therefore consider further the language and learning tools that deaf students bring to the classroom setting and the degree to which those tools put them in a position to benefit from an interpreted education.

COGNITION, LEARNING, AND COMPREHENSION
OF INTERPRETING

Schick (in press) argued that successful educational interpreting requires an understanding of deaf children's cognitive development (see also Detterman & Thompson, 1997; Marschark & Lukomski, 2001; Marschark et al., 2002). Schick emphasized the importance of a deaf child's developing theory of mind, peer socialization, and various other pragmatic language interactions as essential for the acquisition of skills necessary to benefit from interpreting. She acknowledged the likely interaction of these processes, as deaf children may not have the skills necessary to benefit from classroom interpreting, a barrier that in turn affects their learning of additional academic skills. Consistent with the arguments of Marschark et al. (2002), Schick suggested that "the deaf child may need interaction and teaching that is more fine-tuned to their level of skills and understanding" (draft, p. 21), a rare occurrence in classrooms where an interpreter serves primarily as a conduit for instruction designed for hearing children. The question here is how educational interpreters should deal with this issue—or whether they should.[8] In either case, they have to be aware of it.

Given the interactions of experience, language development, and cognitive development, consideration of the cognitive processes involved in sign language interpreting must take into account the nature of the to-be-processed material and its mental representation as well as individual characteristics and experience. Deaf children, for example, have been shown to have more difficulty processing and retaining sequentially presented information relative to both simultaneously presented material (e.g., Todman & Seedhouse, 1994) and spatially related information (O'Connor & Hermelin, 1972). Spoken language appears to confer an advantage in retention of sequential information, even among deaf people (Burkholder & Pisoni, in press; Lichtenstein, 1998; see Marschark, 2003, for a review). Let us consider two related domains in more detail.

Visuospatial Considerations for Educational Interpreting

Lack of hearing early in life has significant impact on the development of the nervous system and organization of function within the brain. Tharpe, Ashmead, and Rothpletz (2002) accordingly proposed stronger or weaker forms of a *sensory compensation hypothesis* by which, because deaf individuals lack hearing, they should be particularly adept in the visual domain. Adherents of such a position would argue that the visual advantage among deaf individuals would increase over time and visual experience. In general, however, there is no overall enhancement of vision, visual perception, or visuospatial processing skills in deaf individuals (see Emmorey, 2002, chap. 8, Marschark, 2003, for reviews). Nonetheless, vision is the primary modality for learning by deaf students, and it is incumbent on us to determine how the characteristics of visuospatial cognition among deaf individuals would affect learning via interpreting. For example, deaf adults who use sign language show relatively better performance in some aspects of visual perception relative to both hearing individuals and deaf individuals who use spoken language: the ability to rapidly shift visual attention or scan visual stimuli (Corina, Kritchevsky, & Bellugi, 1992; Rettenback, Diller, & Sireteanu, 1999), visual detection of both motion (Neville & Lawson, 1987) and sign language (Swisher, 1993) in the periphery, and face recognition (Bellugi, L. O'Grady, Lillo-Martin, M. O'Grady, van Hoek, & Corina, 1990). Although there do not appear to be any studies indicating that deaf individuals have lesser visual attention skills than hearing individuals, it would not be surprising to find that deaf individuals suffer more from eye fatigue and relax their visual attention (i.e., reduce vigilance) more often. Alternatively, because hearing individuals can utilize their hearing, they may take advantage of redundancy in visual and auditory messages but be less visually vigilant than deaf individuals.

An environment rich in stimulation and connections between different sense modalities enhances the development of visual attention skills. While sound appears to contribute to some aspects of (visual) perceptual and cognitive development (Burkholder & Pisoni, in press;

Quittner, Smith, Osberger, et al., 1994; Smith, Quittner, Osberger, & Miyamoto, 1998; Tharpe et al., 2002), signed communication does too. Emmorey and her colleagues, for example, have shown that skilled signers are faster in generating and manipulating mental images than either later (deaf or hearing) signers or hearing non-signers (Emmorey, Klima, & Hickok, 1998; Emmorey, Kosslyn, & Bellugi, 1993; Emmorey & Kosslyn, 1996; see also Talbot & Haude, 1993). Visuospatial skills of this sort might be utilized in the multifaceted visual environment of the classroom, enhancing access to information by deaf students who sign by allowing them to more readily perceive, process, and retain visual information from different sources.

Cognitive Considerations for Educational Interpreting

Related to the issue of how deaf students coordinate multiple sources of visual information is the question of how they deal with relations among visual displays, course materials encountered outside of the classroom, and instructors'/interpreters' productions in the classroom. That is, deaf and hearing individuals appear to make differential use of relational versus individual-item information. Ottem (1980) reviewed more than 50 studies involving various kinds of memory, learning, and problem-solving tasks and found that when tasks involved only a single stimulus dimension, deaf individuals usually performed comparably to hearing individuals. When a task required simultaneous attention to two or more dimensions, the performance of hearing individuals usually surpassed that of their deaf peers.

Most likely a result of early educational experiences, many deaf individuals appear to focus on individual items or events within a context, rather than on relations among items, an orientation shown to affect performance in a variety of cognitive tasks (e.g., Marschark, 2003; Richardson. McLeod-Gallinger, McKee, et al., 1999). Banks, Gray, and Fyfe (1990), for example, found that although deaf and hearing students recalled equal amounts of read text, the deaf students tended to remember disjointed parts rather than whole idea units. Findings suggest that, at least in some contexts, deaf students are less likely than hearing peers to attend to or recognize relational information. Interpreters may be implicitly aware of this situation and adjust accordingly, for example, in describing the location, shape, and function of part of a building (Johnson, 1991). Analyzing the productions of interpreters relative to what an instructor says thus might reveal that various relations and inferences are supplied, even if they were not stated explicitly. Such provision might occur more often during interpreting than transliteration, because interpreters often feel they have more flexibility in the former, not being as closely tied to the literal production of the speaker (Frishberg, 1986). However, understanding which inferences are relevant (or necessary), which are intended by the teacher, and which are likely to be drawn by the deaf student without assistance presents a challenge even when the interpreter is familiar with both the content and the student. At present, it is unclear how interpreters are to decide on the correctness and helpfulness of their elaborations—or whether they are even aware of them.

Anecdotal reports from a number of educational interpreters suggest that they see such activity as an important part of their roles, as deaf students often do not seem to make those connections themselves.[9] In the short term, one would expect that providing information beyond that given by an instructor (or other speaker) would facilitate comprehension, perhaps even giving them an advantage relative to hearing classmates. In the longer term, however, providing relational/inferential links for deaf students may discourage them from doing so themselves in other settings or perhaps even being aware that such links are helpful.

Marschark (in press) argued that such narrow approaches to learning on the part of deaf students likely would be the consequence of the limited language interactions among deaf children and their hearing parents, lower expectations and less consistency in classrooms with hearing teachers, and lesser quality in K-12 interpreting. Nonetheless, the behaviors of well-meaning interpreters might also be an important contributor in that regard. If sign language interpreters supply such inferences and relations explicitly, deaf students still have to learn to engage in such higher-order processing on their own (Bebko, 1998). An interpreting strategy of this sort also may preempt the instructional strategies of teachers who set up situations that explicitly require students to go beyond the information given, thus fostering problem-solving and learning skills. Ultimately, both the frequency of such strategies by interpreters and their positive or negative consequences are empirical questions, precisely the kind that we should be asking about the impact of interpreting on teaching and learning.

Convergence of Visuospatial and Cognitive Considerations in Educational Interpreting

One more issue is in need of consideration in the context of ways that deaf students' visual and cognitive abilities might influence learning via interpreting. The increasing use of multimedia tools in academic settings has been bolstered by research demonstrating the utility of combining verbal and visual information (e.g., Gellevij, van der Meij, Jong, & Pieters, 2002; Paivio, 1986; Tiene, 2000). But research has not yet adequately addressed the fact that deaf students are unable to simultaneously attend to both visual displays and sign language in the classroom. The enhanced peripheral vision and speeded visual attention shifts by deaf students who are skilled signers may offset this challenge, but the pairing of interpreting and visual instructional technologies appears likely to create a barrier to deaf students' full participation in the classroom.

Matthews and Reich (1993) argued that deaf students' relatively poor academic performance could be explained in part by the visual demands of classroom communication. They examined communication in high school classes at a school for the deaf, a setting in which one would presume that both teachers and students would be particularly sensitive to communication needs. Analyzing sign production and gaze direction from videotaped segments of classes, however, Matthews and Reich found that when they were signing, teachers were being looked at by students an average of only 44% of the time, and students were looked at by their peers only 30% of the time. Students who were specific targets of a production by a teacher visually attended to the teacher only about 50% of the time. Matthews and Reich thus concluded that "even with well-trained teachers and relatively sophisticated students, the level of possible reception of transmitted messages is disappointingly low, somewhat below 50%" (p. 16).

In a second relevant study, Siple, Steve, Sapere, Convertino, Seewagen, and Marschark (in preparation) examined the information available to deaf students during an interpreted class in which an instructor used a projected computer display to teach a software package. Detailed analyses included relations among the instructor's use of the display, the interpreter's behavior, and student attention. Most obviously, ongoing descriptions frequently did not restate what happened on the screen, but rather explained actions, directed attention, or provided supplementary information (e.g., "So we click on this and drag it over here...you can [selecting from menu] change its appearance..."). Attending to the interpreter thus often meant that deaf students would miss other information. At the same time, attending to the screen could result in missing both the explanation of a demonstration and supplementary information from the instructor.

Siple and colleagues examined the instructor's spoken language in terms of his computer demonstrations, revealing that if deaf students had watched the interpreter only, they would have missed almost half of the information contained in the demonstration. Similarly, the relation of demonstrated actions to the instructor's spoken production was such that if students were watching the screen only, they would have missed approximately half of the information communicated by the instructor. Finally, because students could not watch both the interpreter and the screen at the same time, Siple and colleagues examined the amount of information accessible via one source or the other, taking into account what the interpreter heard from the instructor (some actions were not accompanied by speech), what the interpreter produced, and whether or not students appeared to be looking at the interpreter or the screen. Overall, that analysis indicated that, indeed, the deaf students would have had the opportunity to receive only about half of what was available to hearing peers.

Consistent with earlier findings (e.g., Johnson, 1991), Siple and colleagues' results indicate the need to better understand the interactions of students, interpreters, and settings if mainstream education is to be successful. While research on such issues is continuing, it is clear that learning via sign language interpreting adds another layer to the interplay of cognitive linguistic, and situational factors in teaching and learning. Further, adding to this complexity is consideration of deaf students' communication preferences.

WHAT DO DEAF STUDENTS WANT?

Rolling Stones musicians Mick Jagger and Keith Richards (1967) noted that while people cannot always get what they want, they sometimes get what they need. In part, investigations like those of Livingston and colleagues (1994) and Marschark, Sapere, and colleagues (2004, 2005) reflect a frequent assumption in interpreting that deaf clients should get the former (what they want) regardless of what they need. At the same time, skilled interpreters working in educational settings claim (confidentially, of course) that many deaf students who request ASL in the classroom have little notion of what it really is and do not understand it. Despite the fact that our research has consistently found that even those students who prefer signing with English word order and claim not to be skilled in ASL understand ASL interpreting just as well as transliteration, there are larger issues involved. We will not deal here with the ethical questions surrounding the responsibilities of interpreters to give students what they want by way of interpreting. Instead, we will focus on the extent to which interpreting can provide deaf students access to academic settings.

Surprisingly, the relative value of direct instruction versus interpreted (or mediated) instruction has not been considered in any depth, although the matter clearly depends on both the content knowledge and communication skills of students, interpreters, and instructors (Lang, McKee, & Conner, 1993). One aspect of this issue is the frequent assumption that deaf students prefer direct instruction to interpreted instruction, but there does not appear to be any empirical support for this belief. What about comprehension in interpreted and direct-instruction mainstream classrooms? Quinsland and Long (1989) examined students' understanding of a college science lecture from either an instructor signing for himself (via simultaneous communication) or interpreters designated as "skilled" or "unskilled" based on their RID certification. Quinsland and Long found that students learned about twice as much with a skilled interpreter relative to an unskilled one, but there was no difference between direct instruction and instruction via a skilled interpreter. Test scores were comparable to those in the interpreting studies described previously, with deaf students' scores about 84% of those obtained by hearing peers.

Use of simultaneous communication (SimCom) in the Quinsland and Long study might make it suspect, and the issue of SimCom versus natural sign language in the classroom is not at issue here. Nevertheless, Cokely (1990) also failed to find any comprehension differences when deaf college students saw lectures presented via SimCom, sign language alone, or interpretation, and there is apparently no published research to support the frequent claim of interpreters and teachers of deaf students alike that interpreted education cannot be as beneficial as direct instruction. Although we have already noted that the relative benefits of the two modes of education will depend on instructor communication skills as well as student, interpreter, and setting characteristics, discussion surrounding the chapters of this volume indicate that we are far from agreement on this issue (see Sapere et al., this volume).

Lacking any quantitative evidence for the benefits of direct instruction over interpreting or vice versa, there also is the question of what mode of interpreting students prefer in the classroom, what mode of interpreting interpreters think students prefer in the classroom, and what actually benefits the students more. Our results thus far suggest that, at least for individual lectures, interpreting and transliteration are equally effective, regardless of student preferences. So let us address the other two questions.

Napier and Barker (2004) conducted a qualitative study in which they examined deaf university students' preferences for "free interpretation" (primarily Auslan) versus "literal interpretation" (primarily transliteration). They found that students who preferred Auslan in social settings and some academic settings nevertheless wanted transliteration in more technical courses so that they could acquire the same vocabulary as hearing peers. That consensus was consistent with Napier's (2002) finding that university-level interpreters routinely code-switch in order to provide deaf students with information necessary for their academic success.

In an unpublished study, we recently examined both deaf students' mode preferences for interpreting and interpreters' beliefs about those preferences. Over 400 deaf students attending Rochester Institute of Technology (RIT) chose whether they would prefer interpreting or transliteration (each of which was explained fully) in three different settings: social and co-curricular situations, liberal arts courses, or science and engineering courses. In addition, they completed a checklist for each situation containing 14 possible reasons for their preferences. Forty RIT interpreters completed the same survey, indicating what they thought the "typical RIT deaf student" would prefer in those settings and why. Consistent with interpreters' predictions, students reported preferring ASL to transliteration in social settings. However, the preference was not a large one, as ASL was preferred by only 51% of the students, while 93% of the interpreters predicted that a typical deaf student would prefer ASL. The interpreters were also correct in predicting that students would prefer transliteration over interpreting in science and engineering courses, although again, students' 65% to 35% preference for transliteration was not as strong as expected by the interpreters, 80% of whom expected deaf students to prefer transliteration. The greatest differences were observed with regard to liberal arts courses, where 63% of students preferred to receive instruction through transliteration, while 73% of the interpreters predicted that they would prefer ASL interpreting. Students' reasons for choosing one kind of interpreting or another in different settings are somewhat complex (e.g., students who prefer transliteration in liberal arts courses were more likely to cite "better pacing" as a reason for their choice, whereas interpreters predicted that students would choose ASL for the same reason). Across comparisons, however, the important finding is that their reasons are quite different than those assumed by interpreters (see Lang et al., 1993, for similar findings with regard to students' and teachers' perceptions of instruction preferences).

These findings leave us with a dilemma. It is clear that interpreters' expectations about the communication preferences of deaf students do not match those reported by the students themselves. At present, there is no evidence that student preference for interpreting is related to their actual comprehension or recall of interpreted material. Indeed, at least as judged by comprehension of individual lectures, deaf students understand just as much regardless of whether the mode of interpreting matches their preferences or not (Livingston et al., 1994; Murphy & Fleischer, 1977; Marschark, Sapere, Convertino, et al., 2004). So, is this just a matter of comfort (interpreter or student), or might preferences be more important over the term of an entire course than a single, brief lecture? At present, there is no way to know, but clearly the matter warrants further investigation. Why no one has addressed these issues is almost as interesting as the educational questions themselves.

When Students Prefer Not to Have Interpreters

Before leaving the issue of student preferences in educational settings, it is important to note the increasing numbers of students requesting online text presentation (e.g., captioning, CART, C-Print) as a means of gaining access to the classroom. This trend may reflect either an increasing pressure from hearing parents (and hearing peers) for deaf students to appear more "hearing" in school settings or the shortage of skilled interpreters (Baily & Straub, 1992; Jones et al., 1997; Schick et al., 1999). Examination of recent data concerning deaf students' literacy skills, however, reveals that they still read significantly below hearing peers (Traxler, 2000), and it is unclear whether they would be able to benefit any more from captioning than from sign language interpreting. Jelinek Lewis, and Jackson (2001), for example, found that even when reading level was controlled, deaf students (in 4th, 5th, and 6th grades) comprehended less of a captioned video than hearing peers, apparently because "deaf students lag behind hearing students in their ability to generalize information or to use prior knowledge" (p. 49) (see also, Jackson, Paul, & Smith, 1997; Oakhill & Cain, 2000).

One early study in this area by Stinson, Meath-Lang, and MacLeod (1981) compared deaf students' comprehension of a lecture that was either interpreted or provided in printed form. They reported that students recalled significantly more information when the material was presented in print rather than interpreted. However, only 19% of the idea units was recalled from text, compared to 12% from interpreting, suggesting that neither mode of classroom communication was very effective. Furthermore, without information concerning the reading or sign language skills of the students in the Stinson and colleagues study, it is difficult to know how those results should be interpreted. More recently, Everhart, Stinson, McKee, and Giles (1996) found that deaf students reported understanding significantly more in class when using C-Print rather than an interpreter, but the accuracy of those reports was not assessed (cf. Marschark, Sapere, Convertino, et al., 2004). Stinson, Kelly, Elliot, Colwell, Liu, and Stinson (2000) compared deaf students' comprehension and memory of an interpreted introductory sociology lecture with presentation of the same information using C-Print and failed to show any significant difference between conditions, although students who were better readers scored higher overall.

In short, while it remains unclear just how much sign language interpreting "levels the playing field" in educational settings, there are not yet any convincing data that the use of text materials in the classroom (e.g., via captioning) offers a more viable alternative. Indeed, just as some proponents of captioning argue that not all deaf students know sign language sufficiently well to benefit from interpreting, it is very clear that most deaf students do not read well enough to benefit from the typically fast pace of captioning (see Marschark, 2001, for discussion). It is important to note, however, that both the studies mentioned in this section and those described earlier with regard to sign language interpreting have involved only single lectures, and the effects of these support services over an entire course or after multiple presentations on the same topic remain to be determined. These issues all clearly need to be addressed, taking into account the extent to which these alternatives actually mesh with students' knowledge, communication skills, and learning strategies.

SUMMARY AND CONCLUSIONS

The research described in this chapter emphasizes the need to better understand the complex personal and functional interactions of students, instructors, interpreters, and settings if educational interpreting— and interpreted education—is to be optimally beneficial for deaf students. We are sensitive to the fact that findings of the sort described here make an already difficult situation seem even more so. Ultimately, however, if some of the factors that have previously been assumed important turn out not to be, we may be able to significantly improve the effectiveness of educational interpreting without overwhelming the interpreter or shortchanging the student.

There is now convincing evidence that deaf students do not comprehend as much as their hearing peers in the classroom, even when provided with highly qualified sign language interpreters in controlled settings where competing visual information is not at issue. Several analyses provided here have addressed the issue of whether such findings are specific to sign language interpreting or indicative of more general teaching/learning challenges in educating deaf students. The answer remains to be determined. Examination of deaf students' comprehension of interpreting indicates that they are not as accurate as hearing peers in assessing their own comprehension. Whether this result is specific to sign language interpreting is not entirely clear, but in any case a metacognitive gap of this sort would impede full understanding of ongoing communication in the classroom. One would expect that at least a partial resolution of this issue could be found by looking at how accurate deaf students are in predicting their reading comprehension (e.g., from captioning). Despite a variety of studies concerning metacognition and reading in deaf students (see Strassman, 1997), this rather obvious question apparently has not been asked.

Much of the research described here has been conducted with deaf college students, and it has not yet been extended to community or K–12 settings. Overall levels of comprehension may be much the same, but deaf adults in the community may well show greater comprehension when the mode of interpreting (ASL versus English-based) is more commensurate with their preferences and reported skills. Although such differences have not been demonstrated in studies involving college students, deaf students involved in the research described here represent a relatively limited range of experimental participants. Yet, results thus far are consistent across students enrolled in 2-year and

4-year programs, different universities and methodologies, students who varied in their sign language exposure, and the content areas of material presented. Students who learned to sign earlier sometimes score higher on comprehension tests than peers who learned to sign later, but they still perform at levels below hearing peers.

If students' interpreting preferences are not related to improved understanding of interpreted lectures, the comprehension gap between them and their hearing peers may derive from several different sources. One possibility lies in their language skills. More than 95% of deaf students have hearing parents, so it may well be that variable language exposure during childhood has left them with lesser language flexibility or language comprehension skills below those of hearing peers. Although there do not appear to have been any rigorous studies of comprehension via oral interpreting, cued speech, or speechreading in classroom settings, such investigations are clearly important and would be informative in several respects. If the observed comprehension challenges are specific to sign language interpreting, we should be able to work with interpreters and interpreter educators to alter interpreting methods and compensate in areas of documented (content or language) difficulty. If the comprehension challenges prove a product of general language fluencies, we expect interpreters and instructors to recognize that fact and address it as well as possible (hopefully together), student by student, in different settings.

Closely related to a general language comprehension barrier to interpreting success is the possibility that deaf students' conceptual knowledge, world knowledge, or information processing strategies differ from those of hearing students in ways that create barriers to comprehension of interpreting (Marschark, 2003; Marschark et al., 2004; McEvoy et al., 1999). In that case, it may be that the structure of information conveyed by an instructor will not match the cognitive structures of deaf students in the class[10] or, perhaps less correctable, deaf students may lack sufficient background knowledge and vocabulary to grasp ongoing classroom lectures/discussions as rapidly as hearing peers. Many deaf students depend on other sources of educational support, such as tutors, text materials, and instructor time, to facilitate their academic success. Interpreters who are familiar with course content and their student clients might be able to provide additional support for them in mainstream settings where teachers are unfamiliar with the needs of deaf students (see Harrington, 2000; Johnson, 1991), although professional and practical considerations currently prevent their doing so. The distinction between the interpreting role and other possible roles makes good sense in a variety of community settings (see Cokely, this volume), but it may be less of a service to deaf individuals in educational settings.

Another possible reason why deaf students might learn less from interpreted lectures than hearing peers do from spoken lectures may lie in some basic differences between direct instruction and mediated instruction. There are a variety of intuitively appealing arguments for direct instruction for deaf students through some form of signed communication, and one obvious explanation of our findings is that interpreters simply can never really hope to duplicate the knowledge and nuances that a good instructor brings to a classroom lecture by virtue of teaching experience and content knowledge (i.e., that interpreting cannot duplicate its source).[11] However, there have not yet been any demonstrations that direct instruction is superior to interpreted instruction or any evidence that deaf learners prefer it. Furthermore, there is mounting evidence that deaf and hearing learners process information differently, have different content/conceptual knowledge, and different knowledge organization than hearing peers (and, presumably, hearing instructors). Hearing instructors with experience teaching deaf students and who sign for themselves in the classroom may well recognize those differences, implicitly or explicitly, and adjust for them. The fact that almost twice as many deaf students graduate from the National Technical Institute for the Deaf and Gallaudet University than other college programs could be taken as support for that argument (independent of the issue of sign language skill). Alternatively, it also may be that the difficulty of courses taken in those settings and/or the level of instructors' expectations for those deaf students are somewhat different than are encountered in mainstream settings. In any case, if either instructors or interpreters were aware of differences between deaf and hearing learners and could modify instructional content accordingly, it seems likely that student comprehension and learning would improve. As yet, however, few instructors, interpreters, or interpreter educators seem willing to recognize such differences, let alone develop collaborative strategies for dealing with them.

Finally, regardless of the extent to which any of the preceding alternatives contribute to academic barriers for deaf students, the lack of research into interpreting and its outcomes surely is a significant factor in deaf students' challenges in academic settings. Much more research is needed, and it requires the support and participation of all stakeholders in the interpreting enterprise. As noted at the beginning of this chapter, whether due to the relative youth of the interpreting profession or the ambiguous role of interpreters, there are many important questions that have not been asked. Even where information has been obtained with regard to deaf learners, there has yet to be any concerted attempt to incorporate the relevant psychological and educational research into interpreter education. Some interpreters take relevant courses as part of their own professional development, but findings like those discussed in this chapter suggest that a course on deaf learners (or appropriate study materials) should be a requirement for any program that trains interpreters who work in educational settings and instructors who have deaf students in their classes. To do otherwise either regards ignorance as acceptable or hides it behind a mask of political correctness. Both are equally detrimental to deaf students, depriving them of educational opportunities and squandering their potential.

ACKNOWLEDGMENTS

Preparation of this report and research reported herein was supported by grants REC-0207394 and REC-0307602 from the National Science Foundation. Any opinions, findings and conclusions, or recommendations expressed in this material are those of the authors and do not necessarily reflect the views of the National Science Foundation. We thank Harry Lang and Jemina Napier for comments on an earlier draft of the chapter.

NOTES

1. Unless otherwise noted, references to interpreting situations throughout this chapter assume that the deaf individuals involved are fluent in the relevant language and that the interpreting is of the highest quality, even if the meanings of "quality," "skill," and "fluency" are open to debate. In practice, of course, neither of these assumptions necessarily holds. In research, it is therefore incumbent on the investigators either to select participants who meet these criteria or clearly indicate when they do not hold—political correctness notwithstanding.

2. Although most of the work in this regard has been done in English-speaking countries, "ASL" and "English" henceforth will be used generically to refer to natural sign languages and their vernacular-based variants. There may be some subtle variations across different spoken and signed languages with regard to the issues addressed in this chapter, but they are beyond the current goals and have yet to be empirically discerned.

3. Note that because signed versions of comprehension tests did not improve deaf students' performance (Marschark, Sapere, Convertino, et al., 2004, experiments 1 and 2), written tests were used in subsequent experiments.

4. There are also some fascinating cultural, epistemological, and developmental aspects to this matter; for example, if the lack of any interpreting/transliteration differences is the consequence of experience with relatively poor interpreting in K–12 settings. These issues are beyond the scope of the present discussion but clearly in need of investigation.

5. Instructors vary widely in their knowledge and skill in working with deaf students as well as in their ability and willingness to make special accommodations for them. In a study conducted at RIT, we found that instructors in two academic units were perceived as less supportive of deaf students and less cooperative with interpreters. Deaf students taking courses in

those two units had the lowest grades of all units studied, although the causal relations in those findings remain unclear.

6. Prior content knowledge on the part of interpreters also might affect students' comprehension, a possibility currently under investigation.

7. In a similar fashion, Leybaert and her colleagues have found that young deaf children who are exposed to cued speech both at home and at school show significant improvement in their acquisition of French Sign Language, but exposure in only one setting or the other does not provide such marked benefits (Leybaert & Alegria, 2003).

8. In our view, interpreters are responsible for ensuring that teachers are made aware if students have apparent difficulty understanding communication in the classroom. Although some interpreters argue that such behaviors violate their role (see Dean & Pollard, this volume), they also complain that instructors place too much responsibility for communication on them. Clearly, this issue is in need of discussion and resolution.

9. Opinions on this issue do not appear to be a function of experience in the field, and study of educational interpreters' beliefs about what they are doing and why would be most informative.

10. The matching of cognitive structures here refers both to the situation where information from a hearing instructor matches the conceptual structure of hearing students but not deaf students (Marschark, Sapere, Convertino, et al., 2004) and the situation in which the diverse learning strategies and variability in knowledge organization makes it difficult or impossible to accommodate several deaf students in a single class.

11. The possible issues of poor teaching, lack of support for the special needs of deaf students, and instructor resistance to sign language interpreters are not at issue here.

REFERENCES

Baily, J., & Straub, S. (1992). Interpreting services. *ASHA, 34,* 51–53.

Banks, J., Gray, C., & Fyfe, R. (1990). The written recall of printed stories by severely deaf children. *British Journal of Educational Psychology, 60,* 192–206.

Bebko, J. (1998). Learning, language, memory, and reading: The role of language automatization and its impact on complex cognitive activities. *Journal of Deaf Studies and Deaf Education, 3,* 4–14.

Bellugi, U., O'Grady, L., Lillo-Martin, D., O'Grady, M., van Hoek, K., & Corina, D. (1990). Enhancement of spatial cognition in deaf children. In V. Volterra & C.J. Erting (Eds.), *From gesture to language in hearing and deaf children.* New York: Springer-Verlag, pp. 278–298.

Burkholder, R.A., & Pisoni, D.B. (in press). Working memory capacity, verbal rehearsal speed, and scanning in deaf children with cochlear implants. In P.E. Spencer & M. Marschark (Eds.), *Advances in the spoken language development of deaf children.* New York: Oxford University Press.

Cokely, D. (1990). The effectiveness of three means of communication in the college classroom. *Sign Language Studies, 69,* 415–439.

Corina, D.P., Kritchevsky, M., & Bellugi, U. (1992). Linguistic permeability of unilateral neglect: Evidence from American sign language. In *Proceedings of the Cognitive Science Conference.* Hillsdale, NJ: Erlbaum, pp. 384–389.

Detterman, D.K., & Thompson, L.A. (1997). What is so special about special education? *American Psychologist, 52*, 1082–1090.

Easterbrooks, S.R., Lytle, L.R., Sheets, P.M., & Crook, B.S. (2004). Ignoring FAPE, a costly mistake: The case of F.M. & L.G. versus Barbour County. *Journal of Deaf Studies and Deaf Education, 9*, 219–227.

Emmorey, K. (2002). *Language, cognition, and the brain*. Mahwah, NJ: Lawrence Erlbaum Associates.

Emmorey, K., Klima, E.S., & Hickok, G. (1998). Mental rotation within linguistic and nonlinguistic domaines in users of American sign language. *Cognition, 68*, 2221–2226.

Emmorey, K., Kosslyn, S., & Bellugi, U. (1993). Visual imagery and visual-spatial language: enhanced imagery abilities in deaf and hearing ASL signers. *Cognition, 46*, 139–181.

Emmorey, K., & Kosslyn, S. (1996). Enhanced image generation abilities in deaf signers: a right hemisphere effect. *Brain and Cognition, 32*, 28–44.

Everhart, V.S., Stinson, M.S., McKee, B.G., & Giles, P. (1996, April). *Evaluation of a speech-to-print transcription system as a resource for mainstreamed deaf students*. Paper presented at the annual meetings of the American Educational Research Association, New York.

Fleischer, L.R. (1975). *Language interpretation under four interpreting conditions*. Unpublished doctoral dissertation, Brigham Young University.

Frishberg, N. (1986). *Interpreting: An introduction*. Silver Spring, MD: Registry of Interpreters for the Deaf.

Gellevij, M., van der Meij, H., Jong, T.D., & Pieters, J. (2002). Multimodal versus unimodal instruction in a complex learning context. *Journal of Experimental Education, 70*, 215–239.

Harrington, F. (2000). Sign language interpreters and access for deaf students to university curricula: the ideal and the reality. In R.P. Roberts, S.E. Carr, D. Abraham, & A. Dufour (Eds.), *The critical link 2: Interpreters in the community*. Amsterdam: John Benjamins.

Jacobs, L.R. (1977). The efficiency of interpreting input for processing lecture information by deaf college students. *Journal of Rehabilitation of the Deaf, 11*, 10–14.

Jackson, D.W., Paul, P.V., & Smith, J.C. (1997). Prior knowledge and reading comprehension ability of deaf adolescents. *Journal of Deaf Studies and Deaf Education, 2*, 172–184.

Jagger, M., & Richards, K. (1967). You can't always get what you want. LP *Let it Bleed*. London: Decca.

Jelinek Lewis, M.S., & Jackson, D.W. (2001). Television literacy: Comprehension of program content using closed-captions for the deaf. *Journal of Deaf Studies and Deaf Education, 6*, 43–53.

Johnson, K. (1991). Miscommunication in interpreted classroom interaction. *Sign Language Studies, 70*, 1–34.

Jones, B.E., Clark, G., & Soltz, D. (1997). Characteristics and practices of sign language interpreters in inclusive education programs. *Exceptional Children, 63* (2), 257–268.

Karchmer, M.A., & Mitchell, R.E. (2003). Demographic and achievement characteristics of deaf and hard-of-hearing students. In M. Marschark & P.E. Spencer (Eds.), *Oxford handbook of deaf studies, language, and education*. New York: Oxford University Press, pp. 21–37.

Kersting, S.A. (1997). Balancing between deaf and hearing worlds: Reflections of mainstreamed college students on relationships and social interaction. *Journal of Deaf Studies and Deaf Education, 2,* 252–263.

Krinsky, S.G. (1990). The feeling of knowing in deaf adolescents. *American Annals of the Deaf, 135,* 389–395.

Kruger, J., & Dunning, D. (1999). Unskilled and unaware of it: How difficulties in recognizing one's own incompetence lead to inflated self-assessment. *Journal of Personality and Social Psychology, 77,* 1121–1134.

La Bue, M.A. (1995). Language and learning in a deaf education classroom: Practice and paradox. In C. Lucas (Ed.), *Sociolinguistics in Deaf Communities,* Washington, DC: Gallaudet University Press, pp. 164–220.

Lang, H.G. (2002). Higher education for deaf students: Research priorities in the new millennium. *Journal of Deaf Studies and Deaf Education, 7,* 267–280.

Lang, H.G. (2003). Perspectives on the history of deaf education. In M. Marschark & P.E. Spencer (Eds.), *Oxford handbook of deaf studies, language, and education.* New York: Oxford University Press, pp. 9–20.

Lang, H.G., Biser, E., Mousley, K, Orlando, R., & Porter, J. (2004). Tutoring deaf students in higher education: A comparison of baccalaureate and sub-baccalaureate student perceptions. *Journal of Deaf Studies and Deaf Education, 9,* 189–201.

Lang, H.G., McKee, B.G., & Conner, K.N. (1993). Characteristics of effective teachers: a descriptive study of perceptions of faculty and deaf college students. *American Annals of the Deaf, 138,* 252–259.

Leybaert, J., & Alegria, J. (2003). The role of cued speech in language development of deaf children. In M. Marschark & P.E. Spencer (Eds.), *Oxford handbook of deaf studies, language, and education.* New York: Oxford University Press, pp. 261–274.

Lichtenstein, E. (1998). The relationships between reading processes and English skills of deaf college students. *Journal of Deaf Studies and Deaf Education, 3,* 80–134.

Livingston, S., Singer, B., & Abramson, T. (1994). A study to determine the effectiveness of two different kinds of interpreting. *Proceedings of the Tenth National Convention of the Conference of Interpreter Trainers—Mapping our course: A collaborative venture,* pp. 175–197.

Marschark, M. (2001). *Language development in children who are deaf: A research synthesis.* Alexandria, VA: National Association of State Directors of Special Education.

Marschark, M. (2003). Cognitive functioning in deaf adults and children. In M. Marschark & P.E. Spencer (Eds.), *Oxford handbook of deaf studies, language, and education.* New York: Oxford University Press, pp. 464–477.

Marschark, M. (in press). Developing deaf children or deaf children developing? In D. Power & G. Leigh (Eds.), *Educating deaf students: Global perspectives.* Washington, DC: Gallaudet University Press.

Marschark, M., Convertino, C., McEvoy, C., & Masteller, A. (2004). Organization and use of the mental lexicon by deaf and hearing individuals. *American Annals of the Deaf, 149,* 51–61.

Marschark, M., Lang, H., & Albertini, J. (2002). *Educating deaf students: From research to practice.* New York: Oxford University Press.

Marschark, M., & Lukomski, J. (2001). Cognition, literacy, and education. In M.D. Clark, M. Marschark, & M. Karchmer (Eds.), *Context, cognition, and deafness.* Washington, DC: Gallaudet University Press, pp. 71–87.

Marschark, M., Sapere, P., Convertino, C., & Seewagen, R. (2005). Access to post-secondary education through sign language interpreting. *Journal of Deaf Studies and Deaf Education, 10,* 38–51.

Marschark, M., Sapere, P., Convertino, C., Seewagen, R., & Maltzen, H. (2004). Comprehension of sign language interpreting: Deciphering a complex task situation. *Sign Language Studies, 4,* 345–368.

Matthews, T.J., & Reich, C.F. (1993). Constraints on communication in classrooms for the deaf. *American Annals of the Deaf, 138,* 14–18.

Mayberry, R.I., & Eichen, E.B. (1991). The long-lasting advantage of learning sign language in childhood: Another look at the critical period for language acquisition. *Journal of Memory and Language, 30,* 486–512.

Mayer, R.E. (1983). Can you repeat that? Qualitative effects of repetition and advance organizers from science prose. *Journal of Educational Psychology, 75,* 40–49.

McEvoy, C., Marschark, M., & Nelson, D.L. (1999). Comparing the mental lexicons of deaf and hearing individuals. *Journal of Educational Psychology, 91,* 1–9.

Monikowski, C., & Winston, E.A. (2003). Interpreters and interpreter education. In M. Marschark & P.E. Spencer (Eds.), *Oxford handbook of deaf studies, language, and education.* New York: Oxford University Press, pp. 347–360.

Murphy, H.J., & Fleischer, L.R. (1977). The effects of Ameslan versus Siglish upon test scores. *Journal of Rehabilitation of the Deaf, 11,* 15–18.

Napier, J. (2002). University interpreting: Linguistic issues for consideration. *Journal of Deaf Studies and Deaf Education, 7,* 281–301.

Napier, J., & Barker, R. (2004). Access to university interpreting: Perceptions, preferences, and expectations of deaf students. *Journal of Deaf Studies and Deaf Education, 9,* 228–238.

Neville, H.J., & Lawson, D. (1987). Attention to central and peripheral visual space in a movement detection task: An event-related potential and behavioral study. II. Congenitally deaf adults. *Brain Research, 405,* 268–283.

Oakhill, J., & Cain, K. (2000). Children's difficulties in text comprehension: Assessing causal issues. *Journal of Deaf Studies and Deaf Education, 5,* 51–59.

O'Connor, N., & Hermelin, B. (1972). Seeing and hearing and time and space. *Perception & Psychophysics, 11,* 46–48.

Ottem, E. (1980). An analysis of cognitive studies with deaf subjects. *American Annals of the Deaf, 125,* 564–575.

Paivio, A. (1986). *Mental representations: A dual coding approach.* Oxford: Oxford University Press.

Quinsland, L.K., & Long, G. (1989, March). *Teaching, interpreting, and learning: Implications for mainstreaming hearing-impaired students.* Paper presented at the annual meeting of the American Educational Research Association, San Francisco.

Quittner, A.L., Smith, L.B., Osberger, M.J., Mitchell, T.V., & Katz, D.B. (1994). The impact of audition on the development of visual attention. *Psychological Science, 5,* 347–353.

Ramsey, C. (1997). *Deaf children in public schools*. Washington, DC: Gallaudet University Press.

Rawson, K.A., & Kintsch, W. (2002). How does background information improve memory for text? *Memory & Cognition, 30,* 768–778.

Redden, M.R., Davis, C.A., & Brown, J.W. (1978). *Science for handicapped students in higher education: Barriers, solutions, and recommendations*. Washington, DC: American Association for the Advancement of Science.

Rettenback, R., Diller, G., & Sireteanu, R. (1999). Do deaf people see better? Texture segmentation and visual search compensate in adult but not in juvenile subjects. *Journal of Cognitive Neuroscience, 11,* 560–583.

Richardson, J.T.E., MacLeod-Gallinger, J., McKee, B.G., & Long, G.L. (1999). Approaches to studying in deaf and hearing students in higher education. *Journal of Deaf Studies and Deaf Education, 5,* 156–173.

Schick, B. (in press). Educational interpreting and cognitive development in children: Potential relationships. In E. Winston (Ed.), *Educational interpreting: How it can succeed*. Washington, DC: Gallaudet University Press.

Schick, B., Williams, K., & Bolster, L. (1999). Skill levels of educational interpreters working in public schools. *Journal of Deaf Studies and Deaf Education, 4,* 144–155.

Seal, B.C. (2004). *Best practices in educational interpreting*, 2nd. ed. Boston: Allyn and Bacon.

Sinkavich, F.J. (1995). Performance and metamemory: Do students know what they don't know? *Journal of Instructional Psychology, 22,* 77–87.

Siple, L., Steve, M., Sapere, P., Convertino, C., Seewagen, R., & Marschark, M. (in preparation). Visual access in the high-tech classroom: a challenge for deaf students?

Smith, L.B., Quittner, A.L., Osberger, J.J., & Miyamoto, R. (1998). Audition and visual attention: The developmental trajectory in deaf and hearing populations. *Developmental Psychology, 34,* 840–850.

Stewart, D.A., & Kluwin, T.N. (1996). The gap between guidelines, practice, and knowledge in interpreting services for deaf students. *Journal of Deaf Studies and Deaf Education, 1,* 29–39.

Stinson, M.S., Kelly, R., Elliot, L., Colwell, J., Liu, Y., & Stinson, S. (2000, April). *C-Print, interpreting and notes, and memory of lectures*. Paper presented at the annual meetings of the American Educational Research Association, New Orleans.

Stinson, M.S., & Kluwin, T. (2003). Educational consequences of alternative school placements. In M. Marschark & P.E. Spencer (Eds.), *Oxford handbook of deaf studies, language, and education*. New York: Oxford University Press, pp. 52–64.

Stinson, M., Meath-Lang, B., & MacLeod, J. (1981). Recall of different segments of an interpreted lecture by deaf students. *American Annals of the Deaf, 126,* 819–824.

Strassman, B. (1997). Metacognition and reading in children who are deaf: A review of the research. *Journal of Deaf Studies and Deaf Education, 2,* 140–149.

Swisher, M.V. (1993). Perceptual and cognitive aspects of recognition of signs in peripheral vision. In M. Marschark & M.D. Clark (Eds.), *Psychological perspectives on deafness*. Hillsdale, NJ: Lawrence Erlbaum Associates, pp. 229–265.

Talbot, K.F., & Haude, R.H. (1993). The relationship between sign language skill and spatial visualizations ability: Mental rotation of three-dimensional objects. *Perceptual and Motor Skills, 77*, 1387–1391.

Tharpe, A., Ashmead, D., & Rothpletz, A (2002). Visual attention in children with normal hearing, children with hearing aids, and children with cochlear implants. *Journal of Speech, Hearing and Language Research, 45*, 403–413.

Tiene, D. (2000). Sensory mode and information load: examining the effects of timing on multisensory processing. *International Journal of Instructional Media, 27*, 183–198.

Todman, J., & Seedhouse, E. (1994). Visual-action code processing by deaf and hearing children. *Language and Cognitive Processes, 9*, 129–141.

Traxler, C.B. (2000). Measuring up to performance standards in reading and mathematics: Achievement of selected deaf and hard-of-hearing students in the national norming of the 9th Edition Stanford Achievement Test. *Journal of Deaf Studies and Deaf Education, 5*, 337–348.

4

Linguistic Features and Strategies of Interpreting: From Research to Education to Practice

Jemina Napier

INTRODUCTION

Over the years "researchers [have] increasingly realized that interpreting is an active process of communicating between two languages and cultures and that theoretical frameworks of social interaction, sociolinguistics, and discourse analysis are...appropriate for analyzing the task of interpreting" (Roy, 2000a, p. 8). Based on research findings, interpreter educators have refined their teaching approaches, and this has ultimately led to the more sophisticated practices of sign language interpreters worldwide.

Educational interpreting is a genre of sign language interpreting that has been widely discussed (see Hurwitz, 1998; Jones, Clark, & Soltz, 1997; Seal, 1998). It is an area that is considered a specialty of sign language interpreters because of its unique approach to providing interpreting services for deaf people in the classroom, as opposed to within the educational "milieu," which is more common within the spoken-language interpreting profession (e.g., between teachers and parents of children).

Educational interpreting for deaf children has emerged as a need due to the philosophical shift in education toward integration and inclusion (Byrnes, Sigafoos, Rickards, & Brown, 2002). It is therefore common to find deaf children educated in local schools alongside their hearing counterparts, with support from interpreters and note-takers (Bowman & Hyde, 1993). Consequently, sign language interpreters are often found working in classrooms with deaf students, interpreting between the students and the teacher. Educational interpreters face different challenges when working with deaf children compared to deaf adults due to differing linguistic needs of deaf children (Schick, 2001), the specific interpreter competencies needed (Schick, Williams, & Bolster, 1999), ethical conflicts (Scheibe & Hoza, 1986), role confusion (Hayes, 1992), linguistic isolation (Storey & Jamieson, 2004), and occupational overuse injuries (DeCaro & Hurwitz, 1992).

The introduction of antidiscrimination legislation in many Westernized countries has led to a specialized area of educational interpreting in the form of higher education interpreting. In many countries, deaf people are in a legal position to demand access to university education through interpreters. University interpreting has its own challenges. Several studies have explored the linguistic and communication issues in accessing higher education through sign language interpreters (Harrington, 2000, 2001; Johnson, 1991; Livingston, Singer, & Abrahamson, 1994; Locker, 1990). University interpreting places extra demands on interpreters, particularly in terms of the linguistic strategies they can employ in order to ensure that deaf students are accessing lecture content in the same way as hearing university students. Lang (2002) highlights the need for more research into higher education interpreting to further investigate the relationship between interpreting and learning.

Due to the demands of this interpreting niche, there is a need for linguistic research into university interpreting in order to better inform interpreter educators. Utilizing this knowledge, interpreter education programs can better prepare graduating interpreting students for the linguistic and communicative challenges involved. Higher standards of preparation can then lead to improved practice in higher education and can also be applied to interpreting in other contexts.

This chapter explores the linguistic features and strategies of interpreting (primarily in higher education), through the description of various research projects involving Australian Sign Language (Auslan)/English interpreters[1] and their application to the education and practice of sign language interpreters. Although the research, education, and practice to be discussed are specific to the Australian context, findings and suggestions are applicable to sign language interpreters working in higher education worldwide. The findings may also be applicable to sign language interpreting in other contexts, and to some extent spoken language interpreters working in a range of settings. (See Davis, this volume, for discussion of the implications of linguistic strategies used by educational interpreters working with deaf children.)

University Interpreting in the Australian Context

The sign language interpreting profession in Australia is relatively young when compared with other Westernized countries, with the first training course offered in 1986, followed by the establishment of the Australian Sign Language Interpreters' Association in 1991.

Auslan interpreters receive accreditation through the National Authority for the Accreditation of Translators and Interpreters (NAATI), which accredits all language interpreters.[2]Accreditation is earned by passing a one-off test or by completing a NAATI-approved training course. Accreditation is available at two levels: (1) Paraprofessional level—basic competence in interpreting for non-specialist dialogues; and (2) Professional Interpreter level—competence in interpreting for specialist dialogues and monologues requiring linguistic sophistication. The U.S. system of certifying interpretation and transliteration separately is not replicated in Australia, as they are not recognized as separate processes (see the next section for definitions of transliteration and interpreting). Therefore, Auslan interpreters receiving accreditation are expected to use either one of these interpreting approaches to best meet the needs of the deaf consumer.

The provision of Auslan interpreters in university settings varies from state to state, with some universities having formal employment structures in place, and others recruiting interpreters on an ad hoc basis. There are no current figures available to indicate how many deaf students are studying at university and using Auslan interpreters to access lectures, however, the general demand is increasing (Ozolins & Bridge, 1999). The customary recommendation for university interpreters is that they should be accredited at NAATI Professional Interpreter level. However, due to issues of supply and demand, Paraprofessional interpreters are also often employed.

Before discussing various Australian research on university interpreting, it is necessary to establish the theoretical foundation of each of the studies in relation to translation style.

Translation Style

The term "translation" refers either to the process of specifically changing a written text in one language to a written text in another language, or is used as a generic term to discuss the process of changing a message produced in one language into another language (regardless of the mode). The term "interpretation," however, typically refers to spontaneous translation between two spoken languages, or a signed and spoken language. Therefore, the two terms are often used interchangeably (Davis, 2000).

There are two key translation styles or interpretation methods discussed in ASL interpreting literature: "interpretation" and "transliteration." "Interpretation" is the process of changing a message produced in ASL into spoken English, or vice versa; where as "transliteration" is the process of changing a message produced in English into English-based signing, or vice versa (RID, 2004). More recent literature borrows from spoken language interpreting theory and describes processes of "free interpretation" and "literal interpretation" (Metzger, 1999; Napier, 2002a). Free interpretation focuses on meaning as well as linguistic and cultural equivalence, but not the form of the message, as opposed to literal interpretation, where the form of the source text influences the form of the target text (Napier, 2002a). Much of sign language interpreting literature refers to literal interpretation as "transliteration" (Cerney, 2000).

Typically, a free interpretation approach has been endorsed as the most effective method, as the translation focuses on conveying the message so that it is linguistically and culturally meaningful and gives consideration to the fact that participants communicating through an interpreter may bring different life experiences to an interaction (Metzger, 1999; Napier, 1998; Roy, 2000b). Nevertheless, it is also recognized that a literal interpretation approach is appropriate in some contexts—especially in higher education (Pollitt, 2000); for example, in order to provide access to English terminology by producing signs in English word order and incorporating fingerspelling and English mouth patterns.

All the research discussed in this chapter refers to free and literal interpreting styles as a basis for analyzing linguistic features and strategies of Auslan interpreting.

RESEARCH

Linguistic Features Used by Auslan Interpreters

Research has been conducted on the following areas: linguistic features used by Auslan interpreters when interpreting for dense information, the relationship between interpreters' language and that of the Deaf Community, and features of language contact used by interpreters and deaf people in university settings. Each of these research studies provides insight into the linguistic features used by interpreters and deaf people when dealing with a more "formal" register of language. Halliday (1978) states that formal presentations in spoken English (such as university lectures) are often presented using a structure of language more characteristic of written, rather than spoken, text—which makes the text "lexically dense." Research has demonstrated that sign languages used in more formal situations are highly influenced by the dominant spoken language and incorporate greater use of mouth patterns from the spoken language and fingerspelling than would be expected in other contexts (e.g., informal conversation) (Fontana, 1999;

Lucas & Valli, 1990). This is a typical form of "language contact," whereby the dominant majority language impacts on the structure of the minority language in particular contexts. Interpreters working in university lectures will therefore potentially be interpreting for lexically dense text in a language-contact environment.

Interpreting Lexically Dense Text

In a discussion of linguistic features of university interpreting, Napier (2002b) analyzed the output of ten interpreters when interpreting an extract of a lexically dense university lecture from English into Auslan. Lexically dense text is identified by measuring the ratio of lexical (content) and grammatical (function) words to the total number of words in a text. Written text tends to be more lexically dense than spoken text, since it relies less on the use of function words (Halliday, 1985). Ure (1971) found that a typical spoken lecture had a lexical density of 39.6%. The university lecture used in this study had a lexical density of 51%. Six of the participants were native signers, with the other four having learned Auslan as an adult. Six had completed university education, two were studying toward undergraduate degrees at the time of the research, and two had never studied at university. All of the interpreters had some experience with university interpreting, but only five of the participants were familiar with the lecture topic. The lecture topic focused on the language acquisition of deaf children and was presented by a university professor as part of an ongoing series of lectures to a group of students training to become teachers of the Deaf.

Napier (2002b) found that the interpreters tended to be dominant or extremely dominant in one translation style or another (i.e., free or literal) and that some of the interpreters "code-switched" between styles at key points in the text. There was a relationship between the interpreters' translation style and what words were fingerspelled in the interpretation, with a difference in the level of "linguistic transference" as opposed to "linguistic interference," as found by Davis (1990, 2003) in studies of ASL interpreters. Interpreters using a dominant free approach signed a concept freely in Auslan, then switched to a more literal style to fingerspell certain lexical items and thus "transferred" linguistic features of English into the Auslan production in order to introduce English terminology. Those interpreters dominant in a literal approach, however, only fingerspelled the subject-specific content words and did not translate the meaning. They also fingerspelled English function words that would not ordinarily be fingerspelled in Auslan; thus the linguistic features of English were "interfering" more with their interpretations.

The occurrence of linguistic transference was more prevalent in parts of the text with higher than average lexical density. The more complex the concept, the more content (rather than function) words were used in a sentence in the form of subject-specific or academic terms, and the higher the lexical density of that sentence. Napier (2002b) surmised that the density of the text had an impact on the translation style used and the use of fingerspelling as a linguistic feature of interpretation. It was argued that those interpreters who incorporated use of fingerspelling (i.e., linguistic transference) for key lexical items of the text were using an appropriate translation style for a university lecture. It was suggested that interpreters should switch between different styles as a linguistic strategy for dealing with the context of situation, and that interpreters should be trained in both translation styles in order to effectively meet the needs of deaf consumers in different contexts, particularly in university settings. Pollitt provides perfect examples to illustrate this point:

> In some contexts it may be more suitable to focus on texts rather than discourse, and here a more literal (conduit) approach to interpretation may be required.... The student studying for ... English Literature will not benefit from a free, discourse (interactive) type interpretation of a Shakespearean text if the purpose is to memorise it verbatim for the forthcoming exam.... English Literature classroom discussions [also] focus on understanding the purpose and meaning of whole chunks of Shakespeare, and here the interpreter will be required to tread carefully, choosing interactive or literal interpreting strategies as appropriate. Lectures, documentaries and factual broadcasts ... are all contexts in which the interpreter might need to be adept at switching between strategies. (2000, p. 62)

The research study just described focused on the linguistic features used in the interpretation of dense university lecture text. There are many other text types outside of the university context, however, that interpreters may encounter which are also lexically and informationally dense. The speed of production and density of texts can provide a challenge for all interpreters, regardless of their experience level (Scullion, 2002). Media text (i.e., spoken text on television) is an example of such a challenge.

Interpreting Media Text

Napier and Adam (2002) reported on linguistic features used in the interpretation of media text in the form of a news report. News reports are particularly challenging to interpret because "the language must be efficient and concise so precision enables information to be presented in as short a time as possible" (Morris, cited in Steiner, 1998, p. 104). Steiner discusses the world knowledge that television viewers need to have in order to fully access a news report and how this impacts on deaf viewers' access. The purpose of the Napier and Adam study was to identify similarities and differences of language use between British and Australian sign language interpreters. British Sign Language (BSL) and Auslan are closely related languages, both using a two-handed fingerspelling alphabet (Johnston, 2002). Five BSL and five Auslan interpreters of equal qualification and experience were filmed interpreting the same piece of news text, taken from a British current affairs program. The topic of the report was the scandal involving former U.S. president Bill Clinton and an intern, Monica Lewinksy. The text was particularly dense, as it incorporated the typical linguistic features of a news report—a fast rate of delivery, a high number of content words, and use of more typical patterns of written rather than spoken English.

The interpreters' use of the following linguistic features in their interpretations was analyzed: classifiers, fingerspelling, role-shift, and placement. It was found that the BSL interpreters used more classifier signs and role-shift, but less fingerspelling, than the Auslan interpreters. The BSL interpreters tended to use initialization (i.e., spelling the first letter of a word to accompany the English mouth pattern), rather than fingerspelling full lexical items. The Auslan interpreters tended to use placement less frequently and less consistently than the BSL interpreters.

Napier and Adam (2002) identified that the language use of the interpreters reflected the language use of the Deaf communities in each of the two countries. They concluded that "from general observation in the Deaf communities in the UK and Australia, it seems that Auslan exhibits a greater degree of fingerspelling use than does BSL ... and this is reflected in the use of fingerspelling in the five Auslan interpreted texts, and BSL in turn exhibits a greater degree of initialization of words than does Auslan" (p. 28). They acknowledge, however, that even though BSL and Auslan are visual-spatial languages, the interpreters used role-shift and placement differently than has been observed with deaf people, which "may not be seen as a true reflection of language use" (p. 28). They surmised that the interpreters' pattern of substituting fingerspelling for placement and role-shifting, or vice versa, "may only be restricted to interpreters as opposed to those in the language group who would represent a totally different but equally revealing study" (p. 28).

So what linguistic features do interpreters and deaf people have in common in their use of sign languages? Do interpreters accurately reflect the language use of the Deaf Community? The Napier and Adam (2002) study hints at a relationship, but no analysis of the sign language use of deaf people was presented for comparison. The following study by Napier (2003a) focuses on the linguistic features used by interpreters and deaf presenters in university lectures, providing a direct comparison of the two groups.

Linguistic Features of University Lectures

Napier (2003a) reported the findings of a study that explored the influence of language contact on the interpretations of Auslan/English interpreters and compared it with the influence of language contact on deaf Australians producing text[3] in Auslan. Because the research focused on the analysis of only four individuals, it was presented as a preliminary case study of such language contact phenomena, with a view to a wider study at a later date.

Napier established that one form of language contact involves "code-switching," common in spoken-language bilinguals, where a person literally changes from one language to another during a conversation, and it can occur inter-sententially or intra-sententially (Clyne, 2003). A more common form of language contact between a signed and a spoken language is that of "code-mixing." As mentioned earlier, Lucas and Valli (1990) describe code-mixing between ASL and English, whereby English words are mouthed on the lips or manually coded (fingerspelled) while the signer is still using linguistic features of ASL (e.g., spatial mapping and metaphor, role-shift, non-manual markers, etc.). Various investigators have discussed code-mixing between a signed and spoken language (Fontana, 1999; Hauser, 2000; Sofinski, 2002); and Davis (1990, 2003), Detthow (2000), and Winston (1989) have all described how interpreters introduce language contact features of fingerspelling and mouthing in more formal contexts. See Davis (this volume) for a detailed discussion of language contact, code-mixing, and linguistic transference.

Valdes and Angelelli (2003) noted that research on spoken language interpreting "provides valuable insights about complex aspects of language contact" (p. 58), and language contact has been identified as occurring in different "sites" or contexts, such as religious (Spolsky, 2003) and business (Harris & Bargiela-Chiappini, 2003). A common "site" for language contact between signed and spoken languages is university lectures. Spoken lectures tend to incorporate a "formal" register, with use of technical terms, longer sentences, strategic pausing, and little interaction with the audience (Joos, 1967; Goffman, 1981). Roy (1989) and Zimmer (1989) have found that lectures produced in ASL adopt similar features: fingerspelling, pausing, larger signing space, and use of particular signs as discourse markers to establish a new topic. Napier (2003a) hypothesized that deaf academics, presenting university lectures in Auslan, would use particular language-contact phenomena and that Auslan interpreters would produce similar linguistic features in their interpretation of a university lecture from English to Auslan.

Four Auslan university discourse texts were analyzed: two were produced directly in Auslan by deaf people (one a native signer, the other a non-native signer), and two were interpretations from English into Auslan by hearing interpreters (one was a native signer, and the other non-native). Excerpts of the first few introductory minutes from each text were analyzed for language-contact features of mouthing and fingerspelling. Each source text was a genuine university lecture produced in a language-contact environment, where both Auslan and English users were present.

Contrastive analysis was used to count the total number of signed lexical items, the number of fingerspelled items, and the number of English mouthed words. Any patterns of words mouthed or finger-spelled (i.e., nouns, verbs, etc.) were noted, with the identification of marked (unusual) and unmarked (typical) patterns. Comparisons were then made between deaf presenters and interpreters, and native and non-native language users.

The results showed that the non-native signers mouthed more English words than native signers. The two native signers tended not to mouth English patterns with verbs, but used appropriate non-manual features; however, they frequently used English mouthing for nouns. This supports findings of Schembri and colleagues (2000) and Johnston (2001) in their discussion of noun-verb pairs in Auslan.

The non-native signers produced more English mouthed words than actual lexical signs—mostly due to adding English lexical items such as pronouns, determiners, auxiliary verbs, and prepositions. The follow-ing example illustrates this point, as the signer mouthed 19 English words, but produced only 15 signs.

A lot of that Maybe	American so	maybe not	relevant
MANY DET MAYBE PRO AMERICA		MAYBE NOT R-E-L-E-V-A-N-T	
here but	a lot of interesting	things	there too.
HERE BUT BIG INTERESTING	THING	DET SAME //	

All participants used mouthing for nominal groups, especially for terminology and names of people or places, and some mouthing for prepositions, pronouns, and determiners.

The native signers' use of fingerspelling tended to be unmarked (i.e., spelling lexical items that would be expected in Auslan), whereas the non-native signers produced more marked fingerspelling choices where sign choices existed (e.g., "relevant"). The native signers used more spatial mapping than the non-native signers, indicating less English influence on the grammatical sign order. In particular, the native signers made more use of rhetorical question strategy, which is a common "topic-comment" structure in sign language grammars (Sutton-Spence & Woll, 1998) (e.g., WILL TALK OVER WHAT? LANGUAGE ACQUISITION). The non-native signers, however, tended to follow a more "subject-verb-object" structure typical of English.

Although there were limitations to Napier's study (2003a), the basic conclusions are worth considering in relation to the linguistic features used by interpreters and deaf people in university lectures, as a point of comparison for further studies. Napier concluded that there was evidence of code-mixing (transference) rather than code-switching (interference), and that the distinction was not necessarily between interpreters and deaf people, but rather between native and non-native signers. Although some features were more common to native signers and others to non-native signers, since the Deaf Community is made up of both native and non-native signers, and interpreters also comprise both groups, it can be suggested that interpreters do incorporate language-contact phenomena into their interpretations in the same way as deaf people when presenting university lectures.

In summary, studies like those described above provide a preliminary foundation of knowledge for interpreter educators in being able to identify key linguistic features used by interpreters in university settings. Student interpreters can draw on this knowledge in order to identify appropriate linguistic features to be used to effectively convey a message in language appropriate to the university context. Identification of these linguistic features may also serve interpreters in other contexts, whether in educational interpreting in general, or community or conference interpreting.

Thus far, discussion has centered on the linguistic features used by interpreters, particularly in terms of fingerspelling and mouthing. Another aspect of interpreters' output is shown by the linguistic strategies used when interpreting in higher education.

Linguistic Strategies of Interpreting in Higher Education

Interpreters' strategic use of linguistic and cultural knowledge to manage interpreted interactions has been investigated and discussed by both signed and spoken language–interpreter researchers (e.g., Metzger, 1999; Roy, 2000b; Pöchhacker, 2004; Wadensjö, 1998).

Napier (2002a, 2002b, 2002c) analyzed the translation styles of Auslan interpreters in a university lecture and described how interpreters switched between free and literal translation styles in order to ensure that deaf university students effectively accessed the content of lectures and subject-specific terminology. The Auslan interpreters that dominantly used a free interpretation approach used linguistic transference as a linguistic strategy, and switched to a literal approach in order to complement paraphrasing with a fingerspelled lexical item and enhance the contextual force of a message. Davis (this volume) further elaborates on the consequences of translation style (or code) choices.

Interpreting Omissions

Napier (2002a; 2002c; 2003b; 2004) and Napier and Barker (2004a) discuss the production of omissions as a linguistic strategy in university
lectures. Ten Auslan interpreters were filmed interpreting a segment of
a university lecture, and their interpreting omissions were noted and
analyzed through a process of task review and retrospective interview.
A spectrum of omission types was identified based on the metalinguistic commentary provided by the interpreters during the task review
as to why certain omissions had occurred, their level of consciousness
about making the omission, and whether it was a proactive or reactive
measure. These omission types were classified as follows:

- Conscious strategic,
- Conscious intentional,
- Conscious unintentional,
- Conscious receptive, and
- Unconscious.

The research showed that interpreters produce omissions strategically
as a linguistic mechanism, as well as in error, and that omission production may be influenced by a combination of familiarity with the
context of situation (i.e., academic discourse) and familiarity with the
subject matter. Commentary from the interpreters involved in the research indicated that those who had completed university qualifications felt that they were better able to linguistically cope with the
interpretation of the university lecture. Although the research was
conducted in a university setting, it is suggested that the findings are
applicable to sign language interpreters working in any context and
that awareness of omission types can enhance interpreters' understanding of the interpreting process. It was also highlighted that interpreters are highly aware of the linguistic decisions they make while
interpreting, and again, that this knowledge augments the success of
interpretations.

Research discussed thus far has focused on linguistic strategies of
interpreting in higher education in terms of the output of sign language
interpreters. But what are deaf university students' perceptions of the
university interpreting services that they access? What are their preferences and expectations of interpreters in higher education?

Deaf Consumer Preferences

Napier and Barker (2004b) report the details of a small panel discussion
with Australian deaf university students, providing insight into deaf
university students' perceptions and preferences of Auslan interpreters'
translation style in the university context, and their expectations in

relation to the educational backgrounds and qualifications of university interpreters.

Four deaf university students of differing linguistic backgrounds (all of whom used Auslan as their first or preferred language) were shown two extracts of interpretations of a university lecture, one in which the interpreter used a literal translation style, and the other a free translation style. The panel members were asked to discuss their perceptions of the different styles, their preferences, and reasons for those preferences. They were also asked to comment on their expectations regarding interpreters' qualifications if working in higher education.

Although the panel preferred information to be interpreted conceptually into Auslan for ease of understanding, they also wanted access to English terms, thus endorsing the notion of interpreters switching between free and literal translation styles as a linguistic strategy to deal with the complexity of the information received and the demands of the context of situation. The notion of perceptions and preferences vis á vis actual comprehension is a potentially contentious issue, especially when considering the study of Marschark and colleagues (2004). After conducting three experimental studies comparing deaf university students' reported communication preferences and their comprehension of lecture content through interpretation (free interpretation) or transliteration (literal interpretation), Marschark and colleagues found that the deaf students were equally competent in comprehending the lectures through both translation styles, regardless of reported sign language skills and preferences. However, the deaf students gained less from lectures than their hearing counterparts. This highlights the need for further research on interpreting in higher education in order to establish the most appropriate and accessible provision for deaf students.

The Australian deaf student panel advocated for interpreters to have a university qualification in general, but especially if they work in a university context (Napier & Barker, 2004b). This has been a recommendation of many interpreter researchers and educators (such as Patrie, 1993; Sanderson, Siple, & Lyons, 1999). More recently, interpreter regulatory bodies (such as the Registry of Interpreters for the Deaf [RID] in the United States, Council for the Advancement of Communication with Deaf People [CACDP] in the United Kingdom) have also recognized the importance of interpreters having university qualifications. Aquiline (2000) cites the World Federation of the Deaf policy statement on the education of deaf people, and specifically states that interpreters should never accept work that involves interpreting at an educational level higher than they have achieved themselves. Surveys in the United Kingdom and Australia have shown, however, that many sign language interpreters do not possess a university qualification, and many interpreters working in higher education have never accessed that level of education themselves (Harrington & Traynor, 1999; Napier & Barker, 2003). This emphasizes the need for sign language–interpreter education programs to be based in higher education institutions to ensure that interpreters are academically educated as well as vocationally trained.

EDUCATION

Historically there has been much debate in the sign language–interpreting field as to the type of training that all interpreters should undertake. This debate is facilitated by the Conference of Interpreter Trainers (United States) biannual convention and subsequent publication of proceedings, whereby the structure and content of ASL interpreter education programs are discussed at length. In the United States, United Kingdom, and many other countries, sign language–interpreter education programs have long been established as Associate's, Bachelor's, or Master's degrees. There are approximately 150 postsecondary ASL interpreter education programs in the United States (RID, 2004), although the overwhelming majority are offered in community and technical colleges rather than universities. It has been acknowledged that "[sign language interpreter] graduates of university programs with bachelors' and more especially masters' degrees are prepared for most interpreting tasks" (Frishberg & Wilcox, 1994, p. 18). In Australia, this has not been the case because of the lack of university programs.

The accreditation authority NAATI (National Authority for the Accreditation of Translators and Interpreters) has always advocated that interpreters and translators should be trained (Bell, 1997). Attendance at a training course is not currently mandatory, meaning that many interpreters receive accreditation without being trained. Several graduate diploma and degree courses exist for interpreters of spoken languages (Ozolins, 1998), but historically Auslan interpreter training has only been available to the Paraprofessional level and has only been offered in community colleges.

Napier (1999) questioned the training available to Auslan interpreters and made a series of recommendations in order to improve the standards of the profession. All Auslan interpreters should do the following:

- Complete a course of study at the tertiary level, preferably in a subject related to interpreting (e.g., linguistics, English);
- Receive some formal instruction in Auslan, even native signers, as well as informal exposure within the community; and
- Have access to a training course made available for Auslan interpreters at university level.

Since these recommendations were made, the Postgraduate Diploma in Auslan/English Interpreting was established within the Linguistics Department at Macquarie University—the first ever university training course for sign language interpreters in Australia. Now that the program has been established, Auslan interpreters accredited at NAATI Paraprofessional level can access a university education and further develop their interpreting skills to Professional Interpreter level. One of the major consequences of this access is that many of the problematic issues identified in the Australian-based research will be alleviated. In addition, the research findings are applied in the teaching of the program in order to enhance the critical, metalinguistic, theoretical, and practical skills and knowledge of the interpreting students. Students are taught to identify the linguistic features and strategies they use in their interpretations, particularly the use of, and switching between, free and literal translation styles in different contexts. The application of research into teaching ultimately informs the practice of all interpreters.

PRACTICE

Witter-Merithew and Maiorano (1996) define "practice" as "the actual performance or application of skills, knowledge and attitudes related to a specific task; the systematic exercise for proficiency . . . the exercise of a profession" (p. 48). The implementation of research into the pedagogical framework of the Auslan interpreting program provides significant and tangible benefits to the practice of Auslan interpreters, making them better equipped to incorporate appropriate linguistic features and strategies into their work in higher education.

These skills can also be applied in other contexts when interpreting with deaf professionals, since interpreters can use the same linguistic features and strategies to provide access to English in professional settings, such as business meetings. Interpreting work with deaf professionals is a growing area (Liedel & Brodie, 1996), as a result of larger numbers of deaf people completing higher education and obtaining professional jobs. As stated by Hodek and Radatz (1996, p. 140): "As Deaf professionals become increasingly involved in advocacy and politics, community issues and public speaking . . . the skills and flexibility needed by interpreters change rapidly." In a survey of American deaf people working in professional arenas, Viera and Stauffer (2000) found that deaf professionals preferred more access to English through a literal translation style in order to use the same terminology and expressions as their colleagues. Therefore, a better understanding of the linguistic features and strategies used in higher education will consequently benefit all sign language interpreters' practice in working with deaf professionals.

Rather than simply reporting perceptions of how interpreters' practice is enhanced by the application of research into education, it is worthwhile considering comments from practitioners, student interpreters, and deaf consumers themselves. A few Auslan interpreters, Auslan-interpreting students, and deaf professional consumers were approached and asked to provide comments. Students were asked to comment on how their understanding of research and theory has impacted on their practice, and how the training they have received has made a difference to their practice. The responses were varied, but the following examples illustrate how the students clearly felt the benefits of their study:

> The main benefit I've noticed from undertaking postgraduate studies in interpreting is that I have become much more aware of what it is I'm doing as an interpreter. This has benefited my skills as an interpreter because I am more able to reflect on what it is I do and make improvements to my skills/practice where necessary. Additionally, I am able to talk about what it is I do with others; particularly less experienced interpreters or those who have never worked with interpreters before. In this way I am able to more confidently represent interpreters and participate in the continued professionalization and growth of the profession. Undertaking this course of study has also enhanced my analytical skills during an assignment. Having a solid basis in translation/interpretation theory provides a foundation where I can justify the decisions I make as I interpret.

> Study has enabled me to develop a greater appreciation for and understanding of the Code of Ethics and my role as an interpreter. In my experience, an awareness and understanding of theory fosters development of practical skills, while the converse may not be true. Studying has shown me that interpreting practice, the interpreter's role, and Code of Ethics have changed over time (and may continue to change), therefore continued study is imperative to remain an informed professional.

All of the students had already been working as Paraprofessional interpreters before commencing their study at Macquarie University (this is a mandatory entry requirement); therefore, they already had a level of practical experience. The following comments show how the students feel their interpreting practice has improved as a direct consequence of their study:

> In studying the theory of interpreting and translation I feel that my practice has been enhanced. I know of a greater range of strategies and theoretical justification for these strategies. Previous to the course if I were to use some of these strategies I would have done so unconsciously and perhaps seen them as errors. The course helped me to move from a level of "unconscious incompetence" to at least a

level of "conscience incompetence" and perhaps even moments of effectiveness.

Study of translation and interpreting theory has really improved my understanding of what I do as an interpreter, what choices I have and what strategies I have at my disposal that I can select consciously. Beforehand, I think I could recognise strategies or approaches that worked or didn't work but couldn't necessarily understand or explain why. As well as extending my "interpreter's toolkit" of strategies and options, understanding the theories has given me the language and the tools to reflect on my interpreting work in a more considered and informed way.

One of the key ways that the course has impacted on my practice is simply that I have a greater awareness (whilst I am actually interpreting) about the language used by all participants and the impact that it has on the interaction and the participants.

One student was so inspired about what she had learned, that she began practicing full-time as an interpreter:

My study has had a profound impact on my skills and abilities as a practitioner. This has been achieved through enhanced knowledge and understanding of Auslan and English, discourse analysis, and the interpreting process. I was an accredited Paraprofessional Auslan interpreter for 5 years prior to attending the course at Macquarie University. During this time I worked as an interpreter on a casual basis. Work undertaken was mostly linked to my position in a Deaf-specific welfare organization. I often resisted offers for freelance interpreting work. Contributing factors included a lack of confidence and feeling stunted in my knowledge about the interpreting process, linguistics, and the management of the interpreted discourse event. The Diploma has given me access to literature, peer discussion, and practical experience in a variety of discourse settings. After the Diploma, I left my place of full-time employment to undertake freelance interpreting on a full-time basis. I have applied knowledge and skills learnt during the Diploma to my work, and I have enjoyed greater job satisfaction and received several encouraging remarks from users of my service. I am very confident making linguistic choices and employing strategies in my work as an interpreter to ensure successful interpreted discourse events.

The students obviously feel the benefit of research-based pedagogy on their interpreting practice. This benefit also extends to other practitioners in the field. Practitioners were asked to comment on their perceptions of how the available training was impacting on their experience of team-working with these interpreters in the field. All responses were favorable, with interpreters commenting that students who have completed the Diploma are generally more professional and more self-aware about their interpreting skills. One interpreter made the following comment:

> The biggest difference that I have noticed in interpreters that have come through the program is that they are far more able to articulate about, and reflect on, the processes inherent to the task. The most palpable benefit to me as a fellow practitioner is the strategies that they now bring before, during, and after assignments.

Ultimately, research on interpreting and education for interpreters is obsolete if the consumers of interpreting services do not feel the direct benefit. When asked how research and training have made an impact on Auslan interpreters' practice, deaf consumers gave a favorable response, noting improved professionalism and delivery of service and higher levels of satisfaction. A few examples of comments follows:

> I have, in the last year or so, noticed a clear and growing trend in those interpreters undertaking the course at Macquarie University to think more carefully about their translation from English to Auslan and vice versa. Their analysis of the interpreting situation is more pronounced, clearer, and most certainly more professional. The end result of each piece of translation from these students is a careful and thought-out process and with a far more accurate translation than I have experienced in the past.

> There has been a noticeable improvement in the quality of interpreting services from the interpreters who have had training. Because my needs for academic acquisition during my time at university were of utmost importance, I was pleased that the interpreters, who were well-trained, were able to deliver the right vocabulary and information in the strictly academic environment. They satisfied my expectations.

> Having had the opportunity to work with one of the students at a recent large meeting, I was impressed with the quality and clarity of the interpreting work. I had the opportunity of working with the student before the course was up and running and could see the marked difference. The difference was that the interpreter was much more confident and able to take the work up to a higher level.

Although these comments are subjective, Deaf consumers anecdotally have noticed a change in the quality of interpreting as a consequence of the training the interpreters have received. Overall, it can be seen that by incorporating knowledge from research on linguistic features and strategies used by Auslan interpreters into the interpreter education program, students, interpreters, and consumers feel the benefit in terms of interpreting practice.

In order to guide research agendas, however, researchers and educators need to observe practice and identify gaps in knowledge or understanding of the interpreting process. Educators need to observe interpreting students' skills development and identify gaps in training techniques, which may be assisted through further research. This is a cyclical process, with each component relying on the others. Research on interpreting informs interpreting education, which informs interpreting practice, which informs research.

A RESEARCH AGENDA

A chapter of this sort would not be complete without giving some thought to key research questions and directions for future investigation. There is an obvious need for further research in the sign language–interpreting field, but there is a greater need for completed research to be disseminated as widely as possible. We need to understand more about what makes communication effective, and therefore what makes interpreted communication achievable. The only way to achieve this level of understanding is through further collaboration among interpreting researchers, educators, and practitioners.

Interpreter Fieldwork Research

I would encourage practitioners in particular to become researchers, but not necessarily researchers in the traditional sense. In the same way that teachers have been encouraged to participate in "classroom research" (Angelo, 1991), interpreters can become involved in what I call "interpreter fieldwork research."

The purpose of "classroom research" is "to contribute to the professionalization of teaching, to provide knowledge, understanding, and insights that will sensitize teachers to the struggles of students to learn. [It] consists of any systematic inquiry designed and conducted for the purpose of increasing insight and understanding of the relationships between teaching and learning" (Cross, 1990; cited in Angelo, 1991, p. 8). This approach is known as "practitioner research" in the area of language teaching (Allwright, 2003), whereby practitioners engage in "exploratory practice"—developing their own research agendas and exploring them in the classroom, thus contributing to the knowledge and understanding in the field.

In applying the definition of classroom research to interpreting, it could be said that the purpose of "interpreter fieldwork research" is to contribute to the professionalization of interpreting—to provide knowledge, understanding, and insights that will sensitize interpreters to the challenges of Deaf and hearing consumers to access communicative events—through systematic inquiry designed and conducted for the purpose of increasing insight and understanding of the relationships between language, culture, discourse, and interpreting. Interpreters are out there in the field—doing it. They know what the problems or "puzzles" (Allwright, 2003) are that need to be investigated. More interpreter fieldwork research will enable us to see what is happening at the coalface; that is, where the "real interpreting" (Turner, this volume) occurs. "Interpreter fieldwork research" is already evident in various publications where authors have reflected on personal interpreting experiences and the decisions made or strategies used (see Bergson & Sperlinger, 2003; Cragg, 2002; Hema, 2002).

Interpreter fieldwork researchers can decide on a research agenda that interests them. What issues do they confront in their everyday work? Is there anything that intrigues them about their work? Do they have any questions about reoccurring "puzzles"? Interpreter educators can ask similar questions about their teaching and engage in "practitioner research" as teachers. What teaching strategies are most effective and why? Are there any changes that need to be made and how can these changes be introduced? Action research is an ideal framework for researching and recording educational outcomes.

Action Research

"Action research" is a research methodology popular in education. It is a cyclical, reflective process that responds to the context and involves ongoing identification and investigation of practices requiring improvement or enhancement; development of practitioners' skills in problem identification and problem solving; assurance that results of enquiry actually get translated into practice; greater collaboration among practitioners; and development of strategies for change that take into account or seek to influence positively the particular culture, conditions, and context(s) in which innovation is to occur (Scott, 1999).

Action research can be an effective catalyst for change (Arnold, 1998) and promotes "reflection in and on action" (Schön, 1995). In a study of long-term outcomes of educational action research projects, Kember (2002) identified six benefits of action research:

1. Lasting improvements in teaching in terms of deeper understanding of teaching and willingness to employ more innovative teaching strategies;
2. A shift toward more student-centered teaching approaches and a better understanding of students' needs;
3. Teachers' development of action research abilities and recognition of action research as a natural framework for the educational change process;

4. Improved capacity and competence to reflect upon, and monitor, quality of one's own teaching;
5. Development of team-work skills; and
6. Changing attitudes and development of valuable skills.

Examples of action research projects include the following:

1. Changing the delivery of the Macquarie University Auslan interpreting program to external mode through consultation with stakeholders (i.e., practitioners, students, university teachers, and administrators), researching the literature and other program formats, and piloting a new program structure and resources (Napier, forthcoming).
2. Developing a new curriculum for the provision of generic interpreting skills training to potential interpreters of rare spoken languages[4] through consultation with service providers, examiners, teachers, and practitioners; observations of teaching practices and student responses; practitioner evaluations of fieldwork experience; and interviews with students and teachers (Slatyer, Chesher, & Napier, 2004).

Action research is particularly successful on a small local scale, but perhaps more difficult to replicate at a centralized level (i.e., nationally or internationally). Therefore researchers, educators, and practitioners need to collaborate on identifying, conducting, and disseminating research to ensure that local issues can be considered worldwide.

Suggestions for fieldwork and action research do not negate the need for traditional academic research; thus, some research ideas are provided for more traditional studies in order to enhance the knowledge gleaned from research discussed in this chapter and to further our understanding of the processes and products of sign language interpreting.

Research Ideas

The specific research suggestions given here focus on the potential to understand more about linguistic features and strategies used by sign language interpreters—so as to improve both access to education by Deaf individuals and more efficient and effective interpreter education—and could be carried out by researchers, educators, or practitioners.

- Language contact—Film various Deaf people presenting a lecture in Auslan (or other natural signed language) on the same topic. Then film a hearing person presenting on the same topic and ask several interpreters to interpret from English into Auslan. All presentations should occur in front of a mixed audience of Deaf and hearing people. This process would provide more reliable data to compare the linguistic features used by Deaf people and interpreters in university settings. In addition, Deaf people and interpreters could be filmed in more informal situations and the results compared with findings of university lecture language contact features. Do the patterns identified in university lectures only occur in formal settings?

- Interpreting omissions—Replicate Napier's study (2004) of interpreting omissions in other interpreting contexts. This would create a picture of the different discourse factors that impact on the use of conscious strategic omissions and the production of erroneous omissions; for example, in a medical appointment, at a job interview, in a conference setting, or in a meeting situation. The research could then be taken one step further, contrasting interpreters working in identical situations who had received more preparation.

- Educational interpreting—Many discussions of interpreters and education rely on an assumption that interpreters who do not have postsecondary qualifications will struggle with the language and terminology used in such educational settings. It is also consistently stated that interpreters familiar with topics of lectures will be in a better position to understand and interpret the meaning. A proposed study could test interpreters' comprehension of lecture content before assessing the effectiveness of their interpretations of the same lecture content. If the data were collected from a range of interpreters with differing qualifications, it would be possible to identify any patterns of correlation between educational qualifications held, area of expertise, and the effectiveness of interpretations.

- Comprehensibility—The majority of sign language–interpreting research focuses on interpreters' output or on descriptions of consumer preference. Only a few empirical studies of interpreting comprehension have been conducted, including studies on ASL interpreters by Marschark and his colleagues (see Marschark et al., this volume) and one on BSL interpreters by Steiner (1998). This issue is currently being investigated under the auspices of a Macquarie University Research Fellowship. The aim of the project is to provide evidence for the linguistics strategies used by interpreters to ensure the comprehensibility of interpretations from English into Auslan. A new tool for the objective assessment of sign language–interpreting comprehensibility is much needed. This research will investigate studies and models of achieving understanding in discourse, studies of comprehension of text, language performance assessment tools, and the effect of discourse on language comprehension in order to draw on spoken language parallels and develop a new sign language–specific tool. The expected outcomes include the identification of why some Auslan interpreters are more understandable than others, in relation to the appropriate and strategic use of discourse features in Auslan. The results will be invaluable in the training of sign language interpreters both in Australia and worldwide.

In addition, our research agenda needs to be informed by considering the following questions: (1) What comparisons can we make between the linguistic features and strategies that Deaf and hearing interpreters use, and what can we learn from each other? (2) What linguistic features and strategies do spoken language interpreters use, and how similar or different are they from those used by signed language interpreters?

SUMMARY AND CONCLUSIONS

This chapter has explored the linguistic features and strategies of interpreting, particularly in higher education, through the description of various research projects involving Auslan/English interpreters, and their application to the education and practice of sign language interpreters. The research studies discussed focused on the linguistic features used by Auslan interpreters when interpreting dense information, the relationship between interpreters' language and that of the Deaf Community, features of language contact used by interpreters and Deaf people in university settings, linguistic strategies of Auslan interpreters when interpreting for a university lecture, and the use of translation style and omissions as strategies within the university discourse environment. It also focused on Deaf students' expectations of university interpreting and interpreting strategy, as well as the educational backgrounds of interpreters in relation to their ability to interpret in higher education. The benefits of research-based pedagogy has been discussed in terms of interpreter practice, whereby interpreters are better equipped to incorporate appropriate linguistic features and strategies when working in higher education and with Deaf professionals. Suggestions for further research on sign language interpreting have been provided, outlining a clear research agenda for the field. In particular, practitioners have been encouraged to carry out "interpreter fieldwork research" and educators to conduct "action research" in order to expand the amount of available research on sign language interpreting and education, which will inform academic researchers, educators, and other practitioners.

ACKNOWLEDGMENTS

The studies reported here were only made possible with funding from the following sources: Australian Federal Government Department of Education, Training and Youth Affairs Commonwealth Scholarship (1998–2001); Victorian Services for Deaf Children Deafness Research Fund (1999), Macquarie University Postgraduate Research Fund (2000), and the Macquarie University Generic Skills Integration Grants Scheme (2003); and in-kind support from Renwick College (affiliated with the University of Newcastle). I would particularly like to acknowledge Dr. Eddie Ronowicz, convener of the Translation and Interpreting program at Macquarie University, for his support in setting up the Auslan Interpreting program; and Professor Chris Candlin, Associate Professor Trevor Johnston, and Dr. Adam Schembri for supporting my research in the area of Auslan interpreting. Thanks also to Helen Slatyer for the many in-depth discussions on interpreting. Finally, I would like to thank Karin Banna, Andy Carmichael, Danielle Fried, Marcel Leneham, Trevor Maggs, Alastair McEwin, Geraldine Shearim, Brett Trenery, and Andrew Wiltshire for their contributions to this chapter.

NOTES

1. For expediency, henceforth referred to as Auslan interpreters.
2. See http://www.naati.com.au.
3. Here the term "text" is used to refer to the production of Auslan as the equivalent of a piece of spoken or written text.
4. Also known as "languages of limited diffusion."

REFERENCES

Allwright, D. (2003). Exploratory practice: Rethinking practitioner research in language teaching. *Language Teaching Research, 7*(2), 113–141.

Angelo, T.A. (1991). Introduction and overview: From classroom assessment to classroom research. *New Directions for Teaching and Learning, 46,* 7–15.

Aquiline, C. (2000, July). *World Federation of the Deaf: Toward a policy on deaf education.* Paper presented to the International Congress of Educators of the Deaf, Sydney, Australia.

Arnold, D. (1998). Action research in action: Curricular articulation and integrated instruction. *National Association of Secondary School Principals Bulletin, 82,* March (596), 74–78.

Bell, S.J. (1997). "The challenges of setting and monitoring the standards of community interpreting: An Australian perspective." In R. Roberts, A. Dufour, & D. Steyn (Eds.), *The critical link: Interpreters in the community.* Philadelphia: John Benjamins, pp. 93–108.

Bergson, M., & Sperlinger, D. (2003). "I still don't know what I should have done": Reflections on personal/professional dilemmas in sign language interpreting. *Deaf Worlds, 19*(3), 6–23.

Bowman, J., & Hyde, M. (1993). Manual communication as support for deaf students in the regular classroom. *Australian Teacher of the Deaf, 33*, 32–46.

Byrnes, L.J., Sigafoos, J., Rickards, F.W., & Brown, M.P. (2002). Inclusion of students who are deaf or hard of hearing in government schools in New South Wales, Australia: Development and implementation of policy. *Journal of Deaf Studies and Deaf Education, 7*(3), 244–257.

Cerney, B. (2000). The ten C's of effective target texts. *Journal of Interpretation*, 131–150.

Clyne, M. (2003). *Dynamics of language contact: English and immigrant languages.* Cambridge: Cambridge University Press.

Cragg, S. (2002). Peeling back the skins of an onion. *Deaf Worlds, 18* (2), 56–61.

Davis, J. (1990). Linguistic transference and interference: Interpreting between English and ASL. In C. Lucas (Ed.), *Sign language research: Theoretical issues.* Washington, DC: Gallaudet University Press, pp. 308–321.

Davis, J. (2000). Translation techniques in interpreter education. In C. Roy (Ed.), *Innovative practices for teaching sign language interpreters.* Washington, DC: Gallaudet University Press, pp. 109–131.

Davis, J. (2003). Cross-linguistic strategies used by interpreters. *Journal of Interpretation*, 95–128.

DeCaro, J., & Hurwitz, A. (1992). Educational interpreters at risk. *Journal of Interpretation, 5*(1), 95–98.

Detthow, A. (2000). Transliteration between spoken Swedish and Swedish signs. In M. Metzger (Ed.), *Bilingualism and identity in deaf communities.* Washington, DC: Gallaudet University Press, pp. 79–94.

Fontana, S. (1999). Italian sign language and spoken Italian in contact: An analysis of interactions between deaf parents and hearing children. In E. Winston (Ed.), *Storytelling and conversation: Discourse in deaf communities.* Washington, DC: Gallaudet University Press, pp. 149–161.

Frishberg, N., & Wilcox, S. (1994). Issue paper: Differentiating training from education, technical and professional. In E. Winston (Ed.), *Mapping our course: A collaborative venture, Proceedings of the 10th National Convention of the Conference of Interpreter Trainers*, pp. 15–20.

Goffman, E. (1981). *Forms of talk.* Oxford: Basil Blackwell.

Halliday, M.A.K. (1978). *Language as a social semiotic: The social interpretation of language and meaning.* London: Edward Arnold.

Halliday, M.A.K. (1985). *Spoken and written language.* Burwood, Australia: Deakin University Press.

Harrington, F. (2000). Sign language interpreters and access for deaf students to university curricula: The ideal and the reality. In R. Roberts, S.A. Carr, D. Abraham, & A. Dufour (Eds.), *The critical link 2: Interpreters in the community.* Philadelphia: John Benjamins.

Harrington, F. (2001). Deaf students and the interpreted classroom: The effect of translation on education? In F.J. Harrington & G.H. Turner (Eds.), *Interpreting interpreting: Studies and reflections on sign language interpreting.* Coleford, UK: Douglas McLean, pp. 74–88.

Harrington, F., & Traynor, N. (1999). *Second-hand learning: Experiences of deaf students in higher education.* Paper presented at the *Pathways to Policy: Deaf Nation 2 symposium*, University of Central Lancashire, Preston, UK, July 1999.

Harris, S., & Bargiela-Chiappini, F. (2003). Business as a site of language contact. *Annual Review of Applied Linguistics, 23*, 155–169.

Hauser, P.C. (2000). An analysis of code-switching: American sign language and cued English. In M. Metzger (Ed.), *Bilingualism and identity in deaf communities*. Washington, DC: Gallaudet University Press, pp. 43–78.

Hayes, L. (1992). Educational interpreters for deaf students: Their responsibilities, problems and concerns. *Journal of Interpretation, 5*(1), 5–24.

Hema, Z. (2002). Dialogism. *Deaf Worlds, 18*(2), 62–65.

Hodek, B., & Radatz, J. (1996). Deaf professionals and sign-to-voice interpretations: Chaos or success? In *A celebration of the profession: Proceedings of the 14th National Convention of the Registry of Interpreters for the Deaf, August 1995.* Silver Spring, MD: RID Publications, pp. 140–151.

Hurwitz, A. (1998). Current issues: Interpreters in the educational setting. In A. Weisel (Ed.), *Insights into deaf education: Current theory and practice.* Tel Aviv: Academic Press of the School of Education, Tel Aviv University, pp. 237–253.

Johnson, K. (1991). Miscommunication in interpreted classroom interaction. *Sign Language Studies, 70*, 1–34.

Johnston, T. (2002). BSL, Auslan and NZSL: Three signed languages or one? In A. Baker & B. van den Bogaer de E&O. Crasborn (Eds.), *Proceedings of the 7th International Conference on Theoretical Issues in Sign Language Research.* Hamburg: Signum Verlag, pp. 47–69.

Johnston, T.J. (2001). Nouns and verbs in Australian sign language: An open and shut case? *Journal of Deaf Studies and Deaf Education, 6*(4), 235–257.

Jones, B.E., Clark, G., & Soltz, D. (1997). Characteristics and practices of sign language interpreters in inclusive education programs. *Exceptional Children, 63*(2), 257–268.

Joos, M. (1967). *The five clocks.* New York: Harbinger Books.

Kember, D. (2002). Long-term outcomes of educational action research projects. *Educational Action Research, 10*(1), 83–103.

Lang, H. (2002). Higher education for deaf students: Research priorities in the new millennium. *Journal of Deaf Studies and Deaf Education, 7*(4), 267–280.

Liedel, J.A., & Brodie, P. (1996). The cooperative dialogue model: Redefining the dynamics between deaf professionals and interpreters. In D. Swartz (Ed.), *A celebration of the profession: Proceedings of the 14th National Conference of the Registry of Interpreters for the Deaf.* Alexandria, VA: RID Publications, pp. 97–104.

Livingston, S., Singer, B., & Abramson, T. (1994). Effectiveness compared: ASL interpretation versus transliteration. *Sign Language Studies, 82*, 1–54.

Locker, R. (1990). Lexical equivalence in transliterating for deaf students in the university classroom: Two perspectives. *Issues in Applied Linguistics, 1*(2), 167–195.

Lucas, C., & Valli, C. (1990). ASL, English and contact signing. In C. Lucas (Ed.), *Sign language research theoretical issues.* Washington, DC: Gallaudet University Press, pp. 288–307.

Marschark, M., Sapere, P., Convertino, C., Seewagen, R., & Maltzen, H. (2004). Comprehension of sign language interpreting: Deciphering a complex task situation. *Sign Language Studies, 4*(4), 345–368.

Metzger, M. (1999). *Sign language interpreting: Deconstructing the myth of neutrality.* Washington, DC: Gallaudet University Press.

Napier, J. (1998). Free your mind—the rest will follow. *Deaf Worlds, 14*(3), 15–22.

Napier, J. (1999). *Auslan interpreter training and testing: Past, present & future.* Paper presented at the National Conference of Interpreter and Translator Educators Association of Australia (CITEAA), Melbourne, 28–30 October 1999.

Napier, J. (2002a). *Sign language interpreting: Linguistic coping strategies.* Coleford, UK: Douglas McLean.

Napier, J. (2002b). University interpreting: Linguistic issues for consideration. *Journal of Deaf Studies and Deaf Education, 7*(4), 281–301.

Napier, J. (2002c). Linguistic coping strategies of interpreters: An exploration. *Journal of Interpretation,* 63–92.

Napier, J. (2003a). *Language contact phenomena: Comparing Auslan/English interpreters and deaf Australians.* Paper presented at the Australasian Deaf Studies Research Symposium 2, Renwick College, Sydney, 2–29 September 2003.

Napier, J. (2003b). A sociolinguistic analysis of the occurrence and types of omissions produced by Australian Sign Language/English interpreters. In M. Metzger, S. Collins, V. Dively, & R. Shaw (Eds.), *From topic boundaries to omission: New research in interpretation.* Washington, DC: Gallaudet University Press, pp. 99–153.

Napier, J. (forthcoming). Making learning accessible for sign language interpreters: a process of change. Submitted to *Educational Action Research.*

Napier, J. (2004). Interpreting omissions: A new perspective. *Interpreting: International Journal of Research and Practice in Interpreting, 6*(2), 117–142.

Napier, J., & Adam, R. (2002). A comparative linguistic analysis of Auslan and BSL interpreting. *Deaf Worlds, 18*(1), 22–31.

Napier, J., & Barker, R. (2003). A demographic survey of Australian sign language interpreters. *Australian Journal of Deaf Education, 9,* 19–32.

Napier, J., & Barker, R. (2004a). Sign language interpreting: The relationship between metalinguistic awareness and the production of interpreting omissions. *Sign Language Studies, 4*(4), 80–120.

Napier, J., & Barker, R. (2004b). Accessing university education: Perceptions, preferences and expectations for interpreting by deaf students. *Journal of Deaf Studies and Deaf Education, 9*(2), 228–238.

Ozolins, U. (1998). *Interpreting and translating in Australia: Current issues and international comparisons.* Melbourne: Language Australia.

Ozolins, U., & Bridge, M. (1999). *Sign language interpreting in Australia.* Melbourne: Language Australia.

Patrie, C. (1993). A confluence of diverse relationships: interpreter education and educational interpreting. In *A confluence of diverse relationships: Proceedings of the 13th National Convention of the Registry of Interpreters for the Deaf.* Silver Spring, MD: RID Publications, pp. 3–18.

Pöchhacker, F. (2004). *Introducing interpreting studies.* London: Routledge.

Pollitt, K. (2000). On babies, bathwater and approaches to interpreting. *Deaf Worlds, 16*(2), 60–64.

RID (2004). Registry of Interpreters for the Deaf [online]. Available: http:// www.rid.org. [Accessed March 16, 2004].

Roy, C. (1989). Features of discourse in an American sign language lecture. In C. Lucas (Ed.), *The sociolinguistics of the deaf community.* New York: Academic Press, pp. 231–252.

Roy, C. (2000a). Training interpreters—past, present and future. In C. Roy (Ed.), *Innovative practices for teaching sign language interpreters.* Washington, DC: Gallaudet University Press, pp. 1–14.

Roy, C. (2000b). *Interpreting as a discourse process.* Oxford: Oxford University Press.

Sanderson, G., Siple, L., & Lyons, B. (1999). Interpreting for postsecondary deaf students: a report of the National Task Force on Quality of Services in the Postsecondary Education of Deaf and Hard of Hearing Students. Northeast Technical Assistance Center, Rochester Institute of Technology.

Scheibe, K., & Hoza, J. (1986). Throw it out the window! (The code of ethics? we don't use that here): Guidelines for educational interpreters. In M. McIntire (Ed.), *Interpreting: The art of cross cultural mediation.* Silver Spring, MD: RID Publications, pp. 128–134.

Schembri, A., Wigglesworth, G., Johnston, T., Leigh, G., Adam, R., & Barker, R. (2000). The test battery for Australian sign language morphology and syntax project: Noun-verb pairs in Auslan. In A. Schembri, J. Napier, R. Beattie, & G. Leigh (Eds.), *Deaf Studies, Sydney 1998: Selected Papers from the Australasian Deaf Studies Research Symposium, Renwick College, Sydney, 22–23 August 1998.* Sydney: North Rocks Press, pp. 99–118.

Schick, B. (2001). Interpreting for children: How it's different. *Odyssey: Directions in Deaf Education, 2*(2), 8–11.

Schick, B., Williams, K., & Bolster, L. (1999). Skill levels of educational interpreters working in public schools. *Journal of Deaf Studies and Deaf Education, 4*(2), 144–155.

Schön, D.A. (1995). The new scholarship requires a new epistemology. *Change, 27*(6), 26–34.

Scott, G. (1999). *Change matters: Making a difference in education and training.* St Leonards, New South Wales: Allen & Unwin.

Scullion, R. (2002). Distance from the source text. *Deaf Worlds, 18*(2), 39–49.

Seal, B.C. (1998). *Best practices in educational interpreting.* Needham Heights, MA: Allyn & Bacon.

Slatyer, H., Chesher, T., & Napier, J. (2004). *Researching a curriculum model for generic training in interpreting skills.* Poster presentation given to Critical Link: 4th International Conference on Community Interpreting, Stockholm, Sweden, May 20–23, 2004.

Sofinski, B.A. (2002). So, why do I call this English? In C. Lucas (Ed.), *Turn-taking, fingerspelling, and contact in sign languages.* Washington, DC: Gallaudet University Press, pp. 27–52.

Spolsky, B. (2003). Religion as a site of language contact. *Annual Review of Applied Linguistics, 23,* 81–94.

Steiner, B. (1998). Signs from the void: The comprehension and production of sign language on television. *Interpreting, 3*(2), 99–146.

Storey, B.C., & Jamieson, J.R. (2004). Sign language vocabulary development practices and Internet use among educational interpreters. *Journal of Deaf Studies and Deaf Education, 9*(1) 53–67.

Sutton-Spence, R., & Woll, B. (1998). *The linguistics of British sign language.* Cambridge: Cambridge University Press.

Ure, J. (1971). Lexical density and register differentiation. In G.E. Perren, & J.L.M. Trim (Eds.), *Applications of linguistics: Selected papers of the 2nd International Congress of Applied Linguistics.* Cambridge: Cambridge University Press, pp. 443–452.

Valdes, G., & Angelelli, C. (2003). Interpreters, interpreting, and the study of bilingualism. *Annual Review of Applied Linguistics, 23,* 58–78.

Viera, J.A., & Stauffer, L.K. (2000). Transliteration: The consumer's perspective. *Journal of Interpretation,* 83–100.

Wadensjö, C. (1998). *Interpreting as interaction.* London: Longman.

Winston, E. (1989). Transliteration: what's the message? In C. Lucas (Ed.), *The sociolinguistics of the deaf community.* Washington, DC: Gallaudet University Press, pp. 147–164.

Witter-Merithew, A., & Maiorano, J. (1996). ASL form interpreters: Contextualization features of ASL discourse style. In *A celebration of the profession: Proceedings of the 14th National Convention of the Registry of Interpreters for the Deaf, August 1995.* Silver Spring, MD: RID Publication, pp. 43–60.

Zimmer, J. (1989). Toward a description of register variation in American sign language. In C. Lucas (Ed.), *The sociolinguistics of the deaf community.* New York: Academic Press, pp. 253–272.

5

Code Choices and Consequences: Implications for Educational Interpreting

Jeffrey E. Davis

Language interpretation is a multifaceted endeavor involving many factors and numerous demands. This chapter examines the variety of linguistic choices encountered during interpreting work, especially in educational contexts. Interpreting work occurs in a context that is best characterized as an intensive language-contact situation and involves numerous linguistic consequences. It reviews numerous research studies that describe the wide range of linguistic variation encountered and various language and communication strategies available to interpreters.

In most bilingual or multilingual communities around the world, there has been prolonged contact between two or more languages. These language-contact situations result in a specific set of sociolinguistic outcomes. The most salient linguistic features of language contact are code-switching and lexical borrowing. Other sociolinguistic pressures, such as language dominance or cultural hegemony, may lead to an "intensive" language-contact situation. These sociolinguistic pressures represent a special set of challenges for interpreters who work in these language-contact communities. The outcomes are shaped by the diversity of participant characteristics and the varieties of language available (or not available) to these participants. Not only is there linguistic transference (rule-governed bilingual behavior); there may also be language interference (the results of inadequate first- and/or second-language acquisition and difficulty keeping the contact languages separate). How interpreters deal with these linguistic challenges has major implications for interpreter education, evaluation, practice, and research.

The consequences of language contact between signed and spoken languages, and understanding that these are universal occurrences, have significance for deaf people, educators, and interpreters worldwide. The focus here is interpreting in K–12 educational contexts (for post-secondary issues, see Napier, this volume). The linguistic demands and strategies described are applicable across a wide range of interpreting settings and are relevant to both signed and spoken language interpreters. Given the variety of signed and spoken language-contact situations around the world, American Sign Language (ASL) and English are used in this chapter as generic cover terms to illuminate some of the universal linguistic outcomes.

ISSUES OF DEFINITION

Various approaches may be followed in the study of language interpretation, and the present discussion concentrates on language-contact studies—a branch of sociolinguistics. Depending on the discipline, there are different meanings assigned to the term "code." In sign language studies, the term is typically used to refer to any number of invented manual codes representing spoken language and which linguists distinguish from naturally evolved and acquired signed language. In the field of sociolinguistics, however, "code" is used as a generic cover term "to refer not only to different languages, but also to varieties of the same language as well as styles within a language" (Romaine 1995, p. 121). Code-switching, for example, refers to the alternate use of two languages within a communicative event.

The term "consequences" refers to the results or outcomes of language contact and the choices between language codes and varieties (e.g., code-switching, mixing, lexical borrowing, etc.). Myers-Scotten (1998, p. 3) defines code and variety as "cover terms for linguistic systems at any level, from separate languages to dialects of a single language to styles or substyles within a single dialect." Such labels, while sometimes problematic, are necessary to distinguish linguistic characteristics within the multilayered and multidimensional complex of language and communication. These distinctions appear to be even more complex in cross-modality and cross-cultural sociolinguistic contexts (e.g., spoken-signed language contact). Signers have both manual and oral channels available for the coding of linguistic information.

Spoken-signed language contact studies suggest that "true" code-switching means a *complete switch from one language to another*—that is, a switch in linguistic modality (e.g., Davis 1989, 1990a; Lucas & Valli, 1992). In other words, someone stops signing and starts speaking, or vice versa. However, the definitions offered by Romaine and Myers-Scotten suggest a broader view. A broader interpretation is necessary to account for one of the unique outcomes of spoken-signed language contact. Signers sometimes *simultaneously* represent spoken language words or phrases with mouth movement or fingerspelling during signed language production (i.e., code-mixing).

In terms of the oral channel, signers appear to *alternate sequentially* between using mouth configurations specific to the signed language and those representative of the spoken language. At another level, the alternation between sign-driven and speech-driven linguistic output can be seen as a type of code-switching (e.g., when one alternates between signing more like ASL and signing more like English). These forms of cross-linguistic transference have been reported for dozens of signed languages (e.g., Ann, 2001; Bergman & Wallin, 2001; Boyes-Braem & Sutton-Spence, 2001; Lucas & Valli, 1992; Woll, 2001) and are reflected during interpreting work (e.g., Davis, 2003; Napier & Adam, 2002). This research indicates that these bilingual behaviors are highly patterned, cross-linguistic strategies differing from linguistic interference—a result of inadequate second-language acquisition (see Napier, this volume, for further discussion of the strategic use of these linguistic behaviors among interpreters).

The prolonged contact between spoken and signed languages, along with pressures for deaf people to acquire spoken language, leads to an "intensive" language-contact situation. Such intensive contact may lead to extraordinary efforts (e.g., language policy and planning) to keep the languages separate and to keep the dominant language from exerting pressure on the minority language. There are numerous consequences (or outcomes) of prolonged and intensive language contact. These may be as dramatic as language shift, language death, and the emergence of pidgins and Creoles—or as commonplace and predictable as code-switching and mixing, foreigner talk, and lexical borrowing. Language contact studies offer a useful theoretical and analytic framework to explore the numerous linguistic outcomes, demands, and choices encountered by interpreters—particularly in educational contexts.

LANGUAGE CONTACT STUDIES

The study of language-contact outcomes is one of the most complex areas of linguistic inquiry. Numerous approaches may be taken in the study of language contact (e.g., second-language acquisition, bilingualism, and sociolinguistics).[1] Regardless of theoretical approach, language, or modality, a substantial body of research reveals that the most common consequences of language contact involve code-switching, mixing, and lexical borrowing, and that these are bilingual rule-governed behaviors (e.g., Auer, 1995; Gumperz, 1982; Kachru 1992; Muysken, 2000; Myers-Scotten, 1992, 1993 a & b, 1997; Myers-Scotten & Jake, 1995, 2000; Poplack 1980; Poplack, Sankoff & Miller, 1988; Poplack & Sankoff, 1988; Romaine, 1995; Sankoff 1998).

We are still in the early stages of researching linguistic consequences of contact between spoken and signed languages and between signed languages. However, the evidence thus far strongly suggests that in addition to the universal outcomes found between spoken languages (and apparently between signed languages), contact between a signed and spoken language involves unique cross-linguistic and cross-modality phenomena (e.g., lexicalized fingerspelling and mouth configurations) (see Ann, 2001; Battison, 1978/2003; Boyes-Braem & Sutton-Spence, 2001; Bridges & Metzger, 1996; Davis, 1990a; Lucas, 2001; Lucas & Valli, 1989, 1990, 1992; Mulrooney, 2002; Padden, 1991, 1998; Quinto-Pozos, 2002; and Sofinski, 2002 for more discussion).

Additional research shows the language-contact features that are highly characteristic of deaf peoples' sign language are also used by their interpreters. Specifically, interpreters use code-switching and lexical borrowing as linguistic strategies to clarify the message, convey accurate meaning, and accommodate the audience (Davis, 1990a, 2003; Napier, 2002a & b, and this volume; Sofinksi, Yesbeck, Gerhold & Bach-Hansen, 2001). The wide array of code choices faced by interpreters, particularly in educational contexts, requires distinguishing code-switching as a linguistic strategy (i.e., *transference*) from other possible outcomes—for example, *interference* from the source language during interpretation.

Notions of Transference and Interference

Code-switching, mixing, and lexical borrowing may be viewed negatively by many, including bilinguals themselves. Some individuals believe it shows a deficit or a lack of linguistic mastery, while others attribute it to laziness or sloppy language. However, few bilinguals keep their languages completely separate, and code-switching is universal, highly patterned, rule-governed, and a valuable linguistic strategy. Thus, bilinguals tend to intermittently mix their languages even in the "monolingual mode." Scholars suggest that perfectly balanced bilingualism is a rare occurrence and few bilinguals have native competency in both languages (e.g., Grosjean, 1992, 1996; and Romaine, 1995).

Typically, the first or dominant language influences the second language. When such influence appears to be the result of inadequate second-language acquisition and performance, it is considered "interference." However, linguistic transference (code-switching and lexical borrowing) may be viewed as a bilingual discourse strategy and is distinguishable from linguistic interference (i.e., source language–retained forms that may interfere with the propositional content of the target language message). Linguistic transference means that source-language forms appear to be "consciously" retained to elucidate or disambiguate the message (Davis 1990a & b, 2003; Napier 2002a & b, and this volume).

Examples of linguistic *transference* are evident when interpreters intentionally represent English words or phrases with fingerspelling, lip movement, or a literal sign for word rendition (e.g., the literal representation of an English idiom). Davis (1990b, 2003) described how ASL interpreters mark the cross-linguistic transfer of material from the source language (in this case, English) in very specific ways (e.g., using quotation markers or by indicating that it is a literal English rendition).[2] This research shows that transfer between ASL and English can take place without the phonological parameters and linguistic rules of the target language (in this case, ASL) being violated (i.e., the transfer is sign-driven). See Napier (2002a) for details about the use of this strategy in a study of Australian Sign Language, or Auslan, interpreters. Transference or interference may occur at any linguistic level—phonological, morphological, syntactic, or even pragmatic.

Interference implies that a linguistic rule in the target language is violated or that the material being introduced from the source language into the target language is considered intrusive by the intended audience. The following patterns are examples of interference: overuse or overgeneralization of mouthing and/or fingerspelling; using literal vs. semantically correct sign choices,[3] and glossing of ASL signs during interpretation.[4]

Language Bases

In code-switching studies, the language used predominantly is called the *primary, base, or matrix* language, while the language from which the linguistic forms originate is the *source, donor, or embedded* language. A major defining characteristic of signed-spoken language contact is that the signed language typically forms the base language (i.e., the spoken language is generally the source of the transfer material). For example, it is much more common to see English-like features in ASL discourse than ASL forms in English. As such, ASL appears to borrow heavily from English, but there is a disproportionate amount of borrowing from ASL into English (cf. Davis, 1990a, 2003; Lucas & Valli, 1992). This type of asymmetry is a common occurrence in minority-majority language-contact situations. Naturally, the transfer of linguistic material does occur in both directions, and there are some cases where the spoken language forms the base, with the source material originating from the signed language. This most commonly occurs among hearing ASL-English bilinguals (e.g., children of deaf adults or interpreters).

Anecdotal evidence suggests that when hearing ASL-English bilinguals interact with each other in English, there are many instances of code-switching and mixing with ASL. However, not much research has been conducted in this direction. In one such study of this type, Miller (2003) follows Myers-Scotten's (1997, 1998) Matrix Language Framework to analyze the code-switching patterns of hearing ASL-English bilinguals interacting with each other in English. Miller's study describes patterns consistent with other contact situations and patterns unique to this context (e.g., signing and speaking simultaneously). The notion of what constitutes the base (or matrix) language and how this shapes the linguistic outcomes has implications for language-contact studies and for bilingual and interpreter education.

Distinguishing Language-Contact Phenomena

The term "code-mixing" is sometimes used to refer to "pieces" from one language being embedded into the sentences of another language—in contrast to "code-switching" where there is a clearer break between clauses, sentences, or longer stretches of discourse (Kachru, 1978, 1992). When pieces from one language appear within a single clause or sentence in another, various problems of incongruence arise—such as word-order differences, morphological disparities, semantic differences, and literal vs. idiomatic interpretations. In systematic studies of bilingual communities, it has been observed that speakers tend to avoid switches in places that would result in ungrammatical sentences (Poplack, 1980; Poplack, Wheeler, & Westwood, 1989; Sankoff & Poplack, 1981). The challenge is to differentiate linguistic transfer material that appears within sentences (code-mixing) from switches that take place at or between sentence boundaries (code-switching).

Lexical Borrowing

In order to understand the range of lexical and morphological choices available to interpreters it is important to understand the process of lexical borrowing. Researchers have gone to great effort to distinguish the process of lexical borrowing from code-switching. Sankoff, Poplack, and Vanniarajan (1986, p. 3) posit that "it is often impossible, in a given sentence, to tell whether a genuine switch has taken place; if a single word from one language appears in a sentence in the other, this may constitute a switch, but it may also be a loanword." Borrowing and code-switching represent different linguistic processes and involve different constraints and conditions. In the case of lexical borrowing, individual words (or compounds functioning as single words) from the donor language are repeatedly used in the host or recipient language until they become fully assimilated and indistinguishable from the native vocabulary.

In addition to frequency of occurrence, loanwords have generally achieved recognition and acceptance. Loanwords typically indicate some new cultural or technological concept or refer to some established notion in a new way. Preference on the part of speakers for simpler lexical items to express the same referent and a desire for synonyms to distinguish registers has been proposed as motivation for borrowing. It has also been proposed that bilingual ability and language contact are key predictors of lexical borrowing (Mougeon et al., 1985; Poplack, Sankoff, & Miller, 1988; Sankoff, Poplack, & Vanniarajan, 1986).

Morphemic Mouth Movements

Modality shapes lexical borrowing between a signed and spoken language, leading to unique phenomena—for example, lexicalized mouth configurations. Davis (1990a, b; 2003) described how the mouth is used to convey linguistic meaning during ASL interpretation, whether in the rich articulation of ASL non-manual signals (such as adjectives and adverbs) or in the visual representation of certain English words (primarily nouns). The rich use of morphological mouth configurations appears to be a major defining characteristic of intensive language contact between a signed and spoken language and is an example of simultaneous code-mixing (cf., Davis, 1990a; Lucas, 2001; Lucas & Valli, 1992). Rather than sequentially switching from one language to the other, certain features of both languages are produced simultaneously. For example, the lexicalized English mouth movements that accompany some ASL signs (e.g., LATE, HAVE, WANT, LIKE, FINISH, WHO, etc). In contrast, ASL mouthing bears no apparent relationship to English (e.g., the adverbial modifiers MM, TH, PAH, CHA, etc.). For linguistic descriptions, see Bridges and Metzger (1996), Davis (1990, 2003), and Marshcark, LePoutre, and Bement (1998).

Mouth patterns similar to those found in ASL appear to be evident in other signed languages. Boyes-Braem and Sutton-Spence (2001) have edited a book on the use of the mouth in European sign languages and report broad consensus among the contributors that there are at least *two* clearly identifiable types of mouth patterns in sign languages. As these researchers put it: "Mouth patterns used in a sign language may be derived from a spoken language or they may have formed from within the sign languages and bear no relation at all to the mouth movement of a spoken language" (p. 1). European researchers refer to the patterns related to spoken languages as "mouthings" and patterns from within signed languages as "mouth gestures." Preliminary research suggests that the movements of the hand and body drive (and are synchronized with) the movements of the mouth—that is, mouthings borrowed from the spoken language are restructured to fit the patterns and constraints of the signed language (cf. Bergman & Wallin, 2001) and "mouth gestures derive from the actions of the hands" (Woll, 2001, p. 87).

Lexicalized Fingerspelling

Scholars have argued that fingerspelling, by its very nature, is a signed language phonological event (e.g., Davis, 1989, 1990a & b; Lucas & Valli,

1992; Mulrooney, 2002; Padden, 1991; Padden & Gunsauls, 2003). Battison (1978/2003) first described and analyzed the process of English words becoming "fingerspelled loan signs" and hypothesized that a "borrowing" occurred when fingerspelled English words were made into ASL signs. He analyzed the lexical restructuring of 93 "fingerspelled loan signs" such as #YES, #JOB, #BACK, #WHAT, #EARLY, #DOG, #RARE, etc.[5]

Davis (1989) and Lucas and Valli (1992), following an idea originally made by S. Liddell (personal communication, 1989) argued that fingerspelling is essentially an ASL phonological event (prior to this, the assumption was that fingerspelling was English). Therefore, the representation of English with fingerspelling entails lexical restructuring and is a productive lexicalization process in ASL. In a pattern parallel to lexical borrowing, an English word can be fingerspelled repeatedly until it becomes an ASL sign. In other words, a fingerspelled word can undergo systematic phonological, morphological, and semantic changes— that is, the word eventually becomes an integral part of the ASL lexicon. This suggests that ASL fingerspelling is a rich and productive way to represent English literacy events and to derive new ASL lexicon.

Initialized Signs

ASL fingerspelling is used to represent abbreviations and acronyms commonly used in professional, technical, and educational contexts. In addition, fingerspelled letters may be used to "initialize" the citation form of a sign to correspond to the first letter of an English word that has the same or similar connotation. According to Padden (1998, p. 41) "initialization is one of the most productive word-building processes in ASL, used widely for technical or professional purposes." The linguistic process of sign initialization appears to be highly patterned and widely used in the adult Deaf Community. Some initialized signs are used primarily by individual consumers in a specific setting (e.g., occupation or profession related).

Initialized signs are also ubiquitous in educational contexts. English-based signing and transliteration rely heavily on sign initialization. However, overgeneralization of this linguistic feature and violation of morpheme structure constraints are a concern and can lead to misunderstandings (which are an example of interference). This happens when other consumers and interpreters are expected to know the initialized signs that were created for a specific context without the benefit of preconferencing. Educational interpreters need to be aware of the linguistic and sociolinguistic processes that govern sign initialization and how this feature is generally used by members of the ASL signing community. For example, Kelly (2001, p. 48) cautions transliterators to follow the initialized signs already established by deaf adults and that "if an initialized sign is created, then that sign should remain in that specific context and not be used in another setting without being properly established."

CODE CHOICES AND CONSEQUENCES IN THE EDUCATIONAL CONTEXT

The types of code-switching and lexical borrowing characteristics of bilingual discourse are also available to interpreters as a linguistic strategy (see Davis, 1990a, 2003; Napier 2002a & b, and this volume). More research is needed to account for the range of coding systems intended to represent English that are commonly used in educational contexts. In addition to conventional orthographic means, finger-spelling, cued speech, initialized signs, and English-based signing may be used. There may also be times when the interpreter is required to transliterate or sign and speak simultaneously. These coding mechanisms for English comprise the general linguistic repertoire of educational interpreters who may be expected to apply them to varying degrees depending on numerous educational and sociolinguistic factors. During a typical day, interpreters are faced with making frequent linguistic choices and decisions about the approach they take to interpreting work. Freelance interpreters enter a wide range of settings and encounter a variety of topics and participants from diverse backgrounds (social, economic, educational, cultural, and sociolinguistic). For many interpreters, such variety may have been one of the things they found most appealing about the interpreting profession.

Interpreters working in specialized settings (e.g., educational, legal, or medical) are faced with making critical decisions about language choice and interpreting approaches on a continual basis. The nature of interpreting work involves multiple contexts and a variety of participants, with demands arising from several sources. Some demands stem from the languages or communication modes being used, and others from non-linguistic factors, such as environmental, interpersonal, and intrapersonal demands. Dean and Pollard (2001, and this volume) offer a cogent way to sort through these demands. This approach helps interpreter practitioners and educators describe the source of these demands and encourages effective decision-making.

During a single day, interpreters may be called upon to translate, interpret, transliterate, or "code" English in various visual-manual forms (i.e., transcodification). The pressures in the educational domain for the development and maintenance of English literacy lead to demands for literal English coding and transliteration. This raises issues concerning language policy and planning, language dominance and cultural oppression, and how much consumers understand the translation/interpretation/transliteration process. This also raises such questions as "At what age are deaf children best served by educational interpreters?" "How are deaf children taught to work with an interpreter?" (for further discussion of issues in educational interpreting, see Fleetwood, 2000).

The Question of Best Practice

Challenges have emerged from recent legislation in several countries, the educational inclusion reform movement, and the ever-increasing consumer demands for qualified interpreters. Before delving into the wide array of code choices that are evident in educational contexts, it is informative to see what researchers have said about the sociolinguistic nature of interpreting work, particularly in educational contexts (Cokely, 1992, and this volume; Foster, 1989; Harrington, 2000; Johnson, 1991; La Bue, 1995, 1998; Ramsey, 1997, 2000; Winston, 1990, 1994, 2004). This research suggests that deaf students, even with support from interpreters, may become unintentionally marginalized participants in the educational mainstreamed context. Notwithstanding this issue, Seal provides the following overview:

> The scope of practice for educational interpreting is both broad and deep. Any teaching-learning situation can be an educational interpreting situation. Consider a 40-year-old taking scuba diving lessons, a 25-year-old in a Lamaze class, a 62-year-old taking "Alternatives to Smoking" classes, or an 8-year-old in a summer soccer camp. Educational interpreting can and does occur in each of these settings; but only one setting, the school setting, provides a scope of practice that can include units on scuba diving, natural childbirth, the dangers of smoking, and the basics of soccer in the same 6-hour day that also includes units in mathematics, reading, writing, and on and on. Educational interpreting itself is *all-inclusive*. (2004, p. 6)

Adding to the complexity of educational contexts is the fact that children who are deaf represent a very heterogeneous sociolinguistic group. Contributing to this linguistic variation are factors relative to hearing loss (e.g., degree and age of onset), family background (signing/non-signing, deaf/hearing parents or siblings), and educational placement (full inclusion, mainstreaming, school for the deaf, etc.). The high degree of language variation found among deaf children is also evident in the general Deaf community. Thus, the microcosm of the classroom is reflected in the larger linguistic community of deaf adults. In other words, many of the consequences that emerge from educational placement and communication practices continue well into adulthood (see Marschark, Sapere, Convertino, & Seewagen, this volume).

The Need for Adequate Preparation

Current trends in educational placement of deaf children necessitate interpretation in multiple languages (e.g., ASL, English, and even Spanish or other languages if necessary) and through multiple communication modes (e.g., manual, oral, written, and electronic media)—thus the need for highly trained and qualified educational interpreters. As the situation dictates, the need may arise for translation, interpretation, transliteration, or transcodification (e.g., cued speech or manually coded English [MCE]). One of the greatest challenges facing Interpreter Preparation Programs (IPPs) in the United States is selecting qualified applicants and preparing interpreting students who are proficient in both ASL and English (and there is also an ever-increasing need for interpreters who are fluent in Spanish). Only a small number of applicants are truly ASL-English bilingual.[6]

Regardless of degree type (Associate or Bachelor), formal interpreting preparation typically takes place in a 2- to 3-year time frame. Given such time constraints, priority is given to language preparation, teaching about the interpreter's role, code of ethics and business practices, interpreting and discourse processes, and interpreting practice. Thus, students are faced with acquiring ASL proficiency, improving English skills, and learning to interpret during a relatively brief degree program. Considering the wide range of sociolinguistic variation in educational settings and within the larger Deaf Community (e.g., gender, age, ethnic, regional, and educational), most IPPs are most concerned with teaching individuals to become skilled interpreters in a wide a range of settings. However, a significant number of graduates find jobs in educational contexts that necessitate the ability to transliterate and to work with English-based sign systems.

Most IPPs do not focus on a particular specialization, nor do they concentrate on teaching transliteration or manually coded English. Interpreters are trained as generalists, which means they face acquiring specialty skills in the field, through continuing education, preparation for certification, or additional degree studies. For example, it is not uncommon for some IPP graduates to also have other degrees (e.g., teaching or law degrees) or for those with Associate degrees in interpreting to subsequently complete a Baccalaureate degree in interpreting. To address the gap between preparation and entry into the field, Dean and Pollard (this volume) offer a problem-based approach to interpreter preparation and new approaches to interpreter training through observation-supervision. Most interpreter educators and practitioners recognize that it is essential that preparation be maintained in the field along with continuing education and mentoring. The need for higher education and more rigorous preparation is reflected in the degree requirement passed at the 2003 Registry of Interpreters for the Deaf (RID) Conference in Chicago.[7]

What Is Transliteration?

Because transliteration is most commonly found in the educational interpreting arena, it warrants discussion. In the United States, transliteration is the label used to account for the way interpreters attempt to visually represent English words and grammar. The recognition of English-based (i.e., literal) renditions can be traced back to the emergence of the interpreting profession, prior to the understanding of the underlying psycholinguistic processes (that continue to evolve along with the argot). Since the establishment of the RID national evaluation and certification system for sign language interpreters in 1972, candidates have been awarded either interpreting and/or transliterating certification (see Cokely, this volume).

Winston (1989) conducted the first in-depth linguistic analysis of transliteration work. Her research described a complex combination of ASL and English features that appear to be a conscious strategy used by interpreters. Winston proposed that transliteration balances the pragmatic, linguistic, aesthetic-poetic, and ethnographic goals of translation work. This suggests that transliteration is the ability to incorporate ASL features in English word order. More recently, Sofinski, Yesbeck, Gerhold, and Bach-Hansen (2001) conducted an in-depth linguistic analysis of the transliterated output of 15 educational interpreters. For the study, Sofinski and colleagues borrowed the concept of two different types of Simultaneous Communication (SimCom) proposed by Stewart, Akamatsu, and Bonkowski (1988): *speech-driven*, where primary emphasis is given to the spoken English portion of the linguistic output, and *sign-driven*, where primary emphasis is given to the meaning, or semantic base, of the signed portion of the linguistic output.

The results of Sofinski, and colleagues' study (2001) were that interpreters rendering a transliterated product can be divided into at least two groups: sign-driven and speech-driven. A third hybrid group (a mixture of both) also emerged. This suggests that transliteration parallels what other researchers have found in SimCom. Sign-driven transliteration incorporates more ASL features (such as those identified by Winston, 1989),[8] while speech-driven transliteration uses more English features (e.g., constant English mouthing, manually coded English-bound morphemes, predominant use of initialized signs, and English word order). The third group identified suggests that in some cases transliterators switch between signing that is more ASL or English-like.

Some scholars (e.g., Metzger, 1999; Napier 2002a), recognizing that translation, interpretation, and transliteration share similar underlying processes, borrow the terms "free" and "literal" from spoken-language interpreting to account for the two main forms of interpreter output. Napier (2002a, p. 28) defines "free interpretation" as "the process by which concepts and meanings are translated from one language into another, by incorporating cultural norms and values; assumed knowledge about these values; and the search for linguistic and cultural equivalents." In contrast, transliteration is described as "literal interpretation," which means it closely follows the patterns of the source language in the target output. Research conducted by Napier (2002b) on post-secondary educational interpreting suggests that interpreters tend to be dominant in either free or literal translation style, and that some "code-switched" between styles (see Napier, this volume). More research is needed to describe the nature and structure of alternation between "free" and "literal" interpretation, to compare "sign-based" and "speech-based" transliteration, and to identify parallels with spoken-language interpreters.

Kelly (2001) reported that most IPPs focus on language preparation, translation, and interpretation. This follows the general assumption that translation forms the basis for interpreting and that interpretation and transliteration share similar underlying processes (e.g., Davis, 2000). One example of the importance of translation in practice in the educational domain is that interpreters are frequently called upon to provide sight translation (i.e., rendering written texts into signed language). In contrast to signed-language IPPs, most spoken-language IPPs require bilingual proficiency in the working languages as a condition for admission. Signed-language IPPs focus on language preparation, whereas spoken-language IPPs concentrate on the development of translation skills (see Lee and Quinto-Pozos, this volume, concerning issues of language preparation).

Although there is a larger world market for spoken-language translation services, translation-based approaches recognize the importance of developing translation skills as the basis for doing interpreting work. Given the nature of translation work (typically involving frozen texts rather than interpreting live interactions), one would expect students of translation to develop a clearer structural delineation (grammatical and semantic) between the working languages. Generally, translation provides time to produce accurate target language output with less risk of interference from the source language (an issue for simultaneous interpretation). Arguably, after mastering translation, students would be better prepared to consecutively interpret, and then simultaneously interpret. See Russell (2002) for research concerning different outcomes between simultaneous and consecutive interpreting work.

Kelly (2001, p. 2) described transliteration this way: "The task of transliterating is defined as delivering the signed message based on

English grammatical order; basing sign choices on ASL usage, not English gloss; maintaining the meaning and intent of the original English; and understanding that the meaning of the message is more important than the form." Sofinksi (2002, p. 27) pointed out that while recent definitions of transliterating have been expanded to include elements of both English and ASL, the notion of "word-for-sign representations of English using manual communication in English-order" is still central to these definitions. Livingston, Singer, and Abrahmson, (1994) broadened the definition of transliterating to encompass language contact varieties that include both English and ASL linguistic elements.

The rationale for transliteration is that it meets the preferences of a large number of consumers and that federal legislation grants deaf children and adults the right to choose from an array of services that includes interpreting/transliterating. The need for transliteration has been clearly articulated in the literature (cf. Siple, 1997; Napier, this volume). Deaf consumers frequently request transliterating because they want to "see" the English (Kelly, 2001). The need for transliteration raises numerous questions about the role of the interpreter, the interpreting process, and the preparation of interpreters. When should transliteration skills preparation be introduced to students of interpretation? What are the implications of deaf consumers asking to "see" the English? Viera's (2000) survey, for example, suggested that consumers sometimes request transliteration because they want to "learn" English like their hearing peers. How plausible is it that English can be learned through transliteration? How is the interpreter's role to be delineated in educational contexts? Do interpreters serve as linguistic change agents? To what degree is transliterating the product of the requirement to render the message "simultaneously" to an audience who has some degree of English proficiency (or who may be striving for that goal)?

These questions are not raised to minimize or dismiss a deaf person's right to request transliteration. Rather, it becomes a question of how to prepare students of interpretation to accommodate these differences. If the goal is to "see" and "learn" English, when might one consider the use of real-time captioning services rather than transliterating? The expressed desire of deaf consumers to "see" English is consistent with the increase in requests for real-time captioning, although that increase may be the result of the lower cost of text-based services than interpreting. Consumers would benefit from in-service workshops that explain interpretation and transliteration processes, demonstrate the differences between interpreting and transliterating, and discuss the role of the interpreter/transliterator. How often do deaf children or even adults using interpreters have access to this type of information? Can the need for interpreters be replaced by electronic means of communication? What are the nature, structure, and motivation for switching between sign-based and speech-based forms?

English-Based Signing

In addition to transliteration, it is also highly probable that interpreters in educational settings will encounter a variety of English-based signing—collectively referred to as manually coded English—a product of total communication philosophy. Garretson (1976, p. 300) defined total communication as a "philosophy incorporating the appropriate aural, manual, and oral modes of communication in order to ensure effective communication with and among hearing impaired persons." The assumption is that deaf children will acquire English by "seeing" it on the hands, and thus make acquisition of reading and writing English accessible. In practice, the total communication philosophy typically is interpreted to mean that spoken English is represented by a manual code, with each sign intended to correspond to each spoken word. English-based systems borrow heavily from the ASL lexicon, but grammatical structure and sign meanings follow English. ASL signs are altered and new signs are sometimes invented to represent English morphology (oftentimes at the expense of ASL morphology and semantic accuracy). In sum, MCEs are a mixture of signs borrowed from ASL and signs invented to represent English words and morphemes. Again, the signing products of the educational arena have implications for interpreting preparation and practice. The effectiveness and "naturalness" of these English-based sign systems in the education of children who are deaf have been approached from different research perspectives and continues to be a source of ongoing debate (cf., Ramsey, 1989; Schick, 2003; Schick & Moeller, 1992; Supalla, 1991; Wilbur, 2000, 2003).

Though a generation of deaf learners has been taught using artificial sign systems, there has not been a significant increase in literacy scores since the inception of these systems more than three decades ago (see Marschark & Spencer, 2003, for an extensive compilation on the subjects of language, culture, literacy, and other educational issues). On this subject, Akamatsu, Stewart, and Mayer (2002, p. 230) write: "It is arguable as to whether English in a manual form is an apt, or indeed accurate, descriptor of the forms of communication that occur in classrooms because there is considerable variation in how much of the English language is actually represented on the hands." Simply put: What does it mean to "see" English? How does one acquire a spoken language without having ever heard that language?

In reviewing the research on bilingualism and literacy, Mayer and Akamatsu (2003, p. 144), along with other researchers, posit that other "compensatory strategies" can potentially be used to facilitate deaf learners' access to spoken-language literacy. They propose two types of compensatory strategies: those that are speech-based, such as "contact sign, mouthing, or mouthing in conjunction with speech, fingerspelling, or sign"; and those that are sign-based, such as "glossing and finger-spelling." According to Mayer and Akamatsu (2003, p. 144), "This potential needs to be investigated with respect to how, and how well, these strategies mediate the literacy learning process, particularly with respect to how they might operate in concert to support the process of learning to read and write." See Supalla, Wix, and McKee (2001) for a discussion of print as the primary source of English for deaf learners.

Sign-Supported Speech

Signed language linguists have long considered "artificially" invented manual codes for English problematic. Signed and spoken languages are considered "natural" if they (1) develop naturally over time, (2) are acquired through an ordinary course of language acquisition, and (3) are organized according to universal and independent patterns of organization (Stokoe, 1960 cited in La Bue, 1998). Natural language development and acquisition patterns are not evident with sign systems developed by committee and enforced by educational policy. Johnson, Liddell, and Erting (1989) use the term "Sign Supported Speech (SSS)" to encompass MCE and the practice of speaking English while simultaneously signing (i.e., SimCom). In one of the first studies on this subject, Marmor and Petitto (1979) found that SimCom made it extremely difficult for a group of teachers to produce accurate signs and speech. Their research showed that the signed message suffered the most, with the omission, misrepresentation, or misuse of signs that were critical to the meaning of the message. SSS (in the form of MCE or SimCom) appears to "bypass the linguistic, syntactic and semantic patterns associated with signed languages" (La Bue, 1998, p. 9). What language do deaf children perceive and acquire by attempts at representing English through SSS? More research is needed to determine how accurately SSS can represent English in the hands of a highly skilled signer. See Cokely (1990) for further discussion of communication modes—especially a comparison of SimCom and interpreting.

Arguably, the lack of a strong ASL linguistic foundation shapes these outcomes. Based on extensive observational and evaluation data, Schick (2003, p. 219) points out that "teachers and programs differ in how faithfully they represent English via a sign system because of philosophical reasons and less than fluent signing skills." Schick also pointed out another major issue is that children typically learn MCE from hearing educators. This begs the question: Who are the primary linguistic models for children who are deaf—the deaf child's caregivers, members of the educational support team including interpreters, and/or the children's peers? The fact that MCE is a product of "language by committee" and school environments (in contrast to the home and community) diverges from the linguistic principles and acquisition patterns evident in natural languages of the world, thereby raising questions and concerns about its efficacy. This also raises sociolinguistic questions concerning linguistic identity and socialization. For a full account of MCEs, see Bornstien (1990), Schick (2003), and Wilbur (2003).

Approaching the MCE question in terms of the grammatical elements that work well within the visual system and from what deaf children find learnable, Schick concluded:

> When English grammatical structures are converted to a visual form, as with MCE, children appear to have a great deal of difficulty acquiring certain aspects of it, despite special teaching and support. Specifically, they have difficulty acquiring the functional categories and relatively simple morphology of English and produce it in a limited, fragmented manner. This may be due to the restricted input they receive, and the issue of variations in input makes interpretation difficult. (2003, p. 228)

Like researchers who approached this question before her (cf. Gee & Goodhart, 1985; Gee & Mounty, 1991; Singleton, Supalla, Litchfield, & Schley, 1998; Supalla, 1991), Schick concurred that "there may be something about making a spoken language into a visual one that is inconsistent with how visual languages work."

To date, Wilbur (2003) has provided the most extensive linguistic description of what distinguishes naturally evolved signed languages from artificially created signing systems and an overview of the research. She described how natural signed languages are multilayered and make use of multiple manual and non-manual articulation channels (another way of saying that ASL is morphologically complex in ways significantly different than English). Research conducted by Wilbur and Peterson (1998) suggested that signed English lacks the linguistic depth evident in natural sign language and does not have linguistically specified non-manuals of its own. Remarkably, researchers (most notably, Supalla, 1991) have found that deaf children being taught MCE with little or no exposure to ASL frequently enrich their own signing with ASL-like features (classifiers, verb agreement, and spatial mapping). Schick (2003, p. 228), among others, suggests that "this may indicate a core property of visual languages, in that some elements may be able to emerge via gesture, albeit in a rudimentary manner that is not equivalent to the rich, structured morphology of mature ASL." According to the principles that linguists call Universal Grammar, the human brain is suited to the acquisition and use of any language to which a child is exposed regardless of modality, as long as the linguistic form is compatible with certain perceptual and production constraints—that is, it is easy to use and learn (see Fischer, 1998; Lillo-Martin, 1997; Singleton, et al., 1998). Artificially developed signing systems appear to violate these linguistic constraints. According to Wilbur (2003, p. 343), "It is Signed English that demonstrates the importance of the linguistic evolution process because it lacks what natural languages have: efficiency in the modality."

Given the variety of invented codes (including cued speech) involved in interpreting, it would be difficult to prepare students of interpretation for a particular context or to teach any one system that may be encountered at the entry level of the profession. It does seem essential that students of interpreting understand the linguistic underpinnings of "natural" language acquisition and the educational objectives that these contrived systems attempt to achieve. During interpreter preparation, students should be introduced to signed English approaches, review the research on the subject, and evaluate these approaches objectively, following principles of linguistics and language acquisition (specifically, psycholinguistics). If a child or school requires the use of a specific sign system, it is often left up to the individual interpreter to decide if they are qualified for such an undertaking—thus, the need for more meaningful evaluation and field supervision.

REDEFINING THE ASL-ENGLISH CONTINUUM

Given the wide range of code choices encountered during interpreting work, it is useful to reanalyze the traditional continuum used to describe signed-spoken language contact. Woodward (1973) first coined Pidgin Signed English (PSE) to account for sign language variation along the ASL-English bilingual-diglossic continuum. Thirty years later, the term is still in widespread use. However, the emergence of a pidgin is a rarified linguistic situation typically lasting for only one generation before becoming a Creole.[9]

Valli and Lucas have explained why the PSE label is inaccurate and describe the special conditions from which a pidgin arises:

Usually a pidgin is the result of language contact between the adult users of mutually unintelligible languages. The language contact occurs for very specific purposes, like trade. These adult users are usually not trying to learn each other's language, but rather a third language that will help them improve their social and economic status. Often, they are removed from the situation in which they can continue to be exposed to their first language. They also may have restricted access to the language they are trying to learn and may end up learning it from each other. This was the sociolinguistic situation during the slave trade in West Africa and the West Indies, when many pidgins emerged. (2000, p. 186)

Another characteristic of pidgins is a greatly reduced morphology and syntax. A Creole emerges when the children born into these situations acquire it and make it linguistically more complex. Thus, the pidgin notion does not accurately portray the language-contact situation in the Deaf Community. A pidgin is the result of a unique and unstable linguistic situation that represents only one of the numerous possible outcomes of language contact (e.g., bilingualism, lexical borrowing, code-switching, cod-mixing, interference, foreigner talk, convergence, mixed systems, and Creoles).

Lucas and Valli (1992) did extensive research of ASL-English contact and found evidence of code-switching and lexical borrowing. They also found linguistic phenomena unique to sign- and spoken-language contact, such as fingerspelling, fingerspelling/sign combination, mouthing, CODA (children of deaf adults)-speak, and contact signing (code-mixing). They describe a "third system" called "contact signing," which is distinguished by *code-mixing* (see Lucas & Valli, 1992, p. 26). Contact signing is the consequence of intensive contact between English and ASL and has features of both languages. The contact variety (contact signing) gets used by deaf people with hearing people, and by deaf people with each other. Contact signing is described as follows by Valli and Lucas (2000, p. 188): "Its linguistic features include English word order, the use of prepositions, constructions with *that*, English expressions, and mouthing of English words, as well as ASL nonmanual signals, body and gaze shifting, and ASL use of space."

Lucas and Valli's use of the "third system" label to describe this phenomenon is similar to Selinker's (1992) notion of "interlanguage." Finegan provided the following account of interlanguage:

> Some researchers view second-language learners as developing a series of interlanguages in their progression towards mastery of the target language. An interlanguage is that form of the target language that a learner has internalized, and the interlanguage grammar underlies the spontaneous utterances of a learner in the target language. The grammar of an interlanguage can differ from the grammar of the target language in various ways: by containing rules borrowed from the native language, by containing overgeneralizations, by lacking certain sounds of the target language, by inappropriately marking certain verbs in the lexicon as requiring (or not requiring) a preposition, by lacking certain rules altogether, and so on. A language learner can be viewed as progressing from one interlanguage to another, each one approximating more closely the target language. (2004, p. 561)

As with all languages, a great deal of variation exists in ASL. Intensive and prolonged contact between English and ASL has resulted in a signed variety used among adults that is best called "contact signing" (see Lucas & Valli, 1992, p. 100). Most significant is that individuals who use the contact variety appear to be ASL-English bilinguals. Though inaccurate, the PSE label has become commonplace in the field and still appears in much of the professional literature.

Erroneously, many interpreters, teachers, and parents tend to use the PSE term as a "default category" for students who do not sign ASL and do not exhibit complete grasp of one of the manual codes for English (Ramsey, 2000). The "contact sign variety" is not a pidgin or English, and the PSE label is not helpful since it implies the absence, rather than the presence, of language. Central to this debate is language-acquisition base—that is, most children who are deaf do not have English or ASL proficiency. Most caregivers, interpreters, and teachers are not proficient in ASL. Interpreters tend to be the more fluent signers because they are required to complete more sign language preparation and interpreter certification is predicated on language proficiency. Considering these language development circumstances, Ramsey (2000) suggested three probable outcomes for the variety of signing that typically gets assigned the generic "PSE" label: first, the learner signing with ASL as the target; second, the learner signing with MCE as the target; and third, a highly idiosyncratic variety, such as the signing of a late learner who has received delayed or degraded signed input. All this needs to get sorted out from Selinker's (1992) notions of interlanguage (sometimes called learner's grammar).

THE CONTRIBUTION OF EDUCATIONAL SOCIOLINGUISTICS

Educational interpreters encounter a wide variety of sociolinguistic challenges (e.g., language variation, pressures to sign English, linguistic interference, lack of language proficiency among participants, the issue of interpreting into the second language, etc.). The research suggests that interpreting is not equivalent to, nor should it be expected to replace, direct discourse or instruction (e.g., La Bue, 1995, 1998; Ramsey, 1997, 2000, 2004; Winston, 1990, 1994, 2004, this volume). There is a need for more ethnographic-based research grounded in educational sociolinguistic theory. For additional perspectives, see Marschark and colleagues in this volume.

To understand the relationship of communication modes and coding strategies to English literacy development, La Bue (1998) studied the interpreting work of educational interpreters in a large, public, middle through high school program (54 deaf and hard of hearing students, 25 instructional staff). Her research focused on the interpreted discourse in a ninth-grade English class, the relationship between literacy learning and classroom discourse, and the educational interpreters' ability to convey this relationship. La Bue found that instructional discourse features used by the teacher to prompt student participation critical to development of advanced literacy skills were often lost in interpretation.

Stinson and Lang (1994) also suggested the possibility that direct instruction would be better than mediated instruction through an interpreter. It has been discussed that even college-level students who are deaf and rely on the presentation of lecture material through an interpreter are unable to understand and remember as much information as their hearing classmates who receive the information directly from the instructor (see Marschark et al., this volume). La Bue (1998, p. 11) lists three major reasons explaining why deaf students do not comprehend as much using an interpreter: first, the demands of simultaneous interpretation (i.e., processing time); second, deaf students vary in their English and ASL competencies (i.e., language contact variety); and third, "the nature of the signed medium is visual and cannot represent many sound-related literacy-learning practices, such as letter/sound associations or practicing discourse styles that correlate to written composition" (i.e., transliteration). La Bue (1998) suggests that deaf students who succeed academically are fluent in both English and ASL. There is a need for additional research to identify the relationship of sign-based coding strategies (e.g., mouthing, glossing, and fingerspelling) to the development of English literacy skills (see Mayer & Akamatsu, 2003; Singleton et al., 1998; Supalla et al., 2001).

SUMMARY AND CONCLUSIONS

Sorting out language-contact phenomena is a notoriously difficult endeavor. Cross-linguistic and cross-modality differences between signed and spoken language and the coding approaches used in educational contexts make this an even more challenging endeavor. For example, the assumption behind signed English is that deaf children will be able to acquire English by "seeing" it on the hands, making acquisition of reading and writing accessible. However, the research does not support this assumption. The linguistic outcome of manually coded English is a mixture of signs borrowed from the lexicon of ASL and signs invented to represent English words and morphemes. Signed-language linguists have long considered manual codes for English developed by educational committee and enforced by policy problematic because they deviate from universal language-acquisition patterns found in natural language.

A concern in language contact research, and one that has particular relevance to the interpreting field, is to distinguish transference (i.e., rule-governed linguistic behaviors such as code-switching and lexical borrowing) from interference (the deviation from the rules or norms of either contact language due to inadequate language acquisition). Interpreters may use code-switching or mixing as an interpretation strategy (transference), but this may also be an outcome of interpreting into one's second language (i.e., ASL is the second language for most interpreters and for most consumers of interpreting). Moreover, the constraints imposed by simultaneous interpretation (the modus operandi for signed-language interpreters) contribute to interference between the contact languages.

Just as translation forms the basis for interpreting work, the same basic underlying processes are shared by interpretation and transliteration. Depending on various factors, interpreters may provide a freer and more idiomatic equivalency, or one that is more literal (i.e., following the source language forms very closely). Similarly, interpreters tend to alternate between sign-driven and speech-driven renditions. For speech-driven renditions (literal/transliterated), the sign language provides the visual medium for coding the spoken language. For example, ASL fingerspelling encodes English words; handshapes are used to cue speech; signs are initialized for English synonyms; and the ASL lexicon is juxtaposed onto the English morpho-syntactic system. Consequently, there is a range of coding choices used to represent English visually—for example, lip movements, orthographic means, and the aforementioned manual coding devices.

The research presented thus far strongly suggests that fluent bilingual signers (including many deaf people, CODAs, interpreters, etc.) alternate between sign-based and speech-based signing. One of the major outcomes of signed-spoken language contact is lexical derivation in the form of fingerspelling and mouth configurations. Both appear to provide an excellent means of representing spoken-language literacy events and are a productive means for lexicalization. Further research is needed, but at least in American, Australian, and European sign languages, the mouth is used in similar ways. There appear to be three main types of mouth movement that accompany sign language: first, there are mouth movements that bear no obvious relation to spoken language (called "mouth gestures" by some European sign language researchers and "non-manual markers" by some ASL researchers); second, there are lexicalized mouth movements derived from spoken language that always accompany a particular sign; third, there is an alternation of the first two types of mouth movement, with the simultaneous mouthing of spoken language words (i.e., glossing or shadowing) within lexical, phrasal, and discourse boundaries.

Finally, while sign language interpreters may demonstrate these varieties of fingerspelling and mouthing, they are also bound by somewhat different conditions. First, the spoken language is generally their native or primary language; second, when they are listening to the spoken language, they are attempting to simultaneously interpret into the signed language, which is typically their second language. We know from second-language acquisition research that learners are continually striving for more successful approximations of the target language (cf. Campbell, 1998; and Selinker, 1992). The role of immersion, metalinguistic awareness, and feedback that is both supportive and analytical constitutes some of the major ways to achieve the goal of second-language proficiency.

It is problematic to simply divide linguistic coding according to categories of "natural" and "artificial." Like most linguistic phenomena, things are not that cut and dried. Natural and artificial are relative terms, and there exists a range of code choices across linguistic mediums and communication modes. Generally, there are two main types: The first set of choices is cross-linguistic and results from the intensive language-contact situation (e.g., code-switching, mixing, borrowing), and the second set is the cross-modality nature of signed and spoken language communication (e.g., transliteration and transcodification). These two categories are interrelated and seem more productive and descriptive than simply labeling linguistic choices as being natural or artificial. More research is needed to understand these coding compromises and the linguistic and psycholinguistic constraints of the visual signed-based medium to represent speech-based literacy learning.

There are no simple or obvious answers to questions concerning educational interpreters, and there is a need for more educational sociolinguistic, psycholinguistic, experimental, and ethnographic approaches to the study of interpreting work in these contexts. There may be much we still do not know, but at the same time there are many patterns we can observe and describe. We must recognize the ways that interpreting may or may not enhance learning and provide educational access. In the well-intended campaign for inclusion, deaf students, even with support from interpreters, may become unintentionally marginalized participants in the educational mainstreamed context. Due to factors relative to hearing loss (e.g., degree and age of onset) and family background (signing/non-signing, deaf/hearing parents or siblings), there is a great deal of linguistic variation among children who are deaf. These factors lead to sociolinguistic outcomes that pose a challenge for interpreters and interpreter education. Not only is there potential for the successful transference of meaning between languages, there also may be language "interference" (again, issues of first- and second-language acquisition and difficulties keeping the contact languages separate). Interpreters, like the other bilinguals in an intensive language-contact situation, are faced with the challenge of keeping the contact languages separate (i.e., minimizing interference and maximizing transference).

The main shortcomings for educational interpreting have to do with the time and processing constraints imposed by simultaneous interpreting, inadequate first-language base among the participants due to language delay and education policy, and differences between signed- and spoken-language modalities (i.e., the signed medium is visual and cannot represent many sound-related literacy-learning practices). We as interpreter educators, researchers, and practitioners must be aware of these shortcomings, recognize their effects on the participants, and strive for the highest level of language access and equivalency. A strong language base in the contact languages, an awareness of contact signing, and the skill to assess and address the interpersonal communication needs of the participants are tantamount to successful interpretation.

NOTES

1. Clyne (2003, p. 3) reports that the field of language contact studies has evolved into four major areas of research: (1) grammatical aspects of code-switching (Jacobson, 1998, 2001); (2) processing models of bilinguals (De Groot & Kroll, 1997; Nicol, 2001); (3) code-switching in conversations (Auer, 1998); and (4) reversing language shift (Fishman, 2001).

2. Davis (1990b, p. 312) analyzed and described three strategic ways that interpreters represent English words or phrases in the visual modality during ASL interpreting: (1) pronounced mouthing of English words (without voicing) while simultaneously signing ASL; (2) prefacing or following an ASL sign with a fingerspelled word; and (3) marking or flagging a fingerspelled word or the signed representation of an English word or phrase with certain ASL lexical items—for example, the index marker, the demonstrative, quotation markers, etc.

3. A single term in English may convey multiple meanings, whereas ASL may require different signs for the different meanings, or vice versa. For the English word "call," for example, ASL requires different signs to convey different meanings (e.g., NAME, CALL-BY-PHONE, CALL-BY-TTY, TO SHOUT OUT, TO SUMMON, etc.) *Signing the term literally, instead of idiomatically, would be a form of interference.*

4. Here is another example of interference: The ASL verb GO-TO is reduplicated, and the interpreter voices "go, go, go," rather than the appropriate English translation—"to frequent."

5. The convention followed here is that "fingerspelled loan signs" are written in upper-case letters preceded by #.

6. These observations are based on this author's 25 years of faculty service in IPPs at various colleges and universities in the United States. Furthermore, the issue of bilingual proficiency is frequently discussed by interpreter educators in forums such as the Conference of Interpreter Trainers.

7. For more details, see degree requirements at the Registry of Interpreters for the Deaf, Inc.'s website (http://www.rid.org).

8. Sofinski and colleagues (2001) analyzed ten features of *sign-driven* transliteration (adapted from Winston, 1989): sentential rather than textual shadowing; the use of non-manual signals in lieu of consistent English mouthing (i.e., adverbials); listing techniques; use of token and surrogates;

classifier predicates; inflected verbs; ASL semantic-based signs; base/root lexical form; rhetorical questions; and phrasal restructuring.

9. See Fischer (1978) for discussion of sign language and Creolization.

REFERENCES

Akamatsu, C.T., Stewart, D.A., & Mayer, C. (2002). Is it time to look beyond teachers' signing behavior? *Sign Language Studies, 2* (3), 230–254.

Ann, J. (2001). Bilingualism and language contact. In C. Lucas (Ed.), *The sociolinguistics of sign language.* Cambridge: Cambridge University Press, pp. 33–60.

Auer, P. (1995). The pragmatics of code-switching. In L. Milroy and P. Muysken (Eds.), *One speaker, two languages. Cross cultural perspectives on code-switching.* Cambridge: Cambridge University Press, pp. 115–135.

Auer, P. (1998). Introduction: "bilingual conversation," revisited. In P. Auer (Ed.), *Code-switching in conversation. Language, interaction, and identity.* London & New York: Routledge, pp. 1–24.

Battison, R. (1978/2003). *Lexical borrowing in American Sign Language.* New ed. Burtonsville, MD: Linstock Press.

Bergman, B., & Wallin, L. (2001). A preliminary analysis of visual mouth segments in Swedish sign languages. In P. Boyes-Braem & R. Sutton-Spence (Eds.), *The hands are the head of the mouth: The mouth as articulator in sign languages.* Germany: Signum-Verlag, pp.51–68.

Bornstein, H. (1990). A manual communication overview. In H. Bornstein (Ed.), *Manual communication: Implications for education.* Washington, DC: Gallaudet University Press, pp. 21–44.

Boyes-Braem, P., & Sutton-Spence, R. (Eds.). (2001). *The hands are the head of the mouth: The mouth as articulator in sign languages.* Germany: Signum-Verlag.

Bridges, B., & Metzger, M. (1996). *DEAF TEND YOUR: Non-manual signs in American sign language.* Salem, OR: Sign Enhancers.

Campbell, S. (1998). *Translation into the second language.* New York: Addison Wesley Longman.

Clyne, M. (2003). *Dynamics of language contact.* Cambridge: Cambridge University Press.

Cokely, D. (1990). The effectiveness of three means of communication in the college classroom. *Sign Language Studies, 69,* 415–439.

Cokely, D. (1992). *Interpretation: A sociolinguistic model.* Burtonsville, MD: Sign Media.

Davis, J.E. (1989). Distinguishing language contact phenomena in ASL interpretation. In C. Lucas (Ed.), *The sociolinguistics of the deaf community.* New York: Academic Press, pp. 85–102.

Davis, J.E. (1990a). *Interpreting in a language-contact situation.* Unpublished doctoral dissertation, University of New Mexico, Albuquerque.

Davis, J.E. (1990b). Linguistic transference and interference: Interpreting between English and ASL. In C. Lucas (Ed.), *Sign language research: Theoretical issues.* Washington, DC: Gallaudet University Press, pp. 308–321.

Davis, J.E. (2000). Translation techniques in interpreter education. In C.B. Roy (Ed.), *Innovative practices for teaching sign language interpreters.* Washington, DC: Gallaudet University Press, pp. 109–131.

Davis, J.E. (2003). Cross-linguistic strategies used by interpreters. *Journal of Interpretation*, Silver Spring, MD: RID Publications, pp. 95–128.

Dean, R.K., & Pollard, R.Q. (2001). Application of demand-control theory to sign language interpreting: Implications for stress and interpreter training. *Journal of Deaf Studies and Deaf Education, 6* (1), 1–14.

De Groot, A.M.B., & Kroll, J.F. (Eds.). (1997). *Tutorials in bilingualism: Psycholinguistic perspectives*. Mahwah, NJ: Erlbaum.

Finegan, E. (2004). *Language: Its structure and use*, 4th ed. Boston: Wadsworth.

Fischer, S. (1978). Sign language and Creoles. In P. Siple (Ed.), *Understanding language through sign language research*. New York: Academic Press, pp. 309–331.

Fischer, S. (1998). Critical periods for language acquisition: Consequences for deaf education. In A. Weisel (Ed.), *Issues unresolved: New perspectives on language and deaf education*. Washington, DC: Gallaudet University Press, pp. 9–26.

Fishman, J.A. (Ed.). (2001). *Can threatened languages be saved?* Clevedon, UK: Multilingual Matters.

Fleetwood, E. (2000). Educational policy and signed language interpretation. In M. Metzger (Ed.), *Bilingualism and identity in deaf communities, the sociolinguistics of deaf communities series, vol. 6*. Washington, DC: Gallaudet University Press, pp. 161–186.

Foster, S. (1989). Life in the mainstream: reflections of deaf college freshmen on their experiences in the mainstreamed high school. *Journal of the Rehabilitation of the Deaf, 125*, 535–541.

Garretson, M.D. (1976). Committee report defining total communication. *Proceedings of the Forty-Eighth Meeting of the Conference of Executives of American Schools for the Deaf*, Rochester, NY.

Gee, J., & Goodhart, W. (1985). Nativization, linguistic theory, and deaf language acquisition. *Sign Language Studies, 49*, 291–342.

Gee, J.P., & Mounty, J. (1991). Nativization, variability, and style shifting in the sign language development of deaf children of hearing parents. In P. Siple & S. Fischer (Eds.), *Theoretical issues in sign language research: Vol. 2. Psychology*. Chicago: University of Chicago Press, pp. 65–83.

Grosjean, F. (1992). The bilingual and the bicultural person in the hearing and in the deaf world. *Sign Language Studies, 77*, 307–320.

Grosjean, F. (1996). Living with two languages and two cultures. In I. Parasnis (Ed.), *Cultural and language diversity and the deaf experience*. Cambridge: Cambridge University Press, pp. 20–37.

Gumperz, J.J. (1982). *Discourse strategies*. Cambridge: Cambridge University Press.

Harrington, F. (2000). Sign language interpreter and access for deaf students to university curricula: The ideal and the reality. In R. Roberts, S.A. Carr, D. Abraham, & A. Dufour (Eds.), *The critical link 2: Interpreters in the community*. Philadelphia: John Benjamins.

Jacobson, R. (Ed.). (1998). *Codeswitching worldwide*. New York: Mouton de Gruyter.

Jacobson, R. (Ed.). (2001). *Codeswitching worldwide 2*. Berlin: Mouton de Gruyter.

Johnson, K. (1991). Miscommunication in interpreted classroom interaction. *Sign Language Studies, 70*, 1–34.

Johnson, R.E., Liddell, S.D., & Erting, C.J. (1989). *Unlocking the curriculum: Principles for achieving access in deaf education* (Gallaudet Research Institute Working Paper, No. 89-3). Washington, DC: Gallaudet University Press.

Kachru, B.B. (1978). Code mixing as a communicative strategy in India. In J. Alatis (Ed.), *International dimensions of bilingual education*. Washington, DC: Georgetown University Press, pp. 107–124.

Kachru, B.B. (1992). *The other tongue: English across cultures*, 2nd ed. Chicago: University of Illinois Press.

Kelly, J.E. (2001). *Transliterating: Show me the English*. Alexandria, VA: RID Press.

La Bue, M.A. (1995). Language and learning in a deaf education classroom: practice and paradox. In C. Lucas (Ed.), *Sociolinguistics in deaf communities*. Washington, DC: Gallaudet University Press, pp. 164–220.

La Bue, M.A. (1998). *Interpreted education: A study of deaf students' access to the content and form of literacy instruction in a mainstreamed high school English class*. Unpublished doctoral dissertation, University of Harvard, Cambridge, MA.

Lillo-Martin, D. (1997). The modular effects of sign language acquisition. In M. Marschark, P. Siple, D. Lillo-Martin, R. Campbell, & V.S. Everhart (Eds.), *Relations of language and thought: The view from sign language and deaf children*. New York: Oxford University Press, pp. 62–109.

Livingston, S., Singer, B., & Abramson, T. (1994). A study to determine the effectiveness of two different kinds of interpreting. *Proceedings of the Tenth National Convention of the Conference of Interpreter Trainers—Mapping our Course: A Collaborative Venture*, CIT Publications, pp. 175–197.

Lucas, C. (2001). *The sociolinguistics of sign languages*. Cambridge: Cambridge University Press.

Lucas, C., & Valli, C. (1989). Language contact in the American deaf community. In C. Lucas (Ed.), *The sociolingustics of the deaf community*. New York: Academic Press, pp. 11–40.

Lucas, C., & Valli, C. (1990). ASL, English, and contact signing. In C. Lucas (Ed.), *Sign language research: Theoretical issues*. Washington, DC: Gallaudet University Press, pp. 288–307.

Lucas, C., & Valli, C. (1992). *Language contact in the American deaf community*. San Diego: Academic Press.

Marmor, G., & Petitto, L. (1979). Simultaneous communication in the classroom: how well is English represented? *Sign Language Studies, 23*, 99–136.

Marschark, M., LePoutre, D., & Bement, L. (1998). Mouth movement in signed communication. In R. Campbell & B. Dodd (Eds.). *Hearing by eye II: The psychology of speechreading and auditory-visual speech*. London: Taylor & Francis, pp. 243–264.

Marschark, M., & Spencer, P.E. (Eds.) (2003). *Oxford handbook of deaf studies, language, and education*. New York: Oxford University Press.

Mayer, C., & Akamatsu, C.T. (2003). Bilingualism and literacy. In M. Marschark & P.E. Spencer (Eds.), *Oxford handbook of deaf studies, language, and education*. New York: Oxford University Press, pp. 136–147.

Metzger, M. (1999). *Sign language interpreting: Deconstructing the myth of neutrality*. Washington, DC: Gallaudet University Press.

Miller, K.J. (2003). *Did I say that?: An MLF model approach to language choices made by interpreters of ASL and English.* Unpublished master's thesis, University of South Carolina.

Mougeon, R., Beniak, E., & Valois, D. (1985). *Issues in the study of language contact: Evidence from Ontarian French.* Toronto: Center for Franco-Ontarian Studies of Montreal.

Mulrooney, K.J. (2002). Turn-taking, fingerspelling, and contact in signed languages. In C. Lucas (Ed.), *Variation in ASL fingerspelling.* Washington, DC: Gallaudet University Press, pp. 3–23.

Muysken, P. (2000). *Bilingual speech.* Cambridge: Cambridge University Press.

Myers-Scotton, C. (1992). Comparing code switching and borrowing. *Journal of Multilingual and Multicultural Development, 13* 19–40.

Myers-Scotton, C. (1997). *Dueling languages: Grammatical structure in code-switching.* New York: Oxford University Press.

Myers-Scotton, C. (1998). A theoretical introduction to markedness model. In C. Myers-Scotton (Ed.), *Codes and consequences.* New York: Oxford University Press, pp. 18–38.

Myers-Scotton, C., & Jake, J.L. (1995). Matching lemmas in a bilingual language competence and production model: Evidence from intrasentential code-switching. *Linguistics, 33,* 981–1024.

Myers-Scotton, C., & Jake, J.L. (2000). Four types of morphemes: Evidence from aphasia, codeswitching and second language acquisition. *Linguistics, 38,* 53–100.

Napier, J. (2002a). *Sign language interpreting: Linguistic coping strategies.* Coleford, UK: Douglas McLean.

Napier, J. (2002b). University interpreting: Linguistic issues for consideration. *Journal of Deaf Studies and Deaf Education, 7*(4), 281–301.

Napier, J., & Adam, R. (2002). A comparative linguistic analysis of Auslan and BSL interpreting. *Deaf Worlds, 18*(1), 22–31.

Nicol, J. (Ed.). (2001). *One mind, two languages: Bilingual language processing.* Oxford: Blackwell.

Padden, C. (1991). The acquisition of fingerspelling in deaf children. In P. Siple & S.D. Fischer (Eds.), *Theoretical issues in sign language research: Vol. 2, psychology.* Chicago: University of Chicago Press, pp. 191–210.

Padden, C. (1998). The ASL lexicon. *Sign language and Linguistics 1,* 39–64.

Padden, C., & Gunsauls, D. (2003). How the alphabet came to be used in sign language. *Sign Language Studies, 4* (1), 11–33.

Poplack, S. (1980). "Sometimes I'll start a sentence in Spanish y TERMINO EN ESPANOL": toward a typology of code-switching. *Linguistics, 18,* 581–618.

Poplack, S., & Sankoff, D. (1988). A variationist approach to languages in contact. In U. Ammon, N. Dittmar, & K. Mattheier (Eds.), *Sociolinguistics.* Berlin: De Gruyter, pp. 1174–1180.

Poplack, S., Sankoff, D., & Miller, C. (1988). The social correlates and linguistic processes of lexical borrowing and assimilation. *Linguistics, 26,* 47–104.

Poplack, S., Wheeler, S., & Westwood, A. (1989). Distinguishing language contact phenomena: Evidence from Finnish-English bilingualism. In P. Lilius & M. Saari (Eds.), *The Nordic Languages and Modern Linguistics 6, Proceedings of the 6th International Conference,* Helsinki, pp. 33–56.

Quinto-Pozos, D. (2002). *Contact between Mexican sign language and American sign language in two Texas border areas.* Unpublished doctoral dissertation, University of Texas, Austin.

Ramsey, C.L. (1989). Language planning in deaf education. In C. Lucas (Ed.), *The sociolinguistics of the deaf community.* New York: Academic Press, pp. 123–146.

Ramsey, C.L. (1997). *Deaf children in public schools: Placement, context, and consequences.* Washington, DC: Gallaudet University Press.

Ramsey, C.L. (2000, August). *The true confessions of an ex-educational interpreter.* Paper presented at the meeting of the National Educational Interpreting Conference, Kansas City, MO.

Ramsey, C.L. (2004). Theoretical tools for educational interpreters. In E.A. Winston, (Ed.), *Interpreted education: Questions we should be asking.* Washington, DC: Gallaudet University Press.

Romaine, S. (1995). *Bilingualism.* Oxford: Blackwell Publishers.

Russell, D. (2002). *Interpreting in legal contexts: Simultaneous and consecutive interpretation.* Burtonsville, MD: Linstock Press.

Sankoff, D., & Poplack, S. (1981). A formal grammar for code-switching. *Papers in Linguistics 14,* 3–46.

Sankoff, D., Poplack, S., & Vanniarajan, S. (1986). *The case of nonce loan in Tamil.* Centre de researchers mathematiques. Technical Report 1348. University of Montreal.

Sankoff, D. (1998). A formal production-based explanation of the facts of code-switching. *Bilingualism: language and cognition, 1* (1), 39–50.

Schick, B. (2003). The development of American sign language and manually coded English systems. In M. Marschark, & P.E. Spencer, (Eds.), *Oxford handbook of deaf studies, language, and education.* New York: Oxford University Press, pp. 219–231.

Schick, B., & Moeller, M.P. (1992). What is learnable in manually coded English sign systems? *Applied Psycholinguistics, 13* (3), 313–340.

Seal, B.C. (2004). *Best practices in educational interpreting,* 2nd ed. Boston: Allyn & Bacon.

Selinker, L. (1992). *Rediscovering interlanguage.* New York: Longman.

Singleton, J.L., Supalla, S., Litchfield, S., & Schley, S. (1998). From sign to word: Considering modality constraints in ASL/English bilingual education. *Topics in Language Disorders, 18* (4), 16–29.

Siple, L.A. (1997). Historical development of the definition of transliteration. In M.L. McIntire & S. Wilcox (Eds.), *Journal of Interpretation,* Silver Spring, MD: RID Publications, pp. 77–100.

Sofinski, B.A. (2002). Turn-taking, fingerspelling, and contact in signed languages. In C. Lucas (Ed.), *So, why do I call this English?* Washington, DC: Gallaudet University Press, pp. 27–48.

Sofinski, B.A., Yesbeck, N.A., Gerhold, S.C., & Bach-Hansen, M.C. (2001). Features of voice-to-sign transliteration by educational interpreters. *Journal of Interpretation,* Silver Spring, MD: RID Publications, pp. 47–59.

Stewart, D., Akamatsu, C., & Bonkowski, N. (1988). Factors influencing simultaneous communication behaviors in teachers. *ACEHI Journal, 14* (2), 43–58.

Stinson, M.S. & Lang, H.G. (1994). Full inclusion: A parth for integration or isolation? *American Annals of the Deaf, 139* (2), 156–159.

Stokoe, W. (1960). *Sign language structure: An outline of the visual communication system of the American deaf* (Rev. ed.). Silver Spring, MD: Linstock Press.

Supalla, S. (1991). Manually coded English: The modality question in signed language development. In P. Siple & S.D. Fischer (Eds.), *Theoretical issues in sign language research*. Chicago: University of Chicago Press, pp. 85–109.

Supalla, S., Wix, T., & McKee, C. (2001). Print as a primary source of English for deaf learners. In J. Nichol & T. Langendoen (Eds.), *One mind, two languages: Bilingual language processing*. Malden, MA: Blackwell.

Valli, C., & Lucas, C. (2000). *Linguistics of American sign language*. Washington, DC: Gallaudet University Press.

Viera, J.A. (2000). Transliteration: The consumer's perspective. In D. Watson (Ed.), *Journal of Interpretation*, Silver Spring, MD: RID Publications, 83–98.

Wilbur, R.B. (2000). The use of ASL to support the development of English and literacy. *Journal of Deaf Studies and Deaf Education, 5*, 81–104.

Wilbur, R.B. (2003). Modality and the structure of language: sign language versus signed systems. In M. Marschark & P.E. Spencer (Eds.), *Oxford handbook of deaf studies, language, and education*. New York: Oxford University Press, pp. 332–346.

Wilbur, R.B., & Petersen, L. (1998). Modality interactions of speech and signing in simultaneous communication. *Journal of Speech, Language & Hearing Research, 41*, 200–212.

Winston, E.A. (1989). Transliteration: What's the message? In C. Lucas (Ed.), *The sociolingustics of the deaf community*. San Diego: Academic Press, pp. 147–164.

Winston, E.A. (1990). Mainstream interpreting: An analysis of the task. In L. Swabey (Ed.), *Proceedings of the Eighth National Convention, Conference of Interpreter Trainers 1990*. CIT Publication.

Winston, E.A. (1994). An interpreted education: Inclusion or exclusion. In R.C. Johnson & O.P. Cohen (Eds.), *Implications and complications for deaf students of the full inclusion movement*. Gallaudet Research Institute Occasional Paper 94-2. Washington, DC: Gallaudet University.

Winston, E.A. (2004). *Educational interpreting: How it can succeed*. Washington, DC: Gallaudet University Press.

Woll, B. (2001). The sign that dares to speak its name: Echo phonology in British sign language (BSL). In P. Boyes-Braem & R. Sutton-Spence (Eds.), *The hands are the head of the mouth: The mouth as articulator in sign languages*. Germany: Signum-Verlag, pp. 87–98.

Woodward, J.C. (1973). Some characteristics of Pidgin Sign English. *Sign Language Studies, 3*, 39–46.

6

The Research Gap: Getting Linguistic Information into the Right Hands—Implications for Deaf Education and Interpreting

Robert G. Lee

This chapter looks at issues surrounding the linguistic study of American Sign Language (ASL) and the possible implications for both the education of deaf students and the education of ASL-English interpreters. While there have been major strides in the understanding of ASL in the field of linguistics, much of this information has yet to make it to those whom it most affects—deaf people themselves. The lack of accurate information about the linguistics of ASL (and other signed languages) affects the language used by interpreters in the myriad settings in which they work, including educational settings with deaf students.

This chapter begins with an overview of ASL linguistic research to date. We then turn to look at recent findings that run counter to two common misconceptions about the nature of ASL and how such misconceptions can have a detrimental effect on the ability of deaf people (and interpreters) to acquire and use the language. Finally, we present some suggestions for addressing the stated problems.

It should be noted that while this chapter looks specifically at *American* Sign Language, the nature of the concerns addressed can be applied to all sign language communities.

MYTHS AND FACTS ABOUT ASL LINGUISTICS

Background on the Linguistic Study of ASL

The linguistic study of the signed languages of deaf people is a fairly recent enterprise. Systematic study from a linguistic perspective really only began in the 1960s (Stokoe, 1960; Stokoe, Casterline, & Croneberg, 1965). The initial thrust of early research was to provide evidence to the broader linguistic community that ASL in particular, and signed languages in general, were naturally occurring human languages with all the complexity of spoken languages. Later work in the areas of phonology, morphology, and syntax (see, for example, Baker-Shenk, 1983; Battison, 1974; Brentari, 1998; Cogen, 1977; Corina & Sandler, 1993; Klima & Bellugi, 1979; Liddell, 1977; Neidle, Kegl, MacLaughlin, Bahan & Lee, 2000; Padden, 1983) has uncovered both the underlying commonalities of signed and spoken languages as well as modality-specific differences. ASL is an underlying Subject-Verb-Object (SVO) language that is highly inflected and allows null subjects and objects.

ASL (and other signed languages) are governed by the same fundamental organizing principles as spoken languages. Research on ASL has been helpful in the broader understanding of languages in that some modality-specific differences in expression of linguistic features have helped to shed light on more universal linguistic questions such as the nature of syntactic features as well as the structure of questions (Neidle, Kegl, MacLaughlin, et al., 2000).

Another major focus of research has been the acquisition of ASL by deaf children (see, e.g., Braem, 1990; Goldin-Meadow & Mylander, 1983; Hoffmeister, 1978; Loew, 1984; Mayberry & Fischer, 1989; McIntire, 1977; Newport & Meier, 1986; Petitto, 1983; Singleton & Newport, 1987). Because only about 10% (or less)[1] of deaf people are born to deaf parents, many deaf people go through a different language acquisition process than their hearing peers. Lack of access to the limited pool of natively acquiring children (or large corpora of transcribed data as is available for spoken languages) has slowed progress in this area somewhat.

Recently, more and more hearing interpreters are learning ASL as adults, thereby compounding the variety of languages in and around the Deaf Community. To date, very little work has been done to examine the issues surrounding second-language learning of ASL by hearing adults (see, however, Quinto-Pozos, this volume). Two major factors complicate this situation: (1) as mentioned above, the understanding of how native signers use the language is still in its infancy, and (2) in addition to the large gaps in linguistic knowledge about ASL, many misconceptions about the structure of the language abound. (The latter will be discussed in detail in the following sections.)

Finally, a major obstacle to all work in ASL linguistics has been an inability to handle the data efficiently. Researchers working on spoken languages have the ability to use either the orthographic system of the language (if there is one) or the International Phonetic Alphabet to transcribe recorded data. Even the recording of sign language data is cumbersome; video recorders are becoming smaller and easier to transport, but they can still be more intrusive than an audio tape recorder. In addition, no standardized transcription analogues exist yet for signed languages. The lack of such tools has hampered the field's ability to standardize the representations of data[2] as well as make corpora of signing available. Recent advances in digital technology should prove beneficial to sign language researchers. The ability to capture, store, analyze, and search through data quickly will hopefully speed research.[3] An increase in both the speed of research as well as quality of findings can have a direct impact on knowledge and language practices of interpreters, especially in educational settings. It is also conceivable that tools developed by linguistic researchers could be modified for use by deaf students (and interpreters) in the analysis of their own language.

Recent Findings versus Previous Beliefs about ASL

Even with ongoing research work on the grammar of ASL, some characterizations of the language, based on older analyses, still abound. It is vital that interpreters and other professionals working with deaf people have accurate, up-to-date information about the structure of the language.

This section presents recent findings that are counter to some commonly held beliefs about the grammar of ASL. Interestingly, the two misconceptions described herein are often used to show the *differences* between ASL and English. While contrastive analysis is helpful in assisting in the learning of languages, it is only beneficial when the statements about the languages are true. Since a major goal of education is the achievement of language competence, accurate information about the current state of knowledge of ASL and other signed languages is vital for deaf students, teachers of the deaf, and interpreters in educational settings.

The following discussion looks at two areas of the grammar of ASL: the expression of grammatical tense and the existence of determiners (equivalent to the English words "the," "a," and "an"). In both cases, these are areas of the grammar that have been claimed to be different from forms in spoken English. The data presented show that ASL does indeed have these forms, and the understanding of how they are expressed can be beneficial to interpreters as well as teachers of the deaf.

ASL Lacks Grammatical Tense

Languages can differ in how they express the notion of tense; that is, the expression of the time of an event. Some languages mark tense morphologically on the verb (like German and the English past tense *-ed*). Other languages make use of lexical tense markers; that is, individual words occurring in a position after the subject and before the verb (like the English *will* in "John will go home tomorrow"). Other languages (like Chinese) lack a grammatical expression of tense altogether, using instead temporal adverbs.

One common misconception is that ASL (like Chinese) lacks *grammatical* tense markers (Fischer & Gough, 1978; Friedman, 1975; Padden, 1983; Perlmutter, 1991), and that only temporal adverbs are used to mark time distinctions in the language. Recent work (Neidle et al., 2000) has shown that there are indeed lexical tense markers that occur in the expected position in the clause.[4] One possible reason for this misconception about ASL is that the forms of some of the tense markers are similar in articulation to temporal adverbs (and indeed may have been derived from adverbial forms). However, tense markers and temporal adverbs can be distinguished by their distribution (i.e., where they can and cannot occur in a sentence) and their articulation.

For example, the future tense marker in ASL (glossed as FUTURE$_{TNS}$ in the following examples) is articulated with the dominant hand open, with a flat handshape moving from over the shoulder to a position out in front of the signer. This tense marker occurs after the subject and before negation (if it is present).[5]

(1) JOHN FUTURE$_{TNS}$ BUY HOUSE

'John will buy a house.'

$$\overline{\phantom{\text{JOHN FUTURE NOT BUY}}}^{\text{Neg}}$$
(2) JOHN FUTURE$_{TNS}$ $\overline{\text{NOT BUY HOUSE}}$

'John will not buy a house.'

Other orderings are ungrammatical:

(3) * JOHN BUY FUTURE$_{TNS}$ HOUSE

(4) * JOHN NOT FUTURE$_{TNS}$ BUY HOUSE

A sentence can contain a temporal adverb with a similar articulation; however, this occurs at the beginning of the clause.

(5) FUTURE$_{ADV}$ JOHN BUY HOUSE

'John will buy a house in the near future.'

Note that the articulation of the adverbial can be modified to express greater or nearer distances in time; such modifications include an additional non-manual marking as well.[6] In (6), the FUTURE$_{ADV}$ sign is articulated with a short movement near the body; in contrast, in (7), the articulation is longer and slower.

$$\overline{\phantom{\text{FUTURE}}}^{\text{cs}}$$
(6) $\overline{\text{FUTURE}}$ $_{ADV}$ JOHN BUY HOUSE

'John will buy a house in the near future.'

(7) $\overline{\text{FUTURE}}^{\text{bl}}_{\text{ADV}}$ JOHN BUY HOUSE

'John will buy a house much later in the future.'

A sentence can contain both a temporal adverb and a lexical tense marker.

(8) $\text{FUTURE}_{\text{ADV}}$ JOHN $\text{FUTURE}_{\text{TNS}}$ BUY HOUSE

'John will buy a house.'

Note that the sign $\text{FUTURE}_{\text{TNS}}$ (and other lexical tense markers that occur in this position) can never modify its articulation to express degree of time.

(9) * JOHN $\overline{\text{FUTURE}}^{\text{cs}}_{\text{TNS}}$ BUY HOUSE

Additional evidence for interpreting these items as lexical tense markers comes from the fact that they are in complementary distribution with modals.

(10) JOHN CAN BUY HOUSE

'John can buy a house.'

(11) JOHN $\overline{\text{CAN'T BUY HOUSE}}^{\text{Neg}}$

'John can't buy a house.'

(12) * JOHN $\text{FUTURE}_{\text{TNS}}$ CAN BUY HOUSE

(13) * JOHN CAN $\text{FUTURE}_{\text{TNS}}$ BUY HOUSE

The same facts about the allowable location and inability to modify their articulation applies to other tense markers as well (see Neidle et al., 2000, for details).

While the details of all possible manifestations of tense in ASL remain to be uncovered, it is clear that there are lexical tense markers located in the same position that they are found cross-linguistically. This knowledge can be very useful in helping deaf children understand parts of English structure through correlates found in ASL.

ASL Lacks Determiners

Another common myth about ASL (often brought up in contrast to English) is that there are no determiners in the language. Although Zimmer and Patschke (1990) noted the use of the index sign as functioning as a determiner, they looked broadly, not limiting the variety of functions of the index in ASL sentences. Recent work by MacLaughlin (1997) has shown that ASL does indeed have both a definite and an indefinite determiner. As with tense markers, part of the reason for claiming the lack of determiners may stem from the fact that the form of the definite determiner (an index, glossed here as IX_{DET}) is similar in articulation to other items in the language, including locative adverbials (IX_{ADV}) and pronouns (IX_{PRO}).[7] While indexes occur in a variety of places in a sentence, those occurring prenominally point to the location in space associated with the given noun, and such referents are interpreted as being definite. Indexes in other locations (e.g., postnominally) give information about the referent, but not about definiteness or indefiniteness.

(14) JOHN SEE BOB IX_{ADV}

'John sees Bob over there.'

(15) JOHN SEE [IX_{DET} MAN]

'John sees the man.'

(16) JOHN SEE [IX_{DET} MAN] IX_{ADV}

'John sees the man over there.'

When a sentence contains an index that points to a spatial location associated with a noun, but there is no articulation of a sign for the noun, it is interpreted as a pronoun (consistent with other claims in the literature, see note 7).

(17) JOHN SEE [IX_{DET} MAN]

'John sees the man.'

(18) JOHN SEE IX_{PRO}

'John sees him.'

As was seen with lexical tense markers and temporal adverbials, determiners and locative adverbials differ in the ability to modify their articulation. Determiners do not allow any modification of their articulation whereas adverbials do; compare the grammaticality of (19) with the ungrammaticality of (20).

$$\overset{cs}{}$$
(19) JOHN SEE [IX_{DET} MAN] $\overline{IX}$ ADV

'John sees the man right over there (nearby).'

$$\overset{cs}{}$$
(20) * JOHN SEE $\overline{IX}_{DET}$ MAN IX_{ADV}

While the (seeming) optionality of the definite determiner remains to be studied, it is clear that the prenominal index in the above examples functions as such. MacLaughlin (1997) also found that ASL has an *indefinite* determiner (not previously discussed in the literature and glossed as SOMETHING/ONE because the meaning is akin to the English "something" or "someone"). This sign, like the definite determiner, occurs prenominally. The sign is similar to the sign SOMETHING, articulated with an index finger pointing upward and moving with a circular movement. Interestingly, while the definite determiner is associated with a *point* in space (associated with the noun), the form of the indefinite determiner is associated with a *region* in space. The larger the "uncertainty" or "identifiabilty" of the referent, the larger the region of articulation of the sign. For very identifiable referents (e.g., from a closed class), there is a slight circular movement and a squinting of the eyes. For more unidentifiable referents, the circular area is larger and the eye aperture is wider. In addition, there is an associated non-manual marking that co-occurs with SOMETHING/ONE; it is marked primarily by an upward wandering eye gaze.

Context: A teacher leaves her classroom full of students for a few moments. When she returns, she sees that her text book is gone from her desk. She knows one of the students in the class must have taken it. She says:

(21) _____^{squint}

SOMETHING/ONE PERSON STEAL POSS-1p BOOK

'Someone (of you) stole my book.'

Context: A teacher leaves her empty classroom to go to lunch. When she returns, she sees that her text book is gone from her desk. Many people could have had access to the room, since it was unlocked. She says:

wandering gaze_____

(22) SOMETHING/ONE PERSON STEAL POSS-1p BOOK

'*Some*one stole my book.'

Note that in ASL, the distinction between the identifiabilty of the referent is marked non-manually as well as with a change in the articulation of the sign. In English (as represented in the translations), this distinction is marked with vocal prosody.

These same non-manual markings and articulatory changes are seen in verbs with indefinite objects. When a sign like GIVE is used with an indefinite object, the final articulation of the sign is spread, articulated toward a region rather than a point. In addition, the wandering eye gaze is present. Contrast the following (note that "a" and "b" refer to the locations in space associated with each noun):

(23) JOHN$_a$ $_a$GIVE$_b$ [IX$_{det}$ MAN]$_b$ BOOK

'John gave the man a book.'

In this example, the indirect object is definite; it has a definite determiner as well as being associated with a point in space.

wandering gaze

(24) JOHN$_a$ $_a$GIVE$_{indef}$ $\overline{[SOMETHING/ONE_{DET}}$ MAN] BOOK

'John gave some man a book.'

In this example, the indirect object is *in*definite; it has an indefinite
determiner as well as being associated with a wider region in space.
Note that if the direct object (in this case, BOOK) were indefinite, it
would occur with a prenominal indefinite determiner.

wandering gaze

(25) JOHN$_a$ $_a$GIVE $_b$ [IX$_{det}$ MAN] $_b$ $\overline{[SOMETHING/ONE_{DET}}$ BOOK]

'John gave the man some book.'

As with the definite determiner, when the indefinite determiner
occurs without a noun following, it is interpreted as a pronoun.

(26) JOHN SEE [SOMETHING/ONE $_{DET}$ MAN]

'John sees some man.'

(27) JOHN SEE SOMETHING/ONE $_{PRO}$

'John sees someone.'

In summary, contrary to former descriptions of the language, ASL has
a class of determiners, definite and indefinite. The facts about the distribution of the signs themselves, along with their associated non-manual
markings, point to a rather robust system of determiners in the language.

The previous section looked at two common misconceptions (based
on earlier analyses) about the nature of ASL as a language. There are
many "folk" linguistic explanations for different languages (including
spoken English), so why should there be concern for this in ASL? The
status of ASL as a minority language,[8] as well as the lack of stan-
dardization in the teaching of ASL, makes misconceptions about the
language particularly troubling. Because the myths involve both ASL
and English, they can have a negative effect on deaf people's learning
of English as well as hearing people's learning of ASL and, by exten-
sion, interpreters in the educational setting.

This problem is not unique to ASL and spoken English. Similar
problems exist in all areas where there is a little-studied sign language
with a majority spoken language. While research into many signed
languages is ongoing, it must be noted that misconceptions about the
nature of such languages reflects—often negatively—upon the deaf
people who use them.

IMPLICATIONS

Having accurate information about the language of instruction (or the language used by an interpreter) is vital to the correct transmission of information in all settings, including educational ones. Some implications about the effect of misconceptions are discussed in the next section.

The Problem of Discussing Language

The recent findings presented earlier recast our understanding of the grammar of ASL. Indeed, the structures mentioned (lexical tense markers and determiners) are attested to in English, but had not been attested to in ASL. In both cases, the items were something seemingly "missing" in the language.[9] While the attempt may be to be contrastive, that is, discussing something that exists in English but does not in ASL, the overall effect can be to make ASL appear to be inferior, both to those who are naïve about the language as well as to actual users of the language, deaf and hearing alike. While it is true that there are certain linguistic devices that exist in English but not in ASL, it may be more informative to contrast ASL with those languages with which it *shares* features.

In some ways, it seems, the prevailing opinion of ASL has shifted from "is not a true language like (the majority) spoken language— English" to "it is a true language, but it is deficient in X, something that English has." Older ideas about signed language not being true languages may have been replaced with inaccurate representations of how the languages actually function. When these types of negative misconceptions enter the classroom via interpreters, the impact on the generation of deaf students currently receiving mediated educations can be immense.

Let us look now at another specific example. One major difference between ASL and English is that English uses a copula verb ("to be") in sentences like "John is a doctor." I have found that I often will use this type of example to point out (to someone who knows little about ASL) the fact that ASL is indeed a different language. However, his statement, while true, can convey the idea that ASL is somehow inferior; as if it is lacking something that is central to a language like English. I have found it somewhat more helpful to express this key difference in a way that situates ASL among other languages, not just English. So for example, saying, "English has the verb 'to be' as in 'John is a doctor'; that is called a copula verb. Some languages do not make use of such a verb; for example, Russian, in the present tense doesn't use one; Hungarian doesn't use one for third-person subjects, and Maori and ASL do not have one at all." By comparing ASL with a broader range of languages, we can emphasize its commonality with other human languages. Another way of saying this is that English, because of the nature of its grammar, has to use *more* words (like a copula) in comparison to some other languages. In either case, it is important that we are able to situate signed languages among the many other languages with which they share features, not just the minority language with which it coexists.

Another way to lessen the potential negative impact of discussing signed versus spoken languages is, for example, to compare what features and devices ASL *has* that it shares with other languages, but not with English. One example would be the use of so-called *right-dislocated pronouns*. These are unstressed pronouns that occur at the end of a sentence and refer back to a previous noun phrase. The function of this construction is to keep a specific referent active in the discourse. This is a type of construction that does not occur at all in English (see the ungrammatical example [28]) but is very common in ASL, as well as French and Norwegian:

(28) *English*

      * John$_i$ left, him$_i$.

(29) ASL

      JOHN$_i$ LOVE MARY, IX$_i$
      'John loves Mary, *he*.'

(30) French

      Jean$_i$ est parti, lui$_i$
      'John left, *him*.'

(31) Norwegian

      Anton$_i$ har vært I Egypt, han$_i$
      'Anton has been to Egypt, *he*'
      (Fretheim, 1996)

Showing examples of constructions that exist in ASL but do not occur in English can help avoid the possibility of negative attitudes toward ASL. The way discussions about ASL (and other signed languages) are framed can have a huge impact on how the language is viewed by both signers and non-signers. In this case, it is *how* the information is being presented as opposed to *what* information is being presented. In addition, the use of such examples in the classroom can give deaf students a more positive view of their language, since it is not only being compared with the minority languages but with other languages of the world.

Further complications could come in the realm of educational interpreting. First, how an interpreter describes the language used by a deaf student to non-signing faculty and staff can have a significant effect on the opinions about and expectations of the student. In addition, if an interpreter is not equipped to accurately interpret the signed message of a student into the dominant spoken language, incorrect assumptions about the student's content-area knowledge as well as linguistic abilities could be inadvertently conveyed. Likewise, if the interpreter is not able to produce these features in signed interpretations, the student will not receive an accurate interpretation. Broad-based knowledge of the languages used in the classroom is crucial not only to what the interpreter does, but to the overall educational experience of the deaf student—from the ability to understand and express content knowledge, to attitudes about the signed and spoken languages of her environment.

Implications for Language Acquisition

In order to acquire a language, a child must be exposed to a variety of appropriate *accessible* linguistic stimuli over a period of time. Children generalize from the input they are provided with during the acquisition of their native language. If the input is impoverished (i.e., there are no exemplars of a variety of constructions), the output, the child's end state language, will be impoverished as well. If deaf children are not exposed to the full range of complex constructions in the naturally occurring sign language of the adult Deaf Community, there is a danger that their end state language will be deficient. Incorrect assumptions about what is "grammatical" in the language can affect what the child will ultimately be exposed to. It is vital that those who are the *de facto* language models in the child's educational environment (teachers, interpreters, and possibly other school staff) be able to use the range of constructions both at the child's level of understanding as well as to model more complex constructions as an adult user of the language.

In addition, because most deaf children do not have full-time access to native signers, the school environment is often the primary locus for accessible linguistic stimuli. In mainstream settings, this can mean that an interpreter serves as the *de facto* language model for deaf students. If an interpreter's language is lacking in the broad range of constructions in ASL, or if those misconceptions discussed previously are prevalent, the input that the child receives is severely limited. Also, an interpreter's assumptions about how a variety of constructions are expressed in the signed language can negatively impact how given utterances are interpreted in the classroom. Incorrect assumptions about similarities and differences between the signed language and the majority spoken language can affect both how classroom content is interpreted as well as a how the deaf student, the teacher, and interpreter understand each other.

The Problem of Metalinguistic Skills

In educational settings for deaf children, ASL is rarely the language of instruction or of interpreting, let alone a language of study in and of itself. For example, in the United States, while their hearing peers receive content-area instruction (e.g., math and social studies) in English as well as 12 years of classes in the study of English grammar, literature, and writing, deaf students rarely have classes in ASL discussing ASL. The lack of such instruction, grounded in the facts of the language, puts deaf students at a severe disadvantage in their ability to develop *meta*linguistic skills; that is, the ability to use language to think about and discuss language. In addition, the lack of structured classes in ASL for deaf students means that there is no venue for new discoveries about the language to be disseminated. Thus, deaf students do not grow up with an expectation that one's language is something to be discussed and thought about and expanded. The lack of development of metalinguistic skills could negatively impact a student's ability to think in abstract, higher-order ways.

Implications for Interpretation

As stated earlier, many interpreters are adult learners of ASL and are dependent on interpreter education programs (initially) as well as the Deaf Community for learning ASL. If interpreters are being presented with incorrect or inadequate information about the language they are learning, it is obvious that this will impact the language they end up using when they interpret. Also, if an interpreter is exposed to a deaf student (perhaps a native signer) using constructions that the interpreter has not been exposed to, there can be serious miscues in the interpretation based on a lack of understanding of the deaf student's language. For a case in point about the potential harm from a misunderstanding of the nature of tense in a legal situation, see Shepard-Kegl, Neidle, and Kegl (1995).[10]

The two myths discussed in this section—the lack of both grammatical tense and determiners in ASL—as well as the many others that abound, are extremely problematic. If an interpreter is unsure about the ways in which the language expresses such fundamental concepts as time and definiteness, other more nuanced areas could be lacking as well. It is terrible to think that language professionals could be working without a clear understanding of basic forms. As deaf people move more fully into areas of mainstream society and interpreters find themselves working in more challenging environments, the knowledge gap exemplified by these misconceptions could have more detrimental effects on the lives of deaf people and the hearing people with whom they interact.

SUMMARY AND CONCLUSIONS

The previous sections have discussed common myths about ASL from a linguistic point of view, as well as some implications for those misconceptions. Because recognition of sign languages as languages in their own right is fairly new, there is a need for not only continued study of these languages, but for the channeling of research results to the larger community.

Improved Dissemination of Research Results

While most research on ASL (and other signed languages) is reported in the linguistic literature, not much ends up in the hands of those who need it: educators, interpreters, and deaf people themselves. There is an obvious need for a connection between theoretical research programs, educational institutions, and those who work every day with deaf children and interpreters. The creation of videotaped materials, accessible to all who would benefit, could be a good way to both disseminate results and start discussions on a local level for professionals and students.

More inclusion of deaf people in the ranks of research teams will be enormously helpful in guiding research, as well as developing appropriate ways of discussing and disseminating this information. The use of knowledgeable deaf adults as language models and teachers in schools as well as interpreter education programs can help to increase the skill of all language users. In addition, the creation of venues for cross-linguistic discussion can help to shed more light on the structure and use of both ASL and English as well as broader discussion about the deaf consumer-interpreter relationship.

As mentioned earlier, technological barriers have hampered the ability to create large corpora of ASL data for distribution. It is hoped that more researchers will make use of digital media and the Internet for the sharing of research results as well as primary data. The use of the Internet as a method of dissemination can also address the problem of research results being limited solely to professional journals.

Improved Curricula

In order to aid in the development of the metalinguistic abilities of deaf children, formal courses in the structure of ASL need to be developed to enable students to discuss, analyze, and ponder their own language. The inclusion of a wide range of deaf adults can provide a broad range of language models for deaf students. The availability of such courses would have the added benefit of providing potential career models (e.g., ASL teacher, language researcher) for deaf students. Just as other bilingual children in schools can help researchers understand how children can natively acquire two different languages, these courses could be helpful in following the progression of deaf children's language acquisition.

Functionally speaking, interpreters are applied linguists; they make use of their linguistic knowledge to accomplish a task, that of interpretation. Just as language teachers need to be very familiar with the structures of the languages they teach (as well as, perhaps, something about the native language of their students), so should interpreters. To increase the skill and knowledge of interpreters, interpreter education programs need to include up-to-date information about the linguistic structure of both ASL *and* English. Because hearing interpreters are often asked about ASL by linguistically naïve hearing people, it is imperative that interpreters be armed with accurate up-to-date information about ASL. Having interpreter education programs partner with local programs for deaf children (in such classes as mentioned earlier) and other deaf professionals can help to bridge the gap between learners of both languages.

Currently Working Professionals

Last, it is not only students that need to understand linguistic facts about ASL. Currently working professional interpreters and educators need to keep abreast of any developments in the field of ASL linguistics. Certified interpreters in the United States are required to obtain Continuing Education Units to maintain their certification, however there is currently no requirement for the specific *types* of information, other than the broad categories of "General Studies" or "Professional Studies" Professional associations of deaf people, interpreters, and educators should take the lead in providing avenues for currently working professionals to obtain up-to-date information as well as disseminating guidelines about the areas practitioners need to know. In addition, those of us providing continuing education workshops for our peers need to stay as current as possible. By providing accurate, comprehensive, accessible information about the nature of signed languages to professionals working with deaf students, we can hope to see an increase in the quality of the education of deaf children.

NOTES

Much of the linguistic work reported here has come from the American Sign Language Linguistic Research Project based at Boston University (http://www.bu.edu/asllrp), directed by Carol Neidle. This research has been supported by grants from the National Science Foundation (Grants #IIS-0329009, #EIA-9809340, and #IIS-9912573). Data from many of the group's publications are available on the website as QuickTime movies. The author is grateful to the native signers who have helped to shed light on the nature of the human language faculty as it is expressed through sign languages.

1. While the number 10% has been received wisdom for many years, a recent study (Mitchell & Karchmer, 2004) suggests that the number may be less than 5%. In any case it is clear that the number of deaf children born to deaf parents is significantly lower than those born to hearing parents.

2. Indeed, examples presented in this chapter follow the standard, but problematic, representations of a visual language in a written form. Signs are glossed using the closest English approximation. Non-manual markings are shown only to illustrate the intended point, even though the examples contain much richer non-manual expressions. Some subscripts are use to indicate co-referential information (such as a noun and a pronoun) or parts of speech. Following linguistic convention, ungrammatical examples are preceded by a '*'.

3. The American Sign Language Linguistic Research Project at Boston University has developed a program for the transcription of sign language data. The program, called SignStream, allows for the creation of searchable databases of transcribed signing. In addition, researchers at University of California, Berkeley, are in the process of transcribing children's signing for integration with the CHILDES database, used for the study of acquisition of spoken languages.

4. Because it is, crosslinguistically, the location of lexical tense markers, the tense projection is assumed to be located after the surface subject and before negation and aspect. Word order facts support this prediction.

5. Note that some glosses contain information about the part of speech; thus, the future tense marker is marked with a TNS subscript and the future adverbial is marked with an ADV subscript. Also, a line indicates non-manual markings over the signs with which they co-occur.

6. The 'cs' non-manual marking expresses proximity in either time or space. It is articulated by bringing the cheek to the shoulder while articulating the lexical item being modified. The 'bl' non-manual marking consists of a puffing of the cheeks and a release of air through the lips. Both markings are coterminous with the individual signs they modify.

7. This is consistent with other work suggesting that pronouns are actually a form of determiner (e.g. Abney, 1987; Postal, 1969).

8. For a discussion of the commonalities among minority languages, see, for example Simpson (1981).

9. This has been described by the anthropologist Michael Agar as a possible response when one encounters a member of a different culture; that is, "the deficit theory." He says that people "notice all the things that the other person lacks when compared to you, the so-called deficit theory approach . . . the view that differences between self and others are signs of the other's deficiencies. Someone who isn't like me lacks something" (1994, p. 23). While a common reaction to both language and culture, it can be a barrier to fuller understanding.

10. This article was an analysis of the deposition of a deaf plaintiff showing that miscues in the interpretation—mostly related to tense—may have been related to a misunderstanding of tense in ASL by the interpreter. For example when asked a question like "Did you understand [at the time you signed the document] that . . . ?" the plaintiff was instead answering a question about his *current* state of knowledge. Obviously, in the educational setting, as well as

throughout the rest of a person's life, knowledge of speaking about the time of events is vital for interaction.

REFERENCES

Abney, S.P. (1987). *The English noun phrase in its sentential aspect.* Unpublished doctoral dissertation, MIT.

Agar, M. (1994). *Language shock.* New York: Morrow.

Baker-Shenk, C. (1983). *A micro-analysis of the nonmanual components of questions in American sign language.* Unpublished doctoral dissertation, University of California, Berkeley.

Battison, R. (1974). Phonological deletion in American sign language. *Sign Language Studies, 5,* 1–19.

Braem, P.B. (1990). Acquisition of handshape in American sign language: A preliminary analysis. In V. Volterra & C. J. Erting (Eds.), *From gesture to language in hearing and deaf children.* New York: Springer-Verlag, pp. 107–127.

Brentari, D. (1998). *A prosodic model of sign language phonology.* Cambridge, MA: MIT Press.

Cogen, C. (1977). On Three Aspects of Time Expression in ASL. In L. Friedman (Ed.), *On the other hand: New perspectives on American sign language.* New York: Academic Press, pp. 197–214.

Corina, D.P., & Sandler, W. (1993). On the nature of phonological structure in sign language. *Phonology, 10,* 165–207.

Fischer, S., & Gough, B. (1978). Verbs in American sign language. *Sign Language Studies, 18,* 17–48.

Fretheim, T. (1996, October). *Pragmatic functions of right dislocation—the Norwegian story.* Handout from a talk presented at Boston University.

Friedman, L.A. (1975). Space, time and person reference in ASL. *Language, 51,* 940–961.

Goldin-Meadow, S., & Mylander, C. (1983). Gestural communication in deaf children: Noneffect of parental input on language development. *Science, 221,* 372–374.

Hoffmeister, R.J. (1978). *The development of demonstrative pronouns, locatives, and personal pronouns in the acquisition of ASL by deaf children of deaf parents.* Unpublished doctoral dissertation, University of Minnesota.

Klima, E.S., & Bellugi, U. (1979). *The signs of language.* Cambridge, MA: Harvard University Press.

Liddell, S.K. (1977). *An investigation into the syntax of American sign language.* Unpublished doctoral dissertation, University of California, San Diego.

Loew, R.C. (1984). *Roles and reference in American sign language: A developmental perspective.* Unpublished doctoral dissertation, University of Minnesota.

MacLaughlin, D. (1997). *The structure of determiner phrases: Evidence from American sign language.* Unpublished doctoral dissertation, Boston University.

Mayberry, R., & Fischer, S. (1989). Looking through phonological shape to lexical meaning: The bottleneck of non-native sign language processing. *Memory and Cognition, 17* (6), 750–754.

McIntire, M.L. (1977). The acquisition of American sign language hand configurations. *Sign Language Studies, 16* (6), 247–266.

Mitchell, R.E., & Karchmer, M.A. (2004). Chasing the mythical ten percent: Parental hearing status of deaf and hard of hearing students in the United States. *Sign Language Studies, 4* (2).

Neidle, C., Kegl, J., MacLaughlin, D., Bahan, B., & Lee, R.G. (2000). *The syntax of American sign language: Functional categories and hierarchical structure.* Cambridge, MA: MIT Press.

Newport, E.L., & Meier, R.P. (1986). The acquisition of American sign language. In D.I. Slobin (Ed.), *The crosslinguistic study of language acquisition, vol. 1: Theoretical issues.* Hillsdale, NJ: Lawrence Erlbaum, pp. 881–938.

Padden, C.A. (1983). *Interaction of morphology and syntax in American sign language.* Unpublished doctoral dissertation, University of California, San Diego.

Perlmutter, D. (1991, March 28). The language of the deaf. *New York Review of Books,* 65–72.

Petitto, L. (1983). *From gesture to symbol: the acquisition of personal pronouns in American sign language.* Unpublished doctoral dissertation, Harvard University, Cambridge, MA.

Postal, P.M. (1969). On so-called "pronouns" in English. In D.A. Reibel & S.A. Schane (Eds.), *Modern studies in English: Readings in transformational grammar.* Englewood Cliffs, NJ: Prentice-Hall, pp. 201–224.

Shepard-Kegl, J., Neidle, C., & Kegl, J. (1995). Legal ramifications of an incorrect analysis of tense in ASL. *Journal of Interpretation, 7* (1), 53–70.

Simpson, J.M.Y. (1981). The challenge of minority languages. In E. Haugen, J.D. McClure, & D. Thomson (Eds.), *Minority languages today.* Edinburgh: Edinburgh University Press, pp. 235–241.

Singleton, J., & Newport, E. (1987). Constraints on learning: Studies in the acquisition of American sign language. *Papers and Reports on Child Language Development, 23,* 1–22.

Stokoe, W.C. (1960). Sign language structure: An outline of the visual communication systems of the American deaf. *Studies in Linguistics Occasional Papers,* vol. 8. Department of Anthropology and Linguistics, University of Buffalo. Buffalo, NY.

Stokoe, W.C., Casterline, D.C., & Croneberg, C.G. (1965). *A dictionary of American sign language on linguistic principles.* Silver Spring, MD: Linstok Press.

Zimmer, J., & Patschke, C. (1990). A class of determiners in ASL. In C. Lucas (Ed.), *Sign language research: Theoretical issues.* Washington, DC: Gallaudet University Press, pp. 201–210.

7

Factors that Influence the Acquisition of ASL for Interpreting Students

David Quinto-Pozos

In universities, colleges, and high schools throughout the United States, students are enrolling in American Sign Language (ASL) courses in record numbers. A Modern Language Association report of fall 2002 foreign language enrollments in higher education claims that ASL is the fifth most commonly studied language at colleges and universities in the United States and that there were more than 60,000 students enrolled in ASL courses during the semester for which the numbers were reported (Welles, 2004).[1] Additionally, between 1998 and 2002, 187 new ASL programs (or initial offerings of the language) were created in colleges and universities across the country to meet the growing demand. Some of those who enroll in ASL classes plan to use the language in a professional manner by becoming, for example, ASL/English Interpreters (Peterson, 1999), educators for the Deaf, social workers, speech-language therapists, or audiologists. There are also those students, according to Wilcox and Wilcox (2000, p. 133), who "take ASL specifically to make themselves better qualified or more employable in non-deafness-related careers." Some students take ASL because it fulfills a foreign language requirement, and still others take it because they are fascinated with visual characteristics of the language and want to learn it in order to communicate with deaf individuals who use it.[2]

As student enrollments continue to increase and the need for skilled language users becomes necessary (e.g., to enter into the professions mentioned earlier), it is incumbent upon educators to critically evaluate the success of the teaching methods that they employ. However, many people believe that classroom instruction may not be the optimal way to learn a language and that learning must also take place by using the language with members of the target language community (see Monikowski and Peterson, this volume). This approach to language acquisition, referred to here as community- and service-based learning, can be a complementary mechanism to classroom-based instruction—both seek to promote high levels of communicative competence for the student. Essentially, by improving classroom teaching methodologies, our programs could provide a vital component of fostering higher levels of proficiency for the students who are enrolled in ASL classes—especially those who are on an academic path to become interpreters for the Deaf.

ASL, like many other languages of the world, is not an easy language to master for the adult language learner. Jacobs (1996) has analyzed ASL as a Category 4 language for English-speakers, which means that learning it is similar to a native English speaker learning Chinese or Japanese. The "foreignness" of ASL makes it more difficult to learn than, perhaps, Spanish or French. Category 4 languages, according to Jacobs, require that the student commit approximately 1,320 hours of learning in order to reach a level where she is able to "satisfy most work requirements with language use that is often, but not always, acceptable and effective" (p. 213). Based on anecdotal accounts that have been reported to her by ASL and interpretation instructors, Jacobs suggests that it requires between 6 and 15 years, on average, for a student to become comfortably proficient in the language. If those anecdotal accounts are accurate, the expectation that interpreting students will possess the proficiency in the language after 4 years or less of classroom instruction to perform appropriately as interpreters should be re-examined. In spite of claims such as that articulated by Jacobs, we must continue to find ways to improve the language proficiency of our students by drawing on positive aspects of classroom language instruction as well as community-based exposure to the language.

Some parts of ASL grammar are more difficult than others for the adult language learner. One of the areas in which learners commonly experience difficulties is in their acquisition of what have frequently been termed "classifiers," but which I will refer to throughout this chapter as *polycomponential signs*, or PSs.[3] According to McKee and McKee, ASL instructors have noted that PSs in ASL are challenging for students and that even advanced students have trouble using such constructions effectively. For example, "one teacher notes that even students at the most advanced level (and also experienced interpreters) have serious deficiencies in using classifiers effectively in their expressive ASL, which he considers to be 'the heart of the language,' or at least a defining characteristic of fluency" (1992, p. 142).

McKee and McKee also report on the comments of another deaf instructor:

> Another teacher says that although he feels confident in his methods for teaching classifiers, students continue to find the acquisition of classifiers very problematic. "Students are still very reluctant to try using classifiers, even at the advanced level...They understand my demonstrations well, but when it comes to incorporating it into an overall story themselves, they just don't get it quite right—they pick the wrong classifier, or don't quite manipulate the movement appropriately, or don't know when to represent a person with a classifier or body movement." (p. 142)

Anecdotal accounts from instructors of ASL and interpretation frequently refer to similar struggles that students have with PSs, but those accounts also include reference to other communicative devices such as *referential shift* and *constructed action* as loci of difficulties for the student.[4] Like PSs, referential shift (hereafter RS) and constructed action (hereafter CA) are difficult to master for the ASL student. For these reasons, I will discuss the use of PSs, RS, and CA as ASL devices that should be focused upon in future second-language acquisition research and as content material in the design of ASL curricula.

PSs, RS, and CA are used frequently in ASL and other signed languages and are extremely valuable tools for the sign language interpreter. Turner (this volume) discusses the fact that interpreters should have a number of linguistic resources from which to choose for any specific purpose, and PSs/RS/CA are among those choices. They are particularly important when showing how a certain action is performed, and they are part of the communicative competence that a sign language interpreter should possess. If an interpreter cannot recognize or use PSs/RS/CA appropriately, then an interpretation can suffer greatly. Additionally, the degree of PS mastery has been claimed to be a predictor of English literacy in deaf adults (Anthony, 1999). Thus, the importance of PSs/RS/CA is evident for any signer of a natural sign language—regardless of the hearing status of the signer.

The difficulty of reaching a high level of proficiency in ASL—whether it be in PSs/RS/CA use or in a command of other parts of the grammar—has clear implications for the profession of sign language interpretation. Many interpreting students who graduate from interpreter training programs do not posses the language skills to perform effectively in some situations and with some clients. As an example, Schick, Williams, and Bolster (1999) assessed the linguistic skills of educational interpreters who work in public schools and found that, in general, the interpreters performed better on vocabulary assessment than on those areas that evaluated skills at a grammatical or discourse level. The authors suggest that "interpreters hear a spoken English word and then search in their mental dictionary for the sign that represents the spoken word. This produces an interpreted message that is often wrong or poorly expressed. These data provide verification that even a fairly substantial interpreter vocabulary does not predict the ability to produce grammatically correct discourse" (p. 151). PSs, RS, and CA are exactly the type of communicative devices that interact with the grammar of ASL and play an important role at the level of discourse.

Monikowski and Winston (2003) emphasize that exemplary skills in both ASL and English are important for students who are studying to become interpreters. The implication is that students should possess at least a certain level of proficiency in both languages before entering into an interpreter training program. While that approach is ideal (and happens to be the practice of many spoken-language interpreting programs), there are many programs that do not require an entry-level proficiency in the languages prior to beginning the study of interpretation. As Monikowski and Winston state, "The challenge remains of teaching students how to interpret when they do not have adequate language skills" (p. 356). The authors also comment on the fact that extensive research does not exist on the characteristics of the ASL skills of interpreting students.

One related issue worth noting is that interpreters frequently work with deaf consumers who may themselves be acquiring ASL—a situation common in educational interpreting. In such a situation, the deaf consumer might not have the language skills to produce (or, in some cases, comprehend) complex linguistic and communicative devices such as PSs, RS, or CA. It would appear that the interpreter, in these situations, functions as a language model—in some cases the *only* language model—whether or not she is even aware of the fact that she may be providing input to the student that would influence his language acquisition. In those instances, it becomes particularly important for interpreters to possess strong skills in the linguistic and communicative devices in question.

Because of the importance of solid language skills for the work in which signed language interpreting students will be engaged, I believe that it is our responsibility as a profession to encourage and support research-based models of language instruction. Most of what we know about the ways in which adults acquire a signed language (especially if they are raised using a spoken language) is anecdotal; it is time that we begin to address, in earnest, how research can inform our ASL pedagogy. In this chapter, I highlight some areas that, I believe, are particularly important to address at the present time—both in our language instruction and our research on the adult acquisition of ASL. As mentioned previously, I will focus upon PSs, RS, and CA for portions of this chapter.

THE ROLE OF VARIOUS FACTORS IN SECOND LANGUAGE ACQUISITION

Adult language learning and ultimate acquisition is claimed to be influenced by many factors,[5] including those that appear to be unchangeable by educators who wish to facilitate the language acquisition by a student. But, there also appear to be factors that the educator can control by developing specific methods for language use and interaction with the student as well as by determining what demands on student language use would most successfully encourage language learning and ultimate acquisition. While there are likely factors that are not considered here, an attempt has been made to focus on various topics that surface regularly in the literature on second language acquisition (SLA).

Factors That Appear Unchangeable

As humans we are born with various abilities, some of which are evident from birth (e.g., the ability to cry when hungry) and others that usually come to fruition within a given time span (e.g., the ability to crawl and eventually walk). Most (if not all) of these abilities are contingent upon our neural development, which plays a primary role in the development of language. Neural development and neural structures can be implicated in the various ways that adult language learners successfully acquire language structures but also in ways in which the same learners struggle with some language structures. This section highlights some factors that may play a large role in the acquisition of ASL by hearing adults.

The Role of the Native Language (L1)

One of the most common culprits accused of negatively influencing ASL acquisition is the native language of most hearing adult learners of ASL: namely, English. Instructors of ASL and interpretation frequently remind students that they seem to be "thinking in English and not in ASL" when they produce grammatical structures that mirror the words and word order of English but fail to take advantage of the use of space in ASL for expression of their propositions. Skilled use of the signing space may lead to sign-order structures that do not match the commonly used subject-verb-object order of English and the order of lexical items in other phrases (e.g., see Lee, this volume). As Schick, Williams, and Bolster (1999) mentioned, and as quoted earlier in this chapter, interpreters often attach ASL signs to English words without producing grammatically correct discourse in ASL. English can thus be seen as a barrier to correct ASL production.

The phenomenon described briefly here is frequently referred to as first language (L1) transfer, and there are many empirical studies that address a myriad of ways in which structures from a person's native language can influence second language learning and acquisition.[6] The types of errors that second language (L2) learners produce, the learning rates of L2 learners, and the particular path of learning that a student takes in learning a language are discussed in these studies. Other studies suggest that one's L1 is not the main factor that influences L2 acquisition, but the effect of L1 transfer can hardly be refuted.

One point to keep in mind is that not only does English differ in structure, in many ways, from ASL (see Lee, this volume, for specific examples of syntactic differences between English and ASL), but it is also produced and perceived in an entirely different modality (visual-gestural versus auditory-oral) than that of English. There remains much to be done in exploring the influence of acquiring a language in a modality that differs from one's native language modality.

Influence of a "Natural" Sequence of Acquisition: The L1 Acquisition by Native Signers

Another factor that has been implicated in adult L2 acquisition as influencing learning and acquisition is the common sequence in which a native user of a language acquires various structures in that language. The basic claim is as follows: The order of acquisition of various structures for the child who acquires the language natively may be the optimal sequence of structures to which an L2 learner should be exposed.[7]

A substantial amount of research has been conducted on deaf individuals' acquisition of ASL, and that research has addressed both native and non-native signers. Based on a recent examination of national statistics, Mitchell and Karchmer (2004) conclude that between 4% and 8% of deaf children have deaf or hard-of-hearing parents. We can imagine that many of these can be classified as native signers because they receive signed language input from their deaf caregivers. However, close to 92% or more of deaf children assumedly do not receive signed language stimuli early in their development, due to the fact that they are born to hearing parents who likely do not use ASL or another sign language; children from the latter group are often referred to as non-native signers.

Several authors have claimed that native signers acquire signed language following the same general milestones that hearing children follow in their acquisition of spoken languages that are comparable in structure (Meier, 1991; Newport & Meier 1985; Petitto, 2000). This is not only true for deaf children, but for hearing children who are raised in environments in which a natural signed language is among the language stimuli in the environment (Petitto, 2000).

The Acquisition of Polycomponential Signs. Research on PSs is limited, and only a handful of studies have explored ways in which they are acquired by deaf children. Unfortunately, there is little information about sequences of PS acquisition in non-native signers (either deaf or hearing). Three of the commonly cited studies that discuss data from deaf children of deaf parents who are acquiring ASL are Kantor (1980), Supalla (1982), and Schick (1987). Slobin and colleagues (2003) also provide examples of the production of PSs by children learning ASL and children learning Sign Language of the Netherlands (SLN). Unfortunately, the authors of these studies are not in total agreement about the sequence and relative ages of acquisition of various PSs.

One common theme through some of the works is that the mastery of PSs occurs quite late in development.[8] Schick (1987) presents data that suggest that even children ages 7;5 to 9;0[9] have difficulty producing correct (i.e., adult-like) forms at least 40% of the time. Kantor (1980) examined three PSs and claimed that the children in that study did not master those forms until they were 8 or 9 years old. Supalla (1982) also claimed that mastery of PSs requires several years, which was evidenced by some errors by the oldest subjects in his study.[10] However, Slobin and colleagues (2003) and Lindert (2003) claim that their data indicate that the acquisition of PSs occurs more quickly (and perhaps earlier) than what had been suggested previously. Nonetheless, it should be noted that Slobin and his colleagues also suggest that it takes many years to master the use of PSs in discourse—especially with the combined use of perspective shifts (or RS/CA). In this regard, the use of PSs and perspective shifting exemplify the use of discourse strategies that must be learned/acquired by L2 learners. Slobin and colleagues' claim is particularly important for interpreter training programs since the common practice, as mentioned earlier, is to provide 4 years or less of education (both in ASL and in interpretation) before graduation, and then the interpreting student is left to continue to build language skills on her own.

Another important question regarding PS acquisition is "What is the sequence of types of PSs that characterize native acquisition?" The response may depend on what aspect of the PS one is considering. Schick (1987) notes that "Entity" forms[11] (those that are used to represent an object or class of objects, such as a 3-handshape in ASL to designate a vehicle) generally appear to be the most difficult for children on measures of adult-like production and the correct use of space. However, she also notes that handshapes and movement morphemes in Entity forms are produced more accurately than in other PSs such as "Handle" forms (those that portray the action of handling/manipulating an object or the characteristics/shape of an object that is being handled/manipulated) and SASS forms (commonly referred to as size-and-shape specifiers used to describe the physical dimensions of an object). Schick seems to suggest that Entity forms can be phonologically more complex than Handle and SASS forms because, in Entity forms, the hands are often required to articulate two different nominals (perhaps two different handshapes and hand/arm movements that are not symmetrical with respect to each other).[12] Conversely, SASS and Handle two-handed forms frequently display the same handshapes and have symmetrical movements with respect to each other, which suggests that they may be easier to articulate. Slobin and colleagues claim that Handle forms (specifically Manipulative Handle forms) are acquired the earliest, but they suggest that it is because "they represent the movement of the hand(s) in manipulating an object that is referred to" (2003, p. 279). Based on anecdotal accounts from several ASL instructors, it seems that Entity forms are among the most difficult PSs for ASL students to master. Even though we have a few accounts of PS acquisition, a great deal of work remains to be done in this area.

The Acquisition of Referential Shift and Constructed Action.   As one deaf instructor claimed (McKee & McKee, 1992), students often do not know when to represent a person with PSs or "body movement." It is likely that the instructor was referring to either RS or CA or to a combination of both.[13] The use of CA also involves the frequent use of PSs— especially Handle forms. As with PS use, it would be useful to review studies of the acquisition of these devices by children.

A few studies have addressed the acquisition of these devices— some by deaf children of deaf parents and another by deaf children of hearing parents who are in the process of also learning a sign language. Emmorey and Reilly (1998) examined the acquisition of RS and CA in 15 deaf children who were in the process of acquiring ASL as a native language. They found that the use of direct quotations by the children in their study was mastered significantly earlier than the fluent use of CA. For instance, the 7-year-olds had completely mastered the use of RS for quotation, but they had not done so for CA. Reilly (2000) supported the earlier finding by claiming that, based on data from 28 deaf children acquiring ASL as their first language, children as young as 3 years old are able to include at least some direct quotations (i.e., elements of a RS) in their narratives. However, the mastery of manual and non-manual signals for direct quotations does not occur until years later—normally by age 6. Additionally, Slobin and colleagues (2003) reported that children at approximately age 5 have difficulty changing viewpoints, which means that they stay within a given fixed perspective. But, as they become older, they develop the skills necessary to shift in and out of various perspectives and to mark different points of view, which are "mark[s] of a competent signer" (p. 293), according to the authors.

What these findings indirectly suggest is that interpreting students may also struggle for years with these complex communicative devices that have been analyzed as discourse strategies by some authors

(Metzger & Bahan, 2001). According to Slobin and colleagues (2003, p. 291), "[p]erspective, or viewpoint, thus presents major challenges to the sign language learner." As is clear from the acquisition data, children take years to master these devices; the same is likely true for adults acquiring ASL. Further support for this claim is provided by Metzger (1995, p. 263), who notes that "[d]irect action [a type of CA] seems to be a relatively straightforward construction in ASL. However, though often labeled as mime-like, this type of construction is not generally easily mastered by second language learners, as one might expect, since mime-like gesturing is a genre accessible to all linguistic communities." The difficulty of acquiring these forms is irrefutable.

The use of PSs, RS, and CA as discourse strategies in ASL are particularly important for the sign language interpreter. Additionally, the use of these devices by interpreters has been reported in academic articles (see Frishberg, 2000, for a detailed account of one of the pioneers of interpreter education, Lou Fant, producing an interpreted message that includes the significant use of PSs and CA). Since competence in these devices is important to the sign language interpreter, questions about the adult acquisition of these devices must be investigated.

The Critical Period Hypothesis

Most linguists would not argue with the claim that a time span exists in a person's life in which it may be optimal to be exposed to a language in order to acquire it and posses the competence of a native or near-native user of that language. This time span was labeled as the *critical period* by Eric Lenneberg (1967).[14] Endpoints of that time span are an issue of constant debate, but many researchers would agree that the critical period, as it has been advanced in the literature, likely ends in a person's mid to late teens. From the idea of a critical period that influences language acquisition comes the Critical Period Hypothesis (CPH). Some authors (e.g., DeKeyser & Larson-Hall, in press) describe the CPH as the idea that language acquisition from mere exposure is severely limited in older adolescents and adults, which is not the case for children who acquire any natural language from mere exposure to it and interaction with its users. In their review of various studies, Dekeyser and Larson-Hall support the CPH concept by claiming that across many studies, there is a strong negative correlation between age of acquisition of a language and proficiency in that language. That is, as one becomes older, her ability to acquire a language implicitly, or without overt instruction, declines, which has implications for the ultimate attainment that one can reach in a language.

The CPH might seem to suggest that the majority of sign language interpreting students (i.e., those who begin to learn a sign language in their late teens or beyond) may never reach native-like competence in the sign language that they begin to learn as adults. However, one of the important things to remember is that Lenneberg's original claim, and that of other researchers working in this field, was that language attainment from *mere exposure* is limited after a certain age. Perhaps the case is somewhat different for language attainment from exposure in a principled fashion—the type that one might find in an ASL classroom. Also, keep in mind that the research that has been performed in this area mostly claims that a critical period exists, but there is little agreement as to how that critical period can be explained. In other words, it has been established, for the measures that have been used, that there is a strong negative correlation between age of acquisition and various measures of proficiency in a language, but explanations for such a concept are not as clear. Perhaps we might be able to find ways to mitigate the influence of purported critical-period effects on the second language learners of ASL.

Differential Cognitive Abilities of Children vis-à-vis Adults: The Less Is More Hypothesis

Another way to account for differences between native and non-native signers is to focus on the differential cognitive skills that infants, toddlers, and young children have in comparison with older children and adults. The basic claim is that adults learn language differently (and, perhaps, incompletely) because of the various cognitive processes that are occurring while they are learning a language (Cochran, McDonald, & Parault, 1999; Newport, 1988, 1990). This claim was advanced by Elissa Newport in a series of articles that compared the linguistic skills of L1 versus L2 learners and in a work in which she presented a mathematical model of this phenomenon (Goldowsky & Newport, 1993); the theory is known as the "less is more hypothesis."[15] This view that adults have superior cognitive skills to those of children and the implications for eventual language acquisition is of particular interest to adult second language learners of signed languages who aspire to become sign language interpreters.

Rather than provide a long-term advantage for learning an L2, Newport might claim that the superior cognitive skills of adults tend to create limitations to the attainment of native-like language skills in an L2. Children, because of their smaller processing capacity (e.g., memory and perhaps reasoning limitations), focus on and retain only portions of a linguistic string whereas adults learning an L2 attempt to focus on the entire string in order to understand the meaning of the utterance. The act of focusing on smaller linguistic units of the message (i.e., individual phonological and morphological components) may allow children to learn/acquire language more successfully than adults who learn the strings or words holistically and without the robust acquisition of individual linguistic units. As children mature and their cognitive capacities improve, they are able to produce more phonologically and morphologically complex forms, but these complex forms are buttressed by the robust acquisition of basic forms. Whereas the language production of adults learning an L2 may suggest that they are learning linguistic forms quickly at first, their ultimate mastery of the language is not as good as that of L1 learners. Thus, the theory is that there is an "advantage to getting off to a slow start for high final attainment" of language acquisition (Cochran, McDonald, & Parault 1999, p. 31).

The Influence of Aptitude

While aptitude does not appear to play a significant role in first language acquisition (i.e., most people acquire their native language completely regardless of other cognitive abilities that they may possess), it has been implicated in L2 learning by adults. For instance, DeKeyser and Larson-Hall (in press) suggest that verbally gifted adults are good at grasping certain abstract patterns of a language that can be made explicit through language teaching. Harley and Hart (1997) claim that success among adults who are learning a language depends strongly on aptitude—in comparison with children where success may depend more on memory. In essence, the late language learner must rely on aptitude a great deal more than a child who is learning her first language.

The claim of the role of aptitude in second language learning might suggest that our ASL students who possess the right type of analytical skills may indeed be successful in language learning and their eventual attainment of language competency. In fact, one interpretation of the Johnson and Newport (1989) findings, in light of a few high achievers in their study whose age of arrival in the United States was beyond the age of 20, is that adult (or late) language learners can perform well; perhaps those high performers were participants with high levels of aptitude. Of course, many would argue that aptitude is not only necessary for language learning but that it also figures prominently in the skill of interpretation, and our students should be of the highest caliber in order to meet the high demands of the interpreting task. The ugly truth is that some students may not possess the aptitude to succeed as L2 learners of ASL and achieve the skill of interpretation.

Differences Between Typical L1 and L2 Acquisition

Differences Between "Native Acquisition" and Adult Learning

There are a number of ways in which the adult learning of ASL differs from the native acquisition of ASL by a child. For example, Morford and Mayberry (2000) suggest that an advantage of early language exposure for the development of the phonological system prior to the development of the lexical-semantic and morphosyntactic systems is influenced by at least three factors: neural development, attention characteristics, and the type of language to which children—as opposed to adults—tend to be exposed. Two of these factors appear to be related to each other.

Regarding neural development, Morford and Mayberry claim that exposure to a language early in development will shape the neural connections that are being created in a child's brain.[16] The ways in which these connections are formed, according to the authors, influence the perceptual capacities of the child. We might assume that the authors are indirectly claiming that late language acquisition must differ, in part, from early acquisition because the neural connections of an adult have been established and such connections cannot be easily changed.

As far as attention characteristics are concerned, the basic claim is that children are attracted to the language production of adults because of certain prosodic qualities of the signal. However, the same may not necessarily be true for adults and the ways in which they attend to linguistic signals. Children may attend to parts of the linguistic signal that adults ignore, which will influence the overall acquisition of the language for children in comparison with adults.

In addition to children being attracted to certain qualities of a linguistic signal, Morford and Mayberry (2000) claim that there are advantages to the type of language to which children tend to be exposed. For instance, deaf parents will interact with their deaf children in very different ways than they interact with other deaf adults. An example of this is the register of *motherese*. Characteristics of motherese, or *child-directed signing*, have been identified for environments where signed language is used as the primary means of communication (Holzrichter & Meier, 2000; Masataka, 2000). Some characteristics of child-directed signing in an ASL home include slower sign speed, longer sign duration, and repetitiousness (Holzrichter & Meier, 2000). However, language production that can be characterized in this way is perhaps not only directed at deaf children. These characteristics (and others that differ from "typical" interaction between deaf adults) may very well be present in the signed language communication from a deaf individual to an adult learner of ASL.

Keeping in mind the points advanced by Morford and Mayberry, I suggest that an inventory can be made of purported differences between native language acquisition (i.e., child acquisition) and adult acquisition of signed languages. The list presented in table 7.1 includes the claims of Morford and Mayberry and others that are pertinent to the topic of L2 acquisition of a signed language by an adult.[17]

Differential Stages of Acquisition

We know that the linguistic development of infants begins with reception of language stimuli; children are not born with a capacity to

Table 7-1: Some Differences Between Native-User and Adult Language Acquisition of American Sign Language

1. Adults do not normally go through the various stages of language acquisition that children do.

2. The general cognitive abilities of a child differ from those of an adult.

3. Children's early exposure to the language is *quantitatively* different than an adult's early exposure to the language.

4. Children's early exposure to the language may be *qualitatively* different than an adult's early exposure to the language.

immediately produce linguistic messages. Based on research performed on hearing children who acquire a spoken language, we know that infants are sensitive to various aspects of an ambient auditory linguistic signal during their first year of life, and this period of development has been implicated in the ways in which children form the phonological inventory of their language (Kuhl & Meltzoff, 1997; Werker & Tees, 1999). Adult language learners, however, do not usually have this period of language development in which they only perceive the language rather than having to produce it as well. Morford and Mayberry (2000) believe this to be one of reasons that L2 learners fare worse, in the long run, than native learners: Adult learners have not had the critical time required in which perception of a language shapes the neural structure of that language for the learner.

In terms of language production, the vocal babbles of hearing children are believed to be very important precursors to the production of first words (Locke, 1980, 1983), whereas the manual babbles of signing infants are important for the production of first signs (Cormier, Mauk, & Repp, 1998; Meier & Willerman, 1995; Petitto & Marentette, 1991). Since adult learners of ASL do not normally go through periods of manual babbling in their acquisition of ASL, nor do we force them to imitate the manual babbles of children, it can be argued that they are deprived of a vital part of the development necessary to build a robust and native-like phonology of the language.[18] Using the claims given in Morford and Maryberry, it may be possible to suggest that adult learners do not acquire their language completely because they did not robustly acquire the phonology of the language prior to the development of the lexical-semantic and morpho-syntactic linguistic systems.

Quantitative Differences

The early exposure to language that a child learning her first language and an adult learning an L2 receive is substantially different, in terms of quantity of stimuli, in at least two ways: (1) infant learners attend to the language signal for a period of time before they begin to produce the language, and (2) adult learners of an L2 (especially those who learn it in an academic environment) are likely not exposed to the language for the same amount of time as children who learn it from their caregivers. As Morford and Mayberry (2000) suggest, the fact that an adult is not given the opportunity to develop a phonological system in the same way that a child is given that opportunity through repeated exposure to that system early on results in a higher level of mastery of the language by the children. An important point to keep in mind is that adults who learn a language academically do not have the frequency of exposure to that language than children who acquire it natively do. This fact likely influences the ultimate mastery that adult learners will achieve in the language. For this reason, service- and community-based learning should be explored in order to, among other things, provide the student with more exposure to the language.

Qualitative Differences

Deaf parents often interact with their deaf children in very different ways than they interact with other deaf adults. That interaction can be described both in terms of various aspects of the linguistic signal (the form of the signal) as well as the various types of statements and questions that are made by the language models to the learner (the meaning of the signal).

Adult learners of ASL may or may not be exposed to language models who produce ASL with the same characteristics of child-directed signing. However, we could imagine that some language models (either deaf or hearing) do use characteristics of child-directed signing when interacting with adult language learners. The degree to which this is done and whether or not it supports language acquisition is not known.

There are certainly other characteristics of adult (or language model) language use directed to the language learner that can be referred to as qualitative differences. Such differences can be described with reference to *what* is communicated, not *how* it is communicated. For instance, the degree to which a language model uses *negative feedback* (i.e., correction of ungrammatical or poorly formed utterances) likely differs between adult-child and adult-adult interaction. One of the primary mysteries of native language acquisition for a child is that she is usually not corrected by an adult (or mature language model) when producing an ungrammatical sentence, although correction does often occur if the truth-value of a child proposition is in question.[19] Despite the lack of negative feedback, a child manages to acquire the rules of a language, including all of the exceptions to the rules, without much difficulty. In a language learning environment for an adult (such as an ASL classroom or the Deaf Club), however, language models frequently do provide negative feedback to the learner. Whether or not the adult learner is able to incorporate such feedback effectively is another question for research. The point is that adult-child and adult-adult language use likely differs in terms of these qualitative differences.

Social-Psychological Factors

Dekeyser and Larson-Hall (in press) suggest that a number of variables that they term social-psychological can be predictors to success in a second language—especially in naturalistic contexts. The factors that they mention include integrative motivation, risk taking, self-consciousness, attitudes toward the L2 community, and identification with the L2 culture. *Integrative motivation,* or the desire to acquire the language and social customs of the community that uses that target language, has been implicated strongly in successful acquisition of an L2 for spoken languages (see Masgoret & Gardner, 2003) and also for the acquisition of ASL (Lang et al., 1996 a and b).

With regard to ASL, Lang and colleagues (1996a) presented faculty and staff at a large post-secondary program for deaf students with a questionnaire designed to obtain information about the participants' motivation to learn ASL, cultural attitudes toward deafness, and medical attitudes towards deafness. Their results indicate that there is a positive correlation between integrative motivation and sign language proficiency for the adult learners of ASL who participated in the survey, and there is also a positive correlation between a positive cultural attitude toward deaf people and proficiency. There was also a strong positive correlation between integrative motivation and cultural attitudes. All of this suggests that there is a clear relationship between possessing integrative motivation to learn ASL, having a positive attitude toward deaf people and the Deaf community, and one's proficiency level in ASL. Since Lang and his colleagues focused on faculty and staff whose need to learn ASL is intricately tied to their employment, their results may differ from what students in a typical post-secondary environment would have to say about integrative motivation and cultural attitudes toward deaf people and the Deaf community. Peterson (1999) explored questions of student motivation in the learning of ASL and found that nearly 75% of his participants ($n = 1,086$ who responded to that question) either agreed or strongly agreed that they would like to learn sign in order to get to know deaf people better. Investigations of the role of motivation in ASL learning can prove to be quite informative.

DeKeyser and Larson-Hall (in press) also suggest that risk taking and self-consciousness play a role in language learning. One could imagine that those students who are risk takers may be more willing to place themselves in situations where they have to interact with deaf individuals—an action that if performed often, most would argue, fosters language learning and acquisition. Even in the classroom, there is a need to take a risk at times—especially if one is unsure about her language production or comprehension. The risk sometimes results in frustration since a language form may not be produced correctly or may not be understood by the instructor or fellow students; this can lead to a self-consciousness that may affect subsequent language learning. There are also cases of students being ridiculed unnecessarily for the incorrect production or non-comprehension of ASL. Some students may be able to take their frustration and transform it into the fuel for further language learning, while others remain self conscious to the degree that their future language learning may be hampered. These themes, of course, are intricately related to the idea of motivation. As many researchers have noted, these are issues that must be addressed when considering the adult learning of language since they can have a significant effect on the outcomes.

General Factors that Appear to Be Within Our Control

As opposed to any of the purportedly unchangeable factors, or factors that are at least difficult to change, that play a role in L2 acquisition by adults discussed in this chapter, there are ways in which it seems possible to positively influence the language acquisition of an adult L2 learner. Those ways are intricately tied to the language input that the learner receives, the type of language production that the learner is expected to produce, and teaching strategies that are designed, in theory, to facilitate language acquisition for the learner. It is here that we must consider the factors discussed earlier and how the claims that have been made shape the way in which instructors and students interact in the classroom—both in casual conversation and in focused language learning activities.

The Role of Input and Interaction

The following question has puzzled researchers and instructors alike and continues to be a source of great debate: What type of language directed at the language learner (i.e., input) is optimal for language learning? Put more simply, how should a skilled language user (e.g., instructor, teaching assistant, language lab tutor, etc.) produce language that will make language learning the most efficient for the adult L2 learner? A related question is: What type of output should a language learner—especially at the initial stages of language learning—be encouraged to produce?

If we consider PSs in the context of what type of input and interaction is optimal, there are several questions that can be considered. For instance, would it be optimal for beginning ASL students to be exposed to the polycomponential forms that tend to be acquired early by native signers and then move on to the more difficult ones after a period of time? If so, how could that be done in the context of inter-action with the student? Also, what method would one use to provide input to the student that would be optimal for the learning and eventual acquisition of the parts of PSs (rather than having the learner focus on the holistic message and missing the parts), and would it be best to present the student with forms that could be analyzed with the least amount of effort? Exploration of these questions could lead to more usable input forms for the language learner.

The Role of Various Strategies for Instruction

The goals of language instruction may be varied in nature. One goal would be the student's attainment of native-like language skills. While this may or may not even be possible, the question of language instruction goals is an important one for language programs that are training stu-dents to be interpreters. In spoken language interpretation, high stan-dards of language fluency are the norm, and some interpreting programs will simply not admit students who do not already posses native or near native fluency in both languages. As we know, this has not been the paradigm for the training of sign language interpreters. Despite this, our interpreter education programs have succeeded at being the foundations for many qualified (and, in some cases, stellar) interpreters over the years. Yet, if we hope to improve the skill levels of our interpreters as they complete our programs, we must continuously improve our language instruction and set high goals for our students. As Doughty and Williams (1998, p. 202) put it, "[e]ven if a learner's eventual language attainment falls short of native speaker status, there is still much work to be done along the way to largely fluent and accurate target language use."

Two seemingly competing philosophies of second language learning/ acquisition revolve around the following question: Which is more ef-fective in language learning: explicit learning or implicit learning? Ac-cording to Ellis,

> Implicit learning is acquisition of knowledge about the underlying structure of a complex stimulus environment by a process which takes place naturally, simply and without conscious operations. Explicit learning is a more conscious operation where the individual makes and tests hypotheses in a search for structure. Knowledge attainment can thus take place implicitly (a nonconscious and automatic abstrac-tion of the structural nature of the material arrived at from experience of instances), explicitly through selective learning (the learner search-ing for information and building then testing hypotheses), or because we can communicate using language, explicitly via given rules (assimilation of a rule following explicit instruction). (1994, pp. 1–2)

According to Doughty and Williams (1998), rules of a grammar of a language can, for example, be made explicit by the instructor (or language model) in several ways: an instructor can plan drills and exercises to focus on a specific rule(s) or type of construction in the language (commonly referred to as *proactive focus on form*), attempt to focus on a particular rule or type of construction when a learner's need is presented (commonly referred to as *reactive focus on form*), or correct a student each time she makes a mistake in production—without any focus on a particular rule or type of construction. Some strategies of explicit language learning are in accord with current techniques of language instruction that are used widely, such as Communicative Language Teaching (e.g., see Terrell, 1991).

In opposition to an *explicitness* view would be the idea that the most effective way for students to learn language is to be presented with various types of *comprehensible input*, or language input that is at the learner's level or slightly above that level; this is the *implicitness* view of language learning. Examples of an instructor engaging in activities that would include high degrees of comprehensible input include the following: an instructor can share narratives with the students, have the students engage in comprehension activities (either of a live language model or of a video of a signer), or have students involved in conversation activities (although this might trigger explicit language learning as well). This philosophy is consonant with the Natural Approach (also known as the Natural Method or the Direct Approach) of language instruction. Krashen (1994) claims that focus on comprehensible input is more effective than focus on strategies for learning language explicitly.

Current teaching methodologies for ASL likely contain activities and strategies that encourage both explicit and implicit language learning. A question that we should address is "What combination of explicit and implicit learning is most effective for our language learners?" Of course, the response may depend on the skill level a language learner has achieved. For instance, novice learners of ASL may benefit more from strategies that encourage explicit language learning, whereas intermediate and advanced learners may fare better with strategies that foster implicit language learning. Purely implicit learning has been implicated in the underproduction of some grammatical morphemes (e.g., the use of third-person singular [s] as a verb conjugation for English by immigrants to the United States who have not engaged in formal study of English). However, mostly explicit learning—such as classroom instruction with little Community interaction—might cause a learner to oversupply some grammatical morphemes (e.g., the use of the subjunctive mood vowel alternations for Spanish). It seems that a balance of both implicit and explicit language learning may be ideal. Implicit language learning, some would argue, is the type of learning that is achieved when a learner involves herself in community activities such as service- or Community-based learning or other types of activities in which the learner interacts with members of the target language and culture regularly.

The decision to utilize implicit or explicit techniques in the classroom may also be dependent on the particular rule or part of the grammar that is being emphasized. For example, some rules are perhaps more easily learned than others. Basic word order is one example of a part of grammar that seems to be learned easily (Doughty & Williams, 1998) and one that even late learners of ASL seem to master (Newport, 1990). Alternatively, morphology is a part of the grammar of ASL that is not mastered by late learners (Newport), which is particularly significant for the discussion of PSs, RS, and CA in this chapter. We might expect that, based on the complexity of PSs/RS/CA, our language instruction should employ at least some strategies for explicit language learning. But perhaps implicit language learning is also effective, and we must devise ways in which to allow students to unconsciously acquire the morphological rules that govern PSs in conjunction with CA. These are questions that can be tested informally in the classroom and also by means of more formal investigations.

IMPLICATIONS FOR OUR RESEARCH AND INSTRUCTION

As noted earlier, one of the main areas in which students of ASL and interpretation struggle is in the use of PSs, RS, and CA. It is thus our charge to develop teaching methodologies that would improve our students' success in these areas. One of the goals of our profession should be to foster the development of robust language skills for our students. As one can imagine, there are many possible directions for future research on the adult acquisition of ASL (or any signed language). Based on the research that I have briefly summarized in this chapter and the headings under which the various types of research have been categorized, I propose four primary areas of such research on the adult acquisition of a sign language:

1. Experimental and classroom studies investigating the role of factors that appear to be unchangeable.
2. Experimental and classroom studies investigating instructional strategies that attempt to mitigate the apparent differences between typical L1 and the adult acquisition of an L2.
3. Studies investigating the role of social-psychological factors.
4. Experimental and classroom studies investigating the role of input, interaction, and various strategies for instruction.

One characteristic common to these four research areas is the type of investigations that should take place: We need to examine how our language teaching methodologies affect short-term outcomes, but, more important, we need to learn how they affect later language development and eventual levels of proficiency in the language. Essentially, we must begin to perform longitudinal studies in addition to those that provide us with synchronic data.

Since it has been implicated regularly, future studies must address the role of one's first language in the adult learning of ASL, which happens to be English in the case of most interpreters in the United States. Empirical research may suggest that there are ways in which English affects the learning and acquisition of ASL, but there may also be ways in which we might be able to take what seems to be an unalterable factor and create strategies that mitigate its negative influence on acquisition.

If we were to draw on the literature of typical L1 acquisition of PSs, RS, and CA, we could explore the orders in which L2 learners most effectively acquire such communicative devices. Research of that nature could inform our ASL curricula as we continue to refine the order in which new material is presented to students. In the meantime, perhaps using previous studies as a guide can help us to design our current curricula. As reported earlier with regard to PSs, some children tend to produce Handle forms before Entity forms. Thus, having a progression that begins with Handle forms, moves on to SASS forms, and then completes PSs with Entity forms (i.e., those forms that have been reported to be difficult for children acquiring ASL) may be optimal to other sequences. Activities that focus on how different Entity PSs interact with each other in the sign space would likely come next. Finally, the instructor should include stimuli that would encourage the use of RS and CA along with the production (either sequential or simultaneous) of PSs. Slobin and colleagues (2003) believe that bringing these different discourse strategies together is quite difficult for a learner to master, and a high level of proficiency with these forms requires several years. As with young students acquiring the language, these strategies would be for the novice learner of ASL. Intermediate stages may call for different strategies that encourage more implicit learning of the language—such as community- and service-based learning activities.

As mentioned previously, aptitude seems to play a role in SLA for the adult learner. However, there are also high-aptitude students who struggle with L2 acquisition; this raises interesting questions and issues regarding the role of aptitude in second language learning—questions that should be explored. For instance, is acquiring a signed language as a hearing adult different from acquiring a second spoken language, and what role does aptitude play? Are there people who, based on their cognitive skills, can acquire signed languages more easily than spoken languages? Are there people who, based on their cognitive skills, experience more difficulty in acquiring signed languages as opposed to spoken languages? Do deaf individuals find it easier to acquire a signed language as adults? If so, why? For instance, does the ability to hear (and easily switch into spoken language mode) hamper the language acquisition process for hearing individuals versus deaf individuals? These are but a few of the questions that can be addressed in this area of inquiry.

Regarding the influence of cognitive skills on language acquisition, one path of future research could be continued investigation of the "less is more" hypothesis (Goldowsky & Newport, 1993; Newport 1988, 1990) as it would apply to adult learners of ASL. If the hypothesis holds true, this line of research could be very instrumental in the development of robust methodologies for teaching ASL. As has been a theme of this chapter, we particularly need work that addresses the adult acquisition of PSs, RS, and CA. In particular, experimental and classroom-based studies could examine a variety of factors that may influence language learning and acquisition using the "less is more" hypothesis for curricula development. For instance, one method of language instruction that subscribes to the "less is more" hypothesis may attempt to expose adult learners to small units of language structure, thereby avoiding the necessity to focus on larger units that could cause them to purportedly learn things holistically rather than in smaller pieces.[20] One challenge of such an approach is how to make the stimuli as natural as possible in order to avoid the pitfalls of older language instruction methods that focused on language drills and exercises (see Krashen, 1994, for a discussion of the comparative success of strategies that do not emphasize grammar exercises and drills). Another factor that must be kept in mind is that an instructor may not see evidence of the benefits of such a strategy at first. Cochran, McDonald, and Parault (1999, p. 55) suggest that, by following such an approach, "adults would be trading in initial rapid learning for the long-term mastery of internal structure." Despite the slower initial process of learning, our students may benefit in the long run. Another factor to consider is that adult learners may find such instructional techniques boring and difficult to focus on. Nevertheless, research in this area could potentially provide clues to whether or not such an approach is successful and practical from various viewpoints.

Another area of future inquiry could examine differences between typical L1 and the adult L2 acquisition of language. For instance, it may be the case that instructional strategies for mitigating such differences might prove to be fruitful for L2 learners. As mentioned earlier, however, one issue to keep in mind is the need to create language stimuli that are as natural as possible—if indeed naturalness is determined to be a criterion for successful L2 acquisition for an adult. It may be the case that adults would benefit from certain methods of instruction, despite the fact that those methods would create highly unnatural language use, since the learning mechanisms for the adult learner and the child acquiring an L1 may be shown to be different.

As an example of investigating differences between typical L1 and the adult L2 acquisition of a language, teaching methodologies that focus on providing certain amounts of sign language production with characteristics of child-directed signing could prove to be a very beneficial area for research. As was claimed previously, exposure to a second language after a certain age differs qualitatively from exposure to a first language from birth. If that is true, what would happen if, for a period of time, the second language stimuli would resemble typical first language stimuli? Answers to this question could provide valuable information that would inform our classroom teaching strategies. Until such studies are conducted, perhaps allowing more time for our beginning signed language students to focus on reception without having to introduce a significant amount of production would be beneficial. This additional time to focus on reception might aid the learners in the development of a more robust signed language phonology. Additionally, reliably using some techniques of child-directed signing (such as slower signing, longer sign duration, and repetitiousness; Holzrichter and Meier, 2000) may be beneficial to students.

Social-psychological factors must continue to be investigated as well. Research on students who would like to become interpreters and their levels of integrative motivation for learning ASL is limited. Some possible questions are as follows: How do students' short- and long-term goals influence their drive to succeed? Do students who are risk takers and know how to overcome frustration acquire the language better than those who do not like to take risks and who have difficulties dealing with frustration? Also, how do learners identify with deaf people and the Deaf Community and does that have any affect on the language proficiency of students in an ASL or interpreter training program? Questions such as these should be addressed in future work on the adult learning of ASL and other sign languages.

Spoken language instruction and research have a history of model-testing and theory creation via experimental and classroom-based studies. Signed language instruction and research must begin to focus attention on the success of the models that are used to teach sign languages. For instance, how and when are explicit and implicit models of language learning best used in our instructional curricula?

One interesting question that we usually do not consider is how a native signer would learn a different signed language: Would an adult learner experience all the difficulties of learning another signed language that a hearing adult has with learning another spoken language? Based on anecdotal accounts of such learning occurring outside of the classroom, it may be the case that such language learning/acquisition would follow a different course than that of hearing adults learning another spoken language. Despite that, the case of a native signer learning another signed language as an adult may inform our studies of the acquisition of ASL by adults. Additionally, native or near-native signers who become interpreters can also be extremely informative as we continue our investigations of how PSs, RS, and CA are used—both in regular discourse and in interpreted discourse. For instance, the work that Certified Deaf Interpreters perform on a regular basis (see Forestal, this volume) might prove to be quite informative to research on how to teach PSs, RS, and CA to students of ASL and interpretation.

There are certainly other areas that can be explored, but as mentioned earlier, based on discussions in the literature of the effects of these differences, these topics are appropriate for immediate attention. Other possible topics that should also be addressed in the future include the following: the frequency of exposure to the language and predictable results from such exposure, the optimal amount of time per week in which classroom instruction should take place, and the use of extracurricular activities such as deaf mentors (Bryant, 2003). Essentially, the language acquisition trends and questions presented herein, in conjunction with general philosophies of language instruction, can be synthesized to create general suggestions for our future research programs.

CONCLUSION

The time has come for the creation of research-based suggestions for our curricula development—suggestions that would ultimately improve the reliability and success of our language instruction methodologies. The methodologies for teaching interpreting students the use of PSs, RS, and CA, which have proven to be a difficult part of ASL, could benefit tremendously from such research. I suggest that there is a great deal that can be learned from native acquisition of a signed language and the many ways in which native users use various devices for optimal and efficient communication. Sign language interpreters must have competency in the production and reception of PSs, RS, and CA, and deaf students in educational settings will benefit from interpreters having high levels of skill in the use of such signs. At times, a deaf student may actually be learning facets of PSs/RS/CA use from the interpreter, which suggests that interpreter skills in these very important areas of signed communication should be sophisticated—not areas of interpreter weakness. By taking advantage of research on a variety of topics that may influence second language acquisition, we can build more robust models for the acquisition of ASL by adults and continue to test those models in search of increasingly better ways of teaching ASL to adult learners—many of whom will likely become our future interpreters.

NOTES

The other contributors to this volume provided helpful comments and insights that have caused me to consider various viewpoints on the topic. Any errors or misrepresentations are, of course, my own.

1. Welles (2004) reports that there was a 432% increase in enrollments between 1998 and 2002, but she notes that that figure is partially a result of differences in reporting. In 2002, the survey asked specifically for ASL enrollments, whereas in 1998, ASL enrollments that were reported were included in the category labeled "other languages."

2. There are, of course, those students who take ASL because they think or have been told by a friend or advisor that it will be an easy language to learn and use as fulfillment of a language requirement. Sometimes these students have difficulties learning spoken languages, so they try to learn ASL instead. These situations present issues that must be addressed because they have an impact on interpreter training programs, but they are beyond the scope of this chapter.

3. I adopt the term "polycomponential signs," following Slobin and colleagues (2003) and Schembri (2003), although the latter used the term "polycomponential verbs," to refer to the linguistic devices that have previously been referred to by various labels such as classifiers, classifier predicates, classifier constructions, and so forth. As the term "polycomponential" suggests, the signs that it refers to are typically composed of more then one meaningful component (e.g., handshape, movement, etc.), but the status of some of those components as morphemes has been questioned. Schembri argues that the claim that these signs include classifier morphemes akin to constructions that are referred to by the same label in some spoken languages is open to question, which is why the term "polycomponential" seems more appropriate for these devices.

4. The term "referential shift" will be used to refer to communicative devices frequently referred to by other terms (e.g., role shift, direct quotation, perspective marking, etc.). This commonly refers to the use of various manual and nonmanual devices to show the reported dialogue of a character. The term "constructed action" (following Liddell & Metzger, 1998; Metzger, 1995) will be referred to as instances in which the signer portrays the actions of a character or object usually without the simultaneous use of signs, but perhaps with the simultaneous use of PSs.

5. The terms "learning" and "acquisition," when used together in this fashion, refer respectively to the processes of developing an understanding or knowledge of various structures of a language versus the unconscious ability to comprehend and produce those structures in normal discourse. When used in isolation, I intend the term "acquisition" to encompass both phenomena.

6. A related but different topic is that of the role of universal grammar (UG) in language learning. Some researchers would claim that UG, as it has been advanced by many researchers in the Chomskyan tradition, influences SLA by guiding one's acquisition through a small set of choices that govern all languages. However, other researchers would claim that, even if it exists, there is little to no influence from UG on SLA. This topic is beyond the scope of this chapter.

7. Yet, some researchers claim that there also exists a natural and, perhaps, optimal order of acquisition for an L2 learner of a language, and that order may differ from the order in which a child natively acquires the same language.

8. However, recent studies (Lindert, 2003; Slobin et al., 2003) suggest that deaf children, and even their hearing mothers who are learning a sign language, can use linguistically complex signs (i.e., PS) with relatively little exposure (less than 4 years) to the language.

9. As is customary, the first number in the sequences of age reporting represents years and the number after the semicolon indicates months.

10. The Supalla (1982) study included three children who, at data collection, ranged in age from 3;6 to 5;11.

11. Schick uses the term "CLASS" rather than "Entity" for these forms.

12. These constructions have been referred to as "Figure/Ground" constructions by some authors (e.g., Lessard 2002, 2003; Schick, 1990).

13. Slobin and colleagues (2003), Quinto (2001), and Quinto-Pozos (2003) have described instances of a signer depicting the actions of an object as examples of shifts in *perspective*, but the term "point of view" (Lessard, 2002, 2003) has also been used—all of which generally refer to the signer producing CA.

14. Some researchers claim that "critical period" is not the best label for the phenomena that it seeks to describe. Alternative terms that have been suggested are "optimal period" and "sensitive period," both of which imply that language acquisition could take place after the time frame in focus, but that language learning may not be optimal. The term "sensitive period" has been used to refer to other developmental phenomena as well. Some accounts claim that there are even separate *critical periods* for various linguistic phenomena.

15. Possible examples of differential cognitive skills that adults possess in comparison with those that young children have include the following: adults have superior memory skills to children; adults who already possess an L1 may try to make sense of an L2 linguistic message via their L1 (i.e., their L1 may act as a "filter" through which linguistic information from the L2 is processed); and adults have different reasoning abilities than children.

16. For discussions of various neural studies of language acquisition and cognitive development, see Emmorey (2002).

17. There are likely other differences between native language acquisition and adult language acquisition that are not included in Table 7-1, but these are differences that have been discussed or alluded to in the literature. One other possible difference that should be mentioned is that of the motor skills of children versus adults. Some authors (e.g., Hamilton & Lillo-Martin, 1986; Lupton & Zelaznick, 1990) have addressed the roles of various motor skills in acquisition of a signed language, and Mirus, Rathmann, and Meier (2001) have addressed proximalization and distalizaton of sign movement in adult learners of signs from two signed languages—ASL and German Sign Language (DGS).

18. However, one question that is raised is that hearing adult learners of ASL have acquired a spoken language phonology natively, but in many cases they have not been exposed to a signed phonology (i.e., a different modality) in order to have those types of linguistic structures established cognitively.

19. An additional difference might be that the types of events and situations that comprise the content of language production likely differ between

adult-adult interaction and adult-child interaction. Whether or not that results in differences of acquisition is unknown.

20. However, as Liddell (2003) suggests, some PS forms may actually be lexical signs that cannot be decomposed into smaller units. Further work is this area can help to shed light on the best approach to teaching what we have traditionally called "classifiers."

REFERENCES

Anthony, M. (1999). The role of classifiers in predicting English literacy among deaf adults. In A. Greenhill, H. Littlefield, & C. Tano (Eds.), *Proceedings of the Twenty-Third Annual Boston University Conference on Language Development.* Somerville, MA: Cascadilla Press, pp. 20–31.

Bryant, R. (2003). *Introduction to ASL mentoring.* Presentation at the 2003 Pennsylvania American Sign Language Teachers Association (PA-ASLTA) Meeting. Mount Aloysius College, Cresson, PA.

Cochran, B.P., McDonald, J.L., & Parault, S.J. (1999). Too smart for their own good: The disadvantage of a superior processing capacity for adult language learners. *Journal of Memory and Language, 41,* 30–58.

Cormier, K., Mauk, C., & Repp, A. (1998). Manual babbling in deaf and hearing infants: A longitudinal study. In E.V. Clark (Ed.), *The Proceedings of the Twenty-Ninth Annual Child Language Research Forum.* Stanford, CA: CSLI, pp. 55–61.

DeKeyser, R., & Larson-Hall, J. (in press). What does the critical period really mean? In J.F. Kroll & A.M.B. de Groot (Eds.), *Handbook of bilingualism: Psycholinguistic approaches.* New York: Oxford University Press.

Doughty, C., & Williams, J. (1998). Pedagogical choices in focus on form. In C. Doughty & J. Williams (Eds.), *Focus on form in classroom second language acquisition.* New York: Cambridge University Press, pp. 197–261.

Ellis, N.C. (1994). Implicit and explicit language learning—an overview. In N.C. Ellis (Ed.), *Implicit and explicit learning of languages.* London: Academic Press, pp. 1–31.

Emmorey, K. (2002). *Language, cognition, and the brain.* Mahwah, NJ: Lawrence Erlbaum Associates.

Emmorey, K., & Reilly, J. (1998). The development of quotation and reported action: Conveying perspective in ASL. In E. Clark (Ed.), *Proceedings of the Twenty-Ninth Annual Stanford Child Research Forum.* Stanford, CA: CSLI, pp. 81–90.

Frishberg, N. (2000). An interpreter creates the space. In K. Emmorey & H. Lane (Eds.), *The signs of language revisited: An anthology to honor Ursula Bellugi and Edward Klima.* Mahwah, NJ: Lawrence Erlbaum Associates, pp.169–192.

Goldowsky, B.N., & Newport, E.L. (1993). Modeling the effects of processing limitations on the acquisition of morphology: The less is more hypothesis. In E.V. Clark (Ed.), *Proceedings of the Twenty-Fourth Annual Child Research Forum.* Stanford, CA: CSLI, pp. 124–138.

Hamilton, H., & Lillo-Martin, D. (1986). Imitative production of ASL verbs of movement and location: A comparative study. *Sign Language Studies, 50,* 29–57.

Harley, B., & Hart, D. (1997). Language aptitude and second language proficiency in classroom learners of different starting ages. *Studies in Second Language Acquisition, 19* (3), 379–400.

Holzrichter, A.S., & Meier, R.P. (2000). Child-directed signing in American sign language. In C. Chamberlain, J.P. Morford, & R.I. Mayberry (Eds.), *Language acquisition by eye*. Mahway, NJ: Lawrence Erlbaum Associates, pp. 25–40.

Jacobs, R. (1996). Just how hard is it to learn ASL: The case for ASL as a truly foreign language. In C. Lucas (Ed.), *Multicultural aspects of sociolinguistics in deaf communities*. Washington, DC: Gallaudet University Press, pp. 183–226.

Johnson, J., & Newport, E. (1989). Critical period effects in second language learning: The influence of maturational state on the acquisition of English as a second language. *Cognitive Psychology, 21*, 60–99.

Kantor, R. (1980). The acquisition of classifiers in American sign language. *Sign Language Studies, 28*, 193–208.

Krashen, S.D. (1994). The input hypothesis and its rivals. In N.C. Ellis (Ed.), *Implicit and explicit learning of languages*. London: Academic Press, pp. 45–77.

Kuhl, P.K., & Meltzoff, A.N. (1997). Evolution, nativism and learning in the development of language and speech. In M. Gopnik (Ed.), *The inheritance and innateness of grammars*. Oxford: Oxford University Press, pp. 7–44.

Lang, H.G., Foster, S., Gustina, D., Mowl, G., & Yufang, L. (1996a). Motivational and attitudinal orientations in learning American sign language. *Journal of Deaf Studies and Deaf Education, 1* (2), 137–144.

Lang, H.G., Foster, S., Gustina, D., Mowl, G., & Yufang, L. (1996b). Motivational factors in learning American sign language. *Journal of Deaf Studies and Deaf Education, 1* (3), 202–212.

Lenneberg, E. (1967). *Biological foundations of language*. New York: John Wiley & Sons.

Lessard, P. (2002) *Classifiers: A closer look*. Instructional curriculum. San Francisco: Treehouse Video LLC.

Lessard, P. (2003). *Taking a closer look at classifiers. Thinking visually, creating visual realities*. Workshop presentation at the 2003 Registry of Interpreters for the Deaf Biannual Conference. Chicago, Illinois.

Liddell, S.K. (2003). Sources of meaning in ASL classifier predicates. In K. Emmorey (Ed.), *Perspectives on classifier constructions in sign languages*. Mahway, NJ: Lawrence Erlbaum Associates, pp. 199–220.

Liddell, S.K., & Metzger, M. (1998). Gesture in sign language discourse. *Journal of Pragmatics, 30*, 657–697.

Lindert, R.B. (2003). American Sign Language "Classifiers": Can hearing mothers learn to use them effectively? In A. Baker, B. Van den Bogaerde, & O. Crasborn (Eds.), *Cross-linguistic perspectives in Sign Language Research: Selected Papers from TISLR 2000*. Hamburg: Signum Verlag, pp. 209–223.

Locke, J. (1980). Mechanisims of phonological development in children: Maintenance, learning and loss. *Chicago Linguistics Society, 16*, 220–238.

Locke, J. (1983) *Phonological acquisition and change*. New York: Academic Press.

Lupton, L.K., & Zelaznik, H.N. (1990). Motor learning in sign language students. *Sign Language Studies, 67*, 153–173.

Masataka, N. (2000). The role of modality and input in the earliest stage of language acquisition of Japanese sign language. In C. Chamberlain, J.P. Morford, & R.I. Mayberry (Eds.), *Language acquisition by eye*. Mahwah, NJ: Lawrence Erlbaum Associates, pp. 3–24.

Masgoret, A.-M., & Gardner, R.C. (2003). Attitudes, motivation, and second language learning: A meta-analysis of the studies conducted by Gardner and associates. *Language Learning, 53* (1), 167–210.

McKee, R., & McKee, D. (1992). What's so hard about learning ASL?: Students' & teachers' perceptions. *Sign Language Studies, 75,* 129–157.

Meier, R.P. (1991). Language acquisition by deaf children. *American Scientist, 79,* 60–70.

Meier, R.P., & Willerman, R. (1995). Prelinguistic gesture in deaf and hearing infants. In K. Emmorey & J. Reilly (Eds.), *Language, gesture, and space.* Hillsdale, NJ: Lawrence Erlbaum Associates, pp. 391–409.

Metzger, M. (1995). Constructed dialogue and CA in American sign language. In C. Lucas (Ed.), *Sociolinguistics in deaf communities.* Washington, DC: Gallaudet University Press, pp. 255–271.

Metzger, M., & Bahan, B. (2001). Discourse analysis. In C. Lucas (Ed.), *The sociolinguistics of sign languages.* Cambridge: Cambridge University Press, pp. 112–144.

Mirus, G., Rathmann, C., & Meier, R.P. (2001). Proximalization and distalization of sign movement in adult learners. In V. Dively, M. Metzger, S. Taub, & A.M. Baer (Eds.), *Signed languages: Discoveries from international research.* Washington, DC: Gallaudet University Press, pp. 103–119.

Mitchell, R.E., & Karchmer, M.A. (2004). Chasing the mythical ten percent: Parental hearing status of deaf and hard of hearing students in the United States. *Sign Language Studies, 4* (2), 138–163.

Monikowski, C., & Winston, E.A. (2003). Interpreters and interpreter education. In M. Marschark & P.E. Spencer (Eds.), *Oxford handbook of deaf studies, language, and education.* New York: Oxford University Press, pp. 347–360.

Morford, J.P., & Mayberry, R.I. (2000). A reexamination of "early exposure" and its implications for language acquisition by eye. In C. Chamberlain, J.P. Morford, & R.I. Mayberry (Eds.), *Language acquisition by eye.* Mahwah, NJ: Lawrence Erlbaum Associates, pp. 111–127.

Newport, E. (1988). Constraints on learning and their role in language acquisition: studies of the acquisition of American sign language. *Language Sciences, 10* (1), 147–172.

Newport, E. (1990). Maturational constraints on language learning. *Cognitive Science, 14,* 11–28.

Newport, E., & Meier, R.P. (1985). The acquisition of American sign language. In D.I. Slobin (Ed.), *The crosslinguistic study of language acquisition. Volume 1: The data.* Hillsdale, NJ: Lawrence Erlbaum Associates, pp. 881–938.

Peterson, R. (1999). *The perceptions of deafness and language learning of incoming ASL students.* Unpublished doctoral dissertation. University of California, Riverside.

Petitto, L.A. (2000). The acquisition of natural signed languages: Lessons in the nature of human language and its biological foundations. In C. Chamberlain, J.P. Morford, & R.I. Mayberry (Eds.), *Language acquisition by eye.* Mahwah, NJ: Lawrence Erlbaum Associates, pp. 41–50.

Petitto, L.A., & Marentette, P.F. (1991). Babbling in the manual mode: Evidence from the ontogeny of language. *Science, 251,* 1493–1496.

Quinto, D. (2001). *Creating life in your interpretations: A look at perspective in ASL.* Professional discussion presentation at the 2001 Registry of Interpreters for the Deaf Biannual Conference. Orlando, Florida.

Quinto-Pozos, D. (2003). *Practicing perspective in ASL: Camera, characterization, action!* Five-hour workshop track presentation at the 2003 Registry of Interpreters for the Deaf Biannual Conference. Chicago, Illinois.

Reilly, J.S. (2000). Bringing affective expression in the service of language: Acquiring perspective marking in narratives. In K. Emmorey & H. Lane (Eds.), *The signs of language revisited: An anthology to honor Ursula Bellugi and Edward Klima.* Mahwah, NJ: Lawrence Erlbaum Associates, pp. 415–433.

Schembri, A. (2003). Rethinking 'classifiers' in signed languages. In K. Emmorey (Ed.), *Perspectives on classifier constructions in sign languages.* Mahwah, NJ: Lawrence Erlbaum Associates, pp. 3–34.

Schick, B.S. (1987). *The acquisition of classifier predicates in American sign language.* Unpublished doctoral dissertation. Purdue University.

Schick, B.S. (1990). Classifier predicates in American Sign Language. *International Journal of Sign Linguistics, 1*, 15–40.

Schick, B., Williams, K., & Bolster, L. (1999) Skill levels of educational interpreters working in public schools. *Journal of Deaf Studies and Deaf Education, 4* (2), 144–155.

Slobin, D., Hoiting, N., Kuntze, M., Lindert, R., Weinberg, A., Pyers J., Anthony, M., Biederman, Y., & Thumann, H. (2003). A cognitive/functional perspective on the acquisition of "classifiers." In K. Emmorey (Ed.), *Perspectives on classifier constructions in sign languages.* Mahwah, NJ: Lawrence Erlbaum Associates, pp. 271–296.

Supalla, T. (1982). *Structure and acquisition of verbs of motion and location in American sign language.* Unpublished doctoral dissertation. University of California, San Diego.

Terrell, T.D. (1991). The role of grammar instruction in the communicative approach. *Modern Language Journal, 75* (1), 52–63.

Welles, E.B. (2004). Foreign language enrollments in United States institutions of higher education, Fall 2002. *ADFL Bulletin, 35* (2), 1–20.

Werker, J.F., & Tees, R.C. (1999). Influences on infant speech processing: Toward a new synthesis. *Annual Review of Psychology, 50*, 509–535.

Wilcox, P.P., & Wilcox, S. (2000). American sign language. In J.W. Rosenthal (Ed.), *Handbook of undergraduate second language education.* Mahwah, NJ: Lawrence Erlbaum Associates, pp. 115–137.

Winston, E.A. (1991). Spatial referencing and cohesion in an American sign language text. *Sign Language Studies, 73*, 397–409.

8

Service Learning in Interpreting Education: Living and Learning

Christine Monikowski and Rico Peterson

In the space of 30 years, the education and training of sign language interpreters has evolved from community endeavor to academic enterprise. Cokely (2000, p. 26) writes, "Whereas two and a half decades ago the vast majority of interpreters/transliterators entered the profession via an interactional route, today the vast majority enters via an academic route." This transition has served to increase the number of people who receive training and has thereby helped to satisfy the growing demand for interpreters, especially in educational settings. While exact figures on employment are not known, in 1986 the Registry of Interpreters for the Deaf (RID) had a membership of "over 3,000 members from the U.S." (Frishberg, 1986, p. 13), whereas today the number stands at 10,412 (RID, 2003). However, it is not clear that as we increase the quantity of interpreters, we have also maintained the quality of their training.

Moving the locus of our learning from the community to the classroom has had another, less desirable effect—that of removing deaf people and their communities from the center of our education. Thus, our migration from community to academy has come at some cost: In spite of the best efforts of the institutions of higher education (IHEs), many students complete their American Sign Language (ASL) course sequence (if not their entire interpreting coursework) without having had significant interaction with deaf people and communities.

We are certainly not the first to note the inherent compromise of institutionalizing learning. In *The School and Society* (1902), the pragmatist philosopher John Dewey wrote movingly of the twin circumstances of social change and education at the turn of the twentieth century:

> [T]he clothing worn was for the most part not only made in the house, but the members of the household were usually familiar with the shearing of the sheep, the carding and spinning of the wool, and the plying of the loom. Instead of pressing a button and flooding the house with electric light, the whole process of getting illumination was followed in its toilsome length, from the killing of the animal and the trying of fat, to the making of wicks and dipping of candles. The supply of flour, of lumber, of foods, of building materials, of household furniture, even of metal ware, of nails, hinges, hammers, etc., was in the immediate neighborhood, in shops which were constantly open to inspection and often centers of neighborhood congregation. The entire industrial process stood revealed, from the production on the farm of the raw materials, till the finished article was actually put to use. Not only this, but practically every member of the household had his own share in the work. The children, as they gained in strength and capacity, were gradually initiated into the mysteries of the several processes. It was a matter of immediate and personal concern, even to the point of actual participation.
>
>   We cannot overlook the factors of discipline and of character-building involved in this: training in habits of order and of industry, and in the idea of responsibility, of obligation to do something, to produce something, in the world. There was always something which really needed to be done, and a real necessity that each member of the household should do his own part faithfully and in cooperation with others. (1990, pp. 10–11)

The reader of this quote will doubtless make the connection between the world Dewey describes and that of the rapidly evolving Deaf culture, where technology has so recently wrought such tremendous change. Dewey went on to explain the problematic nature of classroom instruction and to inspire a basic premise of this chapter (italics added):

> We cannot overlook the importance for educational purposes of the close and intimate acquaintance got with nature at first hand, with real things and materials, with the actual processes of their manipulation, and the knowledge of their social necessities and uses. In all this there was continual training of observation, of ingenuity, constructive imagination, of logical thought, and of the sense of reality acquired through first-hand contact with actualities. The educative forces of the domestic spinning and weaving, of the saw-mill, the gristmill, the cooper shop, and the blacksmith forge, were continuously operative. *No number of object-lessons, got up as object-lessons for*

the sake of giving information, can afford even the shadow of a substitute for acquaintance with the plants and animals of the farm and garden, acquired through actual living among them and caring for them. No training of sense-organs in school, introduced for the sake of training, can begin to compete with the alertness and fullness of sense-life that comes through daily intimacy and interest in familiar occupations. Verbal memory can be trained in committing tasks, a certain discipline of the reasoning powers can be acquired through lessons in science and mathematics; but, after all, this is somewhat remote and shadowy compared with the training of attention and of judgment that is acquired in having to do things with a real motive behind and a real outcome ahead. (pp. 11–12)

It must be said that the faculty of interpreting education programs (IEPs), populated by and large still by people with one foot in the practical world of the deaf and one in the academic, work hard to make opportunities for interaction with deaf people available to today's students. ASL classes routinely require attendance at Deaf events. Many courses include an invitation to deaf guests for a variety of activities. However well intentioned this exposure is, it is difficult to see these opportunities as anything other than stilted and contrived. Members of the Deaf Community in that situation are not interacting with their peers or even with students. Rather, they are appearing as representatives of their community and as such are subject to all the ambassadorial baggage of any envoy. Whatever value these invitations have, they cannot possibly fulfill the students' need to interact directly and meaningfully with individuals with whom they will one day work.

Dewey's view of society reflects the Deaf Community of a previous generation, when deaf people monitored the community of interpreters and controlled who did or did not pass muster. The abject dearth of deaf representation in positions of authority in IHEs speaks volumes about the quality of the bargain made in transferring accreditation from community to college.

Language skill is foremost among the deficiencies found in substituting curriculum for community. Here the deck is already stacked against our students. The classroom is notorious for being an insufficient, frustrating environment in which to learn a language. The study of foreign language as an academic discipline in schools in the United States has been neither popular nor successful. Literature on this topic is in no short supply. Christison and Krahnke (1986), Dornyei (1990), Mantle-Bromley (1995), Oxford and Shearin (1994), Ramage (1990), Reinert (1970), and Roberts (1992) are among the many researchers who have looked at the failings of traditional language learning in the classroom with an eye toward defining the problem and suggesting solutions.

There is some evidence that ASL is even more susceptible to student insensibility than other languages might be. Omaggio (1986, p. 20) suggests that "it takes 720 hours of instruction under ideal conditions to enable a student with a superior aptitude for languages to reach Level 3 [superior] in oral skills in French or Spanish." Although no research supports this information in the study of ASL, it stands to reason that the limited hours our students spend in a classroom (typically anywhere between 90 to 240, assuming 3 to 4 hours per week in 10–18 weeks per quarter/semester) are inadequate. The actual use of ASL with native and near-native users is paramount for the high level of proficiency interpreters require. Jacobs (1996) makes a strong argument that the amount of time the typical student spends studying ASL in the classroom falls far short of standards for learning truly foreign languages. Compromises common to the classroom, in particular the lack of meaningful interaction with the Deaf Community, all too often result in students woefully deficient in two areas of central concern to interpreters: culture and language.

Dewey (1902, p. 15) identifies a "tragic weakness" in classroom instruction. Speaking here of classroom instruction in general (not specifically of the language classroom), he states, "It endeavors to prepare future members of the social order in a medium in which the conditions of the social spirit are eminently wanting." In an effort to address that "wanting," those shortcomings, we have begun to implement a "service learning" approach in our IEP. This chapter continues with a discussion about the distinction between academic learning and experiential learning and then offers our working definition of service learning and examples of efforts that are sometimes confused for it. From that foundation, an overview of our service learning courses is presented, with representative comments from students.

ACADEMIC CLASSROOM OR INTERACTION AND EXPERIENCE?

The limitations of the classroom learning environment have been an issue for almost as long as there have been classrooms. One virtue of classroom learning is that it allows students to have a structured and sequenced access to knowledge. Classroom instruction is a very efficient way to offer standardized instruction to large groups of students. However, recognition of the important distinctions between academic learning and what Rogers (1969; Rogers & Freiberg, 1994) calls "personal" or "significant" learning has led to interesting work in experiential learning. Kolb and Fry created a model of the experiential learning cycle (Cooper, 1975, p. 33), shown in Figure 8.1.

Much work on experiential learning uses a model similar to the one described earlier. Other research has sought to develop the model further. Jarvis (1995) is notable in his exploration of the many possible

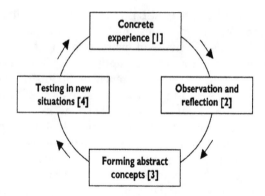

Figure 8.1. Kolb & Fry's Experiential Learning Cycle

individual responses to a given learning opportunity. His model is especially useful in its recognition of the fact that the outcome of potential learning experiences is not always learning, at least not the sort of learning implicit in the instruction. Jarvis organized possible non-learning outcomes into categories including presumption, non-consideration, and rejection, all of which reflect the varying degrees and ways in which a person can experience a learning opportunity and yet remain untouched by the intended learning outcomes.

What combination of experiences, then, both academic and social, will lead to literacy, and to cultural and linguistic competence? Literacy—the ability to function in a culture—can only come from intensive interaction with that culture. Interpreters, per force, work between different cultures. If biliteracy is accepted as a *sine qua non* of qualified interpreters, what can IHEs do to address the shortcomings of classroom and curriculum in preparing interpreters?

SERVICE LEARNING: A DEFINITION

An interesting approach to this question can be found in literature on service learning (SL), a form of experiential learning that emphasizes students' needs to reflect on the dynamic relationship between self and community. We shall, for the purpose of our discussion here, define SL as an approach to teaching and learning that combines credit-bearing academic work with active reflection on the relationship between self and society. Valerius and Hamilton (2001, p. 339) see SL as "characterized by students' engagement in their local communities to apply and learn course concepts." In offering a definition of SL, we should also be forthright in stating what SL is *not*.

First and foremost, we do not construe volunteer interpreting assignments to be proper SL opportunities. Students by definition are deficient in skills that meet the needs of the Community. There are interpreter educators who urge interpreting students to accept unsupervised volunteer assignments, labeling them as low-risk, pro bono opportunities. We question the wisdom of this choice. Anyone who considers Girl Scout meetings, Tupperware parties, or youth sports to be low risk to interpreting students (and their clients) has simply not looked carefully enough at the complexities and pressures these settings present to a student.

The literature on pro bono work in other fields (most notably law and medicine) is written for professionals, not for students. It should be noted here that medical and law students must pass much more strenuous screening than do most interpreting students before gaining admission to their programs and the attendant "pro bono" work therein. There are no real opportunities in these disciplines for those who have not yet developed the skills necessary to perform the task, although most professions require an internship or practicum that, typically, includes direct supervision from instructors or practitioners. Other chances for pro bono work, like those found in organizations such as Habitat for Humanity, happen only under the strict supervision of experienced professionals.

In the field of interpreting, the notion of pro bono work is widely discussed, but is largely absent from the literature. Two significant exceptions are Tipton and Findley (1998), who write of pro bono work as a symbol of the status in our profession and who offer guiding principles for accepting such assignments, and Cokely (2000, p. 34), whose clear and succinct explanation conforms to the perspective of other professions: "When professionals undertake pro bono work, the expectation is that they will perform the work as if they were being paid. Pro bono work can be described as, 'Do the work you do to earn a living, do it just as well, but just don't get paid for it this time.'"

This definition calls into question why so many educators allow students to deceive themselves and the greater Community into thinking they are, indeed, providing a service to the Community. Arguably the hearing community benefits from this volunteer effort because they do not have to pay for interpreting services that might otherwise be unavailable, but it is doubtful that the Deaf Community benefits in any way. How can students "do it just as well" if they cannot yet "do it"?

Moreover, there is little discussion of the potentially deleterious effects of placing students in "interpreting" situations too soon and without adequate supervision. It is demonstrably the case that students lack sufficient language skills. By putting students in low-risk situations, we may be deceiving them (or allowing them to deceive themselves) about the quality of work they are capable of doing. Kruger and Dunning (1999), in a study of metacognition, found that students' self-perceptions were not good predictors of their skill level; those who were unskilled tended to be unable to assess accurately their ability. "Not only do these people reach erroneous conclusions and make unfortunate choices, but their incompetence robs them of the metacognitive ability to realize it" (p. 1121). "Erroneous conclusions and unfortunate choices" is an interesting description. It aptly describes the problem from the perspective of the interpreting student. It does not, however, come close to describing the problem from the perspective of the recipients of this "interpreting." The shibboleth that "something is better than nothing" has no more validity today than it did a generation ago when deaf people were presumed to be grateful for whatever snippets of information people in power cared to toss their way.

It is known that many students come to the study of ASL laboring under gross misapprehensions about the relative difficulty of the subject and about the length of time it will take them to become fluent (Peterson, 1999). To be sure, institutions do little to dispel these misapprehensions. Institutions, are, after all, emplaced to satisfy social needs. Bearing the imprimatur of social probity, who are students, teachers, or the Community to disagree if the institution determines that 2 years is a sufficient time to learn how to interpret? We have yet to explore fully the ramifications of allowing students to engage in volunteer interpreting work for which they lack the basic language skills. A student who volunteers is likely to see him or herself as successful at the task of interpreting. When this success does not translate into similar success in the classroom (or in the grade book), the credibility lost is liable to be that of the teacher and program, at least in the eyes of the student. This paradigm is often seen in ASL classes as well. "But my deaf friends understand me just fine," is a common refrain from students who are frustrated by the important differences between language and communication.

"Community service" is another false synonym for service learning. Community service is commonplace in IEPs. Many interpreters, interpreting faculty, and students make comments such as "I've been doing service learning for years," when most often what they have been doing is better described as community service (i.e., service to a specific community). Students give their time to the Community by assisting with committee work, productions at the Community theater, or holiday events. Certainly there is a need for such a commitment from our profession. However, often without realizing it, when we volunteer, we have a different relationship with members of the Community. "Volunteerism suggests a paternalistic, one-way relationship in which the community is the sole beneficiary of services, while not recognizing the benefits received by students" (Valerius & Hamilton, 2001, p. 340).

Lane (1992, p. 33) clearly saw the problems inherent in a helping relationship: "Whenever a more powerful group undertakes to assist a less powerful one, whenever benefactors create institutions to aid beneficiaries, the relationship is fraught with peril."

We hold that SL is a recursive phenomenon, wherein students learn the significance of membership in a community while reflecting on the importance of reciprocity and the symbiotic nature of learning and living.

SERVICE LEARNING: AN APPROACH TO EDUCATION

By fixing the locus of SL firmly in the domain of experiential learning, we are recognizing the need for practical application outside of the classroom of the skills learned inside the classroom. Service learning is distinct, however, from other forms of experiential learning in two important ways. The most obvious difference is that reflection is a vital component of SL. Students are required not only to participate in community activities, but to also reflect actively on their participation. Through reflection students are able to construct schemas for the Community, for themselves, and for their place in the Community. Ehrlich (1996, p. ix) holds that SL comprises "the various pedagogies that link community service and academic study so that each strengthens the other."

A second way to distinguish SL from other forms of experiential learning is in the primary purpose of the endeavor. In general, experiential learning can be said to be student-centered—its purpose is that students have an opportunity to apply academic learning in a social situation. An example of this in our practice is the common requirement that ASL students attend Deaf events. The premise of such a requirement is that the *student* needs more contact with the Deaf Community. The purpose of SL, however, is to satisfy *community* needs. By demonstrating that the student's need is subordinate to the Community need (the common good), SL students and Community alike affirm their traditional roles in the social contract.

We seek, then, to distinguish SL from those other activities that are common to sign language and interpreting coursework. In requiring thorough reflection and by exalting Community over individual, SL is an approach that has much to offer interpreting education programs. From the perspectives of the IHE and the Community, SL can be seen as a commitment by the institute to recognize and serve the needs of the Community. From the perspective of the program, SL can be seen as a means by which the efficacy of curriculum can be assessed. From the perspective of the student, SL is a guided entrée into the Deaf world.

AN APPROACH TO SERVICE LEARNING
IN INTERPRETING EDUCATION

Having investigated SL programs at other institutions and in other disciplines, we recognize that SL is likely to be more successful as a holistic approach to an entire curriculum than as a single add-on course. The efforts we have made at our school are necessarily prefatory. We look forward to seeing our curriculum infused with an SL perspective.

One of our first steps was to identify a community liaison. We are fortunate to have a large and diverse faculty. One member of the faculty in particular is quite well-established in the local Deaf Community. Working together with her, we were able to establish a number of venues for our students. Community buy-in is essential to the success of a program such as this. We began with placements in the local Deaf Club, where Wednesday nights are favored for Euchre—a popular card game. Approximately fifty deaf individuals attend the weekly competitions. Students at this placement primarily functioned as servers; once the tables were set up and the score pads distributed, drinks were ordered and delivered to tables. We are also fortunate to have a positive (although limited) relationship with the local residential school. Since many of our graduates become educational interpreters, this placement presented students with an opportunity to experience deaf education from an "inside" perspective. Students were placed in the middle school dormitories in situations that matched their skills and the deaf students' needs.

We are still in the early phase of establishing the courses and the approach, so we began with four one-credit courses, presented as electives. The initial course, presented during spring quarter of the 2002–2003 academic year and again during fall quarter of the 2003–2004 academic year, has now become SL II.

Our plan includes four one-credit SL courses to be taken sequentially during the six quarters of the IEP; the ideal schedule will include SL I during the second quarter, SL II during the third quarter, and so on, with students completing the requirements prior to beginning the Interpreting Practicum (in the sixth and final quarter). SL I focuses the student's energy on the general topic of service to the Community. In this regard, students are placed in settings that are not specific to deaf people (i.e., daycare sites, elementary school teacher's aide, clerical support in volunteer office). The purpose is to help students orient themselves toward the reciprocal nature of being a member of the Community. Placements are arranged through our campus volunteer center.[1] At this writing, five students have completed this initial course. SL II is a fairly structured association with the local Deaf Community (either at the Deaf Club or the residential school), and it has been offered three times; nine students have completed the requirements. SL III allows for more flexibility and students play more of a part in determining their own placement(s); three students are currently enrolled. And finally, SL IV will be the student's choice: visiting an isolated deaf elder in a nursing home, answering phones at the interpreting referral agency, "adopting" a deaf family who needs additional child care, etc.; two students are enrolled for the coming quarter.

Analysis of Students' Online Postings

This discussion centers on our initial offering, which has now become SL II; There were five students in that first one-credit section offered in the spring quarter of academic year 2002–2003, and there were two students in the second section, during the fall quarter of the following academic year. Three students were placed at the residential school and participated in a wide range of activities, including pick-up basketball games, supervising homework completion, play rehearsal, moving boxes to prepare for building renovation, and so on. Their orientation included meeting the director of residential life and several dormitory supervisors; times for their weekly visits were established and logistics were explained (each was on a different schedule). The four other students opted to function as servers at the Deaf Club's weekly Euchre games; their orientation included meeting with a deaf faculty member who loosely supervised their work (introduced them, help them explain why they were there, how long, etc.).

In addition to "time on site," each student was required to submit two online postings per week—the "reflection" part of the course. In this initial offering, students responded to the instructor's specific thought questions. We chose the online format for three reasons. First, not requiring a face-to-face meeting (i.e., a typical seminar class), allowed for more freedom in everyone's schedule. Second, traditional classroom participation requires students to perform in front of peers, on cue from the instructor. The online format gave students time to think about their responses; they thought and wrote at their own pace. And third, all the discussions were visible to all the students. They created their own community where they developed trust in their peers and an appreciation for each other's experiences. The students are actively involved in the greater community and they are reflecting upon that involvement; McKeachie espouses the power of the process of writing:

> Why does writing improve thinking? Skill in thinking is like musical and athletic skills. It takes practice to improve—particularly practice that enables one to see what works and what doesn't. Much of our thinking remains in our minds, where it is not exposed to review. The very process of putting thoughts to paper forces clarification; seeing them on paper (or on the computer screen) facilitates our own

evaluation; and receiving comments from peers or teachers provides further help. Note that most of these educational gains do not require that writing be graded. Writing is to facilitate learning and thinking. Thinking in turn results in class discussions that are animated and thoughtful. (2002, pp. 170–171)

The initial postings explained the sites, responsibilities, and so forth; students were required to express their own goals for the experience. Initial postings were also to reflect information gleaned from the required readings. The first posting for the second week was meant to elicit a clear summary of the student's placement and, more important, whether Rubin and Thompson's (1994) chapters 4 and 5 ("Planning Your Language Study" and "The Communication Process") illuminated any initial language issues. Student 1's comments, although a bit long, validated the offering of this course to the instructor! This was a successful student, diligent in his/her work up to this point, but there was never a hint of this depth of analysis when he/she was using ASL in classroom communication; we specifically draw your attention to the italicized comments (italics added). And Student 7's comments relate quite dramatically to Rubin and Thompson (1994, p. 22): "Learning a foreign language in a community where it is spoken . . . offers one of the strongest reasons for learning—the need to communicate."

Student 1: Well, as for my duties at the Deaf Club, they seem to be very easy when they are written down on paper. Basically, my duties are to serve drinks to people playing Euchre. However, when this is put into practice, *it becomes anything but easy*. Within this past week, I have been confronted with many of the issues presented in Chapter 5 of the text along with a few that were not mentioned at all. So far, the vocabulary and grammar have not been all that challenging. I ask them if they would like a drink, and then they tell me what they want. On the other hand, there is *a sense of culture within this environment that I do not believe that I could learn in any formal setting*. Embedded in the simple task that I have described there lies a *plethora of subtle cues* and rules that I am just beginning to understand (i.e., when to wait, when to ask, who to ask, how to ask, and how long to wait before asking again). . . . There are quite a few references in Chapter 5 to social status and how different cultures deal with that. Within this particular setting, there are a number of people with very high social status. I am learning through trial and error what social addresses are appropriate and which are not. . . . Service learning is really giving me a chance to see *what I have learned on a theoretical level put into action in a real life situation*. In this case, however, I feel that I am speaking more of the cultural information that I have learned over the years rather than the linguistically based information. I feel that by the time I have finished my obligation with this assignment, my language proficiency with ASL might improve; perhaps a little or perhaps a lot. I am sure, however, that by the time I finish with these ten weeks *that my understanding and appreciation of Deaf culture* in general and this community specifically can only deepen greatly.

Student 7: My first week at the Deaf Club was different from other visits there. At other times, I entered there as a guest and have always been nervous, feeling a little like an intruder. This time, I was required to be there and although I was still nervous, I was less nervous and for different reasons (what if I spill something?!). Everyone was very kind and if they didn't know why we were there, they would ask. People that I spoke to that I didn't already know always wanted to know if I was an interpreter and why I was there. *It was easy to strike up conversations with anyone.* With the pressure of "I am here to socialize and I must speak to people" taken away, I actually socialized and spoke to people.... Ironically, I had a conversation with someone that night about how *different* it was to go to the Deaf Club and use the language vs. learning it in a classroom. *Even with the best teachers, one cannot create all of the situations that occur in real life.* In learning a language, you have to explore it. A good way to do that is to get stuck and work your way through it. In other words, if I want to discuss something in class, I can plan out my question or my comment before I say it. I can use signs that I know are correct. If I am involved in a real conversation, *I must communicate.* If asked a question, I must answer it. I may not know the correct signs or have time to plan out the answer so I am forced to say something in the best way that I can.

As mentioned in these comments and otherwise in this volume, many students enter IEPs long before they are competent in ASL and English. For this reason, the early SL courses focus on students' metacognitive abilities as language learners, as noted in the italics above.

During the fourth week, the discussion centered on Rubin and Thompson's Chapter 8, "Taking Charge of Your Learning." Students were prompted to consider how they have taken charge of their learning and to consider how they could do so as they look toward their second year. The honesty of Student 2 was enlightening, especially as he/she realizes that second language learning for an interpreter is an ongoing process:

Student 2: Hmmm . . . I am always on the look out for interesting ways to learn this language. I often find myself *impatient with the whole process.* It all started with the prospects of getting into the [IEP]. My first assessment resulted in a recommendation to start ASL I, when all I wanted to hear was I am ready for ASL IV. I can still remember how frustrated I was to hear that I needed ASL I, because this had put my plans of starting the Interpreting Program on hold for a WHOLE year. Now I'm looking back and thinking that was TWO years ago!...Where did the time go??? I can't believe how much I have learned in these two years. *The real revelation is the amount YET to learn.*

And, Student 6 expressed surprise at a deaf person's reactions to the naturalness of his/her signs, just as Rubin and Thompson (1994, p. 59) related: "The language must, in some sense, become a part of you rather than remain an external mechanical system that you manipulate according to a set of instructions."

> **Student 6**: Recently, one of my friends at the Club and I were chatting. At first the conversation was a bit more serious/formal. Eventually, we got into a fun, playful exchange. Without realizing it, I became very relaxed, *wasn't thinking about making a mistake*, and had a great time. Part way through this exchange, my friend said to me, "Why don't you sign like that all the time? I was taken aback and confused by what he said. I asked him to explain what he meant, and he told me that my ASL had become much more smooth and fluent, my body had loosened up, and I was using my space much better....

Later, in the seventh week, the discussion centered around just how much personal information one should share with these new acquaintances (at the Deaf Club): Should one really be trying to establish friendships? How close should one become with one's future "consumers"? These discussions often arise in IEPs and, as far as we know, are addressed appropriately. However, it seems that Student 3 gained some valuable personal insight as he/she reflected on the issue; again, we draw your attention to the italicized segments:

> **Student 3**: *Because I am a quiet person and not very comfortable conversing with strangers (especially in my L2)*, I feel that I am at a disadvantage within the Deaf Community. First there's the obvious fact that the less I participate, the less of that essential interaction I'm getting. *But I've resolved that it will just take me more time.* More to the point of this discussion though, because I'm not outgoing and comfortable, I have felt myself viewed with suspicion, as though I must not really be interested in becoming involved. With hearing people, there is usually a grace period for getting a conversation going, a few minutes of finding what you have in common, etc...I have found that, often with Deaf

people, if it doesn't flow right away they give up and lose interest. And, because I'm not "open," I fear that I am perceived as insincere about my interest in the community. Since I can't change my personality, *I don't know how to remedy this except to keep on going back and prove myself slowly over time.* I don't know if anyone else can relate to this, but it is an aspect of our topic that is very relevant to me.

This student has hit upon the key to success as an interpreter, the success that our profession gained naturally in years gone by, before we became isolated in academia. He/she sees that acceptance cannot be forced and it cannot be accomplished in a short period of time (e.g., one or two visits to an ASL class). Acceptance in the Deaf Community must be earned and the deaf people themselves, as gatekeepers, have the power to accept these new students—or not. This student has decided that acceptance is worth the effort and has decided to "keep on going back and prove myself slowly over time."

Finally, at the end of the quarter, students were required to write a final summary of their service learning experience. We believe it is worthwhile to call attention to several specific comments. When asked if there was anything "unexpected that you learned from your experience about the population you worked with" (Question 2), several students made comments that relate directly to metacognitive abilities, language learning, and on becoming a member of a Deaf Community.

Student 2: Seeing the "life of a deaf student in a residential school" really hit me to see how very structured their lives are during the week. I mean, I have read about residential schools in general, but *to be a part of it was incredible.* I assumed that what I read in textbooks had to be a thing of the past.... For example, I can now set my watch to the time I see the kids leave the school for the day, leave the cafeteria after finishing dinner, begin their study time, rec time, etc.

Student 4: Having been told the difficulty [deaf] kids have learning the English language, it was not totally unexpected when I saw that happen. However, the extent of the problem did surprise me. On a few occasions, I assisted a couple of the girls with their English homework.... [I]t became obvious they had no idea what they were really being asked. I would ask the kids what the question meant and they would shrug their shoulders. It certainly was not easy when I tried to explain it to them. It was obvious how frustrating the whole process was to the kids.... It was a real eye opener *seeing firsthand the struggles the kids had with the language.*

As mentioned here, placement in a residential school opens up numerous possibilities for those interpreting students who will become educational interpreters. That this student has come to this realization through his/her own action confirms the value of SL.

> **Student 6**: *I learned that people who are deaf are human just like people that can hear....* This is something I will take with me as I continue on in my career and in my personal life as I become more involved in the Deaf Community. I will continue to be aware of cultural differences, but will not focus on it so much. I will try to use the point of view, "How would I react/feel if this was a group of hearing people?"

> **Student 7**: I think that I am most surprised by how much [my classmate] and I think alike. So many times our reactions were the same to events or to topics posted. I have wondered about this in the past but *seeing it in writing confirmed it for me.* We all tend to feel as though we are unique in our learning experiences and that we as individuals are the worst at this, that, or the other thing, and it turns out *that we are feeling and experiencing the same things (for the most part).* We are going along the same path and it seems that many of our experiences and reactions are typical. I keep telling myself to take comfort in that but in the midst of a bad day I forget. *It gives me hope to think that I am following a course that others have followed and to see that they have come out successfully.*

Question 3 asked students to consider what they had learned about themselves by participating in this experience.

> **Student 6**: What I learned about myself is that I can persevere. I began this program in December 2001. At that time, my family life was in great turmoil. It has not been easy for any of us, but my family knows that I am doing this because it is my life dream and it will benefit all of us. I have tried to be a role model for my children and display that no matter what the obstacles, you can get through and achieve your goals, but sacrifices must be made along the way. The important thing is to *keep focused on your goals* and try not to lose touch with the things that mean most in your life, your family. My experience at the Deaf Club has been enlightening because even though I felt fairly comfortable around people who are deaf, it was intimidating going to the Deaf Club where I would be one of the only hearing people there. *I was worried that I would not be accepted, or that they would be suspect of my intentions.* Through my continued involvement, I have been accepted and *have made some good friends.*

Student 7: As far as learning about myself, I like the idea that I have taken control of my own learning. Before that topic came up, I had never really thought about it fully. Now I think about it a lot *and it gives me a sense of power.*

Rubin and Thompson begin Chapter 8 (1994, p. 59) quite emphatically: "Remember that unless you can take charge of your own learning, you will probably not succeed in mastering the new language."

Question 4 asked students to consider how this entire experience would impact them now and in the future, and we offer several excerpts from their answers here:

Student 1: I hope that I have made an initial impression on those that frequent the club as someone who might be a little awkward but also someone who is *genuine* and not a threat in any way.

Student 2: I realize the benefits of getting involved in the Deaf Community...I push myself to get involved in events that will start to *make a name for myself* in the Deaf Community.

Student 3: I intend to pursue the *friendships* that have begun with a couple of the dorm ladies.

Student 4: I feel fortunate to have been a *part of something* that is very important to the Deaf Community...the residential school....For both the students and the staff, it is not just school or work. They are family. Now when someone talks to me about his or her experiences at a residential school, I am a *little closer to understanding* what it really means.

Student 5: I believe my involvement in this assignment has provided me with a good opportunity to be recognized and welcomed by many of the people I have met. *It is up to me* to stay connected in some way, so I'm planning to stop in this summer and attend other events as they arise.

Student 6: Last night at the Deaf Club, [one deaf man] announced to everyone that [my classmate] and I had finished our "tour of duty." Everyone gave us a round of applause and thanked us for coming. Many expressed that they were sad to see us go and many hugs and good wishes were given. When I told people that I was a member and they were stuck with me, they expressed surprise and were thrilled that I would continue coming. Of course one of their next questions was, would I be playing Euchre now? Once I told them I was already in the Friday night league, they let me off the hook, but did ask if I was available to sub for them if they needed me. *When I left last night, I did not feel things had ended, but instead a new chapter has begun.*

One comment about the online aspect of this course is necessary, due to the controversial nature of online learning for interpreting students. We have often had other instructors ask, "What was missing?" when we discuss online work. Nothing is missing; certainly, the course is different than a face-to-face experience, but we believe that the reflection that occurs online is far superior to comments made in the classroom. The process of putting thoughts into writing onto the course website facilitates learning and thinking, just as McKeachie said. Using the course website makes this sharing more relevant and timely each week. And the sharing with peers builds confidence and rapport in this young interpreting community.

SUMMARY AND CONCLUSIONS

We find the value of incorporating an SL approach to interpreting education to be self-evident, and we believe the sample of student comments we have included speak for themselves, as do Eyler and Giles (1999, p. 58): "[Students] believe that the service-learning experience added something unique to their understanding of what they were learning in the classroom. Students who participate in service-learning believe not only that they learn more but that the quality of what they learn is different from what they learn from books and lectures alone."

It is an effort to balance the playing field in terms of deaf representation in curriculums and programs. It is a means by which programs can facilitate students' transition into the community of interpreters. There is abundant literature extolling the virtues of SL in today's academy. There is little evidence that SL has found its way into interpreting education. Many programs produce students that work initially, if not primarily, in the field of K–12 educational interpreting. The rush to prepare interpreters for this task has resulted in something of a schism between "educational" interpreters and community interpreters. We offer SL as a natural bridge between the Community and the institutions of learning. The opportunity for placing student interpreters in K–12 SL settings is very promising. By affording students a privileged perspective into the realities of educational interpreting, we are intending that they join into the discussion on a topic that has caused much controversy. As the student comments herein suggest, there is much to be gained by putting students in the way of experiential learning.

We acknowledge that our own program is in the very early phase of implementation. But, as SL gains currency with our community, students, and faculty, we hope to see this approach infused into all of the courses across our curriculum, until SL is seen not as a *thing* students do but as a way of characterizing *everything* that students do. Collier and Lawson (1997) noted that many faculty members indicated increased teaching satisfaction when involved in community work with students, despite the additional time it required. The comments from our initial offering last spring validated our belief that there was a need to reconnect interpreting students with the community with whom they will be working. We believe that the excerpts from the students' postings clearly show their support for this approach to learning. And, in end-of-the-quarter informal meetings with some of the deaf adults (dorm supervisors at the residential school), they expressed their pleasure at having interpreting students participate in routine activities. Also, we know members of the Deaf Club enjoyed the students' participation, as reported in the final student excerpt presented. We are hopeful that this shift, away from rigid and singular classroom learning and back toward interactions with individuals in the Community, will enhance and inform the next generation of interpreters.

APPENDIX A: COURSE DESCRIPTIONS
FOR THE FOUR COURSES

Service Learning I requires the student to participate in a volunteer activity in the general Rochester community (the hearing community, not the Deaf Community). Collaboration is ongoing with the RIT "Student Volunteer Center," which aids in students' on-site placements (http://svc.rit.edu). This course is a pre-requisite to the other Service Learning courses. Courses must be taken in this specific sequence.

Service Learning II requires the student to have a reciprocal relationship with the Deaf Community. The student provides a service to the Deaf Community, applying his or her knowledge of ASL to real interactions. Students *cannot* take Service Learning II unless they successfully complete Service Learning I.

Service Learning III can be either a continuation of Service Learning II or involve a different placement.

Service Learning IV requires the student to develop his/her own project within the Deaf Community. It is assumed that students will have developed contacts within the Deaf Community as well as explore their own preferences (e.g., DEAF elders, residential school, etc).

NOTES

The authors owe a debt of gratitude for the support and encouragement received from our Deaf Community colleagues. We also acknowledge the generosity of spirit and energy of our students. Without the cooperation of both students and community, this project would be impossible.

1. The RIT Student Volunteer Office at the Center for Campus Life is a campus-based clearinghouse for RIT students, faculty, and staff who are in-

terested in making a difference in their community. The center provides information on the volunteer needs of more than 200 agencies in the Rochester community. During academic year 2002–2003, approximately 5,000 student placements were completed.

REFERENCES

Christison, M., & Krahnke, K. (1986). Student perceptions of academic language study. *TESOL Quarterly, 20* (1), 61–79.
Cokely, D. (2000). Exploring ethics: A case for revising the code of ethics. Registry of Interpreters for the Deaf. *Journal of Interpretation,* 25–57.
Collier, C. and Lawson, H. (1997). Toward academically based community scholarship: Ideals, realities, and future needs. *Quest, 49,* 380-393.
Dewey, J. (1990). *The school and society and the child and the curriculum (1902). A centennial publication of the University of Chicago Press.* Chicago: University of Chicago Press.
Dornyei, Z. (1990). Conceptualizing motivation in foreign-language learning. *Language Learning, 40* (1), 45–78.
Ehrlich, T. (1996). Foreword. In B. Jacobs and Associates, *Service learning in higher education: Concepts and practices.* San Francisco: Jossey-Bass.
Eyler, J., & Giles, D.W. (1999). *Where's the learning in service learning?* San Francisco: Jossey-Bass.
Frishberg, N. (1986). *Interpreting: An introduction.* Silver Spring, MD: RID Publications.
Jacobs, R. (1996). Just how hard is it to learn ASL? The case for ASL as a truly foreign language. In C. Lucas (Ed.), *Multicultural aspects of sociolinguistics in deaf communities.* Washington, DC: Gallaudet University Press, 183–226.
Jarvis, P. 1995. *Adult and continuing education.* London: Routledge.
Kolb, D.A., & Fry, R. (1975). Toward an applied theory of experiential learning. In C. Cooper (Ed.) *Theories of group process,* London: John Wiley.
Kruger, J., & Dunning, D. (1999). Unskilled and unaware of it: How difficulties in recognizing one's own incompetence lead to inflated self-assessments. *Journal of Personality and Social Psychology, 77* (6), 1121–1134.
Lane, H. (1992). *The mask of benevolence: disabling the deaf community.* New York: Vintage Books/Random House.
Mantle-Bromley, C. (1995). Positive attitudes and realistic beliefs: Links to proficiency. *Modern Language Journal, 79* (3), 372–386.
McKeachie, W.J. (2002). *McKeachie's teaching tips: Strategies, research, and theory for college and university teachers.* Boston: Houghton Mifflin.
Omaggio, A.C. (1986). *Teaching language in context: Proficiency-oriented instruction.* Boston, MA: Heinle and Heinle Publishers, Inc.
Oxford, R., & Shearin, J. (1994). Language learning motivation: Expanding the theoretical framework. *Modern Language Journal, 78* (1), 12–28.
Peterson, R. (1999). Perceptions of deafness and language learning. In *Proceedings of the 16th National Convention of the Registry of Interpreters for the Deaf.* Silver Spring, MD: RID Publications, pp. 185–237.
Ramage, K. (1990). Motivational factors and persistence in foreign language study. *Language Learning, 40* (2), 189–219.

Reinert, H. (1970). Student attitudes toward foreign language—No sale! *Modern Language Journal, 55* (2), 107–112.

RID (Registry of Interpreters for the Deaf), (2003). Frequently Asked Questions. Available at http://www.rid.org/faq.html. [Accessed November 28, 2003]

Roberts, L. (1992). Attitudes of entering university freshmen toward foreign language study: A descriptive analysis. *Modern Language Journal, 76* (3), 275–283.

Rogers, C. (1969). *Freedom to learn.* Columbus, OH: Merrill.

Rogers, C., & Freiberg, H.J. (1994). *Freedom to learn,* 3rd ed. Columbus, OH: Merrill/Macmillan.

Rubin, J., & Thompson, I. (1994). *How to be a more successful language learner: Toward learner autonomy.* Boston: Heinle and Heinle.

Tipton, C., & Findley, M. (1998). Pro bono interpreting. *Registry of Interpreters for the Deaf VIEWS,* December, pp. 8–9.

Valerius, L., & Hamilton, M.L. (2001). The community classroom: Serving to learn and learning to serve. *College Student Journal, 35* (3), 339–345.

9

Designing a Curriculum for American Sign Language/English Interpreting Educators

Elizabeth A. Winston

What do competent interpreting educators need to know how to do in order to foster the development of competent interpreters? To answer this, it is important to address two underlying issues. First, what do competent interpreters need to know how to do? And from the answer to that, what do competent educators need to know how to do to develop that competence in interpreting students? Interpreters and educators have a body of knowledge and skills that define the content interpreters need to master. However, explicit information about how to lead interpreters to mastery of the knowledge and skills required is not part of that body of knowledge. Underlying all the knowledge and skills is an essential core—the need to develop critical thinking, decision making, and self-assessment in each domain. Educators contributing to the studies reported in this chapter implicitly acknowledge that these processes are crucial. Interpreting educators need to learn how to structure, implement, and assess active learning approaches that will lead to active learning by their students, and, therefore, to competent interpreting.

Sign language interpreting as a profession is a fairly recent development. Until the early 1960s, most interpreters came from families with deaf parents where at least one child became the "default" interpreter, learning American Sign Language (ASL) from birth as a first or second language (see Cokely, this volume). In the 1960s and 1970s, laws such as Section 504 of the Rehabilitation Act of 1973 and PL-94-142 (later IDEA) were established requiring access to various settings via interpreters (Synthesis, 2004). Public schools were suddenly required to educate deaf children, using, when needed, sign language interpreters. Adequate numbers of qualified interpreters were not available, and the federal government established funding to set up training programs to train interpreters. However, there were few experienced and qualified academic instructors of interpreting to staff these programs.

Most such programs were established in community colleges. The great majority of faculty were, and continue to be, hired as part-time adjuncts because they are competent practitioners of interpreting. Their expertise as educators and as interpreting educators was not an essential qualification for hiring; word of mouth was often enough to secure an adjunct teaching position in many programs. Only the relatively few full-time faculty were required to demonstrate any expertise as educators. Most have learned to teach through experience, taking courses occasionally. Many earned degrees beyond high school and college, but few entered teaching as a profession to be mastered. Cokely (this volume), Monikowski and Peterson (this volume), and Monikowski and Winston (2003) raise important questions about the impact of establishing interpreting education in academia.

The shift of interpreting education from the Deaf community and culture in which it had been intricately intertwined into the objective rigors and expectations of academia has led to both positive and negative implications for interpreting education. These implications cannot be ignored. While the shift has resulted in more warm bodies sitting in the interpreter's seat, and has perhaps demystified the process of interpreting to some extent, the negative effects have been an ongoing concern. There is consensus that many of the "warm bodies" leaving these programs are generally not prepared to function independently in many settings (Patrie, 1994). And, as interpreting education has shifted into academia, it has, albeit unintentionally, lost much of the experience and expertise of the Deaf community. Although this loss is not the central focus of this chapter, it is an essential issue that must be addressed by every interpreting educator. This chapter should be read within the context of this issue, with an understanding that any improvement in the education of interpreters must infuse the knowledge and experience of the Deaf community into every aspect of every activity.

Meanwhile, the national interpreting organization, the Registry of Interpreters for the Deaf (RID), is moving toward requiring interpreters to have Bachelor's degrees as a requirement for certification. This means that interpreting faculty must have qualifications sufficient to satisfy the stricter hiring requirements at 4-year institutions. In addition, the national interpreting educators' organization, the Conference of Interpreter Trainers (CIT), has established standards for interpreting education programs, including a section addressing faculty qualifications (Conference, 1995). Unfortunately, these standards do not include a set of guidelines or expectations for independent educators who offer mentoring or workshops around the country. And the standards have not been disseminated widely in order for educators and institutions to access them. There is a need for educators who are skilled and competent not only as practitioners, but also as teachers. This is true regardless of the teaching environment, be it pre-service in academia, or post-service in workshops, mentoring, and training.

WHAT WE KNOW

What We Know from Literature in Education

The field of adult education has made major shifts in recent years, from the behavioral approach of teaching at students who passively sit through lectures, toward a learning-oriented, student-as-active-learner philosophy, where students are held responsible for their own construction of knowledge. Academics are looking beyond behaviorist theory and the static measurement of products and behaviors. They are incorporating cognitive and constructivist theories of learning—approaches such as problem-based learning, cooperative learning, and writing across the curriculum. These approaches are being used to develop critical thinking, analysis, and active cognitive skills. Attempts to provide tangible models for educators to achieve these goals have been developed over the years; the most well known being Bloom's taxonomy (Bloom et al., 1956). Although educators in recent years (and Bloom himself) have provided revisions and expansions on Bloom's basic taxonomy, it is still widely familiar to many educators who are concerned with designing clear educational objectives for leading students from the basic knowledge of facts to the more complex processes of critical thinking (Anderson & Krathwohl, 2001; Bloom et al., 1956; Marzano, 2001).

Bloom's six original categories are knowledge, comprehension, application, analysis, synthesis, and evaluation. They are intended to represent a hierarchical organization of cognitive processes that lead to complex learning. The first or least difficult level in the hierarchy is knowledge, the ability to recall information that has been learned. Verbs that reflect this level in the hierarchy include "name," "list," and "label." Interpreting competencies at this level might include being able to name the four component parts of a sign or listing the tenets of the RID Code of Ethics. Competencies of interpreting educators at this level might include naming types of interpreting to be taught and listing the types of assessment approaches used in interpreting. The second level is comprehension, where learners are expected to understand meaning, explain or restate ideas, or describe a process. An interpreter might be expected to understand the meaning of a sign location to mean "informal." An interpreter educator might be expected to comprehend the different applications of various assessments. The third level of Bloom's taxonomy is application, the ability to use newly learned information effectively. For example, an interpreter would be expected to use the appropriate language register when told the environment and setting. An educator would be expected to apply appropriate assessment approaches when a specific instructional objective is identified.

Bloom's fourth level is analysis, where the learner demonstrates an ability to categorize newly learned information, compare or contrast, or make a decision based on the available facts. At this level, an interpreter would need to determine which factors of a setting might affect the choice of language register. An educator would need to determine which factors would have significant impact on the choice of assessment approaches. Fifth, synthesis is the ability to use newly learned information to create new ideas or discover relationships. An example of an interpreter demonstrating synthesis might be the ability to enter an unknown setting, assess essential factors, and determine new ways to approach the needs of the new situation. An educator, likewise, would need to be able to develop a new assessment approach that fits an individual set of needs, assess a novel interpretation, and prepare an evaluation and justification of its overall effectiveness. Bloom's sixth and final level is evaluation, when learners are able to judge the importance or value of information based on specific criteria. Interpreters, for example, would be able to judge the effectiveness of their own interpretations; educators would be able to judge whether an assessment approach has been effective.

Bloom's taxonomy has been used extensively since it was first disseminated more than 45 years ago, when it was a seminal publication about learning domains and levels of abstraction. More recently, researchers such as Anderson and Krathwohl (2001) and Marzano (2001) have revisited Bloom's taxonomy, providing more depth and understanding of learning processes as research has progressed. Marzano (2001), for example, expands Bloom's one-dimensional hierarchy of learning to a two-dimensional one, in which he separates the realm of knowledge from the processes learners apply as they learn about the uses and relevance of those pieces of knowledge. Anderson and Krathwohl (2001) have refined and expanded the levels of Bloom's taxonomy by adding more explicit explanations of each level. Regardless of the particular perspective on learning, however, it is essential that these be part of any educator's repertoire of teaching expertise.

Vygotsky (1978) also provides interpreting educators with insight about the learning processes experienced by students (see also Daniels, 2000). His writings about student learning, the need for scaffolding new learning on prior or existing learning, and guiding the learner from dependence to independence in learning all relate to interpreting education. As educators work with interpreting students to build interpreting skills from language skills, to expand discourse analysis skills from intra- to interlingual applications, and to develop effective self-monitoring skills, they need to have a broad understanding of how learners, and especially adult learners, actively internalize and synthesize new information and concepts as they construct their own knowledge.

An important aspect of the previous approaches is the need for learners to be able to assess their own learning and abilities. Educators, therefore, need to be able to help them develop these essential self-assessment skills. Boud (1995), a proponent of self-assessment in all learning, writes that competent self-assessment reflects "what is important in teaching and learning in higher education. It stresses the importance of learners constructing rather than receiving knowledge, of promoting the taking of responsibility for learning, of communicating and expressing what learners know and understand and of taking a critical stance to received wisdom" (p. 9). Interpreting educators have long recognized the need to help students develop competence in self-assessment, yet frequently students graduate from programs unable to do this. The education of interpreters must focus on this if interpreters are to develop life-long learning skills; interpreting educators need to understand learning, structure activities based on learners' needs, and asses their own effectiveness as teachers.

Boud sums up the change that is happening in the wider arena of education, especially for adults. It is his claim that "[t]he greatest conceptual shift which has occurred in recent times in higher education has been from a perspective which focused on the teacher and what he or she does, to a perspective in which student learning is central. While much current practice has yet to fully reflect this shift, it is one which is not likely to be reversed" (p. 24).

What We Know from Interpreting Education

A review of interpreting literature indicates that there is a body of knowledge and information about what interpreters need to know and be able to do, and therefore, what educators need to include as content in the courses they teach. The CIT Standards (Baker-Shenk, 1990; Conference, 1995; Members, 1984a & b) the previous curriculum (Baker-Shenk, 1990), and Community wisdom all reflect the belief that these skills can be developed through active, hands-on learning. The expected effect of this active learning is that students will be able to respond critically, make decisions, and assess the effect of those decisions responsibly and professionally. In other words, we expect students to be able to deal with any situation that requires "It depends..." as an answer.

There is also an underlying assumption throughout the literature that interpreters must be aware of and comfortable in the Deaf Community. This belief is so intertwined throughout all the literature that it often remains implicit in discussions and explanations about interpreting education. During the early years when interpreters were apprenticed through Community interaction, accepted through the approval of the Deaf Community, and encouraged to interact within the Deaf Community, the implicit assumptions were implicitly assimilated. In the shift from Community grooming to academic education, the implicit expectations of Deaf Community interaction and acceptance have been paid "lip service." However, realization of them is often weak or nonexistent in practice. There are few deaf faculty in interpreting programs; those who are in interpreting programs are often assigned to teaching ASL exclusively. Anecdotal input in the field indicates that many educators, both deaf and hearing, believe that while there is tremendous input needed from deaf people to teach ASL, there is relatively little deaf educators can effectively contribute in teaching interpreting, since they cannot evaluate both the source and the target messages simultaneously.[1] CIT statistics indicate that only 13% of its membership is deaf or hard of hearing (Directory, 2001–2002).

The implicit expectations and assumptions about the essential value of and need for Deaf Community, deaf faculty, and multicultural competencies exist in stark contrast to the reality reported by CIT membership and by the qualifications of interpreting program graduates. In recognizing the contrast, many interpreting educators are acting to insure that these expectations are moving from the background to the foreground, making them more explicit and expected. In addition to the chapters in this volume from Cokely, Turner, Monikowski, and Peterson that focus specifically on this emphasis, others raise similar concerns. Those chapters about language learning and use all stress the need for native signers and Deaf Community members as essential language and culture models for interpreting students (see Quinto-Pozos, Davis, and Lee, this volume). Public discussions emphasize the need for more deaf faculty who teach interpreting as well as ASL.[2]

However, the ways and means of meeting that need are only beginning to be addressed. Although most interpreting programs incorporate some type of observation and practice requirements, often these requirements are accompanied by somewhat vague instructions, such as "Attend a Deaf event and write a journal about what you saw." More recently, interpreting educators and researchers are investigating more structured and directed approaches to these observations and participations. These are approaches that provide students with the means to benefit more fully from their learning about both their own cultures and the Deaf Community and cultures. Monikowski and Peterson (2003; this volume), for example, offer a systematic approach to infusing Deaf

Community involvement for interpreting students. In addition, their use of service learning addresses something even more basic—the need of interpreters to gain an understanding of any culture, especially their own, as a foundation to understanding another. Dean and Pollard (2001; this volume) offer the systematic structure of demand-control schema for documenting observations that lead to understanding of what students see and experience as they interact within Deaf community and culture. Dean, Pollard, Griffin, and Davis (2002) provide evidence that the structure is effective in interpreting education. Forestal (this volume) provides detailed insight into the roles and experiences of deaf interpreters. It is clear that Deaf community and culture must be an explicit part of the interpreting educator's reality, so that it is infused throughout the now primarily academic approach to teaching interpreting. Any newly designed curriculum will need to include explicit goals and objectives to address this need. Further research about how this is currently being done, and how it can be more effectively accomplished, is needed.

Interpreting education does have a body of knowledge about what interpreters need to know and know how to do. CIT members performed a major task analysis of interpreting (Members, 1984a & b). This document provides lists of terms and descriptions of interpreting tasks like "analysis," self-assess," "analyze content," "decision making," "audience assessment," and "décalage" (Members, 1984a & b). Many of the categories and topics fall into the upper levels of Bloom's taxonomy; for example, reflecting the expectation that interpreting requires complex types of critical thinking. It is a valuable guide for people who already know how to reach these goals, but it does not provide guidance for a practitioner who is new to interpreting education. And unfortunately, this document was not widely disseminated beyond the membership of CIT and has not been easily accessible until very recently, when CIT made it available electronically through their website.

In 1990, Baker-Shenk led a group of experienced interpreting educators in the publication of a curriculum for teachers of interpreting, the Teaching Interpreting Program (TIP). The curriculum provides insight and information about the skills and competencies that were considered essential for competent interpreters at that time. Most recently, CIT has investigated the idea of reviewing and assessing interpreting programs, with a potential goal of accreditation. A set of National Interpreter Education Standards was developed over a period of years, with input from a broad range of interpreting educators, both deaf and hearing, and was approved unanimously by the membership (Conference, 1995). The domains and subdomains of knowledge and skills outlined in the standards provide a comprehensive description of what programs need to teach and, therefore, what competent graduates of these programs must be able to demonstrate. These include domains of professional knowledge, language competencies, interpreting knowledge and skills, and the ability to function effectively in diverse settings. They underscore the need for educators and programs to focus on the more complex processes of learning that result in critical thinking skills.

The literature discussed thus far provides a basis for answering the question, "What do interpreters need to know to be competent?" It does not explicitly address how these competencies are to be taught. Interpreting educators must also master these defined skills and competencies; they are essential prerequisites to becoming educators. But they must master much more. They must master effective approaches for developing these competencies, or rather, for guiding students to accept responsibility for learning, constructing their own understandings about them, and applying their understandings critically by assessing their own thinking and actions critically.

In addition to the literature available to inform this study in interpreting education, we can look to related fields and professionals for input about teaching competencies. A sister organization of CIT, the American Sign Language Teachers Association (ASLTA), is an organization that assesses the competencies of ASL teachers. Although traditionally interpreting and teaching have been viewed as separate fields, it is unquestionably true that the two are closely related. Given that the specific criteria for ASL teachers will be different from those for interpreting teachers, the mastery of approaches that foster student learning, independence, and life-long learning requires similar understanding. ASLTA has established a portfolio system of assessment (ASLTA, no date). Adopting the use of a portfolio indicates a focus on the need for higher-order cognitive skills by this professional group. In addition to the portfolio, applicants for certification must demonstrate their teaching skills—again, a focus on their ability to think about their teaching, decide what constitutes effective teaching, and assess their own work. Each candidate needs to demonstrate, above all else, their own critical thinking about their work, their decision making in choosing portfolio elements, and their ability to assess their own work in order to determine what elements are included. This approach focuses on the underlying processes that ASL educators and interpreting educators need to master and offers educators of interpreting some ideas about how to assess their own teaching competencies.

The field of interpreting education has been in some ways ahead of the shift in adult education discussed previously. Educators like Colonomos (1992) and Gish (1984) have introduced the field to the ideas of Vygotsky and practiced interactive approaches to education.[3] The TIP curriculum implicitly reflects this approach in the types of class and assessment activities it describes (Baker-Shenk, 1990). Consistent with the recent emphasis on active learning approaches that focus on the development of critical thinking, decision making, and self-assessment, Humphrey (2000) suggests the use of portfolios to address the integration and synthesis needs of graduating interpreting students, and as way to bring them into more valuable and effective contact with the Deaf Community. Cokely (personnel communication, June 2002), in his work on decision making and portfolios, embraces active student learning. His new approach to curriculum design that focuses on communication from a discourse perspective promotes critical thinking (Cokely, 2003).

Yet, as current studies indicate, many educators do not understand these approaches and strategies and are not embracing them as the foundation for teaching the interpreting process. Critical thinking, decision making, and self-assessment are still often relegated to secondary importance, focused on only when the "critical" needs of memorizing, testing, knowing, and grading have been accomplished.

TEACHING INTERPRETING: RECENT INVESTIGATIONS

The remainder of this chapter focuses on current knowledge, attitudes, and philosophies of interpreting educators. In order to design and develop a curriculum for interpreting educators that meets the needs of the field, it is essential that a deliberative approach be followed. Data collection from a broad spectrum of stakeholders is essential (Peterson, 2003). Participation and ownership are important features of a successful curriculum at this point in the field.

Three separate investigations in an ongoing deliberative process of curriculum development are reported. The three studies incorporate data gathered through open-ended surveys, a roundtable conference, and focus groups. In each study, input was gathered from instructors who are or have worked in interpreting education and in ASL. They range in experience from first-year teachers to those with many years of experience. They have a range of educational backgrounds and a variety of teaching experiences, ranging from many years in structured classrooms to workshop presentations. They include educators who learned sign language at home from deaf parents or family members and then naturally fell into interpreting and teaching. There are others who learned ASL through academic programs in order to become interpreters. Some have educational backgrounds in curriculum design, second language teaching, adult education, linguistics, and English as a second language. Others have little academic training but a tremendous wealth of experience and insight. Data were collected in a variety of ways from a variety of participants. The following section describes the data collection approaches for each study and discusses the findings.

Study 1: Open-Ended Survey about Teaching Interpreting

Data Collection

Cogen, Monikowski, Peterson, and Winston (2002) developed and distributed a survey for interpreting and ASL instructors. The survey consisted of two sections. The first section posed a series of demographic questions for respondents, including length of time teaching; status as a teacher (full or part time); if they were affiliated with an institution; what academic degree(s), if any, they held; and in what field(s). The second section of the survey asked participants to respond to four open-ended questions. The questions were designed to elicit explanations of activities and the reasons that people used them.

1. Describe your favorite/most effective teaching activity, discuss why, and describe how you assess it.
2. Describe your least favorite/effective activity and discuss why.
3. Tell us about how you grade your courses.
4. Are there other things you want to share about your teaching?

Data collection began in 2002, when the researchers solicited the first group of participants by sending an announcement to CIT, the only interpreting educator organization in the United States. The announcement was sent to their listserv, which is distributed to all members of the organization. The number of members was listed as 272 in 2001–2002 (Directory, 2003–2004). However, many interpreter educators report anecdotally that other faculty in their program, especially adjunct faculty and independent educators, do not belong to CIT, and this number is not considered an accurate reflection of the actual number of interpreting educators in the United States. Although there is no actual count of interpreting educators in the United States at this time, the RID website states that there are approximately 150 interpreting programs (Registry, retrieved March, 2004). Estimates from educators indicate that there may be an average of one to two full-time instructors and one to eight part-time instructors in many programs. Therefore, the members were encouraged to share the information and invite any other educators involved with teaching interpreting, whether as faculty or as workshop presenters and independent consultants.

Over the course of a 3-month period, 21 surveys were submitted. Quantitative analysis of the results is problematic because access to the survey was not restricted by password or other criteria, so the real number of possible respondents is unknown. However, qualitative analysis provides insight into the philosophies of those who did respond.

A second group of participants were recruited in the spring of 2003. A national online roundtable discussion was sponsored by Project

TIEM.Online, entitled "Teaching Interpreting: What Do We Need to Know?" The survey was linked to the website for the roundtable discussion, and registrants of the roundtable were encouraged to respond if they had not done so previously. There were 299 registered participants of the roundtable, and 19 participants chose to respond to the survey.[4] Although access to the survey was restricted to registered participants of the roundtable, registration to the roundtable was not restricted. As with the first round of recruitment, the conditions for collecting these surveys were not controlled adequately for strict quantitative analysis.

In all, 40 surveys were available for analysis. This research collated the demographic information collected from the first section of the survey and analyzed comments made in response to open-ended questions 1, 2, and 4.[5] Participants ranged in teaching experience from 0–5 years: 14; 6–10 years: 13; 11–15 years: 5; and 16+ years: 8. There were 23 full-time faculty members and 17 adjunct or independent educators. Their places of employment ranged from 17 at 2-year institutions, 13 at 4-year institutions, and 10 independent educators not affiliated with any institution. Participants held a variety of academic degrees, including 3 with Associate's degrees, 8 with Bachelor's degrees, 22 with Master's Degrees, 6 with Ph.D.s, and 1 with a high school diploma. Of these, some reported working on advanced degrees in areas such as linguistics, interpreting, teaching interpreting, special education, and adult education.

Respondents were not asked if they were deaf or hearing, nor were they asked about race or ethnicity. Future versions of the survey may include those questions. A few participants self-identified as deaf or hearing. The format of a written English survey, combined with the online environment, meant that some educators did not participate.

Data Analysis

Of the four open-ended questions about teaching interpreting, the responses to three informed this study. The questions about favorite/effective activities, least favorite/effective activities, and additional thoughts provided insight into educators' philosophies and needs for teaching. The question about grading yielded specific information about syllabi and grading policies; responses to this question were not analyzed for this study.

Question 1. Describe your favorite/most effective teaching activity, discuss why, and describe how you assess it? Of the 40 surveys, 33 people responded to this question. All but one described an activity that developed critical thinking, decision making, and/or self-assessment skills. Only one activity described was teacher-centered, designed to simply transfer factual information to a passive student group. Most activities included students working together to analyze problems (either texts or situational questions), self-assessment of interpreting skills, and educator/student interaction that led students to construct knowledge for themselves.

Educators reported that these types of activities were essential in developing the higher-order thinking and analysis skills that interpreters need to be competent practitioners. Although the comments overwhelmingly indicate a sense of the value of these types of activities, they also reflect a range of meta-knowledge about this understanding. Some comments were very articulate statements about the need for developing these skills. Respondent #14, for example, did not describe a specific activity; instead, she wrote: "I think the most beneficial activities in the classroom are grounded in self-analysis. No matter what I am teaching (almost), I go back to asking the students about their experiences, what their challenges were, how they managed the challenges, what they learned in the process, etc. I use this at all levels, and I think it speaks to self-directed growth."

Other comments do not explicitly discuss why these activities promote critical thinking. They merely state that critical thinking and self analysis are the goal of the activity. For example, Respondent #11 discusses an activity that is videotaped, writing: "The student receives feedback from the instructor and fellow classmates, but, more importantly, they get the opportunity to view and provide a self-critique of their own work." Respondent #30 begins her comment very succinctly by stating, "Student self-analysis."

Other comments reflect an understanding that these types of learning activities are effective, but do not identify the underlying processes they foster. Respondent #3 describes two activities that are effective. The first is an interpreting activity where the students "use 'process mediation' (i.e., engage in a discussion of their processing, etc.) using a fishbowl technique in class"; the second is an activity that has students "engage in role plays with Deaf Community members and get direct feedback from these Deaf people and process the experience." Although there is no explanation of why this is important or what process the activity fosters, she adds, "Both course evaluations and student comments (in class) attest to the benefit of these activities."

These comments indicate some level of understanding of the essential need to develop critical thinking and self-assessment in interpreters. More important, they also reflect a need to better understand how to structure and assess the activities. While some participants described their assessment approaches knowledgeably, others were clearly at a loss as to how to do this. Several, after describing their most effective activity, bemoaned the fact that it is too hard to assess, or that they do not assess it at all. Respondent #14, quoted above with a very articulate explanation of the need to develop self-assessment and critical thinking skills, ends her comments by writing: "There is difficulty in assessment with this method, and I feel fortunate that I mainly teach in the workshop setting, so assessment is based less on grading and more on personal growth and movement."

This indicates a possible conflation of assessment and grading and raises the question of whether this educator is aware of approaches to assessment that could be effective in her teaching, regardless of the setting, and of the possibility that effective assessment of these activities could be relevant to grading and teaching.

The comments of two respondents about assessing these activities are striking in their similarity—the activities they describe are central to interpreting, yet they are not evaluated. Respondent #20 describes an activity that pairs students for interactive practice with interpreting skills. She concludes by writing: "This gives the students practice in dual tasking as well as short term memory.... There is really no assessment—this is primarily for skill building." It is revealing that this educator does not assess this activity, which focuses on an essential aspect of our work-skill building.

Respondent #29 describes an effective interactive activity in translation, ending with this thought: "I did not grade the final performance of this activity. This was more for them to get a feeling of the process of changing messages from one language to another." It is interesting to see that the basic, underlying skill of interpreting (i.e., transferring a message), is not assessed in a translation activity.

Comments like these indicate that these participants value activities that lead students toward constructing their own knowledge through critical thinking, decision making, and self-assessment. It is also apparent that both the ability to assess these activities, and the awareness that these are the activities that need to be assessed, need to be developed for some educators. That respondents report their most fun or effective activities as unassessed reflects the need for educators to learn how to approach assessment more effectively, both for the growth of their students and for their own growth as educators.

Question 2. Describe your least favorite/effective activity and discuss why. When asked to describe a least favorite or effective activity, another interesting insight is revealed. Of the 40 participants, 33 responded to this question. Of these, seven did not answer the question specifically enough to be included in the analysis. One such response stated that travel to practicum was the least effective activity (but that once she arrived, the travel was worth it). Another stated that "[m]ost of the theory and foundation courses" were least effective. And one person wrote: "Hard to say. It was my first teaching experience so everything seemed daunting."

Of the remaining 26 responses, all but 2 described an activity that was either primarily teacher-centered or that resulted in a teacher-centered grading of some interactive, student-centered assignment. The activities described here included testing, grading videotapes, rote memorization, grading written papers, scoring journals, and lecturing. The following comment from Respondent #38 reflects the attitude of most: "Watching videotapes of student-interpreted performances. . . . I just find it incredibly tedious to watch all these tapes and provide written feedback."

Several of the participants who mentioned grading tapes go on to state that students benefit from getting written feedback. Unlike the expanded comments about the most effective activities, which included discussions about the value of building critical thinking, none of the comments in this section included a student-learning rationale to support the belief that students benefited from the tedious grading. No one substantiated their statements that they know students use it, learn from it in some way, or even read it.

Several respondents reflect a sense that these teacher-centered activities are being done to satisfy some type of institutional requirement. Respondent #37 reflects this sense, writing: "The only activity I did not like was having to grade when I was teaching some courses as an adjunct. It did not accomplish much other than satisfying university requirements." There is an overall sense that the valuable activities of Question 1 are not assessable, and that the least favorite activities are conducted because they have to be. There is little sense that it is possible to assess the valued learner-centered activities and learning, or that assessment in general provides some valuable benefit for students. As this research and our understanding of interpreting processes goes forward, we clearly need to explore teachers' perceptions of grading and assessment.

Question 3: Are there other things you want to share about your teaching? This question elicited more responses about teaching and learning philosophies and reinforced the sometimes implied philosophies in the previous two sections. Of the 40 participants, 26 responded to this question. Of the responses, not all the comments were relevant to teaching philosophy. For example, Respondent #23 wrote: "I am really more interested in concerns that need to be addressed in establishing an ITP at a 4-year institution."

However, some took the opportunity to explicitly discuss their teaching philosophies. The most common thread expressed was that student-centered learning was the end goal—with critical thinking, an ability to continue learning after the teacher is gone, and ability to make decisions essential to the mastery of interpreting. Participant #3 writes: "I think that the most important thing for students to learn is critical thinking skills. We cannot attempt to provide an absolute model of what an interpreter can/should be; however, we need to instill in students an ability to think quickly... As the saying goes, you can give a person a fish or you can teach the person to fish."

Respondent #33 shared: "I believe that teaching is a discovery and problem-solving process. Sheer fact information, while necessary, is not the optimal goal... Learning how to solve a problem is better than knowing a lot of answers." These comments reflect a philosophy of student-centered learning that builds critical thinking, decision making, and self-assessment. The comments from these surveys indicate that educators recognize the value of learning-centered activities that lead the students to construct knowledge for themselves, learn to think critically, make decisions, and assess themselves. Some participants demonstrate an explicit awareness of this philosophy, while others "know" it but are not articulating the reasons for the value. The ability to express this awareness is fundamental in an educator's repertoire of teaching expertise. An essential part of this is the development of an understanding of assessment as a tool to measure growth, as opposed to simply satisfying institutional expectations.

Study 2: Roundtable Discussion of Educators' Needs

The second study that informs this discussion analyzes input and data from an international online roundtable held in February 2003: "Teaching Interpreting: What Do We Need to Know?" It was designed to collect input for this study by raising the questions and providing a forum for discussion. Experts in the field of interpreter education were identified through their own work in the field of educating interpreters and interpreting educators. Approximately 20 people were invited to submit papers in their areas of expertise, including deaf and hearing educators, ASL and interpreting educators, and U.S. and international educators. Not all were able to submit papers in time for the roundtable, but all were supportive and interested in the topic. In addition, educators were invited to submit papers for discussion. A call for papers was distributed to a variety of e-mail distribution lists in the hopes of contacting as many potential educators as possible. These include the list of CIT members; a list from Project TIEM.Online, which has been collecting and distributing distance information nationally and internationally (approximately 235 addresses); and a list distributed by Direct Learn, Inc., a British consulting firm that offers online learning and discussions on deafness and interpreting (approximately 7,000 recipients worldwide). List members were encouraged to share the information regionally and locally. In all, 299 people registered for the roundtable discussion.

Participants were able to read and discuss the ideas and concepts raised in the papers. Authors went online regularly to respond to and comment on topics and issues raised, and the discussions were summarized. The papers, discussions, and summaries that were produced via the roundtable discussion have been analyzed for input to this discussion.

Discussion Topics.   The comments and questions raised in the papers and ensuing discussions return time and again to two common themes: critical thinking and participation of the Deaf Community in all aspects of interpreter education. Only discussions related to the first theme are discussed here. The second theme was infused throughout the discussions and has been addressed in other chapters in this volume. As noted previously, this is an essential need in the development and implementation of interpreting programs, and therefore in the needs of interpreting educators. Further investigation about how this is being done and can be done is essential. Throughout the discussions, participants stressed the need to bring deaf people and the Deaf Community more deeply into the education of interpreters, emphasizing that students need to experience, interact with, and learn directly from those encounters. This recognition of the power of active student learning in comparison to a more passive, teacher-centered approach comes out in the discussions of each paper, regardless of the topic. Examples of practicums, service learning, and interacting with community groups all reinforce the underlying understanding that students need, first and foremost, to learn though interactive, collaborative experiences with others. These are the types of student-centered learning activities that foster the development of critical thinking, decision making, and self-assessment that are essential to interpreting effectively and competently.

Of the eight papers that constituted the core of the discussions, six directly reflected the understanding that critical thinking is an essential core process that interpreters need to master. Each author discussed the need for this in relation to the topic he or she presented. Peterson, in his opening keynote, "Perspectives on Curriculum Making," discussed different approaches to curriculum design and the impact curriculum design can have on the ability of students and faculty to promote critical thinking, active interaction, and learning. He advocated the idea of curriculum as deliberation—as an explicit focus on what all stakeholders believe to be important in the education of competent interpreters: critical thinking.

Responses to Peterson's paper reinforced the need for educators, both ASL teachers and interpreting educators, to develop a meta-awareness of their knowledge and skill before they can adequately teach it. The need for teachers to have critical thinking skills about their own teaching in order to develop these skills in their students was emphasized.

Gordon, in "Do Students Need to Fail to Succeed?" (2003), examined the traditional behaviorist model of assessing interpreting students, focusing on product rather than process and on dualistic labels of right and wrong. She advocated instead approaches that will lead students to self-assessment, constructing their own learning, and actively incorporating what they learn into a structured, cohesive understanding of interpreting. She thus supported a philosophy of education that fosters "mindful growth."

The discussion about Gordon's paper emphasized again the traditional perspective of education that makes students fit the model or curriculum, an approach that places content above learning. The comments also implicitly raised the issue of guiding students to learn, as participants recognized that value of explicitly helping students to integrate each step of the process of interpreting, rather than simply telling them to do it because the course objectives state it and the grading requires it. Further discussion of Gordon's paper focused on teaching strategies that encourage student learning, while also recognizing that not only educators, but the academic culture itself, do not value student learning above test scores. Developing skills in self-assessment, critical analysis, and decision making were emphasized repeatedly throughout this discussion, as was the critical need for educators to know how to develop these skills.

Winston posted a reading from Forster (1993) that raised the basic questions of "What is teaching?" and "What is learning?" challenging participants to examine their own understandings of these ideas as they think about whether they are teaching at students or leading students to learning. Responses to the Forster reading again recognized and emphasized the need for interpreting educators to focus on student learning rather than teaching. Discussion continued around the need for educators to meet student needs, to provide opportunities for learning to occur, and to recognize the differing levels of growth in each student. Discussants also raised the question of the need to link curriculum design more effectively to support student learning goals and to convince institutions to support more focus on higher-order cognitive skills that are the basis for interpreting.

Cokely's keynote paper, "Curriculum Revision in the Twenty-First Century: Northeastern's Experience," described the curriculum reform undertaken at his program—one that analyzes types of discourse so that interpreting students think critically about the goals and functions of the participants, rather than on the setting, number of participants, and topic. Approaches that encourage underlying assessment of discourse rather than surface-observable factors can lead students to think critically and to make effective decisions about their work. His approach also advocates helping students make critical decisions about their work.

Discussion about Cokely's curriculum included a variety of topics, such as teaching materials, valuing consecutive interpretation, and the underpinnings of the approach. It was noted that the approach reflects thinking and educational practices that are changing as we learn more about second language acquisition and cognitive processing. One thread in this discussion focused on educational interpreting and the growing focus in K–12 education on student learning, collaborative activities, and other approaches intended to stimulate critical thinking. It was suggested that unless educational interpreters also have these skills, they can neither recognize the goals and objectives of the activities, nor can they interpret them effectively either.

Swabey's paper (2003), "Critical Thinking and Writing to Learn in ASL and Interpreter Education," directly addressed the need to develop critical thinking skills for interpreters. She articulated the sense that many educators (and institutions) have that time spent on developing critical thinking will detract from time spent on content. She advocated a focus on the process of developing critical thinking as an essential skill for all interpreters, noting that as students learn to think critically, the begin to assume responsibility for their own learning and analysis.

Swabey's paper elicited discussion supporting the use of writing to develop critical thinking skills for interpreters. Writing was reported to help students learn to organize, analyze, assess, and evaluate not only their own thinking, but also the thinking and subsequent text structure of discourse they will someday interpret. Discussants recognized the process of developing these skills as being highly related to the skills needed by competent interpreters.

Mindess (2003) presented arguments for focusing on intercultural communication in her paper, "Building a Firm Foundation: Intercultural Communication for Sign Language Interpreters." Her discussion of activities that stress student action and practice emphasized the need for interpreters to be able to actively apply their critical-thinking, decision-making, and assessment skills within the Deaf Community and its multiple cultures. Simply presenting students with the facts and information related to such interactions is not enough.

Discussion about Mindess's paper recognized that interpreters need to be able to think critically and assess cultural interactions not only between deaf and hearing interactants, but also among the many cultural, ethnic, religious, and other groups with whom they work. It was also recognized that many white middle-class interpreters do not adequately analyze their own culture and end up learning about other cultures as oddities—something different from normal—while never understanding that their own cultural beliefs, attitudes, and experiences are also essential for understanding communication.

Although each paper and the ensuing discussions approached the question of what we need to know as interpreting educators from a different perspective, the need for student learning rather than teacher "teaching" as the focus of educators was emphasized.

Study 3. Focus Groups of Educators and Consumers

Because both Studies 1 and 2 were text- and technology-based, two face-to-face focus groups were conducted to gather input from those who were not comfortable with these other formats; ASL was the language of communication used in the face-to-face groups.

Data Collection—Focus Group 1.　Focus Group 1 was conducted at the ASLTA convention in Spring 2003. It was one of several concurrent workshops. Attendants were voluntary participants, having chosen to attend the discussion, "What Do Interpreting Educators Need to Know?" The group session was scheduled for 1 hour and was attended by approximately 30 people. It was not possible to determine exactly how many participants were deaf and how many were hearing. However, many of the participants were known to the researcher and to others in the room, and it appeared that participants were evenly divided between hearing and deaf people.

In an opening presentation, the researcher talked about her own background and connections to the Deaf Community and interpreting, the history and background of the questions being asked, the information and input that had been collected up to that point, and the goals of the hoped-for discussion. Participants were then asked to think individually about what interpreting educators need to know and were invited to make written notes on cards if they liked. They were then asked form small groups of three to five people to share their ideas and discuss the ideas of others in the group. Finally, participants came together in the large group to report about what their groups had discussed. The researcher took notes as the participants reported, writing the ideas on an overhead and verifying that her note reflected the intention of the participant. After the discussion closed, participants were invited to leave their written notes.

Input from this group raised the parallel threads of previous input: (1) involving deaf educators in the interpreting curriculum and process and (2) developing higher-order cognitive skills. The majority of this discussion was on the first topic, integrating and infusing Deaf culture and deaf input into interpreting education. Participants discussed the need for interpreters to interact in the Deaf Community, to learn how to effectively assess their work and the context of their work, and to understand the people they work with. Participants also stressed the need for more materials and information that would support teachers who are working in interpreting. The belief that deaf educators are not widely teaching interpreting, and often do not know how to become involved in academic programs, was raised as a concern by many participants. Each of these areas supports the belief that critical thinking is essential for interpreters and for those who participate in their education.

Data Collection—Focus Group 2.   Focus Group 2 had 16 participants. Eleven of the participants were identified and invited based on their current participation in learning and teaching of interpreting, research that focuses on student learning, and involvement of deaf faculty. This group was invited to attend a 2-day meeting with a group of five interpreting faculty who wanted to revise their own curriculum to incorporate the most effective approaches to interpreting education. Of the 16 participants, 3 were deaf and 13 were hearing.

Prior to the face-to-face meeting, each participant contributed a paper, article, or document about their individual focus during the meeting. These written texts were posted in an online conference area, and each participant was expected to read all the postings before arriving at the meeting.

At the face-to-face meeting, a set of questions was offered to the participants, with the understanding that other questions, approaches, and topics were welcome as well. The original questions were as follows: (1) What is the difference between a B.A. and an M.A. program in sign language interpreting? (2) What are entry- and exit-level skills for those programs? (3) What are the requirements for interpreting faculty in general? The group focused on one question at a time, for approximately 1.5–2 hours. For each discussion period, the participants divided into four groups, discussed the topic, and returned at the end of each period to report back to the larger group. Note takers were chosen in each group, and the notes were later typed up for dissemination to the group.

Discussion of Input.   The discussions focused on the general questions of this chapter: What do interpreters need to know and what do faculty need to know? Discussion about the first two questions (what is the difference between a B.A. and an M.A. program, and what are entry- and exit-level skills) resulted in two threads of discussion: specific needs and underlying competencies. The specific needs reflected and expanded on existing information, such as the CIT Task Analysis (Members, 1984a&b), the CIT Standards (Conference, 1995), and the Teaching Interpreting Curriculum (Baker-Shenk, 1990). The participants emphasized that the fundamental requirement for students entering interpreting programs is cultural and communicative competency in each language they will work in. Entering students must already be able to use their skills for critical thinking and self-assessment of those language skills. Thus, they should be able to analyze their own languages and be able to understand what they are doing with them. Likewise, they must be able to think critically about deaf/hearing and other multicultural interactions from a participant's perspective on entry, expanding those critical-thinking skills to apply to interpreting contexts throughout their interpreting program. As one group wrote: "Exiting students must be 'mature—able to reflect on their experiences [as an interpreter].'" All four groups also repeatedly emphasized the need for focus on Community interaction, with service learning, practica, or other interaction being essential. They all expressed the importance of graduating students knowing their own abilities and being able to critically asses which interpreting settings were appropriate for them to work in. And they emphasized the need for exiting students to be able to focus on meaning; for several that meant adding much more translation or consecutive interpretation activities into interpreting programs. All four groups listed the ability to demonstrate students' abilities to think, judge, and asses in some way—either through a portfolio or through other assessment approaches that demonstrate their skills as essential skills at program graduation.

The third question was most directly relevant to this project, asking: What are the requirements for interpreting faculty? The input from all groups served to reinforce the content domains described by previous studies and groups. Educators need to be bilingual, experienced interpreters, experienced educators, and hold some type of advanced degrees. Interspersed with the content areas, knowledge, and skills needed as interpreters, they also emphasized the need for educators to understand adult education and student-learning approaches and to have the ability to foster critical thinking, self-assessment, and decision making. One thing that each group included was an ability to conduct and to read and understand research findings of others. This need reflects the epitome of critical thinking, decision making, and self-assessment—this is what research is all about.

SUMMARY AND CONCLUSIONS

This chapter examined the following question: What do interpreting educators need to know how to do in order to foster the development of competent interpreters? The question is really twofold—in order to answer it, we must answer both its parts:

- What do competent interpreters need to know how to do?
- What do educators need to know how to do to develop that competence?

The existing literature and the data reveal what a few already know, and what many more need to learn about and bring to their students. Documentation of the domains of knowledge and observable skills is available. The task analysis of 20 years ago at CIT, the Western

Maryland TIP curriculum of 1990, and the current CIT Educational Standards provide guidelines. Missing from these resources, however, is an explicit focus on developing the underlying processes for critical thinking, decision making, and self-assessment as the core foundational processes that interpreters must develop and that interpreting educators must learn how to develop in interpreting students.

The frequent focus on content in courses—on the "things" that educators believe need to be taught—has led many to panic and back-peddle when students are allowed to enter interpreting programs without prerequisite language and critical-thinking skills. The allotted educational time during programs is often spent bringing interpreting students up to minimum expectations of language performance and instilling basic information about the field instead of on developing more complex interpreting skills and processes. Educators may try hard to help students develop these; some try to provide learning opportunities that develop decision-making and self-assessment skills. But these goals are often not reached because so much time must be spent building foundational language skills that should be prerequisite to entry. When push comes to shove, the interpreting students must pass a test, get an A on a true/false exam, and spew correct answers on tests. Many educators believe that this is required by the system. Even workshop presenters reflect this attitude, expressing relief that they don't have to worry about "that," they just work with students.

What needs to be made explicit is the understanding that critical thinking, decision making, and self-assessment underlie competency in all areas of competent interpreting. Content, specific texts, and settings are the areas where these abilities need to be applied. Educators need to understand how to develop these skills and processes in interpreting students. This research indicates that many have that "gut feeling." Now it is important for educators to demystify that gut feeling and actively apply this understanding to the teaching and development of competent interpreters.

One goal of this volume is to consider how interpreting educators' needs apply to interpreting and interpreters in education. What are the implications for interpreted educations? Simply put, if educators are not helping interpreters develop their own sense of learning, of critical thinking, and of lifelong learning, and if educators are not demanding that interpreters be able to apply those processes across all knowledge and skill domains of interpreting, then interpreting educators are failing the deaf students in the classroom who ultimately depend on those interpreters. Most observers in the field believe that the least experienced interpreters usually go into K–12 interpreting. The standards for those interpreters in the K–12 setting are low, when they are not lacking completely (Jones, in press; Schick, Williams, & Bolster, 1999;

Winston, 2004). While the expected competence and standards may be higher for post-secondary interpreting, many beginning interpreters do not have adequate processing skills; are unable or unwilling to assess situations, make decisions, and then assess their own work; and may not be adequately competent in assessing the skills and abilities they need to accept or turn down assignments (Jones, in press; Jones, Clark, & Soltz, 1997; Schick, Williams, & Bolster, 1999; Yarger, 2001). Hearing students in the ideal classroom are learning how to construct knowledge, make learning their own, and critically self-assess. If the interpreters mediating between the teacher and the deaf student are not knowledgeable about these processes, they cannot effectively interpret them. Educators who place a primary focus on content, fact, hand movement, and correct grammar instead of on helping interpreters learn to develop the underlying essential processes are failing both the interpreters and the deaf students whose interpreted educations are inadequate and incomplete.

If interpreting education is to lead interpreters to competence, there are several implications for prerequisite skills. Incoming students must be competent in each language before entering an interpreting program and must be able to demonstrate critical-thinking, decision-making, and self-assessment skills using each of the languages or communication modes they intend to use as working languages or modes. Educators must insist that incoming students demonstrate higher-order skills in each language. If this means saying "no" to open door policies, so be it. Educators cannot support the illusion that students can learn both language and interpreting in 2 years and at the same time. When potential interpreters enter interpreting programs, they must be ready to build on pre-existing language skills in order to develop the complex competencies needed for interpreting. If existing programs are not allowed to require sufficient requisite language skills, they need to seriously consider the quality and competence of the graduates they are sending to the Community.

Interpreters graduating from programs need to demonstrate consistent competence in the application of critical thinking, decision making, and self-assessment in each domain of interpreting. Mastery of knowledge, remembering, and understanding are essential foundations for critical thinking. But we must demand that this knowledge and understanding be developed into critical thinking throughout every activity, workshop, course, and curriculum. Activities that begin with memory must still explicitly lead to critical thinking. Activities that focus on text analysis must lead students to learning about the text, constructing their own knowledge, and making effective decisions about that text. Simply telling students what is or is not working through one-way diagnostic work is not enough. The purpose of education is defeated when students are given activities that are graded by the teacher but are not given the opportunity to learn from and through the assessment. Equally important, interpreting education needs to bring the Deaf Community into the academic education that is currently the norm. Competent interpreters need to think critically, make decisions, and assess the consequences of their work within the context of the Deaf Community. They need to understand how interpreting affects the many differing cultures within and outside of the Deaf Community and must be culturally and communicatively competent.

In spite of years of teaching interpreting, in spite of curriculum changes, in spite of a recognized failure to adequately educate interpreters, we continue to do what we do. We accept students into interpreting programs because we are told to, ignoring evidence that it does not result in competent interpreters. We graduate students into the Community, acknowledging that they are not qualified, that there is a gap, and that they need at least a year or two to achieve even "entry level" competence. We recognize that we are barely able to teach them the facts, when what we need are interpreters who can go far beyond the facts; who can go beyond the most simple cognitive skills of remembering and understanding. We recognize that we do not provide enough relevant opportunities for the Deaf Community to influence our work, nor do we provide enough relevant opportunities for interpreting students to learn through and from the Deaf Community. Interpreters need to be able to apply the facts they remember; they need to analyze the situations and interactions they encounter; they need to evaluate the effectiveness of their work; and they need to create an ongoing cycle of learning, critical thinking, and self-assessment that continues throughout their careers. Interpreting educators need to focus on leading students toward developing these essential processes, and interpreting education must be intertwined with the input of the Deaf Community in order to succeed.

NOTES

1. There is no real evidence that hearing educators can do that, either. Many who evaluate effective interpretations attend to only one message at a time; comparing the meaning dynamics sequentially. An important direction for future research is investigating the effectiveness of on-site assessment of interpreting quality compared to studied assessment after the fact.

2. Public discussions in the past have often been ignored unless reported in writing. With the advent of electronic online-discussion formats, the presentations and discussions survive to document the topics and trends discussed. These online discussions have the advantage, as well, of providing a forum for international input from a broad spectrum of participants. Some recent examples include "What Do Interpreting Educators Need to Know to Teach Interpreting?," "Mentoring," and "Service Learning in Interpreting Education,"

sponsored by Project TIEM.Online, and the "Supporting Deaf People," conferences sponsored by Direct Learn, Inc.

3. Although the dates for Colonomos and Gish may appear to indicate that Gish's work occurred first, in fact, Colonomos presented her work much earlier. The 1992 date is the first published version of her work presented and distributed in the field.

4. Although the response rate was low, the results were informative. More information about how advertising for participants was conducted is included in the next section, which reports specifically on the Roundtable discussions.

5. Question 3 about course-wide evaluation did not elicit information directed to the more narrow focus of this study.

REFERENCES

Anderson, L.W., & Krathwohl, D.R. (Eds.). (2001). *Taxonomy of learning, teaching, and assessment.* New York: Longman.

ASLTA. (No date). *Evaluation and certification system for ASL teachers.* Available at http://www.aslta.org. [Accessed February 1, 2004]

Baker-Shenk, C. (1990). *Model curriculum for teachers of American sign language and teachers of ASL/English interpreting.* Available at http://www.asl.neu.edu/tiem.online/curriculum_baker-shenk.pdf. [Accessed January 15, 2004]

Bloom, B.S., Englehart, M.D., Furst, E. J., Hill, W. H., & Krathwohl, D. R. (Eds.). (1956). *Taxonomy of educational objectives. Handbook 1: Cognitive domain.* New York: David McKay.

Boud, D. (1995). *Enhancing learning through self-assessment.* Philadelphia: Kogan Page.

Cogen, C., Monikowski, C., Peterson, R., & Winston, E.A. (2002). *Survey for interpreting and ASL educators.* Unpublished document.

Cokely, D. (2003). Curriculum revision in the twenty first century: Northeastern's experience. In E.A. Winston (Ed.), *What do teachers need to know about teaching interpreting?* Northeastern University: Project TIEM.Online Roundtables available at http://208.185.149.218/, Archived Roundtables. [Accessed September 3, 2004]

Colonomos, B. (1992). *Processes in interpreting and transliterating: making them work for you.* Westminster, CO: Front Range Community College.

Conference of Interpreter Trainers. (1995). *National interpreter education standards.* Available at http://www.cit-asl.org/standard.html. [Accessed September 20, 2003]

Daniels, H. (Ed.). (2000). *An introduction to Vygotsky.* New York: Routledge.

Dean, R.K., & Pollard, R.Q. (2001). Application of demand-control theory to sign language interpreting: Implications for stress and interpreter training. *Journal of Deaf Studies and Deaf Education, 6* (1), 1–14.

Dean, R.K., Pollard, R.Q., Griffin, M., & Davis, J. (2002). *Reforming interpreter education: A practice-profession approach; year one progress report.* Presentation at the biennial meeting of the Conference of Interpreter Trainers, Minneapolis, MN.

Directory of Membership. (2001–2002). Conference of Interpreter Trainers.

Forster, A. (1993). *Professional development program in distance education: Learning at a distance*. Madison: University of Wisconsin Press, pp. 21–41.

Gish, S. (1984). Goal-to-detail and detail-to-goal. In M.L. McIntire (Ed.), *New dimensions in interpreter education: Task analysis—theory and application*. Proceedings of the 5th National Convention, Conference of Interpreter Trainers: RID Publications.

Gordon, P. (2003). Do students have to fail to succeed? In E.A. Winston (Ed.), *What do teachers need to know about teaching interpreting?* Northeastern University: Project TIEM.Online Roundtables. Available at http://208.185.149.218/. [Accessed September 3, 2004]

Humphrey, J.H. (2000). Portfolios: one answer to the challenge of assessment and the "readiness to work" gap. In C.B. Roy (Ed.), *Innovative practices for teaching sign language interpreters*. Washington, DC: Gallaudet University Press, pp. 153–175.

Jones, B.E. (In press). Competencies of K–12 educational interpreters: What we need versus what we have. In E.A. Winston (Ed.), *Educational interpreting: Why it succeeds*. Washington, DC: Gallaudet University Press.

Jones, B.E., Clark, G.M., & Soltz, D.F. (1997). Characteristics and practices of sign language interpreters in inclusive education programs. *Exceptional Children, 63*(2), 257–268.

Marzano, R.J. (2001). *Designing a new taxonomy of educational objectives*. Thousand Oaks, CA: Corwin Press.

Members of Conference of Interpreter Trainers. (1984a). Task analysis of interpretation and response. In M.L. McIntire (Ed.), *New dimensions in interpreter education: Task analysis-theory and application*. Asilomar, CA: RID Publications, pp. 29–69.

Members of Conference of Interpreter Trainers. (1984b). Task analysis of transliteration and response. In M.L. McIntire (Ed.), *New dimensions in interpreter education: Task analysis-theory and application*. Asilomar, CA: RID Publications, pp. 70–102.

Mindess, A. (2003). Building a firm foundation: Intercultural communication for sign language interpreters. In E.A. Winston (Ed.), *What do teachers need to know about teaching interpreting?* Northeastern University: Project TIEM.Online Roundtables. Available at http://208.185.149.218/, Archived Roundtables. [Accessed September 3, 2004]

Monikowski, C., & Peterson, R. (2003). Service learning in interpreter education programs. In *Project TIEM. Online Roundtable*. Available at http://208.185.149.218/. [Accessed September 3, 2004]

Monikowski, C., & Winston, E.A. (2003). Interpreters and interpreter education. In M. Marschark & P.E. Spencer (Eds.), *Oxford handbook of deaf studies, language, and education*. New York: Oxford University Press.

Patrie, C.J. (1994). The "readiness to work gap." In E.A. Winston (Ed.), *Mapping our course: A collaborative venture. Proceedings of the tenth national convention of interpreter trainers*. Charlotte, NC: Conference of Interpreter Trainers, pp. 53–56.

Peterson, R. (2003). Perspectives on curriculum making. In E.A. Winston (Ed.), *What do teachers need to know about teaching interpreting?* Northeastern University: Project TIEM.Online Roundtables. Available at http://208.185.149.218/, Archived Roundtables. [Accessed September 3, 2004]

Registry of Interpreters for the Deaf. (No date). *List of interpreter training programs.* Available at http://filemaker.rid.org/FMPro. [Accessed March 3, 2004]

Schick, B., Williams, K., & Bolster, L. (1999). Skill levels of educational interpreters working in public schools. *Journal of Deaf Studies and Deaf Education,* 4 (2), 144–155.

Swabey, L. (2003). Critical thinking and writing-to-learn in ASL and interpreter education. In E.A. Winston (Ed.), *What do teachers need to know about teaching interpreting?* Northeastern University: Project TIEM.Online Roundtables. Available at http://208.185.149.218/, Archived Roundtables. [Accessed September 3, 2004]

Synthesis of Deaf Education Laws. (No date). *What laws influenced the current early intervention laws?* Available at http://www.deafed.net/PublishedDocs/ 9807pbb.html. [Accessed January 14, 2004]

Vygotsky, L.S. (1978). *Mind in society.* Cambridge, MA: Harvard University Press.

Winston, E.A. (2004). *Language myths of an interpreted education.* Paper presented at the Supporting Deaf People Online Conference at http://208.185.150.197/.

Yarger, C.C. (2001). Educational interpreting: Understanding the rural experience. *American Annals of the Deaf, 146* (1), 16–30.

10

The Emerging Professionals: Deaf
Interpreters and Their Views
and Experiences on Training

Eileen Forestal

Deaf people working as interpreters are emerging as the new professional in the interpreting field. For the past 10 years in Philadelphia, Pennsylvania, all court cases involving deaf persons are required to have an interpreter. Hospitals and any medical emergency facilities in the same area must have one too. Interpreters are showing up in courts, hospitals, work-related sites, training programs, conferences, and theaters. You can find them in classrooms in deaf schools and in mainstream programs for deaf children across the country, primarily in major cities. Interpreters work as translators from spoken or written English to American Sign Language (ASL), international sign language, or in a gestural form in visual orientation. You can find them working with deaf-blind people, at international conferences, and at sporting events such as the World Games of the Deaf using ASL or International Sign Language. The hearing interpreter has more than likely worked with at least one in the past several years. They are now almost everywhere interpreting with deaf people and where ASL-English interpreting occurs. From empirical observations and personal experience as a deaf interpreter, it seems that these roles are evolving so rapidly, we have difficulty keeping up.

Where, when, and how did deaf people get involved in interpreting? Historically, deaf people have been interpreting among each other for hundreds of years. As Bienvenu (1991) noted, deaf people have been doing this since schools came into being for deaf children. Deaf students would clarify, explain, or reinforce by repetition for each other what was being said orally or by signing from the teachers in the classrooms or anyone outside of the classroom. Deaf people understood what it was like to frequently miss information or to not get it clearly, in a manner that can be best understood. Deaf adults would bring letters or vital papers to Deaf Clubs and social events to ask for clarification, explanation, or instructions on what these documents entailed. Often, these important letters or papers would be translated for them. In Deaf Clubs, during meetings, or at lectures, deaf persons who missed some information or came in late would be filled in by people sitting nearby. This was the norm in Deaf Clubs because deaf people trusted each other and provided as much information and assistance as possible. Many deaf adult children of deaf parents translated for their parents. They often felt this was an important factor in becoming bilingual (Bienvenu, 1991; Bienvenu & Colonomos, 1990; Collins & Roth, 1992).

In 1972, the Registry of Interpreters for the Deaf (RID) started awarding deaf persons Reverse Interpreting Skills Certificates (RSCs), originally developed for hearing interpreters who partially passed the certification examination, namely in the area of ASL-to-English interpreting. In the earlier days of interpreting, ASL-to-English interpreting was referred to as "reverse interpreting." Deaf adults needed to be on the panel for the certification examination because RID had a mandate that there be five panelists, three hearing and two deaf, for evaluations (see Cokely, this volume). All the panelists were required to be certified in order to serve as evaluators. RID decided that the only way to get around this was to certify deaf adults who had passed on their own merit with the RSC. The RSC had helped resolve the critical need of recruiting deaf panelists for the evaluations.

Around that time, deaf persons with or without an RSC were gradually being brought in to "help" hearing interpreters with deaf clients and were being called *intermediary interpreters*. With the deaf interpreter serving as intermediary interpreter, the hearing interpreter maintained the role as lead interpreter. Such a title, then, was acceptable and used accordingly. In addition, intermediary interpreters were being encouraged to obtain their RSC if they did not have one.

In 1988, RID suspended awarding RSCs to members while the entire testing and certification systems were being revamped (Frishberg, 1994). Since then, deaf individuals have not been able to obtain a certificate of any kind. RID also developed a Certified Deaf Interpreter (CDI) test, but it was suspended to undergo a complete overhaul when the validity of the written part of the test materials was questioned. While this research project was being conducted, RID's task force completed and scheduled the first nationwide written test. The knowledge portion of the test is now available in both the written format and in ASL on a CD-ROM, and the performance portion will follow soon (*RID Views*, February 2001).

Since the mid 1980s, the demand for qualified and Certified Deaf Interpreters has been growing rapidly. Passage of legislation related to communication accessibility promoted a greater demand for deaf interpreters (Bienvenu & Colonomos, 1990). RID had considered developing a certificate of "relay interpreting," since deaf persons working as interpreters were called "relay interpreters." With the newly emerging field of deaf people working as interpreters, deaf RID members (with support from many hearing members) suggested that it was more appropriate to have certification for deaf interpreters rather than a certificate titled "relay interpreting." In 1994–1995, RID set up the CDI Task Force in order to develop a testing system that would lead to a Certificate in Deaf Interpreting—Provisional (CDI-P). This would rectify the dilemma of deaf interpreters not being able to get a certificate of some kind.

To obtain a CDI-P, deaf persons were required to have 8 hours of training on theories of interpreting and 8 hours of training on RID's Code of Ethics, with a minimum of 1 year's experience working as an interpreter. Since CDI testing has been made available nationally, the CDI-P remains valid for 1 year. CDI-P holders must take and pass the CDI test to remain certified as deaf interpreters (Solow, 2000). The first testing for the written part of the newer CDI test was held on April 21, 2001; the performance portion is to be offered soon, and that will complete the entire process for the CDI test (*RID Views*, February 2001).

TEACHING-LEARNING OF DEAF INTERPRETERS

Moving from the service models of intermediary interpreting to relay interpreting, and now on to deaf interpreting, deaf interpreters have evolved from a secondary position to being an equal team member in a deaf-hearing interpreting team; they may even be the lead interpreter in situations in which deaf interpreters are working. But what do we really know about their roles, functions, and how they work in professional settings since they have become recognized as professional interpreters? Is there a consensus among deaf interpreters about their roles, functions, and necessary training? Is there agreement among educators and trainers as to what is necessary for teaching and how training should be designed for interpreter preparation for deaf persons? Should there be a core curriculum standard for deaf interpreter education, much like there is for hearing interpreter education?

The past 20 years or so have seen fluctuations in available workshops and training programs for deaf interpreters; however, little or no research has been conducted to provide trainers with tangible methods or a theoretical base to develop a core curriculum. So what are the trainers using for teaching? Could this lack of research be viewed as a backward march in the field of interpreting and interpreter education?

Cokely, in this volume, provides further discussion about the roles and the lack of research related to deaf interpreters and interpreting. How does the hearing interpreter view this deaf person working as an interpreter and team member and vice versa? Is the process the same as when a hearing interpreter works solo or is teamed with another hearing interpreter in settings such as the courtroom, a classroom with deaf children, or hospitals? Do deaf interpreters bring in their own "frame" as consumers based on how hearing interpreters have worked with them? Do they bring different power dynamics into the work and within the team? These are all valid questions that need to be explored more as curriculums are developed for teaching deaf interpreting. The purpose for this research is to investigate what deaf interpreters actually learn and need in terms of their training.

DEAF INTERPRETERS IN PRACTICE

Although limited in scope, there are several sources of information on deaf interpreting and deaf-hearing interpreting team processes. Most of the literature sketchily describes the job, role, and function of a deaf interpreter and the certification(s) available to deaf persons working as deaf interpreters. Most research mentions only the settings where deaf interpreters may be working, such as hospitals, courtrooms, and in highly sensitive situations where "trust" would be a major issue. They might also be working with deaf-blind persons and deaf persons who have limited ASL skills, limited use of a foreign sign language, or limited communication skills. Benefits of using deaf interpreters include linguistic and cultural adjustments as well as shared connections with deaf experiences. Misunderstandings could be alleviated, and a deaf-hearing interpreter team could optimize communication and understanding by all the parties, thereby saving time and money (Collins & Roth, 1992; Frishberg, 1994; Mindess, 1999; Sandefur, 1994; Solow, 2000). These sources provide basic information about deaf interpreting, but they do not offer specifics on requisite skills, processes, or training needs.

In a *RID Views* essay entitled "Certified Deaf Interpreter—WHY?" Reggie Egnatovitch stated that there is now more training available for deaf interpreters, though not much for deaf-hearing teams (1999). Likewise, deaf-hearing team training is not included in interpreter training programs of hearing interpreters. Egnatovitch suggested five important benefits a deaf-hearing interpreter team might provide:

- Serve as a double-checking system,
- Provide a grace period of time for processing information,
- Monitor for effect and neutrality,
- Protect the "right to know" for the deaf consumer, and
- Increase the comfort level for the deaf consumer.

Egnatovitch closed with a statement that deaf interpreters must have training in processing and the linguistic study of ASL, be familiar with specific terminology of various settings, maintain the equivalency and integrity of the message, and follow the Code of Ethics. This information is similar to that provided in the previous sources; however, Egnatovitch expanded his discussion on training and functions of a deaf-hearing interpreter team. Even though the article includes somewhat more in-depth discussion about deaf interpreting, it does not provide specific information on how to provide training on processing or the role and functions of deaf interpreter and team processes between a deaf and hearing interpreter team.

Ressler (1999) looked into deaf-hearing interpreting team processes to determine if there were differences between the hearing interpreter's interpretation "fed" to the deaf interpreter and the deaf interpreter's interpretation. She found there was no evidence or research indicating that interpretations by deaf interpreters are more accurate linguistically or culturally than those of hearing interpreters. Ressler points out that the dynamics of the relationship within the deaf-hearing interpreter team add to the complexity of the interpreting task for each team member. She also augmented that there were no guidelines or standards defining team processes, nor were there techniques deaf and hearing interpreter teams could employ to work effectively on their interpretations. Ressler has pointed out the need for more research on the work and more training of deaf-hearing interpreter teams.

Through her review of the literature, Ressler discovered that there was no earlier research to study the processes between the hearing and deaf interpreters or to provide strategies for them to work together. Her research was limited in that it was based on only one deaf-hearing interpreter team, though she hoped there would be other teams to help or refute the results of her study. Her suggestions for future research include making a clear distinction about how deaf interpreters function; deaf-hearing interpreting teams; and the dynamics affecting deaf-hearing interpreter teams with regard to their interpersonal and intercultural relationships. Ressler hoped that her findings would provide some of the basic tools for training she deemed necessary for deaf-hearing interpreter teams and would increase their repertoire. Her work is significant because it seems to be the first project that attempts to research and analyze the processes and interpretation of, and within, a deaf-hearing interpreter team.

Wilcox (2000) focused on the use of deaf interpreters in courtrooms. She discussed how a "deaf multi-lingual interpreter or a multi-culturally aware deaf interpreter" with a hearing interpreter can provide the accurate interpretation in which bilingual-bicultural competence and highly sophisticated cognitive processing skills are required (p. 94). Wilcox highlighted the benefits of having a deaf interpreter in the courtroom to provide linguistic and cultural access, bring "comfort" into the complexities of the courtroom, and remove the cultural and linguistic oppression that has been so apparent and ingrained in the legal systems at all levels. She said that many states were slowly implementing the use of qualified deaf interpreters, which are also growing in numbers. She noted that training for deaf interpreters is infrequent and limited to content. Throughout her article, the following issues were adamantly stressed: emphasis for skills needed for deaf interpreters' nativeness or fluency in ASL; world knowledge from a deaf cultural perspective; understanding of oppression mechanisms within language use, culture, and society; multicultural awareness; and understanding of the legal system.

Bienvenu and Colonomos (1990) provided apparently the only attempt to explain and develop prototypes of deaf interpreting and training of deaf interpreters. Of all the literature reviewed thus far, this is the only article that mentions deaf interpreters using consecutive interpreting as a process and an approach for teaching. It is also the only analysis of deaf interpreting that provides a model of how deaf interpreting takes place. The model shows the "path" of the process of interpreting among the four "players": deaf consumer(s), a deaf interpreter, a hearing interpreter, and hearing consumer(s). This process entailed the rendering of information from the deaf consumer(s) to the deaf interpreter, which was conveyed to the hearing interpreter. The hearing interpreter, in turn, transmitted in the target language to the hearing consumer(s). The process was replicated in turn from the hearing consumer(s) to the deaf consumer(s) via the hearing interpreter and deaf interpreter.

Bienvenu and Colonomos basically delineated the requisite skills for deaf interpreters: linguistic skills, fluent communication skills, cultural sensitivity, and the ability to work in a wide range of bilingual and bicultural settings. Without being conclusive (due to the newness of the field and lack of research data), the authors suggested the following competencies of trainers for deaf interpreting: bilingual and bicultural, experience as deaf interpreter, a model instructor, and the ability to effectively teach both deaf and hearing students. Subsequently, they outlined the fundamental components of a teaching curriculum on deaf interpreting: minority group dynamics and oppression, language acquisition, interpreting process, and team interpreting.

Bienvenu and Colonomos also discussed effective strategies for instruction and training of deaf interpreters. Only two major strategies were mentioned: separate training for deaf persons and consecutive interpreting processes. The rationale of separate training was that in a mixed classroom or workshop with both deaf and hearing students, there would be an imbalance of power and knowledge in the first phases of training. The major difference between deaf and hearing students is that very few deaf persons have opportunities for interpreter education on interpreting and processing theories but are fluent in ASL, whereas hearing students are primarily educated in these theories but are still learning ASL as a second language. Both deaf and hearing students need opportunities to discuss and work on their own issues of the dynamics of oppression.

Another critical section of the paper was a brief discussion of several strategies and some knowledge areas for deaf interpreting. Additional questions were raised on the role of the deaf interpreter and the necessity for a broader scope of roles in various situations. Bienvenu and Colonomos viewed deaf and deaf-blind interpreting as two separate aspects of interpreting and required separate training for each. The reasoning behind this was that deaf-blind interpreting requires skills working between visual ASL and tactile ASL. They concluded with a note that the field was still new and the processes and roles of deaf interpreting need to be further researched and analyzed to be understood in greater depth for training purposes.

Obviously, literature available on deaf interpreting is minimal, with the exception of work by Bienvenu and Colonomos. Most authors attempt to describe the roles, functions, and specific skills of a deaf interpreter and a deaf-hearing interpreter team; however, they frequently fall short in this objective. The preceding review shows that there is no in-depth information related to theories of how a deaf interpreter may process information or work in certain roles. Bienvenu and Colonomos's article was the first to focus, as its primary objective, on the processes and roles of a deaf interpreter and what trainers needed to know for teaching deaf persons and hearing interpreters. In addition, they discussed concisely the theoretical knowledge and skills needed for both trainers and deaf interpreters. They also pointed out emphatically that more analysis and research are needed on this emerging field, because more deaf persons are working as deaf interpreters and many more are seeking training of some kind.

Based on the minimal availability of literature on the actual training of deaf interpreters, coupled with rapidly growing numbers of deaf interpreters, the need for quality training of deaf interpreters is now crucial; this is made even more so with the newly available CDI tests. How can trainers be assured that appropriate theories and skills are being provided in the training?

A QUALITATIVE STUDY OF DEAF INTERPRETERS

This section will focus on the following areas:

- Background, experiences, certification, and length and type of work as deaf interpreters;

- Type and length of training;
- Theories and skills taught in training;
- Resources on deaf interpreting;
- Views of deaf interpreters on training and specific needs of training; and
- Qualifications and competencies of deaf interpreters.

I contacted deaf interpreters, depending on location and scheduling of the research taking place. Contacts were actively working as deaf interpreters and had certification of some kind from RID: RSC, CDI-P, or CDI.

The deaf interpreters were interviewed about their views on what the qualifications and competencies of deaf interpreters should be and recommendations for changes in the training of deaf interpreters.

This study is exploratory; not much has been researched or written about this topic or the population—deaf interpreters as an emerging group of professionals. The goal was to inquire and listen to the interviewees who agreed to participate in this study and to build a picture based on their experiences and ideas. To gather data for this study, in-depth interviews were conducted with 10 deaf persons who were currently working as interpreters or who had worked within the past 5 years.

Interviews took place at various locations within the United States: four in the New England area, two on the East Coast, three in the Southwest, and one on the West Coast. The interviewees were purposely selected to represent the profession of deaf interpreters. Approximately 30 deaf persons were contacted, 28 of whom were eager and willing to participate in the interview. The two who had declined were concerned about privacy and confidentiality due to being videotaped. This is an understandable concern due to cultural, sociopolitical and professional issues within the Deaf Community and the interpreting community. Of those 28, only 10 were available within the time frame chosen. Only nine interviews were successfully recorded on a video camera. It was discovered at the time of video transcription that the tenth video recording did not "take" after the introductory part of the interview was completed. Thus, only about 10 minutes of the preliminary interview were recorded.

Both the interviewees and the interviewer were included on the videotape in order to follow the line of questioning and feedback. The interviews were conducted in a room arranged by the interviewee where there would be no distraction and where the interviewer and interviewee could sit across from each other at a table. The length of the interviews ranged from 1 to 2 or more hours. The interview began with a brief questionnaire, in written English or signed if preferred, for demographic purposes. Afterward, the interview proceeded with questions signed in ASL.

The consent form addressed several considerations that the interviewees might have regarding privacy, confidentiality, ethical issues, and risk assessment. The interviewee may ask or think, "What is in it for me? Why should I participate in this interview? How will this interview affect my work, my reputation, as well as me? How will interviewing help my profession and me? Will my privacy be respected? Who will see the videotape of me?" The consent form was intended to nullify these issues for the interviewee. Interviews do affect people, and the process brings the interviewee's thoughts, feelings, knowledge, and past experiences out into the open; in this case, on training and the process of becoming a deaf interpreter. If the interviewee was not satisfied with the consent form or had some concerns or questions, further clarification or discussion would have been allowed. It was the goal of the study to conduct the interviews in such a manner that the process for the interviewees became reflective and left them knowing more about themselves and their selected profession as a deaf interpreter. The primary focus of the interview was to gather data, not to change the interviewee.

The framework and format for the interview was structured and open-ended. The questions were asked in the same sequence in all the interviews. Two sections, listing specific units of training, ask for a value, using the Likert scale from 1 through 5. One set of values added an option to the Likert scale—having open-ended questions after choosing a rating. All the interviewees answered the same questions, thus increasing comparability of the responses. The data were complete for each person on the topics addressed in the interview. This type of interview reduced "interviewer effects" and bias that can occur when several interviews are used. One disadvantage is its limited flexibility in relating the interview to the particular interviewees. Another is that standardized wording of the questions could constrain and limit naturalness and relevance of questions and answers. The interview guide was a list of questions and probes that maintained the interviewer's flexibility to pursue in-depth conversations along the line of questioning. The interview was more structured than an informal, in-depth interview. From the list of questions, the interviewer could probe for a range of training, experiences, values, benefits, or needs of the training as well as predictions to the future of deaf interpreting and training for deaf interpreters. To reiterate, the interview was conducted entirely in ASL, other than when obtaining the demographic information.

Analysis of Interviews

The videotapes of the interviews were transcribed, which was challenging and time consuming because the process required translation from ASL to written English. Caution was made to include the discourse and cultural implications within ASL, in translating from ASL to written English. This researcher holds an RSC from RID and is qualified to translate from ASL to English. The translations were verified for accuracy by reading back from the translation to what was signed. It is important to note that this was not the focus on the text and discourse analysis; rather, it was the information on deaf interpreting being sought.

The analysis of the individual interviews was carried out separately, and linkages between the interviews were identified toward the end of the analysis. A second dimension of this inductive analysis investigated themes that arose from the questions. In order for this research to be viewed as a pilot study and be completed within the time constraints, six areas were identified as themes within the greater body of data. These themes will be discussed in greater detail in the following section.

Findings

In summarizing this research, several key issues are identified and discussed, including the perceptions of the deaf interpreters and how they were affected by their training or lack thereof, and by their work experiences. The findings will be primarily focused on six areas: (1) background, experiences, certification, and length and type of work as deaf interpreters; (2) type and length of training; (3) theories and skills taught in training; (4) resources on deaf interpreting; (5) views of deaf interpreters on specific needs of training, and (6) qualifications and competencies of deaf interpreters.

To maintain confidentiality, each interview was coded with a letter, though not necessarily in alphabetical order or in order of the interviews. All references to names of schools, agencies, cities, states, names of persons, an so forth were referred to ambiguously (e.g., this state, on the West Coast, Commission of the Deaf and Hard of Hearing, this trainer or teacher, etc.). This was done to maintain the terms as promised in the letter of consent, which was signed by both the interviewees and the researcher.

Background, Experiences, Certification, and Length
and Type of Work as Deaf Interpreters

Of the nine deaf persons interviewed, three received their training from an interpreter education program, three primarily from workshops, and three from a federally funded Deaf interpreting training program that met one full weekend once a month for 3 years. Of the nine interviewed, seven were female and two were male. Four had a Master's degree, three had a Bachelor's degree, one had an Associate degree, and one had a certificate of completion from an interpreter training program and was working toward an Associate degree.

At the time of the interviews, RID's RSC certificates were suspended and the new tests for CDI certification were not available yet. Thus, all the interviewees had a CDI-P. Half of them were hoping to obtain CDI certification when the tests became available. Two wanted to have the CDI tests available in Spanish or a Mexican language. The majority of them were very concerned about the written or signed component of the test and whether they would understand the stimulus questions.

This researcher feels it is noteworthy to mention, based on information obtained during background studies before the interviews, how the interviewees got involved in deaf interpreting. The interviewees were asked how and why they became deaf interpreters. None had planned on deaf interpreting as a career. It was something they either fell into or were pulled into. Some saw it as an opportunity to develop a career, a second career after being downsized or "RIF'd," or as an additional job. In their early years, no one had ever recommended that they consider deaf interpreting as a profession and a job. One took on a part-time job as deaf-blind interpreter as a means of support through college. Another took on a summer job as a deaf interpreter after graduation from college with pending plans to attend a law school, and "the rest is history." One noted that ever since she was a child, she had been involved in clarifying or interpreting to other deaf children and later on with her spouse and friends. Many deaf adults depended on her for simple matters such as completing forms for SSA/SSI/SSD benefits, doctor visits, and simple court matters. There were times when she had been called to emergency rooms and hospitals when hearing interpreters were not able to "connect" with the deaf patients. However, she had never considered that it could become a profession until the "boom" of deaf interpreters. Two made mention that they saw deaf interpreters working at conferences and felt that it would be something they would like to "try out, as it seemed to be a new trend." There seems to be a consensus that all fell into the job from a personal need or from someone needing services such as deaf-blind interpreting or a foreign language, in this case, Sign Language of Mexico (SLM).

Resources on Deaf Interpreting

One question asked about availability and types of resources (books, handouts, videotapes, etc.) used for training as well as any specific resources for deaf interpreters. Based on the outcomes of the interviews, there are no materials specifically designed with deaf interpreting and deaf-hearing interpreting teaming in mind. A lot of handouts and readings were generic and designed primarily for interpreter education of hearing interpreters. No handouts, other than the chart from Bienvenu and Colonomos (1990), were focused on deaf interpreting, although some were focused on the processing models of interpreting between ASL and English. Some videotapes had models of ASL interpreting for deaf persons to practice interpreting from. The following comment from one interviewee captures the feelings of all the interviewees.

> Yes, books and VTs [videotapes] were usually used . . ., but nothing whatsoever on deaf interpreting and showing deaf interpreters working and how they work in teams, etc., nothing in books or VTs for training. We would use the VTs for hand-on for interpreting skills; still nothing to show deaf interpreters working in situations and working with hearing interpreters. We need to see how they work and for us to have models. There is very little where we can go and observe deaf interpreters working. So it is frustrating. It is almost like working in the dark when I have to assume what and how I should function as a deaf interpreter in critical situations.

Interviewees stressed that there was nothing available for them to learn from or to practice with. Even though some videotapes, materials, and activities could be adapted and applied for the learning process toward becoming a deaf interpreter, the interviewees emphasized that there is a critical need to have a theoretical model of deaf interpreting processes, conveyance of the information between the deaf and hearing interpreter team, types of languages and gestures used for specific clients, sight translations, specific situations such as in legal, educational, medical, and mental health realms and how deaf interpreters function in those arenas. Books for ethics, ASL linguistics, and Deaf Culture have been used. Only one book and a videotape on deaf-blind communication techniques were available. Two interviewees mentioned a manual for legal interpreting training that had some basic information for deaf interpreting, including information about interpreter responsibilities, how to explain their role, and reasons for having deaf interpreters in court. But that was the extent of it. One interviewee said, "I am tired of waiting for a book about deaf interpreting and to see videotapes with real deaf interpreters working with hearing interpreters." Two of the interviewees discussed the need for handouts and materials in SLM, since they were natives of Mexico now working in southwestern states and were relied on often for interpreting for deaf individuals from Mexico. Training, for them, was especially difficult since the limited materials that were available were in English.

Another theme that emerged with regard to materials and videotapes was the need to have videotapes of deaf interpreters sharing their experiences. These could provide an excellent tool for learning and understanding the roles and functions of deaf interpreting. There was much concern about working on ethical dilemmas and how much cultural mediation could be applied to specific situations.

The interviewees were also asked about their trainers or teachers, their background and qualifications, and whether they were deaf or hearing. Names were not required or requested. The basis for asking these questions was that trainers/teachers are a vital resource in training deaf interpreters. Most of the trainers/teachers were RID certified and experienced interpreters, as well as trainers or teachers. Those who were hearing had much experience in working with deaf interpreters. Their qualifications were satisfactory to the interviewees. Of all the trainers/teachers, about half were deaf, half were hearing, and one was an adult child of deaf parents.

One interviewee felt that all her hearing trainers were qualified; however, she felt that they did not know enough to delve into a deeper level about how deaf interpreters use their worldview in the interpretation. Another interviewee felt that resources for trainers and training opportunities for teachers were limited and expressed the need for more qualified deaf trainers. It was interesting to learn from the interviews that one or two trainers were still from the "old school of thought" in terms of teaching the Code of Ethics and interpreting processes, meaning that the trainer viewed the Code of Ethics as being rule-based and rigid and the interpretation would be more of "staying close to the form." Based on the comments of the interviewees, there is a critical need for training opportunities for trainers on teaching approaches and strategies on deaf interpreting.

Theories and Skills Taught in Training

The interviewees were then asked about approaches, strategies, and methods used by the trainers in teaching deaf interpreting skills, requisite skills, and deaf-hearing interpreter teaming processes. Interestingly, each of the interviewees felt most successful with hands-on activities, role-plays, and team or group activities that provided opportunities for skill application based on what was briefly explained in the lectures. What was deemed most successful aspect of training was the ability to discuss, analyze, and compare the work from the hands-on or group activities to see how the information was processed for interpretation by the deaf persons in the group activities. Many found it difficult to retain information when being taught primarily through lecturing, and they benefited most from group and individual activities, as they were required to use all their language and cultural skills. The same was true for those who had training on deaf-hearing interpreter team processes. These preferences all relate to active learning using higher-order skills rather than passive learning; these interviews recognized the value of learning to think critically, make decisions, and self-assess (Winston, this volume).

About half of the interviewees recalled that they were exposed to Bienvenu and Colonomos's interpreting model for learning interpreting processes (1990) as well as to Gish's model of processing information. The interviewees reiterated that with only few workshops available, there was not much opportunity to absorb and understand the theories and application of the processes for skills development. One interviewee who graduated from an interpreter education program mentioned that she learned about the theories and was able to develop skills from them; however, it was difficult to know to what depth deaf interpreters should apply them to their work, having no models of deaf interpreters in the interpreter education program. The key factors were learning how to analyze texts and interpret consecutively.

Most of the interviewees felt they learned best when consecutive interpreting was utilized as a teaching strategy and applied in the group activities and in training for deaf-hearing interpreter teams. Consecutive interpreting is not something that deaf persons see regularly within interpreting as a consumer; thus, learning it through this process helped them develop confidence to use it within the legal, mental health, and medical disciplines. Application of consecutive interpreting allows for critical-thinking skill development, a more thorough interpretation using linguistic and cultural adjustments, as well as a dialogue or conference with the team interpreter.

Learning about the Code of Ethics brought up interesting issues for the deaf interpreters. Three of the interviewees commented that the very first workshop they attended "spent too much time on RID's Code of Ethics. Don't get me wrong, it is important to learn about the Code of Ethics. To learn in black and white terms and what we can do, can't, must do or must not do, I realized, was not helpful for me in the real world of interpreting. It was done all in lectures and we were not allowed to ask questions for more clarification. So the lecture was more in a rigid style." Most felt it was vital to learn about ethics in broader terms and critical thinking for ethical decisions. They reported that being provided with analytical approaches toward given situations would be more useful for them as deaf interpreters. It would help them learn how to discuss issues with their team and the hearing interpreter, and it would help them work toward a mutual agreement on ethical decisions. The interviewees believed that learning how experienced deaf interpreters as well as deaf-hearing interpreter teams handled ethical dilemmas would be an excellent tool and model. Opportunities for this have been minimal for the interviewees, other than their interactions with deaf trainers.

It is crucial to share at this point what two interviewees said, because their thoughts were echoed by three-quarters of the interviewees.

All the deaf teachers I had used a lot of group discussions, activities, and role-plays as well as hands-on. They would give a brief lecture and then provide activities and discussions to develop more in-depth understanding and skills. The hearing teachers I had would lecture and have discussions; however, there were no role-plays or hands-on, which would help in applying what was being lectured and discussed. The teachers do have their own styles of teaching and approaches. I feel that deaf teachers seem to help us relate more to our experiences and what we are learning.

You see, I am a visual learner, and being involved in "doing the work" helps me a lot with learning. Show me, show me how to apply, and then let me do it. Afterwards discuss what happened. With the breakdown of the information into parts and a lot of examples used, I can clearly visualize the information and understand a lot more. That is a good teaching strategy, especially for deaf persons.

These comments bring up a serious question on how instruction may be best conducted. They call for a whole new avenue of research on teaching methods, deaf education, and the learning processes of deaf persons, and they emphasize that deaf interpreters find this focus on application and analysis to be essential (Winston, this volume).

Views of Deaf Interpreters on Training and Specific Needs of Training

Interviewees were asked various questions regarding training to elicit their views on those aspects of training they deemed to be critical. A few themes cropped up, and comments from the interviewees provided considerable insight based on their experiences, their training, and how their work as deaf interpreters is reflected from the training. The first question asked if the interviewees felt their training had prepared them for deaf interpreting and in what ways.

Due to the scarcity of workshops and programs specifically geared toward deaf persons on deaf interpreting, there was general dissatisfaction over the availability of training. It was strongly stressed that there wasn't enough training or mentoring programs for deaf interpreters. Also, they expressed a critical need for materials and videotapes showing deaf interpreters working on translations and interpretations, to use as a basis for discussion, practice, and reviews.

Another concern was the RID training requirement for CDI-P certification: deaf applicants had to complete 16 hours of training—8 hours on theories of interpreting and 8 hours on ethics (*RID Views*, February 2001) in order to qualify. Half of the interviewees expressed frustration on this point, as "this sets much lower standards for deaf interpreters." One interviewee aptly said that "this mentality is an insult to deaf interpreters who have put in many hours of training, work, and attending whatever workshops are available, even if it meant going out of state or flying to go to the workshops" and that "the bar needs to be raised" on standards on deaf interpreting, and specialized training for deaf interpreters must be developed. Because the workshops are so few far apart, opportunities are minimal for continued skill development and critical thinking on interpretation and ethical decisions. One interviewee mentioned that when teaming with another deaf interpreter who had no training, work was very difficult and it threw off teamwork. The basis for this observation was that the role and functions of deaf interpreting were not comprehended, so they were not able to discuss processing, interpretation, and analyzing the message. This interviewee went on to say, "All deaf interpreters must be required to have comprehensive training."

Well, one workshop in 1995 was not enough and it was hard to find workshops close to my hometown. But I was told that I could become CDI-P with only 8 hours of interpreting and 8 hours on the code of ethics. But I felt still I did not understand enough about interpreting. I went ahead and started to work because I was already working in interpreting. The agency told me it was fine to have only a CDI-P. I tried to go to some workshops on deaf interpreting. There was another one later on about 3 years later, on deaf interpreting in my state. I went there and it was almost the same as in 1995. Then I heard about your workshops. It helped me understand more about processing, expansion, and how I should wait until I understand what the hearing person is talking about. . . . I learned it is OK to ask the hearing interpreter to work with me and agree on how we can work together. For a long time I thought, as some deaf interpreters still do, that we just become relay interpreters and I cannot discuss with my team person if I had some questions on the process or the information that was conveyed to me. I noticed my work has improved because I feel better and understand more about interpreting . . . I don't think I felt prepared for a long time and had to learn on the job. In the past some hearing interpreters were helpful and explained to me why they interpreted in certain ways . . . I found myself developing ulcers as I tried to follow the rigid techniques from the first workshop in 1995. I just had to let go of what I had learned and depend on my gut feelings. The most recent workshop validated many things I had felt and taught me techniques and strategies and basic skill development for processing.

I am not satisfied and want more. There should be deaf interpreters teaching and training deaf interpreters as we can do more text analysis and discussion as applied to deaf interpreting. I want to have a deaf interpreter trainer for teaching and sharing experiences and to have a depth of knowledge on interpreting,

text analysis, ethical situations, and on handling certain protocol
and situations, etc. I strongly feel that having a deaf interpreter
teaching and training, we can go more into depth on analysis of
our work and texts. Often when I go to interpreting workshops
that are other than deaf interpreting, I am the only or one of very
few deaf persons there; the hearing participants want to use me or
the few of us as a role model or examples which takes away what
we wanted to come for. I came there to learn too, not to be asked
on how we would sign or do some things they want to know
about or practice on us. I wish there would be workshops for only
deaf interpreters where we would have no pressure and we
can be free to open our minds and have intense discussions to
stretch our minds.

These excerpts from two different interviewees reflect the consensus,
experiences, and feelings of most interviewees in this research and help
to conclude this section. They support Bienvenu's and Colonomos's
view that training for deaf interpreters should be separate due to imbalance of power and knowledge between deaf and hearing participants and minority group dynamics. Hearing interpreters may be
ingrained with theories on interpreting and processing, whereas deaf
persons have had very little opportunities to develop their own
thoughts and opinions (1990).

On another important note, the deaf interpreters whose native language is SLM adamantly said that there is a dire need for more deaf
interpreters skilled in SLM and for more teachers, both hearing and deaf,
knowledgeable about training and working with deaf persons who use
sign languages and/or gestures other than ASL. Also, they expressed a
need for workshops on SLM for both deaf and hearing interpreters.

The next two questions asked which professional settings they felt
the most and least prepared to work in. It was interesting and alarming
to this researcher that most of the interviewees felt they were not
prepared for most settings other than "one on one" or what they
deemed "safe." The settings that they felt most unprepared for or least
confident in were mental health, educational, legal, and lastly medical:
"Liability is what scares me." One commented that because there was
so much controversy in educational interpreting within deaf education,
she was reluctant to work in that setting. One interpreter whose primary work is in legal and court interpreting felt she was prepared
because she spent many hours and days attending legal interpreting
workshops, had taken a basic course in law, and had read up on foreign language interpreting. This same interpreter felt that there was
a need for more specialized training on legal interpreting for deaf
interpreters and for more deaf interpreters within the legal realm.

Few of the deaf interpreters reported that they felt comfortable interpreting for deaf-blind persons and that they were reluctant to move into new avenues such as conferences or legal and mental health settings unless more training were provided. It was interesting to learn that many were resistant to doing conference interpreting because most of their training was based on consecutive interpreting and not much was known about the process of simultaneous interpreting while working with a feed/team hearing interpreter.

The next question, related to whether their training had prepared them to work with hearing interpreters as a team, received the following sorts of answers:

> Big time, yes. I have noticed that when I work with hearing interpreters who have gone through the ITP [Interpreter Training Program], we seem to work well and know where we are going during the process. Others that I have worked with who have had no ITP training, we would have a hard time working as a team. They would not understand why I am processing and interpreting the way I am and what I needed from the team. So that made my work difficult.

> [M]ore should be stressed on this, especially for deaf-hearing interpreter teams. I have noticed that many deaf interpreters and hearing interpreters really don't understand what teamwork is all about. There needs to be a lot of processing within the teams.

> Hearing interpreters have their own issues, too. Some hearing interpreters keep up with their skills and professional development and others don't bother to keep up.

> A little. We met only for a short time to role-play a teaming situation. There is no course specifically for deaf-hearing interpreter teams. It is important we have more training so that we can work together better and benefit from each other.

Discussions about working with hearing interpreters focused on the need for training on the part of hearing interpreters and the fact that workshops or courses on this aspect should be offered more often for deaf and hearing interpreters alike. Several issues emerged about hearing interpreters, their willingness to work with deaf interpreters as an equal team member, and their need to take more training. One interviewee made a comment, which seems to reflect the opinions of the other interviewees, that "I know many hearing interpreters 'scream' for more training on teaming and how to use protocol with the team member." Another interviewee said, "Training is needed for monitoring and sharing the 'burden of proof' when one of the team members needs to challenge the interpretation of the other team member. This way the team members can fairly discuss the work and understand more about the spoken/signed text and the interpretation being challenged."

There seems to be a critical issue related to interpreter education programs offering opportunities for teaching hearing interpreters and inviting deaf interpreters to take part in these classes. Interpreter educators may have briefly explained the teaming but have not provided further training through group activities, having deaf interpreters as speakers, and so on. Many learned on the job, so to speak. Concerns were expressed that hearing interpreters often do not understand the role, processes, and functions of deaf interpreting and that deaf interpreters at a loss as to how best explain or justify their decisions with the linguistic and cultural adjustments or mediation.

Qualifications and Competencies of Deaf Interpreters

Few questions were asked of the interviewees regarding what qualifications and competencies deaf interpreters should have. There was general consensus that all deaf interpreters should be native users of ASL, have linguistic and cultural knowledge of ASL and English, have sensitivity to and understanding of other cultures, be bilingual, and know how to take a text and interpret it into ASL. In addition, most stressed that the qualifications should include having interpersonal skills, an appropriate attitude or "attitude training," cultural mediating skills, processing and expansion skills, gestural skills, use of techniques to use pictures and different tools for communication, and finally, respect for the field of deaf interpreting and interpreting in general. All the interviewees were adamant that deaf interpreters need in-depth training, even if it means taking a few years of courses/workshops. They all felt that there needs to be more screening for deaf interpreters and more support through frequent, available, and accessible workshops and training.

A similar question focused on what changes were needed in training for deaf persons. Responses were parallel to what they deemed were necessary with regard to qualifications and competencies. The common themes for recommended changes included more emphasis on processing skills, ASL and gestural skills, expansion techniques and purposes for expansion, ethical decision-making processes, interpersonal training, working with hearing interpreters, hearing interpreters learning to team with deaf interpreters, mentoring, and explanations of roles and benefits of the team to hearing consumers. More text and comparative analysis for translation and processing is critical to provide practice and application toward different interpretation in different settings. Most of the interviewees mentioned that demonstration models of deaf interpreting would be valuable tools for teaching and learning. An underlying theme of frustration among the interviewees was evident when discussion turned to advanced training on deaf interpreting; they couldn't understand why there were not more workshops on advanced deaf interpreting processes. That in itself would satisfy a great need for most of them.

SUMMARY AND CONCLUSIONS

There seems to be very little support or encouragement for deaf interpreting as a career or as a profession. According to the interviewees, they want to see more support from RID, its chapters, and the interpreting community for more intensive training. Most of those who were interviewed decided to get training as deaf interpreters and/or work as deaf interpreters by chance. With the advent of laws requiring accessibility to language and communication, more support and avenues for deaf interpreting should be provided. The means to do that would have to be explored.

Training has been primarily available only through workshops, and only one U.S. college provided a certificate program specifically for deaf persons (this certificate was federally funded and has not been offered again). Workshops are only rarely offered. Many introductory workshops focus on 8 hours of interpreting theories and 8 hours on RID's Code of Ethics, as required for RID's CDI-P and CDI's written tests (*RID Views*, December, 2003). Seldom are workshops on processing, ethical training, protocol, processes of deaf and hearing interpreter teaming, and advanced training for deaf interpreters offered. Based on the interviews, there seems to be a belief that 16 hours of training would suffice for deaf persons to be qualified as deaf interpreters. This view has been influenced by RID's eligibility requirement for obtaining a CDI-P or taking the CDI written test. Based on the interviewees, 16 hours are not enough and deaf persons need more than 16 hours of training. The paucity of training ostensibly limits opportunities for deaf interpreters to become more skilled, knowledgeable, guided, and prepared for specialized areas such as work in the legal, medical, mental health, and educational arenas. The same holds for those who want to be involved in education of deaf children or work with teachers of the deaf or in the mainstream classrooms where deaf children are placed. "There should be a degree in deaf interpreting," one interviewee exclaimed emphatically.

All three interviewees who received their training from an interpreter education program (all different colleges) felt much dissatisfaction because they were the only deaf persons in the classrooms. As Bienvenu and Colonomos (1990) discussed, minority group dynamics affect the learning processes, and in these cases, there was a lack of modeling of deaf interpreters, even though they received much support and encouragement. Two of the three interviewees were aware that much of the curriculum was adapted to allow them to pass written exams and to be waived from working on English texts. All three shared feelings of loneliness and isolation, while hearing students were able to share their learning experiences and the learning of ASL as a second language. While they were more than glad to help the hearing students, they did not feel a sense of reciprocity to enhance their learning needs with regard to deaf interpreting.

There is also a dearth of qualified trainers of deaf interpreters and a lack of workshops to "train the trainers." It is incongruous that deaf interpreters are required to have certification or licensure to work in legal or educational settings and yet there is very little to be had in terms of preparation and training. There is a growing demand for deaf interpreters, and there are growing numbers of deaf persons interested in becoming deaf interpreters. This is a classic Catch-22 scenario in the profession of deaf interpreters.

As revealed earlier, instructional materials related to deaf interpreting are nonexistent, thus leaving a vacuum of curriculum guides and models to use as reference for teaching and to prepare materials, according to objectives on deaf interpreting processes. There is a critical and vital need for videotapes for observing deaf-hearing interpreters at work, deaf interpreters discussing their work and experiences, deaf-hearing interpreters discussing team process, materials and books on deaf interpreting, and curricula for training deaf interpreters and deaf-hearing interpreter teams. Specialized curricula, materials, and videotapes related to legal, medical, mental health, and educational fields need to be developed with a focus on deaf interpreters and their roles, processes, and functions within these specialized settings.

The general consensus of the nine interviewees on the qualifications and competencies required for deaf interpreters lent credibility to their views, since they were all interviewed separately and unknowingly from one another. Their views emphasize that all deaf interpreters have specific qualifications and competencies and need training on specific skills as deemed necessary for deaf interpreting.

What do deaf interpreting processes entail? What is known about these processes? What teaching model—such as Bienvenu and Colonomos, Gish, and/or Cokely—would be more effective in teaching deaf interpreting? Is there a need for an entirely new teaching model? Are deaf interpreters interpreting from ASL to ASL? What should that be called? Can that be considered as "more ASL"? Are there other forms that deaf interpreters are working into—such as a gestural form that is non-language specific, gestures that are culturally specific, idiosyncratic signs, home or in-group signs, or a sign dialect? What are the dynamics that arise from the relationship between deaf and hearing interpreters, and how is the balance of power between the team worked out? All of this needs to be considered and researched further.

Interviewees expressed a serious concern about testing and how deaf interpreters could best prepare themselves for the tests—particularly understanding the language of the test and the stimulus questions. Some asked whether the tests would be available in other languages such as Spanish or Mexican.

Last but not least, more workshops need to be designed and offered to hearing and deaf interpreters to develop team skills, because the nature of such a team presents different and challenging dynamics within the team and in specific settings.

Currently there is little opportunity, if any, for deaf interpreters to have mentoring from experienced deaf interpreters. As one interviewee noted, "I had no mentor to work with me and to provide me encouragement, support, and continued skill development. Now I am mentoring a new deaf interpreter. It would have been nice to have a model of deaf interpreter/mentor to base my mentoring on now." Another interviewee shared an experience when he went to a mentoring workshop where deaf interpreters were allowed to get together by themselves. The experience was wonderful, and the workshop "helped a lot in terms of support, sharing, and learning from each other's experiences. This helped us to see ourselves as deaf interpreters, to respect each other as professionals, to develop a support group because this is our future." No other interviewees mentioned any experience with mentoring.

This study provided a preliminary outline for training of deaf interpreters from interviews with deaf interpreters. With more time, there needs to be a thorough analysis of all the data gleaned from the nine interviews. Only a limited amount of data was used for this chapter. A wealth of information resulted from answers to the wide range of questions. Implications for research along the same line are that specific items for curriculum development and training need to be designed. Development of instructional materials and training for the teachers, especially deaf teachers and deaf interpreters, of deaf interpreting is vital and ripe for further research.

Other areas for further research include the need to work with minority deaf interpreters to determine how they are being recruited and provided with training; research on specialized training in legal, medical, mental health, and educational interpreting; and case studies of deaf interpreting processes and deaf- hearing interpreter team processes. Research also is needed on how deaf interpreters might view the Code of Ethics differently from hearing interpreters and how these views affect ethical decision-making processes. With more mentoring programs and opportunities developing, there is a need for research on availability and effectiveness of mentoring programs specifically designed for deaf interpreters.

Processes between deaf-hearing interpreter teams would also benefit from more detailed investigation than Ressler's (1999) study involving a single team. This would be an excellent opportunity to research the roles, functions, and processes of deaf-hearing interpreter teams.

As ascertained from the interviewees' comments, there is a critical need to develop videotapes demonstrating models of deaf interpreting and deaf interpreters discussing their work as well as the teaming processes between deaf and hearing interpreters. There are implications of videotaping deaf interpreters in their actual work in certain situations, such as in courtrooms and mental-health settings. In these cases, videotaping would not be allowed; thus most of the "work" of deaf interpreters would be "staged." It would be fascinating to do research on what the deaf interpreters bring to their work in terms of their frame of mind and worldview. Another interesting possible research topic has been raised: What "labels" should be used for the work that deaf interpreters do.

Furthermore, we need to look into what deaf interpreters understand about interpreting, what is entailed as a process of interpreting, and how they work with languages and the processes related to interpreting. Ethical matters should be researched, focusing on how deaf interpreters view their training on ethics and the Code of Ethics and how their function and role on the job is affected by their understanding of these constructs.

Furthermore, a larger number of deaf interpreters need to be recruited for interviews and surveys. This research was conducted in early 2001; today, there are more deaf persons working as deaf interpreters.

In conclusion, this research shows a demand for more information and studies about deaf interpreters working in the field already and for the development of a curriculum to establish a good foundation for comprehensive skills development for deaf interpreters. In several years, RID's certification processes will require that candidates, including deaf persons, have an Associate degree and eventually a Bachelor's degree to be eligible to take certification tests.

This research is only the beginning. The possibilities for deaf interpreting as a solid profession in the future will continue to evolve. As one interviewee aptly put it, "Deaf interpreting is a very exciting field. I would like to see interpreter education programs be designed and geared for deaf interpreters. I would like to see the number of trained deaf interpreters grow."

NOTES

Methodology encompasses more than tactics and techniques. It involves the researcher's assumptions and values, which dictate the manner and means by which the study is pursued. I am aware of my own subjective biases, as I am a deaf interpreter, RSC holder, and frequent trainer and consultant of deaf interpreting and deaf-hearing interpreter teaming processes. In my work as a deaf interpreter since 1978, I have witnessed the rapid evolution of the field of deaf interpreters in the professional arena. I have attempted to monitor those prejudices and biases by documenting my beliefs and subjective state through work with a mentor. I feel I have maintained an open mind to the ideas and experiences of those who were targeted for the interviews and the ways those ideas and experiences might temper my beliefs and expectations. The commitment to this research project, my set of beliefs and values, and the ability to maintain a distance from those ideas and experiences positively affected the process of collecting and analyzing the data in this study.

REFERENCES

Bienvenu, M.J. (1991). *Relay interpreting*. Presentation at 1991 RID Convention, Bethesda, Maryland.

Bienvenu, M.J., & Colonomos, B. (1990). Relay interpreting in the 90s. *Proceedings of Eighth National Conference of Interpreter Trainers, 69–80.*

Collins, S., & Roth, H. (July/August 1992). Deaf Interpreters, *TBC News*, Bicultural Center, 1–2.

Egnatovitch, R. (November, 1999). Certified deaf interpreter—WHY? Registry of Interpreters for Deaf, *RID Views, 1*, 6.

Frishberg, N. (1994). *Introduction to interpreting,* 2nd ed. Silver Spring, MD: RID Publications.

Gish, S. (1987). I understood all the words, but I missed the point: A goal-to-detail/detail-to-goal strategy for text analysis, *New Dimensions in Interpretation Education: Curriculum and Instruction.* Silver Spring, MD: RID Publications.

Mindess, A. (1999). *Reading between the signs: Intercultural communication for sign language interpreters,* Yarmonth, ME: Intercultural Press.

Ressler, C.I. (1999). A comparative analysis of a direct interpretation and an intermediary interpretation in American sign language. *Journal of Interpretation, 1999,* 71–102.

RID Views, (February 2001). *Announcement,* Registry of Interpreters for Deaf. National Testing Council.

Sandefur, R. (September 1994). Team interpreting: Deaf and hearing interpreters as allies, *RID Views,* Registry of Interpreters for Deaf, 1, 15.

Solow, S.N. (2000). *Sign language interpreting,* rev. ed. Silver Spring, MD: Linstok Press.

Wilcox, P. (2000). Dual interpretation and discourse effectiveness in legal settings. *Journal of Interpretation, 2001,* 89–98.

11

Consumers and Service Effectiveness in Interpreting Work: A Practice Profession Perspective

Robyn K. Dean & Robert Q Pollard, Jr.

The old adage *Caveat emptor*—let the buyer beware—not only warns consumers about who ultimately will suffer when a product or service fails to meet expectations, but also serves as a call to responsibility. It reminds us that consumers, not purveyors, must drive the process of evaluating and ultimately judging the quality and utility of products and services.

We view interpreting as a *practice profession*, like medicine, law, teaching, counseling, or law enforcement, where careful consideration and judgment regarding situational and human interaction factors are central to doing effective work. We contrast the practice professions with the technical professions, such as engineering and accounting, where knowledge and skills pertaining to the technical elements of a job are largely sufficient to allow the professional to produce a competent work product. Interpreters function more like practice professionals than technicians due to the significance of situational and human interaction factors on their ultimate work product; that is, factors beyond the technical elements of the source and target language (Dean & Pollard, 2001; Gish, 1987; Humphrey & Alcorn, 1995; Metzger, 1999; Roy, 2000a; Wadensjo, 1998). Interpreters cannot deliver effective professional service armed only with their technical knowledge of source and target languages, Deaf culture, and a code of ethics. Like all practice professionals, they must supplement their technical knowledge and skills with input, exchange, and judgment regarding the consumers they are serving in a specific environment and in a specific communicative situation (see both Turner and Winston, this volume).

Beyond the skills and judgment the professional must bring to the work situation, the practice professions are increasingly emphasizing the role of the consumer in effective service provision. In medicine, patients are expected to play a far more active role in their health care than was the case a generation ago. The keys to achieving greater consumer-driven quality in the practice professions are twofold: (1) adequate consumer understanding of the nature of the professional service being rendered, including its challenges and competency requirements, and (2) consumers taking a more active role in the service delivery process.

When the nature of a professional service is not adequately understood by consumers, the stage is set for a variety of untoward consequences, ranging from professional abuses to consumer inability to effectively partake of the service. Medical malpractice versus patient failure to understand and/or adhere to treatment recommendations are examples of the two ends of that untoward consequence spectrum. With any practice profession service, the ideal context for the consumption of services occurs when the nature of the service is clearly apparent to and understood by the consumer—to a degree that they can participate meaningfully in the procurement of that service. This means understanding service realities, professional competence expectations, service options, and the consequences of these various options. The medical profession incorporates such ideals in the rubric of informed consent. Patients who are sufficiently informed; reasonable in their service expectations; and responsible, active participants in their health care are a physician's delight when seeking informed consent and, ultimately, optimal health care outcomes. The same comparison could be made to consumers served by any practice profession, including interpreting.

Do consumers view interpreting services in this practice profession manner and thus participate knowledgeably and actively in interpreting service delivery? We doubt that most consumers, especially hearing consumers, have this perception of interpreting work and the active role they should play in its effective outcome; that is, beyond "generating language" for the interpreter to translate. Many consumers appear to view interpreters as technicians, where the consumer's participation in the interpreting process is limited to generating language, expecting that the interpreter will perform all the technical changes to that language necessary to render an accurate translation.[1] As in the practice professions of law, health care, or financial advising, consumers who participate minimally in goal-setting, choice of service options, outcomes monitoring, and so forth are at risk for receiving ineffective services or services that run counter to their true desires, and they leave the practice professional with an excessive (often unwanted) degree of power.

Where do interpreters learn to deal with limited consumer perceptions of interpreting and the burdens they impose on effective work?
More generally, where do interpreters develop competency in addressing the situational and human factors that influence their professional practice, apart from the technical knowledge and skills they
learn in the areas of language, culture, and ethics? The remainder of
this chapter examines these and related issues, with an emphasis on the
consequences for effective service delivery to consumers as well as
interpreter education.

DIFFERING PERCEPTIONS OF THE COMPLEXITY
OF INTERPRETING

"Interpreting is more than transposing one language to another . . . it is
throwing a semantic bridge between two people from differing cultures
and thought worlds" (Namy, 1977, p. 25). People who speak different
languages and come from differing cultural backgrounds experience the
world in different manners; they have different *thought worlds*. Both
spoken and signed language interpreters work amidst the differing
thought worlds of their consumers and bear responsibility for the
complex task of attempting to construct semantic bridges between
them. At times, the degree of difference between these thought worlds is
substantial, and the resulting semantic bridge constructed by the interpreter is complex (at best) or incomplete to a greater or lesser degree.
At other times, consumers' thought worlds are very similar, so the semantic bridge constructed by the interpreter can be short and sturdy.
While interpreters understand how different people and circumstances
may combine to yield myriad semantic bridging experiences, usually
they are the only individual present in the situation who can see that
bridge from both sides and therefore the only one who perceives how
effective the bridge they have "thrown" between consumers truly is
in terms of linguistic and thought world equivalence. Unless this perception is shared with consumers, there is danger that the service
effectiveness consumers presume is not in fact what occurred.

As noted, we believe that most consumers, especially hearing consumers, perceive the work of interpreters as vastly more easy and
straightforward than it is and therefore do not participate more broadly
and actively in the process. "Just translate word for word what I say"
or "Just tell him/her what I said" are frequent consumer directives or
perceptions. Most hearing and even some deaf consumers assume that
if the interpreter is signing and speaking in an effort to translate between the parties, and if each party understands the language the interpreter is providing *to them*, then the source and target language
messages must be being rendered faithfully and with no significant
deviation from the original message (i.e., literally). Interpreters know

that these presumptions or wishes are not reality (Cokely, 1992; Roy, 2000b; Seleskovitch, 1978; Winston, 1989), but they rarely convey this to consumers. Why not?

One reason is that interpreters typically are not afforded the same respect and deference as are other practice professionals. Providing such instructive input to consumers may be problematic in that regard; it is generally not expected by consumers and may not be heeded or appreciated. Another part of the answer lies in the way some interpreters, especially novices, view the "do not counsel, advise, or interject personal opinions" tenet of the Registry of Interpreters for the Deaf (RID) Code of Ethics (RID, 1994). Taken in its most conservative, literal context, this tenet would seem to preclude interpreter commentary to consumers while on the job, despite arguments that such rigid interpretations of the code are erroneous and harmful (Fritsch-Rudser, 1986) or outdated and in need of significant revision (Cokely, 2000). A joint committee of RID and the National Association of the Deaf is currently revising the Code of Ethics. The present working draft includes language that allows interpreters to provide consultative opinions in some circumstances (RID, no date).

A third aspect of the difficulty in conveying interpreting complexities to consumers is the sheer multiplicity of factors beyond the words (or signs) people use that interpreters must take into account when making translation (and behavioral) decisions. Metzger and Bahan (2001), Roy (2000b), and Winston and Monikowski (2000) describe some of these factors as aspects of discourse analysis. Others include such factors in their broader consideration of sociolinguistics or interpreting in general (Cokely, 1992; Dean & Pollard, 2001; Namy, 1977; Wadensjo, 1998). It is doubtful whether consumers who subscribe to the literal or technical perception of interpreting work recognize how these discourse and extra-linguistic factors impact the moment-by-moment decisions interpreters make in selecting translations and otherwise fulfilling their professional duties.

It is further arguable that interpreters themselves may fail to perceive this broader picture of the extra-linguistic factors that pertain to accurate translation, at least in the early stages of their professional career when efforts to master sign language and the more immediate linguistic aspects of translation consume their attention. To test this hypothesis, 149 interpreters attending the 2001 RID convention were presented with written descriptions of five interpreting scenarios, each of which contained four situational elements not directly related to consumers' language use. The interpreters rated how strongly these extra-linguistic elements would impact their work in the given scenario using a 1–5 Likert scale where $1 =$ no impact, $3 =$ moderate impact, and $5 =$ strong impact. Their average ranking, across all factors and scenarios, was 3.2, indicating that they judged these factors to have more than a moderate impact on interpreting work. Yet when asked where they learned about the importance of such factors in interpreting work, the majority indicated that they learned through on-the-job experience, not from their interpreter preparation program (IPP), continuing education, or supervision/mentorship. Although 50% of respondents had graduated from their IPP within the past 7 years (70% within the past 12 years), 47% of respondents indicated that their IPP was not a source of learning about the impact of such factors. Rather, 65% ranked on-the-job experience as their first or second most significant source of learning about the importance of such factors. When asked where they learned to *deal with* such extra-linguistic factors during interpreting assignments, 75% of respondents failed to rank their IPPs as a source of such learning.

As noted, several factors may contribute to disparities between what consumers think is happening in the interpreting process (i.e., literal translation based only on language utterances) versus recognition of the complex influences on translation and behavioral judgments that interpreters make, and the resulting variation in the effectiveness of their moment-by-moment semantic bridging work product. These include the low-status afforded the interpreting profession, an assumed ethical prohibition from engaging consumers in discussions of the complexity of interpreting work, and the slow on-the-job learning curve that precedes interpreters' recognition of the plurality of factors that influence their work.

Furthermore, if interpreters fail to view their IPPs as a source of learning about interpreting's broader complexities (whether this perception is accurate or not—just because these things were not learned does not verify that they were not taught), then they may not feel at liberty to discuss these complexities with consumers, for fear that the professional establishment will not back them up. This would reinforce a perception that the RID Code of Ethics prohibits such "personal" communication and further impedes consumer education about interpreting services. This establishes dynamics in which consumers and less experienced interpreters may ascribe to perceptions about the nature of interpreting that are simplistic and inaccurate and where seasoned interpreters with a broader viewpoint may not feel free to share these views and challenges with consumers and the profession at large. To the degree that this occurs, it is arguable that the *schema* guiding consumers' and interpreters' views and dialogues regarding this practice profession is in need of clarification or modification.

RHETORIC VERSUS DE FACTO PRACTICE

In the present context, we use the term "schema" to mean the global, conceptual framework that envelopes the condition or topic that a profession deals with. A schema is the profession's overarching viewpoint of the realities that operationalize the professional's task. Schemas drive a profession's understanding of the challenges it faces and how to meet those challenges and train new professionals to do the same. Consumers of a profession's services also are guided by the profession's schema; it is how they understand the need for and the nature of the services they are receiving.

In the history of medicine, schemas of illness have changed periodically, usually through research advancements (e.g., the microscope, genetics) that force the profession, its teachers, and its consumers to periodically reconceptualize their fundamental understanding about what causes illness and promotes health.

One of the greatest dangers in a practice profession is the prevailing schema failing to adequately account for the realities encountered in professional practice. An inadequate professional schema prompts well-meaning practitioners to behave in ways they judge to be more realistic and effective but which run counter to or outside their prevailing professional schema and therefore are not overtly endorsed, or sometimes even discussed by the professional establishment or with consumers (Turner, this volume). This creates a gap between de facto (actual) practice and the prevailing rhetoric or belief system regarding how that profession conducts its work. When significant gaps exist between rhetoric and de facto practice, dangers of unexamined, unregulated, and unethical practice increase.

An example from medicine involves the topic of "medical mistakes." Until recently, the prevailing rhetoric in medicine was that medical mistakes simply shouldn't be made. Accumulating research data regarding medical mistakes ultimately sparked a rather sudden shift in how the medical profession dealt with this topic. Only in the past few years has the admission of a serious problem in medical mistakes been openly acknowledged by the profession. With this openness came new efforts to address the matter, such as research grants for exploring the issue of medical mistakes, and practices that immediately benefited consumers such as writing on the body of a patient about to undergo surgery so that the proper surgical location is clearly identified. This never would have happened 20 years ago because the risk of operating on the wrong body part was not acknowledged as a sufficiently important reality of professional practice. Since it was not, de facto practice was unable to conform with the profession's rhetoric and such mistakes were hidden or dealt with as private matters, not as a significant issue in the general practice of medicine.

When insufficiencies in a practice profession's schema lead to de facto practices that differ from the profession's rhetoric, deception and practitioner stress are inevitable. Furthermore, consumers' risk for receiving ineffective, and even harmful, professional service escalates since professional practice is insufficiently scrutinized and informed by the profession's oversight bodies and researchers and because teachers are not able to train students effectively regarding these hidden realities of professional practice.

Our teaching and practice experiences have led us to conclude that the field of sign language interpreting suffers from significant gaps in rhetoric versus de facto practice. Specifically, many consumers and less experienced interpreters believe that the work is restricted to circumscribed source-to-target language wording and structural changes, where a consumer's immediate word or sign utterances are the only input data necessary for the interpreter to perform a near-literal transposition between languages—one that is devoid of conscious or unconscious influence from the interpreter. The reality (de facto practice) of interpreting work is notably different from this. It is essential that consumers understand this if they are to participate in the effective rendering of this practice profession service.

THE REALITIES OF INTERPRETING WORK

To those who hold perceptions of interpreting work as a near literal process of transposition between languages, and where the utterances of consumers are the only data interpreters need to produce an effective work product, an honest and competent interpreter could reply:

- Translations often do not mirror the words you say.
- Translations often require information to be added or deleted.
- Translations are based on the interpreter's judgment of what consumers mean, not necessarily the words they choose.
- Consumers respond to the interpreter's translation choices, not the original consumer comments, which influences consumers and the resulting dialogue.
- The interpreter's presence and needs influence the flow of the interaction and the relationship between consumers.

While not every situation calls for diversion from the "just translate word for word what I say" directive, these statements more closely reflect the real work of interpreters. The purpose of the following section is to describe and illustrate each of these realities. The descriptions are of routine interpreting practice challenges and common interpreter responses to them (de facto practice). Yet consumers often do not recognize the frequency with which these "realities" occur during interpreting situations nor how or why interpreters handle them the way they do. The descriptions are intended to model how interpreters might explain to consumers the frequent divergence between "just translate word for word what I say" rhetoric and de facto practice. The illustrations of interpreting scenarios offered below are not meant to portray ideal interpreting practices. Many different responses to a given interpreting challenge may be appropriate, although each will have its particular consequences. Rather than prescribing an optimal response or practice, these illustrations are meant to elucidate the thought process that an interpreter might engage in prior to making a translation or behavioral response to an interpreting challenge, because the interpreter's thought process is not likely to be perceived by consumers and is critical to the evaluation of decision consequences.

Translations often do not mirror the words you say. Translations between two languages do not correspond 1:1 for each vocabulary word uttered. Often, words in one language cannot be translated to another language "word for word"; therefore, verbal alterations, additions, deletions, and approximations are a routine aspect of the interpreter's task. This statement should be the most obvious of the five "realities" listed earlier, at least to interpreters (of spoken and signed languages) and to consumers who are sufficiently fluent in two languages to recognize that the alteration of words is imperative to the effective translation of *concepts*.

Translations often require information to be added or deleted. In part due to the aforementioned non-equivalence of individual vocabulary words, the addition of words (or information) often is necessary in translation between any two languages. Furthermore, differences in "fund of information" between hearing and deaf consumers (Pollard, 1998) often requires an interpreter to fill in information gaps (e.g., briefly explain a term or issue that a consumer has referred to) that otherwise frequently would derail communication between hearing and deaf consumers. The deletion of information might occur when limited time for "throwing a semantic bridge" forces interpreters to disregard what they judge to be less significant words or comments while prioritizing the inclusion and perhaps explanation of more significant words or comments (Cokely, 1992; Napier, in press, a and b). When consumers are communicating rapidly or in group situations where several people may be talking at once, judicious decisions must be made about what words or comments to ignore, summarize, or curtail. Additions and deletions of course take place in spoken language interpreting as well.

Translations are based on the interpreter's judgment of what consumers mean, not necessarily the words they choose. Since languages do not equate on a word-for-word basis, interpreters must understand the concepts they hear (or see) in order to translate them. To some, this is obvious; to others—especially those who are not fluent in two languages—it is not. Interpreter understanding is not exclusively fostered by consumers' word choices. Environmental context and immediate aspects of the situation matter greatly when meaning is extracted from language. Roy (2000a) offers an illustration of the varied meanings of the utterance

"Can I help you?" as a function of differing situational contexts and circumstances. If the interpreter does not understand what is said, the consumer probably will not, either. Implications of this reality argue for greater consumer-interpreter collaboration outside of or parallel to the immediate consumer-to-consumer dialogue to assure that interpreter comprehension is coincident with his or her translation work.

To illustrate how meaning, rather than words, guides an interpreter's translation, consider this scenario of a deaf patient undergoing an examination for back pain. After the physician conversed with the patient about the nature of the pain, what tended to cause or diminish it, and so forth, he began to palpate the area. "Tell me if you can feel this," the doctor directed. The interpreter translated this comment in a straightforward manner. The patient described varying degrees of pain as the examination proceeded. Then, the doctor picked up a pin. Again he said, "Tell me if you can feel this" (the exact same phrase as before), and he began gently poking various areas of the patient's back with the pin. At first, the patient repeatedly said "No," which puzzled both the physician and the interpreter. Unless something was amiss neurologically, the patient should have felt the pin, at least some of the time. The interpreter, who was experienced in medical work, recognized that the patient did not understand how the nature of the exam had changed and the *new* meaning of the physician's identical statement, "Tell me if you can feel this." It no longer meant "Tell me if/how this hurts," but now meant "Do you sense this?" After pausing to confirm her judgment with the physician, the interpreter changed her translation strategy and the neurological exam proceeded normally. (See Marschark, et al., this volume, for discussion of interpreters' influence on deaf consumers' cognitions.)

Interpreters base translations on their best judgment of what consumers mean, simultaneously taking into consideration evidence from consumers' language utterances, what they see taking place in the environment (e.g., the physician picking up a pin), the goals and context of the situation, and other factors that may relate to consumers' thought worlds. Whether or not this ultimately results in an *accurate* perception of what a given consumer meant by an utterance is another question. Interpreters, of course, can misunderstand what a consumer meant. This is further support for the frequent need for interpreters to dialogue with consumers or engage in other information-gathering behavior that fosters the accuracy of the interpreter's own comprehension of the communication that is (or might) take place between consumers.

Consumers respond to the interpreter's translation choices, not the original consumer comments, which influences consumers and the resulting dialogue. Consumers are receiving the translations provided to them through the filter of the interpreter; they are not receiving the original comments unaltered. In our experience, consumers (especially hearing consumers) often fail to appreciate how significant the interpreter is in crafting the translations they ultimately receive. As noted, translations necessarily are influenced by the interpreter's perception of the contextualized meaning of the original comments, by the need to add or delete information, by language and sociocultural differences, by consumers' thought world differences, and so forth. When consumers presume that every word coming from the interpreter has originated from the other consumer, misunderstandings can ensue. The following scenario depicts one such situation.

A medically experienced sign language interpreter needed to translate a physician's inquiry as to whether a deaf consumer was "sexually active." In a medical context, these two words carry complex meaning. The term references a wide variety of sexual behavior with either gender and without regard to social, religious, or even legal norms. It is essential in a medical setting for this term to be conveyed with the widest possible scope of behavioral meanings and yet non-judgmentally. It is quite an interpreting challenge, especially when fund of information limitations or other personal or sociocultural factors may constrain a patient's perception of "sex" to mean intercourse alone and/or socially sanctioned sexual behavior (e.g., monogamy or heterosexuality). It also is specifically challenging to translate into ASL because of the vagueness of what "active" may imply and because the term makes no overt reference to a partner. With many deaf consumers, it is difficult to convey sexual activity in ASL without making reference to a partner and, to some degree, a specific activity. Ideally, in consideration of both ASL and fund of information issues with the average deaf consumer, a conversation regarding sexual activity would unfold as a dialogue, not as a "yes" or "no" response to the physician's inquiry.

In light of these complexities, the interpreter's initial translation of the physician's question included the concepts of "either a man or a woman" as possible partners in sexual activity. The deaf consumer replied, "I'm not gay." The physician didn't understand how this response could have resulted from his question about whether the patient was "sexually active." The interpreter explained the details of her translation choice to both parties, whereupon the physician agreed that he indeed had meant sexual activity with either gender. While many other possible translation or behavioral choices could be considered here, this scenario illustrates how consumers' responses can be more directly related to the interpreter's specific translation choice than the original consumer utterance. This happens so frequently in interpreting work that consumers benefit when they anticipate such a situation may occur.

The interpreter's presence and needs influence the flow of the interaction and relationship between the consumers. Great harm in the effectiveness of interpreting service can be caused by consumers' failure to appreciate the influence of the interpreter's presence. The interpreter is not a shadow presence devoid of influence (Metzger, 1999; Roy, 1993, 2000a). On the contrary, the interpreter can play a pivotal role in how the communication situation unfolds. The interpreter influences numerous aspects of consumers' interactions, from the basics of what they understand one another to be saying to more extraneous matters such as communication turn-taking, perceived alliances among the interpreter and consumers, when and how clarifications are requested, and the degree to which language and cultural consultation is provided. Even the dynamics of the interpreter's arriving, leaving, and needing to be compensated for her services can have a significant impact.

The interpreter's role is associated with considerable power. If her presence is diminished or denied, the interpreter retains this power unchecked. Ironically, it was the desire for interpreters to *not* have such power that gave rise to the "just pretend I'm not here" advice that some interpreters still convey to consumers. In contrast, only by embracing the significance of the interpreter's presence can consumers and interpreters more realistically promote the equitable distribution of power that is so important in cross-cultural interaction.

An interpreter was called into an intensive care unit and asked to translate this statement from a doctor to a patient: "There's nothing more we can do for you; we're going to make you as comfortable as possible." While the concepts of abandoning further treatment and instead targeting pain management could be readily translated into ASL, the covert meaning of this medical euphemism—a pronouncement of impending death—might be missed by many deaf consumers. It is unlikely that the physician would know that. Most interpreters would recognize this and not wish to be left with the burden, and power, of choosing whether their translation should (or shouldn't) convey the impending death concept directly, without the doctor's awareness that this choice must be made. If the translation closely parallels the doctor's original words or overt concepts, it risks the patient's failure to recognize the commonly understood (by hearing people) covert implication of this statement. This could deny the patient the opportunity to request religious counsel, family visitation, or make other preparations for death. Alternately, the interpreter could chose to directly convey the covert meaning of this euphemism (impending death) but there are serious consequences to this as well, especially as a unilateral decision that the doctor is unaware of. Both choices leave the interpreter in an undesirably powerful role, to the potential detriment of the doctor, the patient, and the interpreter. In this particular case, the interpreter's choice was to explain to the doctor the nature of the translation dilemma she was facing. The doctor was unaware of the language and cultural factors involved, and he subsequently took responsibility for conversing with the patient in a more direct and clear manner about her impending death and the palliative care plan.

To maximize the equitable distribution of power in interpreting situations, interpreters and consumers must recognize each of the aforementioned realities of interpreting work and accept shared responsibility for the entire spectrum of the communication exchange—from communication initiator to interpreter to communication receiver—and back again.

ETHICS, CONSUMERS, AND EFFECTIVE WORK

"The choices that we make, and the actions that follow from those choices, can uphold or deny the dignity of other people, can advocate or violate the rights of other people, can affirm or disavow the humanity of other people. Given the potential consequences of our choices and the resultant actions, it is reasonable to expect that we constantly re-examine those values, principles, and beliefs that underscore and shape the decisions we make and the actions we undertake" (Cokely, 2000, pp. 27–28).

In our workshops, we often ask interpreters what fundamental ethical tenet underlies medical practice, when distilled to just one statement. "Do no harm" is the correct response that is always given. "Do no harm" as an ethical statement manifests the relationship between ethics and the effectiveness of professional practice. Professional action (or inaction) that is harmful is fundamentally unethical. Consequently, ethical decision making in the practice professions must include consideration of the impact of the professional's decisions and actions on the consumer as well as other matters, such as the concordance between the professional's decisions and actions with the principles and standards of practice in that profession.

Figure 11.1 depicts our view of the relationship between ethics and work effectiveness in a practice profession such as interpreting. In the center of the figure, a range of ethical decisions and actions is depicted that includes those that are more liberal (i.e., active, creative, or assertive) to those that are more conservative (i.e., reserved or cautious). In this central range between the dotted lines any decision or action—from

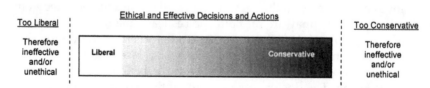

Figure 11.1. A practice-profession model of ethical decision-making

liberal to conservative—may be effective and ethical depending on the circumstances of the situation. Which decisions or actions within this range are *optimally* effective would be a matter of professional debate or perhaps interpersonal consumer or interpreter variation. Practice professionals commonly discuss liberal versus conservative approaches to their work, be it medical care, law enforcement, financial invest-ment, or other topics. Neither end of this ethical and effective range of professional judgment and behavior is inherently better or worse, nor is the median necessarily optimal. Within this ethical and effective range of liberal to conservative practice, qualified practitioners will differ in opinion and approach. Ongoing research and consumer prefer-ences typically inform practitioners' opinions and behaviors in that regard.

Outside the ethical and effective boundaries depicted (beyond the dotted lines) are decisions and actions that are so extreme—on *either* the liberal or conservative end of the spectrum—that they are overtly ineffective and/or unethical. Professional actions on the liberal extreme are most easily recognized. These are bold, intrusive actions that de-viate markedly from professional norms and put consumers at obvious risk of harm. Stories of overly aggressive medical care, policing prac-tices, even financial advice are common in the news.

Less aggrandized but equally harmful are professional actions at the other extreme of the spectrum—those actions that fall outside the ac-ceptable *conservative* boundary of ethical and effective practice. Here is where failing to act or exercise some other aspect of professional judgment leads to consumer harm and, consequently, unethical prac-tice. This end of the spectrum is more difficult to recognize. The impact of what someone has *done* (in being excessively liberal) usually is more apparent than the impact of what someone has *not done* (in being ex-cessively conservative). Yet, overly timid professional decisions can be equally damaging. Doctors who are insufficiently thorough or ag-gressive in treatment planning or teachers whose attentions are biased by student favoritism are behaving beyond the extreme conservative end of the ethical and effective end of this continuum. Why do practice professionals sometimes err in this overly conservative manner? There are many possible reasons, including timidity, ignorance, intoler-ance for risk, fear of taking responsibility, and lack of knowledge re-garding the full range of ethical and effective choices at one's disposal.

Similar to other practice professions, interpreting decisions or be-haviors that fall outside the extreme liberal boundary of the spectrum in Figure 11.1 are easier to recognize. These include active misuses of the interpreter's power, such as providing false translations to effect a certain result, or offering consultation outside the boundaries of one's competency and role (e.g., suggesting a diagnosis to a physician). Much of the content in the RID Code of Ethics (RID, 1994) was written to guard against such excessively liberal interpreter conduct. Such conduct is typically associated with the "helper" model of interpreting practice, which was rejected by the interpreting profession from its beginnings (Frishberg, 1986; Quigley & Young, 1965; Roy, 1993).

But what about the other end of the spectrum? Can interpreters be guilty of excessively conservative professional judgment or behavior? Of course; all practice professionals can, since *bearing responsibility* is an inherent duty in the practice professions but one that can be avoided or insufficiently utilized to the detriment of consumers. Consider an interpreter who knows that communication has been ineffective or that significant misunderstandings have occurred or who was unable to do her job because conditions were not suitable for effective practice, yet fails to speak out, correct the situation, or otherwise convey to the consumers involved that their presumption of effective translation was not accomplished. This is unethical behavior beyond the reasonably conservative end of the continuum because it ultimately is harmful to consumers.

An interpreter working with a deaf psychiatric patient with limited sign language proficiency was asked to interpret for an attorney who was required to inform the patient of his legal rights pertaining to involuntary commitment to the hospital. The attorney read to the patient from a prepared text containing complex legal concepts and instructions on how to assert his rights if he felt they were being violated. It was obvious to the interpreter that she could not effectively convey this information to the patient, not only because of his limited sign language skills but also his impaired mental status. The interpreter properly chose to inform the attorney about this difficulty and the apparent impossibility of accomplishing the desired task in the brief time allotted. The attorney said, "Just interpret what I say the best you can" and, after one more reading of the document, the attorney prepared to leave. The interpreter again expressed her opinion that the patient did not comprehend the information. The attorney said, "The main thing is that he knows he has rights and can contact me if needed." He then wrote a brief note in the patient's chart, asking the interpreter for the spelling of her name. The interpreter was concerned that the treatment team might not be informed of her view that the communication had been ineffective and thereby presume, from the attorney's visit and chart note, that it had been. In our view, for the interpreter to "do nothing" would be excessively conservative and potentially detrimental to the patient, and therefore would be unethical. Many possible choices are open to the interpreter to prevent such harm. One might be to inform the treatment team leader of her opinion that the communication had been ineffective. A more liberal choice might be to add an "interpreter note" to the patient's chart, conveying the same opinion. These and other choices would fall within the "ethical and effective" area of Figure 11.1.

We believe the risk for unethical behavior at the extreme conservative end of the spectrum depicted above in Figure 11.1 is particularly significant in the interpreting profession where, until recent years, the prevailing ethical rhetoric was so polarized against the helper model that the emphasis on inaction and aspirations toward "invisibility" created a deontological ethical rubric (Cokely, 2000; Fritsch-Rudser, 1986; RID, 1994). While interpreting scholarship (Dean & Pollard, 2001; DeMatteo, Veltri & Lee, 1986; Metzger, 1999; Page, 1993; RID, no date; Roy, 1993; Vernon & Miller, 2001) and IPP curricula are now espousing a broader, more flexible view of the interpreter's role, many practicing interpreters trained via older models are at increased risk for such overly conservative professional judgment. As noted earlier, even interpreters trained in the past decade report that their perceptions of the broader realities of interpreting work were gained primarily through on-the-job experience.

While some situations allow, and even call for, conservative interpreting practice, others do not. The effectiveness and consequences of professional decisions and behaviors are the ultimate measures of what is ethical and appropriate in a practice profession. Like other practice professions, interpreting must prioritize "do no harm" and recognize that inappropriate inaction can be as harmful as inappropriate action. Consumers who believe the "just translate word for word what I say" myth, or who believe that the silent, invisible interpreter, in all situations, is the quintessential model of effectiveness, may ultimately be harmed if they compel interpreters to behave in accordance with these beliefs. Improved consumer education, leading to more effective collaboration with interpreters, first depends on the interpreting profession itself confronting these still-common beliefs and subsequently educating consumers, practicing interpreters, and IPP students more effectively about the realities of interpreting work.

As in other practice professions, consumers, teachers, researchers, and practitioners collectively benefit when the nature of that profession—its challenges, presumptions, and practices—are made as explicit as possible. This lessens the gap between rhetoric and de facto practice and fosters critical exchange that can lead to improved professional schemas.

THE DEMAND-CONTROL SCHEMA
AND SERVICE EFFECTIVENESS

The demand-control (D-C) schema for interpreting work (Dean & Pollard, 2001) was adapted from D-C theory, based on occupational health research conducted by Karasek (1979) and Theorell (Karasek & Theorell, 1990). Karasek and Theorell recognized that occupational stress versus work satisfaction and effectiveness arise from the interactive dynamics between the challenges (*demands*) presented by work tasks in relation to the resources (controls or decision latitude) that workers bring to bear in response to job demands. While respecting the central roles of language and culture in the practice of interpreting, the D-C schema focuses on additional factors (demands) that impact effective translation. These include environmental demands, interpersonal demands, paralinguistic demands,[2] and intrapersonal demands. (The acronym EIPI is used when referring to all four demand categories simultaneously.)

Environmental demands are interpreting challenges or success requirements that pertain to the assignment setting (e.g., understanding consumers' occupational roles or specialized terminology specific to a given setting[3] or tolerating space limitations, odors, or adverse weather). Interpersonal demands are interpreting challenges or success requirements that pertain to the interaction between consumers (e.g., cultural differences, power dynamics, differences in fund of information, or consumers' unique perceptions, preconceptions, and interactional goals.) Paralinguistic demands are interpreting challenges or success requirements that pertain to immediate, overt aspects of the expressive communication of consumers (i.e., the clarity of the "raw material" the interpreter sees and hears). Examples of paralinguistic demands are when a hearing individual has a heavy accent or when a deaf individual is signing while lying down or has an object in his or her hands. Intrapersonal demands are interpreting challenges or success requirements that pertain to the internal physiological or psychological state of the interpreter (e.g., the need to tolerate hunger, fatigue, or distracting thoughts or feelings.)

As adapted from Karasek, controls are skills, characteristics, abilities, decisions, or other resources that an interpreter may bring to bear in response to the demands presented by a given work assignment. Controls for interpreters may include education, experience, preparation for the assignment, behavioral actions or interventions, particular translation decisions, (e.g., specific word or sign choices or explanatory comments to consumers), encouraging "self-talk," or the simple yet powerful act of consciously acknowledging the presence and significance of a given demand and the impact it is having on an interpreting assignment. In the D-C schema, the term "control" is a noun, not a verb, and is preferably stated as "control options." We define three temporal opportunities where control options may be employed: pre-assignment controls (e.g., education, language fluency, and assignment preparation), assignment controls (e.g., behavioral and translation decisions made during the assignment itself), and post-assignment controls (e.g., follow-up behaviors and continuing education).

The D-C schema links interpreting theory with professional practice. The model of ethical and effective decision making presented in Figure 11.1 is an integral component of D-C schema supervision and teaching. In a formal D-C analysis, interpreting situations are examined for demands presented by EIPI factors. Then, the value and consequences of various translation and/or behavioral decisions (control options) in response to these factors, ranging from liberal to conservative, are explored and critiqued.

Any schema change in a practice profession must benefit four constituencies: the practitioners, teachers, researchers, and consumers. Among the benefits the D-C schema may offer these constituencies are the following: (1) a structured and objective means of identifying and analyzing a more complete array of factors that impact interpreting practice, (2) a common nomenclature through which to dialogue about these factors, (3) a method for examining the consequences of interpreting decisions that can help interpreters and IPP students hone practice-profession judgment skills, and (4) a stimulus for more open and realistic dialogue about the nature of interpreting work, which could beneficially impact teaching, research, consumer input and participation, and the establishment of qualifying standards for interpreters (either signed or spoken language interpreters).

Each of these purported benefits should be critically examined through empirical investigation. While the schema is still rather new and continues to be refined as it is being implemented in different venues, useful data are beginning to accumulate. Current research on the effectiveness of the D-C schema has two primary foci. The first is on the impact of incorporating the schema and related teaching methods such as "observation-supervision"[4] in IPPs (Dean, Davis et al., 2003, and see http://www.urmc.rochester.edu/dwc/scholarship/Education.htm). The second is examining the utility of the D-C schema and observation-supervision in enhancing interpreting work in specialty practice settings such as mental health (see http://www.urmc.rochester.edu/dwc/scholarship/Interpreter_Training.htm).

Already cited were data indicating that interpreters perceive on-the-job experience, rather than formal training, as their primary source of learning about extra-linguistic (EIPI) factors that impact interpreting work, even those who graduated from IPPs during the past decade when such information was being published and likely included in IPP curricula. Why the majority of these survey respondents failed to credit their IPPs as a source of such learning remains to be elucidated. Perhaps more concerning is the realization that on-the-job learning curves evolve while interpreters are serving consumers, often with limited supervision or access to mentoring (see Monikowski & Peterson, this volume). The consequences for consumers served during early versus later stages of this learning curve should be explored.

The aforementioned survey conducted at the 2001 RID convention also yielded data on the influence of D-C schema training on interpreters' rankings of the importance of EIPI factors in interpreting work. Of the 149 respondents, 58 had taken D-C schema courses or workshops. Participation in D-C schema training was compared with respondents' years of working experience and the number of years since their graduation from an IPP. As might be expected, respondents who participated in D-C schema training ranked EIPI factors as more important in interpreting work than respondents who had not had D-C schema training. Respondents' work experience and their years since IPP graduation were not associated with overall EIPI rankings. Among the four EIPI factors, D-C training had the strongest impact on perceptions of the importance of intrapersonal and interpersonal demands, modest impact on perceptions of the importance of environmental demands, and the least impact on perceptions of the importance of paralinguistic demands. Years of experience had a modest influence on ranking only interpersonal demands as important. Years since IPP graduation had no discernable influence on any of the four EIPI factor rankings.

These data suggest that D-C schema training fosters insights regarding the complexities of interpreting work that practice experience alone does not provide. This is consistent with additional data emerging from another study conducted at the 2003 RID convention and external evaluations of D-C schema training in IPPs (Institute for Assessment and Evaluation (IAE), 2003). However, the training appears more effective in fostering recognition of the importance of intrapersonal, interpersonal, and environmental demands (respectively) than paralinguistic demands. This differential impact of D-C training across EIPI factors, and the finding that work experience alone appears to have modest impact on fostering recognition of the importance of interpersonal factors, raises interesting research questions but also makes intuitive sense. The interpreting challenges presented by deficient or distorted linguistic raw material (paralinguistic demands) may be so obvious as to require no special training to appreciate. The significance of environmental factors, many of which also are obvious, may require less specialized training to appreciate. While D-C schema training appears most influential in fostering appreciation of the importance of intrapersonal and interpersonal demands, work experience alone appears to lead, over time, to a greater appreciation of the importance of interpersonal demands. How this learning might be hastened, including in IPPs, is worthy of investigation, especially given how frequently in recent years interpreting scholarship has emphasized the importance of interpersonal factors in interpreting (Gish, 1987; Metzger, 1999; Roy, 2000b; Wadensjo, 1998). The data herein suggest that this emphasis is not getting through to interpreters until later in their professional careers. D-C schema training appears to hasten that learning. Furthermore, D-C schema training appears uniquely effective in fostering recognition of the significance of intrapersonal demands in interpreting work.

Both D-C schema training and work experience appear to foster interpreters' recognition that factors beyond language per se bear relevance to professional practice (see Roy, Turner, Winston, Marschark et al., this volume). The potential negative consequences for consumers served by interpreters who have not yet developed this broader view of interpreting work are important research and practice issues. We believe these findings lend support for the value of providing D-C schema training to interpreters in IPPs as well as through continuing education, especially interpreters who are early in their professional careers. This conclusion is consistent with reports from our IPP infusion study at the University of Tennessee (Dean, Davis et al., 2003; Dean, Pollard et al., 2003; IAE, 2003), which indicate that student interpreters versed in the D-C schema analyze assignment demands and control options in a manner similar to interpreters with considerable work experience, even though many of these students are not yet fluent in ASL.

Our latest study on D-C schema training for mental health interpreting (which is being conducted in Rochester (NY), Minneapolis, San Francisco, and New York City; http://www.urmc.rochester.edu/dwc/scholarship/Equity.htm) is providing early qualitative data. This project is focused on the observation-supervision approach to interpreter training in specialty practice areas. We are examining not only changes in interpreters' perceived competency in mental health work but also consumers' perceptions of the effectiveness of services provided by interpreters trained through observation-supervision versus interpreters who have not been trained in this manner.

Preliminary data suggest that observation-supervision training has positive impact on interpreters but an impact that differs as a function of their degree of experience in the mental health field. Interpreters with less work experience in mental health settings report that observation-supervision provides them with an appreciation for "big picture" issues (e.g., the nature of a suicide assessment), whereas interpreters with more mental health experience report learning subtle aspects of this specialty practice area (e.g., the importance of a therapist's modeling what words parents should use when speaking to their child in times of stress or conflict). Most interpreter participants are reporting that observation-supervision gives them an enlightened perspective on their own (intrapersonal) reactions to interpreting work, in mental health settings and beyond, underscoring the data cited earlier indicating that D-C schema training appears to have a unique impact on the appreciation of the significance of intrapersonal demands. Even those with many years of experience in the mental health field report new awareness of how their personal reactions to this service environment affect their work and new ways to cope with those reactions during and after work assignments.

Interpreters and mental health professionals who are participating in this project report that the professional-to-professional dialogues they engage in during observation sessions are mutually educational. The interpreters are gaining insight into the thought world of clinicians, while the clinicians are gaining greater appreciation for the nature of interpreting work. This improved collegial relationship may benefit consumers served by such interpreter-clinician teams.

The aforementioned survey and evaluation findings are beginning to document the value of the D-C schema approach to interpreter training. However, this research has not yet expanded beyond investigations of hypothetical or secondhand observed work situations to include actual, in situ work behavior, apart from the qualitative data emerging from our mental health interpreter training study. Nor have we yet analyzed consumer perceptions, experiences, and consequences regarding interpreters who are trained via the D-C schema or observation-supervision. Those investigations will be crucial in further evaluating the utility of the D-C schema and related teaching approaches for interpreters and consumers alike.

SUMMARY AND CONCLUSIONS

The primary reason for the publication of this volume is to provide increased visibility and motivation for the conduct of interpreting research. Both in signed language and spoken language interpreting, there is little research data to guide interpreter education and practice. There is even less empirical study of interpreting as it pertains to consumers, especially consumers outside of educational settings. Interpreters in medical, legal, mental health, and other settings provide a crucial professional service that has profound—even life and death— consequences for consumers. Yet consumers (and researchers) know little about what interpreters really do on the job, how well they do it, and how consumers can more effectively collaborate with these practice professionals toward better service outcomes.

Interest has grown recently in the conduct of research in the related area of doctor-patient communication. As if direct doctor-patient communication were not complicated enough, only a few studies have been published that address the impact of interpreters (usually spoken language interpreters) in medical settings (Bot, 2003; Ferguson & Candib, 2002; Flores, et al., 2003). Given that medical settings are the single largest assignment venue for freelance sign language interpreters (Rivers, 1999), additional study of the added complexities, risks, and benefits associated with interpreter services in these settings is badly needed.

Further empirical study of the validity of D-C schema concepts and the impact of D-C schema training and observation-supervision on the effectiveness of interpreting practice is encouraged. Many topics could be addressed. Is observation-supervision more effective than traditional practicum training for student interpreters? What are optimal ways of advancing consumer education regarding the multiplicity of factors that influence interpreters' translation and behavioral decisions? Is the practice profession model of ethical and effective decision-making (Figure 11.1) useful in fostering dialogue and mentoring on interpreting ethics? What more can be elucidated regarding the learning curve following IPP graduation where interpreters acquire experience and judgment capabilities regarding the EIPI complexities of their work, especially the impact on consumers? Can this learning curve be shortened via modifications of IPP curricula or practicum, internship or continuing education programming?

Offering new models of practice is a common method for critically examining and seeking to enhance the utility of professional work and training. Models make explicit the assumptions and approaches used in an occupation. When models are made explicit, new information—whether from research, consumer input, or other sources—can be used to modify and further enhance a model's utility or, if not, foster the adoption of better models (Hanson & Oakman, 1998). Whether or not the D-C schema for interpreting work ultimately proves to be a useful model for guiding interpreting practice, IPP teaching, and interpreter evaluation will depend on the scrutiny of researchers, practitioners, teachers, and consumers. While some evidence is accumulating to suggest that this schema and observation-supervision are benefiting IPP students and practicing interpreters, ultimately, such benefits are moot unless they lead to more effective interpreting services for consumers.

NOTES

This chapter reports information developed under two grants from the U.S. Department of Education. The first, #P116B010927, "Reforming interpreter education: A practice-profession approach," is from the Fund for the Improvement of Post-Secondary Education. The second, #H133A031105, "Toward equity: Innovative collaborative research on interpreter training, DBT, and psychological testing," is from the National Institute on Disability and Rehabilitation Research in the U.S. Department of Education's Office of Special Education and Rehabilitative Services. However, the contents of this chapter do not necessarily represent the policy of the U.S. Department of Education, and you should not assume endorsement by the Federal government.

The authors gratefully acknowledge the support provided by the Registry of Interpreters for the Deaf in the conduct of the research studies reported herein.

1. Throughout this chapter, we use the term "translation(s)" when emphasizing the linguistic end product of an interpreter's work. Cokely (2002) notes that translation refers to the transfer of ideas from source to target language regardless of form (e.g., written, spoken, or signed). The term "interpretation" is broader in that interpretation includes the complex cognitive process the interpreter engages in prior to deciding upon the final end product, or translation, rendered. Since this chapter primarily deals with the consumer's perspective of that end product, the term "translation" is used.

2. In the 2001 publication, this category was termed "linguistic demands" but that term was changed because language (or translation between languages) is the over-arching *raison d'etre* of an interpreter's work and, in that regard, language is an aspect of all four demand categories.

3. In the 2001 publication, we included terminology (i.e., technical vocabulary) in the (former) category of linguistic demand. We now view technical vocabulary and other specialized terms or phrases as environmental demands, since specialized terminology tends to be dictated by the specific work environment of the interpreter (e.g., a medical, legal, or computer technology setting).

4. Observation-supervision involves interpreter trainees observing potential work situations (e.g., medical appointments) when there are no deaf consumers or interpreters present. Guided in these observations by special forms developed in accordance with the D-C schema, interpreters later gather in semistructured supervision sessions led by mentors well-versed in the D-C schema to conduct EIPI analyses of the observed situations and to propose and analyze the consequences of various control options as they relate to an array of hypothesized deaf consumers who *might have been* in these or similar situations.

REFERENCES

Bot, H. (2003). The myth of the uninvolved interpreter interpreting in mental health and the development of a three-person psychology. In L. Brunette, G. Bastin, I. Hemlin, & H. Clarke (Eds.), *The critical link 3: Interpreters in the community*. Amsterdam: John Benjamins, pp. 27–36.

Cokely, D. (1992). *Interpreting: A sociolinguistic model*. Burtonsville, MD: Linstok Press.

Cokely, D. (2000). Exploring ethics: A case for revising the code of ethics. *Journal of Interpretation*, 25–57.

Dean, R.K., & Pollard, R.Q (2001). Application of demand-control theory to sign language interpreting: Implications for stress and interpreter training. *Journal of Deaf Studies and Deaf Education*, 6 (1), 1–14.

Dean, R.K., Davis, J., Barnett, H., Graham, L.E., Hammond, L., & Hinchey, K. (2003, January). Training medically qualified interpreters: New approaches, new applications, promising results. *RID Views*, 20 (1), 10–12.

Dean, R., Pollard, R.Q, Davis, J., Griffin, M., LaCava, C., & Hinchey, K. (2003). Reforming interpreter education: A practice-profession approach—years 1 and 2 progress report. Presentation at the biennial meeting of the Registry of Interpreters for the Deaf, Chicago, IL.

DeMatteo, A.J., Veltri, D., & Lee, S.M. (1986). The role of a sign language interpreter in psychotherapy. In M.L. McIntire (Ed.), *Interpreting: The art of cross-cultural mediation*. Silver Spring, MD: Registry of Interpreters of the Deaf, pp. 135–153.

Ferguson, W.J., & Candib, L.M. (2002). Culture, language, and the doctor-patient relationship. *Family Medicine, 34* (5), 353–361.

Flores, G., Laws, M.B., Zuckerman, B., Abreu, M., Medina, L., & Hardt, E.J. (2003). Errors in medical interpretation and their potential consequences in pediatric encounters. *Pediatrics, 111* (1), 6–4.

Frishburg, N. (1986). *Interpreting: An introduction*. Rockville, MD: Registry of Interpreters for the Deaf, Inc.

Fritsch-Rudser, S. (1986). The RID code of ethics, confidentiality and supervision. *Journal of Interpretation, 3,* 47–51.

Gish, S. (1987). I understood all the words, but I missed the point: A goal-to-detail/detail-to-goal strategy for text analysis. In M. McIntire (Ed.), *New dimensions in interpreter education curriculum and instruction*. Silver Spring, MD: RID Publications, pp. 125–137.

Hanson, K.C., & Oakman, D.E. (1998). *Palestine in the time of Jesus: Social structures and social conflicts*. Minneapolis, MN: Fortress.

Humphrey, J., & Alcorn, B.J. (1995). *So you want to be an interpreter?* 2nd ed. Portland, OR: Sign Enhancers.

IAE (Institute for Assessment and Evaluation). (2003). *Reforming interpreter education: A practice profession approach. University of Rochester—University of Tennessee (FIPSE) grant project. Report #2.* Knoxville: University of Tennessee.

Karasek, R.A. (1979). Job demands, job decision latitude, and mental strain: implications for job redesign. *Administrative Science Quarterly, 24,* 285–307.

Karasek, R., & Theorell, T. (1990). *Healthy work*. New York: Basic Books.

Metzger, M. (1999). *Sign language interpreting: Deconstructing the myth of neutrality*. Washington, DC: Gallaudet University Press.

Metzger, M., & Bahan, B. (2001). Discourse analysis. In C. Lucas (Ed.), *The sociolinguistics of sign languages*. Cambridge: Cambridge University Press, pp. 112–144.

Namy, C. (1977). Reflections on the training of simultaneous interpreters: A metalinguistic approach. In D. Gerver & H.W. Sinaiko (Eds.), *Language interpreting and communication*. New York: Plenum, pp. 25–33.

Napier, J. (In press). Interpreting omissions: A new perspective. *Interpreting: International Journal of Research and Practice in Interpreting*.

Napier, J. (2003). A sociolinguistic analysis of the occurrence and types of omissions produced by Australian Sign Language/English interpreters. In M. Metzger, S. Collins, V. Dively, & R. Shaw (Eds.), *From topic boundaries to omission: Research in interpretation* (pp. 160–240). Washington, DC: Gallaudet University Press.

Page, J. (1993). In the sandwich, or on the side? Cultural variability and the interpreter's role. *Journal of Interpretation, 6* (1), 107–126.

Pollard, R.Q (1998). Psychopathology. In M. Marschark & D. Clark (Eds.). *Psychological perspectives on deafness*, vol. 2. Mahwah, NJ: Lawrence Erlbaum, pp. 171–197.

Quigley, S., & Young, J. (Eds.). (1965). *Interpreting for deaf people*. Washington, DC: U.S. Department of Health, Education, and Welfare.

Registry of Interpreters for the Deaf. (1994). *RID Membership Directory*. Silver Spring, MD: Author.

Registry of Interpreters for the Deaf. (No date). Draft revised code of ethics. Available at http://www.rid.org/coe.html. [Accessed March 9, 2004]

Rivers, J. (1999 March). Medical interpreting caucus—The need for a healthy body. *RID Views, 3,* 13.

Roy, C.B. (1993). The problem of definitions, descriptions, and the role metaphors of interpreters. *Journal of Interpretation, 6* (1), 127–154.

Roy, C.B. (Ed.). (2000a). Training interpreters—Past, present and future. In C.B. Roy, (Ed.). *Innovative practices for teaching sign language interpreters.* Washington, DC: Gallaudet University Press, pp. 1–14.

Roy, C.B. (2000b). *Interpreting as discourse process.* New York: Oxford University Press.

Seleskovitch, D. (1978). *Interpreting for international conferences.* Washington, DC: Penn and Booth.

Vernon, M., & Miller, K. (2001). Interpreting in mental health settings: Issues and concerns. *American Annals of the Deaf, 146* (5), 429–433.

Wadensjo, C. (1998). *Interpreting as interaction.* London: Longman.

Winston, E.A. (1989). Transliteration: what's the message? In C. Lucas (Ed.), *The sociolinguistics of the deaf community.* San Diego: Academic Press, pp. 147–164.

Winston, E.A., & Monikowski, C. (2000). Discourse mapping: Developing textual coherence skills in interpreters. In C.B. Roy (Ed.), *Innovative practices for teaching sign language interpreters.* Washington, DC: Gallaudet University Press, pp. 15–66.

Afterword: Interpreting and Interpreter Education: Adventures in Wonderland?

Patricia Sapere, Doni LaRock, Carol Convertino,
Laurene Gallimore, & Patricia Lessard

Now, if you'll only attend, Kitty, and not talk so much, I'll tell you all my ideas about Looking-glass House. First, there's a room you can see through the glass— that's just the same as our drawing room, only the things go the other way. I can see all of it when I get upon a chair—all but the bit just behind the fireplace. Oh! I do so wish I could see that bit! I want so much to know whether they've a fire in the winter: you never can tell, you know, unless our fire smokes, and then some comes up in that room too—but that may be only pretence, just to make it look as if they had a fire.

—Lewis Carroll, *Through the Looking-Glass*

As the story continues, Alice climbs up on the mantel, through the drawing room mirror into the looking-glass room, and finds that all was not quite what she expected. But then that is the danger in looking at things closely, analyzing things we take for granted, looking at that bit behind the fireplace.

Over the past 25 years or so, those interested in interpreting and interpreter education have attempted to gain some perspective on the field, only to find themselves staring into cloudy mirrors rather than crystal balls. As Cokely (this volume) describes, we have often seen what we need to do to improve the availability and quality of interpreting, but we have been—or at least felt—powerless to do anything about it. Periodically, however, like Alice in her drawing room, we have to make an attempt to go beyond the here and now; in a workshop on interpreting and interpreter education held in early 2004, a group of experts in the field made an effort to peer beyond the looking-glass. At the risk (and perhaps in the hope) of exposing themselves, their work, and their ideas to critical review by peers, they met to discuss the state of the art in research in the field and develop an agenda for future study and change. This chapter seeks to summarize the discussion in that workshop, rather than the chapters of this volume. The purpose is thus not so much to tie together the writings of the contributors as to provide another perspective on the issues that arose, some of which emerges in the chapters, but much of which remains implicit in the ways that the chapters either connect, or fail to do so.

The workshop presenters and discussants included interpreter educators, educators of deaf students, researchers, and consumers of interpreting services who gathered to share information and perspectives with the goal of providing a catalyst for collaboration and progress. Our role was to stimulate discussion, ask some hard questions, and focus the group on the research issues that need to be addressed. It soon became apparent, however, that the issues of interest were not all strictly related to interpreting. Throughout 3 days of discussion, the topics of language acquisition, the nature of natural sign languages and sign systems, and deaf education surfaced on a regular basis, providing both a context for the discussion and sometimes a distraction from it. In the sections that follow, we consider each of the major themes that wove through the discussion, seeking to capture their essence and the points of greatest agreement and disagreement.

THE CONTEXT AND COMMUNITY SERVED BY INTERPRETERS

It would be difficult to discuss the roles of interpreters and the processes involved in interpreting without considering the deaf individuals they serve. This requires examining the nature of the Deaf community and the diversity of the group, both historically and in the future. Cokely's introductory presentation (see Cokely, this volume) described the changing relationship of interpreters and the Deaf community, and the issues he raised permeated our discussions.

The intended focus of the workshop and this volume was educational access for deaf students. Nevertheless, it was clear that understanding the communication needs of deaf students requires a better understanding of where they come from, how their knowledge and learning differ from hearing peers, and the connection of today's deaf students to the Deaf community. The recent shift from residential schools to mainstream settings, along with new technologies, has created an educational milieu very different from that in which those of us who are "established" in the field gained our training—one in which residential schools and an active role in the Deaf community were the norm, and the effects of technology were seemingly minimal. Although we know that increasing numbers of interpreters are working in K–12 educational settings, we do not have a clear picture of what tomorrow's deaf students will look like, or even whether they will want or need interpreters like us. We know, however, that issues raised in this workshop (and volume) inform our work as interpreters and interpreter educators and ultimately impact deaf children in educational settings.

Beyond academic issues per se, various questions were raised about the social and psychological impact of mediated education and its possible effects on the academic success and personal success of deaf students. These included whether a deaf/hearing interpreting team might improve the educational process, whether deaf students isolated from a critical mass of deaf peers can be meaningfully engaged in extracurricular activities, and whether deaf individuals who were mainstreamed in K–12 feel they have been successfully assimilated into the majority society as a result. With the exception of the first issue (see Forestal, this volume), however, these questions are largely tangential to interpreting and interpreter education.

The mainstreaming issue does, however, relate to interpreting in the community. Many more deaf adults today have had experience with educational interpreters than in the past, thus affecting their expectations of interpreters and interpreting in the workplace and the community. Changes in educational models over the past 25 years also are likely to have changed the language skills of the consumers of interpreting services, even if there do not appear to have been any examinations of such changes over time. It is therefore important that we consider the implications of such changes for the acquisition of American Sign Language (ASL), British Sign Language (BSL), or other natural sign languages by both interpreters and deaf students, even as the Deaf community continues to have a decreasing core of native or near-native ASL users. (Note that both "ASL" and "English" are used generically here to refer to all signed and spoken languages, respectively.) Whether we like it or not, interpreters now are often the primary (sign) language models for deaf students during the school year, and thus interpreters' sign skills take on significance far beyond their effectiveness for interpreting.

MEDIATED EDUCATION: ILLUSIONARY ACCESS?

The workshop included extensive discussion of *mediated education* versus *direct instruction* for deaf students, the latter referring to situations in which instructors communicate directly with deaf students by signing for themselves. Mediated instruction can include the use of supplemental services and technologies (e.g, computers, tutoring, real-time captioning) and full-time services of sign language interpreting or real-time captioning for deaf students in "hearing classrooms." Direct instruction is most common in schools for the deaf and other separate programs for deaf students, but we have little information concerning the sign language skills of those instructors or the effects of these skills on pupils' academic achievement. Nonetheless, a number of workshop participants claimed that direct instruction is superior to mediated instruction (i.e., through interpreters), an assertion also found in the literature but apparently one without empirical support. Indeed, there is at least some evidence that deaf students do not pay much (visual) attention to teachers or deaf peers who do sign in the classroom (Matthews & Reich, 1993), and it may be that an interpreter can command greater attention and facilitate learning better than a signing teacher in some situations. We are not suggesting this to be the case, only emphasizing that carefully conducted research is needed to resolve such sensitive and important issues.

In discussing the question of whether mediated instruction can be as good as or better than direct instruction, a variety of possible research studies were suggested, including a comparison of how fluent ASL signers teach hard-to-interpret material like mathematics or science, how fluent users of simultaneous communication communicate such materials, and how highly skilled interpreters interpret for teachers in these areas. We need signing models in the classroom, and we need to do research on the effectiveness of alternative modes of communication for teaching and learning. However, we must keep in mind that just being deaf does not make a signer's productions fluent or educationally appropriate, and what is successful from the point of view of students' comprehension and language accessibility may not always match their perceptions or preferences—or those of interpreters (see Marschark, Sapere, Convertino, & Seewagen, this volume). Yet for all of the claims that deaf students prefer direct instruction, teaching by deaf faculty, and ASL in the classroom, there appears to be no research evidence to support such assumptions.

Despite our doubts about their accessibility, public school classrooms have now become home to the majority of deaf students (Lang, 2003). With this shift, the demand for educational interpreters has grown much faster than our ability to produce them. Just as serious as this shortage, and perhaps a reflection of it, is the variable quality of classroom interpreting (by certified as well as uncertified interpreters) and the fact that many if not most deaf children come to the classroom lacking fluency in the languages of instruction (signed and spoken) and lacking access to a fluent role model in either. In the United States, relatively few states appear to have competency standards or even assessments for educational interpreters, and what data are available indicate that many interpreters in K–12 classrooms are under- or unqualified (Jones, in press, Jones, Clark & Soltz, 1997; Schick, Williams & Bolster, 1999). How can they support children in fully reaching their educational potentials? Interpreters working in K–12 settings who recognize their lack of skills have few training resources available to them. Meanwhile, high turnover perpetuates the problem of deaf students receiving compromised communication during the time when their educational foundations are supposedly being established.

In this context, the question arose of whether no interpreter might be better than an unqualified or weak interpreter. Participants who had been managers of interpreting services or involved in training interpreters discussed whether the antecedent issue of the "Warm Body Syndrome"—filling interpreting requests regardless of whether the interpreter is qualified—should be, or could be, eliminated. Deaf children (and others with disabilities) in the United States are required to be given "reasonable accommodation" in educational settings. However, administrators who report that "reasonable accommodations" have been lawfully made do not always fulfill the implicit obligation to provide "effective accommodation." This contradiction was mournfully described by workshop participants as "illusionary access," a notion that needs to be challenged and evaluated empirically if it is going to change. Given the shortage of interpreters and our desire to improve as professionals, support also has to be provided for the interpreters who have been under-trained, those who are interpreting without training, and those whose skills have either declined over time or have not kept pace with their changing audience. It was suggested that computer technology might offer methods to support professional development for these interpreters, although there is little evidence concerning the effectiveness of this or any other training methods (but see Storey & Jamieson, 2004).

These issues led to more specific research considerations with both theoretical and applied implications: What can be learned about deaf students' cognitive processing skills by examining their comprehension of sign language interpreters (and vice versa)? What do teachers and interpreters need to know about deaf students' knowledge and learning strategies in order to address potential problems therein? What do deaf students learn from interpreting in the classroom, and how does this compare qualitatively and quantitatively with hearing students and with deaf students who use spoken language interpreters? How do teachers facilitate (or impede) effective communication in the classroom? Research on "interpreting" is not related to the interpreter only, as one discussant reminded us, and the lack of information concerning how and what deaf individuals understand from interpreting is one of the more pressing yet untouched issues.

In addition to communication in the classroom, research also is needed to determine how nonacademic interactions can potentially affect academic achievement and overall language development. For students saddled with the daunting task of learning language along with academic content through an interpreter all day, every day, social contact with peers may be limited and unrewarding (Antia & Kreimeyer, 2003). Interpreting has the potential to support deaf students' inclusion in the extracurricular activities that are important for all students, yet it also carries the risk of having them stand out and potentially makes their integration with hearing peers socially and psychologically more difficult. It remains unclear whether deaf students take full advantage of such opportunities and the extent to which their social interactions benefit when interpreters are present (or not). Do interpreters "get in the way" or do they allow for more successful development of social skills that promote comfortable professional and personal encounters in the post K–12 years?

In short, a mediated education for deaf students has been, and will continue to be, the educational placement of choice for many parents. We believe that research related to this learning environment— including what students are actually receiving from interpreters, how the presence of interpreters affects academic and social functioning, and who the best candidates are for this type of placement—could help lead to more informed choices.

DEAF INDIVIDUALS IN INTERPRETING AND INTERPRETER EDUCATION

Going beyond educational interpreting, workshop participants acknowledged the need to review current practices and evaluate whether we, as interpreters and educators, have created models and practices that provide the best services possible to the Deaf community (see Winston, this volume). In both community and educational interpreting, deaf individuals appear to have great if unexplored potential in roles usually filled by hearing interpreters (see Forestal, this volume). Consistent with other aspects of interpreting and interpreter education, however, most of the previous discussions about the roles, certification, and possible impact of deaf people in those roles have been based on community need and anecdotal information. Both in the context of Forestal's presentation on Certified Deaf Interpreters (CDIs) and more generally with regard to optimizing the language experience of deaf children exposed to sign language interpreters, we considered what exactly is meant by "Certified Deaf Interpreters," when their skills might be more helpful than those of hearing interpreters, and how one would measure their effectiveness. The last of these has not yet received any research attention, and even the definition of "deaf interpreter" had to be left open for future consideration, as the label *interpreter* may not accurately describe current practice by such individuals. *Mediator* was one of the more popular alternatives offered, and Cokely (this volume) discusses others.

Given such uncertainties and lack of agreement concerning the roles of CDIs, relatively little progress was made on this topic despite considerable discussion. Workshop participants agreed on the immediate need for conducting research concerning interactions among CDIs and both the deaf and hearing individuals with whom they work, particularly the potential roles for teams of deaf and hearing interpreters in academic as well as community settings. In this regard, Forestal noted that deaf people often help each other understand ongoing communication, and deaf students in interpreted classrooms frequently look to each other for such clarification. Research also is needed to evaluate the possibility of deaf/hearing teams serving young deaf children (e.g., K–4) in order to provide language and role models for students. The use of such teams would directly improve content access for students and indirectly teach students how to best use hearing interpreters. This kind of exposure during the early years could be followed by "weaning" deaf students from the deaf mediator/interpreting team, using only hearing interpreters in the years to follow.

One might argue about the feasibility of having a third professional in the classroom, besides the (hearing) interpreter and instructor, in light of the additional expense, and such teams admittedly do not appear likely in the present educational and economic climate. The potential benefits of having this team for a limited time could far outweigh the initial outlay of funds both in terms of monies spent in making deaf individuals more self-sufficient through education and access to employment. As a by-product, the presence of deaf individuals involved in public school classrooms would also encourage interactions between hearing instructors and deaf adults. This could serve to enhance the educators' understanding of deaf learners, leading to a potential improvement in teaching/learning strategies for deaf students.

One interesting workshop discussion involved participants recounting their most memorable learning experiences related to interpreting, most of which involved personal interactions with members of the Deaf community. We acknowledged that frustration was a primary motivating factor in improving our communication skills and our understanding of deaf individuals. Currently, however, interpreter education usually lacks anything more than superficial contact with the Deaf community. Interpreters may graduate from an interpreter education program having had minimal if any contact with deaf adults or deaf children, let alone active participation in the community that they are to serve (see Monikowski & Peterson, this volume). *Service learning* was proposed by Monikowski and Peterson as one way to encourage increased interaction between interpreting students and Deaf community members. However, the lack of active Deaf communities in many locales would preclude service learning programs from being established in many areas where interpreter education programs are located.

In this context and a number of others, it was somewhat surprising that participants involved in interpreter education complained that there are too many programs, some of which are of questionable quality. Admittedly, they did not think it likely that calling attention to that fact would make any programs close their doors in favor of a "less is more" approach (see Winston, this volume). Alternatively, we discussed the possibility of several well-established programs creating tracks for educating deaf mediators/CDIs. Such programs would offer deaf and hearing student peers the opportunity to interpret together, begin learning how to support each other as future professionals, and foster sign language fluency among hearing students who lack access to Deaf communities. Indirect cultural learning for both hearing and deaf students also would be encouraged through daily interaction, supported by direct instruction. Still to be determined, however, are answers to basic questions about the ways in which deaf mediators/CDIs can benefit deaf individuals in academic settings, and we have to demonstrate a sound rationale and their effectiveness in education and elsewhere.

Finally, it is noteworthy that in discussions about the roles of deaf individuals in interpreting, as well as broader discussions about improving interpreter education, there was a marked tendency to lean toward problem-solving rather than the empirical bases for proposed changes. Amidst several discussions of the optimal relative positions for carts and horses, however, there was at least tacit acceptance of the need for studies to support any wholesale modifications to interpreter education.

GUIDING CHANGE

The chapters of this book clearly reflect the sentiment of workshop discussions calling for research to guide reform in interpreting and interpreter education, with the ultimate goal of improving educational outcomes for deaf students. But would we have arrived at that point if the workshop had been aimed more generally at interpreting and interpreter education at large, rather than educational interpreting? There have been some directed considerations of research questions in interpreting in academic settings (see Winston, in press), but spontaneous appraisals of how well we provide deaf students with access to formal and informal learning opportunities are rare. All too often, examination of such issues is driven by desires to accommodate new legislation or secure available grant funds; all too seldom do we undertake such efforts simply because it is the right thing to do.

A key factor in the academic success of deaf students, we agreed, is appropriate placement in a program that fosters critical thinking, language, and social development. A variety of alternative educational placements are necessary for deaf children because they vary in their skills and needs far more than hearing peers (Marschark, Lang & Albertini, 2002). A variety of workshop discussions focused on the barriers that deny deaf students academic or personal-social success in various educational placements. Before we could address possible roles for interpreters in dismantling those barriers, we had to consider the many layers of administration involved in educating deaf children.

In the United States, each state has a department that oversees K–12 educational programs; there are administrations at the district level and at the school site where a child is placed. There also may be separate administrators who deal with support services for children with special needs. Similar structures are seen in other countries (although only the United States, Australia, and the United Kingdom were represented at this workshop), sometimes more cumbersome, sometimes less so. A pointed question for future investigations was where in the hierarchy one would direct such research and its dissemination in order to optimize implementation and impact. It was deemed best to keep such decisions at the local level, although greater collaboration across settings would provide for more leverage and more efficiency as we move ahead. The strength of numbers, as well as the power of evidence, is not to be denied.

In discussions of the relative benefits of mainstream and segregated classrooms for deaf students, we speculated about the elements present in "successful" segregated classrooms and whether they could be "imported" into mainstream classrooms. Such an activity would require coordination with and cooperation of mainstream teachers as well as educational administrators. Although it was argued that teachers would need, but likely not obtain, additional training, it may well be that active, on-the-job training with a qualified colleague would be as effective (as well as more likely). Unfortunately, questions concerning the qualifications those individuals would need and the possibility of combining interpreting and educational support into some kind of "educational specialist" role created sufficient discord that no resolutions were in the offing.

During discussions of possible roles for mediator/CDIs, there were suggestions that deaf teachers or other native users of ASL might serve as models in developing new methods of educating deaf students. Once again, there was the caution that language fluency does not confer skill as an educator (although some educational programs appear to assume so), and as a group we already had abandoned the willingness to accept a "something is better than nothing" approach to deaf education. In any case, the question of whether such issues were the province of interpreter education programs, teacher education programs, or some other, yet to be established, alternative was left for a later date. Of more immediate need is the necessity to clearly determine the demands that an interpreter faces in various educational settings and the skills required to satisfy them. An interpreter who received training or practicum experience in primary education is unlikely to be appropriate for the different set of demands presented by a secondary school or university-level setting. Perhaps educational interpreters and their consumers would be better served if certification were awarded according to skill in working with student populations of similar grades and developmental needs, such as K–3, 4–6, 7–9, and so on.

The issues raised regarding the struggles interpreters face in mainstream classrooms led to a variety of straightforward questions that, somewhat surprisingly, have not yet been addressed (at least in published research). Certainly there are a variety of opinions and claims with regard to these issues, but still unclear are basic questions like the extent to which mainstream teachers actually change or need to change the discourse of their classrooms to accommodate deaf students and interpreters, and whether or not they could, even if they were aware. The effects of "accommodations" for deaf students are often said to benefit hearing students as well, but, once again, there appears to be no empirical support for such claims.

The issue of modifying classroom instruction to accommodate student strengths and needs has a parallel in the issue of how we can ensure that standardized academic testing is fair to deaf children. Parents want their deaf children to perform well on state-mandated standardized tests, and to the extent that such tests accurately reflect student achievement and content knowledge, they can be valuable educational tools. We do not know, however, the implications of offering such tests in sign language rather than print, although most U.S. states allow interpreting support for at least some portion of such examinations. (Note that this issue has been a source of debate with regard to intelligence testing for decades, with no resolution to date.) Both reliability and validity issues surfaced in this regard, as did questions of the best way to administer interpreted forms of such tests. Would a child's regular interpreter be able to provide the most accurate support, or would a videotaped, "standard" interpretation be more generally fair? Perhaps a CDI would be the most appropriate means of rendering such a test in sign—either ASL or English-based signing—alternatives that led to their own, animated discussion.

Concerns about the use of video-based rather than live interpreting for standardized testing have been raised in New York and other states. Ongoing research suggests that prerecorded interpreting does not reduce deaf students' comprehension relative to live interpreting, either due to the loss of three-dimensional information or the elimination of student-interpreter feedback. Still, if it was determined empirically that sign language offered a better means for high stakes testing for some deaf students, convincing evidence would have to be presented to parents, administrators, and legislators in a way that investigators typically have not undertaken previously. Then again, we all agreed that change was needed, and it is incumbent upon us as educators and investigators to seek out the answers and communicate them effectively to all audiences concerned, the topic of a following section.

RE-EXPLORING ROLES AND RESPONSIBILITIES

Historically, the term "failure" has frequently been associated with deaf education. In some ways, special schools and programs for deaf students have failed, although the shift in enrollment to mainstream placements has awakened many residential schools to the need for extensive revamping of curricula and instruction methods if they are to survive. At the same time, schools for the deaf have been seen as the placement of last resort for deaf students deemed to have "failed" in mainstream settings, most often because they were placed there for the wrong reasons, without appropriate consideration of their educational needs. From the Deaf perspective, however, there are specific educational priorities for deaf students that seem best served in residential schools (or in mainstream settings that would look very different from those we see today). Discussants and presenters at the workshop argued for a clearer understanding of the problems inherent in the current educational system serving deaf children and the need for in-depth examination of all aspects of the educational enterprise. Deaf individuals must be included in this examination.

Deaf workshop participants emphasized that we must look at how students develop their identities as individuals during the school years. There is some socializing with other students in the classroom, but when deaf students are outside of class, how easy is it for them to communicate with peers, if communication is attempted at all? We need to establish and follow case studies to systematically document the personal experiences of these individuals as they mature from kindergarten through high school graduation, while also examining relations between alternative school placements and academic and social success (Karchmer & Mitchell, 2003; Stinson & Kluwin, 2003).

A variety of studies are available concerning deaf students' perceptions of alternative educational environments (see Marschark, Lang, & Albertini, 2002, for a summary), but it remains unclear how the social dynamics of various settings interact with academic success. We also need to understand how hearing teachers feel about having deaf students in mainstreamed classrooms and how they deal with having to share what has traditionally been seen as their domains with other adults (e.g., interpreters, itinerant teachers). The complex dynamics of such interactions and of teacher-deaf student relationships also should be explored with regard to their impact on achievement. A better understanding of educational interpreting would benefit such investigations, as the relationship between an interpretation and a teacher's original message may vary with the age of the student, the teacher's familiarity with deaf students, and the interpreter's expertise and experience. In short, the role of the interpreter may have many overlapping functions: interpreter, friend, helper, advisor, tutor, and language model. Careful analysis of the multifaceted relationships between educational interpreters and students would greatly help to understand the skills and strategies of both parties, hopefully leading to improvement both independently and in their collaborations.

It would be useful at several levels to explore the alternative modes of communication between parents and deaf children (e.g., ASL, English-based signing, home sign systems) and their relation to educational success. Although we know that children enrolled in early intervention programs that include signing tend to have better developmental and educational outcomes (see Calderon & Greenberg, 1997), there does not appear to be any information available concerning the relation between early communication and later communication during the school years, either at home or at school. We also need to understand better the interactions of deaf students and their (usually hearing) parents with regard to curricular and extracurricular activities. At the end of the day, after sitting and watching an interpreter for hours, what kind of communication occurs in the home when parents' communication with their child is not mutually accessible (whether spoken or signed)?

Importantly, our research agenda must identify the needs of all deaf students who enter the educational system, regardless of where the student is placed. If we systematically and scientifically examine education as a whole, taking care to unpack complex and daunting relations among variables, we will be able to identify what is working in the system and what needs to change. Students, interpreters, teachers, policymakers, and parents all play key roles in the educational system and the academic success of deaf children. By considering these roles and possible interactions among them, we can begin to solve problems that have plagued the education of deaf students for so many years and have affected so many lives.

DISSEMINATION OF RESEARCH: PUBLISH IT
AND THEY WILL READ

Workshop discussions that focused on the role of interpreters in mediated educational settings helped to remind us that the most important beneficiaries of the research activities proposed there and throughout this volume are deaf children. Participants in these discussions sought to apply research findings to the current educational experiences of deaf children in both residential schools and mainstreamed settings. As noted in the previous sections, we recognized that the limited body of research currently available evinces the urgent need to investigate the variety of factors that are involved in mainstream education. It is important to note in this regard that when most interpreter education programs were established, there was little empirical research available to inform or guide them. Few relevant investigations were available, and some of the findings ran counter to beliefs and traditions of interpreter educators.

A feeling also emerged from this workshop that we are at a threshold in the education of deaf students and in the provision of services for deaf individuals more broadly. It is critical that we take that step together. Current research questions and methodologies are becoming more sophisticated and able to address more complex questions that go to the core of understanding the growth of deaf individuals of all ages. These findings need to be incorporated into programs for deaf children, teachers, interpreters, and other stakeholders if we are to be informed participants in the educational enterprise.

Assuming that administrators, teachers, interpreters, and parents can be convinced that the benefit of research will outweigh the time and resources needed, most workshop participants expressed a willingness, if not an a priori desire, to engage in the kind of investigations described here, re-examining our own efforts and educational roles. In looking into the mirror of self-evaluation, participants agreed on the need to validate current methods in interpreter education, deaf education, and ASL/English research, recognizing that we will likely find some things that need to be done differently. With full recognition that such critical self-examination could affect careers, program philosophies, and comfort levels, we agreed that the status quo is no longer an option. We cannot continue to protect our educational fiefdoms and professional egos at the cost of children's educations. In accepting that our methods of interpreting and of training future interpreters are based on belief rather than factual knowledge, contributors to this volume have given up the right of retreat, the comfort of ignoring future results, and standing by rather than being an active player in the changes to come.

In order to reach the diverse audiences we serve, directly or indirectly, technology may be especially helpful in disseminating new research. Web sites, listservs, and e-mail can put research in the hands of parents, teachers, interpreters, administrators, students, and future professionals. If investigators tailor their writing for these specific audiences and choose publication outlets carefully, their work can have far more impact than if they write for other investigators alone. The editors of this volume sought to make its chapters more accessible by urging contributors to remember its audience, avoid jargon, and write in a way that does not require extensive background knowledge to understand. This is a challenge to academics accustomed to writing for their peers, but it is necessary if we are to accept the charge we have given ourselves. Parents, teachers, interpreters, and members of the Deaf community may not read books of this sort or subscribe to traditional research journals, but they might read a more accessible article

in a familiar publication. Our findings may then take on a life of
their own and help speed the evolution of more successful models for
educating deaf students and their interpreters—models infused with
curiosity rather than fears of "failure."

Communication and computer technologies also allow us to conduct
research in ways that were not possible in the past. They can enhance
collaboration among researchers, allow access to databases across
laboratories, and permit alliances between investigators and practitioners around the world. Such avenues for sharing can provide tremendous savings in time and money, cross-cultural confirmation and
elaboration of findings, and support for new investigators and programs so that mistakes of the past need not be repeated.

Finally, the discussion of future research directions had to deal with
"the bottom line." Critical to the discussion of research that needs to be
conducted is the availability of and access to continued funding. Often,
we are willing to continue to invest enormous amounts of money into
already existing programs that have no basis for such support (see
Cokely, this volume). The mere presence of these programs satisfies
most lawmakers who originally sanctioned their existence, and the idea
that we might put our funding in jeopardy in order to re-evaluate the
assumptions on which our programs are based is enough to cause
anxiety in even the most confident academic dean. However, only by
broadening the discussion and bringing our audience into the collaboration can we succeed. Hopefully, the chapters of this volume will
convince readers of the potential for the future and their roles in it.

CONCLUSION

When Alice awoke from her looking-glass dream, she was not quite the
same young lady. Both in analyzing her experiences and in relating
them to the world on "this" side of the looking-glass, Alice had changed
in ways that would not easily be undone. Since the 2004 workshop, we
all have been re-examining that looking-glass adventure, one in which
we saw the world turned around (if not upside down) and where we
were reminded of just how far we have to go. We now have to be willing
to the take steps clearly needed for a metamorphosis in interpreter
education and the educating of deaf students. Findings from current
research need to be used to inform various stakeholders so that consumers of interpreting services and deaf learners of all ages will receive
the best services possible. As we take up the research agenda described
here and in the previous chapters, we need to be inclusive and integrative—willing to go beyond the realm of our own day-to-day activities and the comfort of our traditional assumptions and beliefs. For the
present, at least, the prospect of what can be accomplished easily out-
weighs the effort that will be necessary to do so.

"At any other time, Alice would have felt surprised by this, but she was far too much excited to be surprised at anything *now*" (Carroll, 1960, p. 336).

REFERENCES

Antia, S.D., & Kreimeyer, K. (2003). Peer interactions of deaf and hard of hearing children. In M. Marschark & P.E. Spencer (Eds.), *Oxford handbook of deaf studies, language, and education*. New York: Oxford University Press, pp. 164–176.

Calderon, R., & Greenberg, M. (1997). The effectiveness of early intervention for deaf children and children with hearing loss. In M.J. Guralnik (Ed.), *The effectiveness of early intervention*. Baltimore: Paul H. Brookes, pp. 455–482.

Carroll, L. (1960). Through the looking-glass. In M. Gardner (Ed.), *The annotated Alice*. New York: Bramhall House.

Jones, B.E. (in press). Competencies of K–12 educational interpreters: What we need versus what we have. In E.A. Winston (Ed.), *Educational interpreting: How it can succeed*. Washington, DC: Gallaudet University Press.

Jones, B. E., Clark, G., & Soltz, D. (1997). Characteristics and practices of sign language interpreters in inclusive education programs. *Exceptional Children, 63* (2), 257–268.

Karchmer, M.A., & Mitchell, R.E. (2003). Demographic and achievement characteristics of deaf and hard-of-hearing students. In M. Marschark & P.E. Spencer (Eds.), *Oxford handbook of deaf studies, language, and education*. New York: Oxford University Press, pp. 21–37.

Marschark, M., Lang, H.G., & Albertini, J.A. (2002). *Educating deaf students: From research to practice*. New York: Oxford University Press.

Matthews, T.J., & Reich, C.F. (1993). Constraints on communication in class-rooms for the deaf. *American Annals of the Deaf, 138,* 14–18.

Schick, B., Williams, K., & Bolster, L. (1999). Skill levels of educational inter-preters working in public schools. *Journal of Deaf Studies and Deaf Education, 4,* 144–155.

Stinson, M.S., & Kluwin, T.N. (2003). Educational consequences of alternative school placements. In M. Marschark & P.E. Spencer (Eds.), *Oxford handbook of deaf studies, language, and education*. New York: Oxford University Press, pp. 52–64.

Storey, B.C., & Jamieson, J.R. (2004). Sign language vocabulary development practices and Internet use among educational interpreters. *Journal of Deaf Studies and Deaf Education, 9,* 53–67.

Winston, E.A. (Ed.) (in press). *Educational interpreting: How it can succeed.* Washington, DC: Gallaudet University Press.

Index

CPSIA information can be obtained
at www.ICGtesting.com
Printed in the USA
LVHW050804300623
751144LV00005B/341

9 780195 176940